To Judy,

whose constant support helped inspire this book and so much more.

[illegible]

Flunking Democracy

Flunking Democracy

Schools, Courts, and Civic Participation

MICHAEL A. REBELL

THE UNIVERSITY OF CHICAGO PRESS CHICAGO AND LONDON

The University of Chicago Press, Chicago 60637
The University of Chicago Press, Ltd., London

Published 2018
Printed in the United States of America

27 26 25 24 23 22 21 20 19 18   1 2 3 4 5

ISBN-13: 978-0-226-54978-1 (cloth)
ISBN-13: 978-0-226-54981-1 (paper)
ISBN-13: 978-0-226-54995-8 (e-book)
DOI: https://doi.org/10.7208/chicago/9780226549958.001.0001

Library of Congress Cataloging-in-Publication Data

Names: Rebell, Michael A., author.
Title: Flunking democracy: schools, courts, and civic participation / Michael A. Rebell.
Description: Chicago: The University of Chicago Press, 2018. | Includes bibliographical references and index.
Identifiers: LCCN 2017044531| ISBN 9780226549781 (cloth: alk. paper) | ISBN 9780226549811 (pbk: alk. paper) | ISBN 9780226549958 (e-book)
Subjects: LCSH: Civics—Study and teaching—Law and legislation—United States. | Courts—Social aspects—United States. | Judicial process—United States.
Classification: LCC KF4124.5 .R42 2018 | DDC 344.73/077—dc23
LC record available at https://lccn.loc.gov/2017044531

♾ This paper meets the requirements of ANSI/NISO Z39.48-1992 (Permanence of Paper).

TO HANNAH, JULIA, MADELINE, AND OLIVER, WITH THE HOPE AND EXPECTATION THAT THEY WILL ALL GROW UP TO BE CAPABLE AND COMMITTED CITIZENS

Contents

Acknowledgments

The idea for this book emerged from my conversations over several years with Danielle Allen, who is now the director of the Edmond J. Safra Center for Ethics and James Bryant Conant University Professor at Harvard University. Danielle was intrigued to learn that the New York Court of Appeals, in an education adequacy case I had litigated, held that the purpose of public education is to provide students the skills they need to function productively as civic participants. She encouraged me to explore the full implications of that ruling, and when she became director at the Center for Ethics, she offered me a fellowship and an opportunity to fully research the issues of what the schools need to do to prepare students adequately for civic participation in the twenty-first century, and what role courts might play in inducing them to do so.

One of the many benefits of the time I spent in Cambridge was meeting and working with Peter Levine, who graciously shared with me the research that he and his colleagues at the Center for Information and Research on Civic Learning & Engagement at Tufts University had undertaken over many years, and who patiently read and commented on many chapter drafts. Insights and comments on early drafts from James Ryan and Meira Levinson at the Harvard Graduate School of Education, and from other fellows at the Edmond J. Safra Center for Ethics, especially Liav Orgad and Elizabeth Beaumont, added much to my understanding of the issues. I also am indebted to Bill Koski and David Long for their penetrating analyses and comments on the legal issues covered in the book.

President Susan Fuhrman and Provost Tom James, of Teachers College, Columbia University, also were instrumental in enabling me to write this book, both by providing me with a sabbatical opportunity to pursue the research and by their personal interest and insights into the questions of civic preparation. President Fuhrman has now established civic education as a major priority for Teachers College, and the roundtable discussions involving a broad array of Teachers College faculty that she organized to commence this initiative deepened my thinking on many issues as I was completing the manuscript. My colleagues at the Center for Educational Equity at Teachers College have been enormously supportive, both in helping me develop ideas for this book and in working with me to establish a project that will continue to research a number of the themes raised in this book and attempt to put some of these reforms into effect.

I am especially grateful to Jessica Wolff for both her substantive suggestions and her patient editing assistance, and to Joe Rogers for his penetrating insights into many of the issues. I owe many thanks to Jaylan Elrahman, Esther Cyna, and John Sludden for their persevering research assistance and to Paloma Garcia and Rachel Miller and other members of staff at the Center for Educational Equity for their support and assistance. Elizabeth Branch Dyson, my editor at University of Chicago Press, encouraged me to pursue this idea from the first and has provided numerous helpful suggestions and worked diligently with her assistant Dylan Montanari to expedite the publication process. Katherine Faydash's excellent copyediting skills have also substantially enhanced the text.

My wife, Sharon Rebell, encouraged me from the first to write this book and has been continuously supportive throughout, both in encouraging me to keep my prose readable and in being a patient listener and an insightful reactor and critic as I was developing my ideas.

I am also grateful for the financial assistance provided by the Smart Family Foundation that has made this project possible.

Introduction

The extent to which we take the commitment to democracy seriously is measured by the extent to which we take the commitment to education seriously. — Hilary Putnam

The 2016 presidential election campaign underscored some very troubling trends in the present state of our democracy: the extreme polarization of the electorate, the dismissal of people with opposing views, the failure of many voters (and, quite often, candidates) to focus on substantive policy issues, and the widespread acceptance and circulation of one-sided and erroneous information.[1] Other disturbing trends have been present for decades: the proportion of eligible voters who actually vote is substantially lower than in most other developed countries, the number of citizens who actively participate in local community activities has dramatically declined, and Americans are increasingly neglecting basic civic responsibilities like jury service.

The fact that these worrisome practices have become prevalent in our society also raises serious questions about how well the schools in recent decades have carried out one of their core traditional responsibilities: preparing young people to be good citizens, capable of safeguarding our democracy and stewarding our nation toward a greater realization of its democratic values. As former U.S. Supreme Court justice Sandra Day O'Connor has put it, "We are failing to impart to today's students the information and skills they need to be responsible citizens."[2]

The ability of the schools to carry out their historical role of civic preparation has been further undermined by the disparities in opportunities for effective civic preparation that are available in many schools; this opportunity gap has resulted in a large "civic empowerment gap" for many students in poverty and students of color. Donald Trump's victory in 2016 also highlighted the degree to which the white working class felt not only economically but also culturally neglected and believed that the public schools did not reflect their values.[3]

The premise of this book is that, for at least the past half century, the schools have failed to perform properly their critical role of preparing students to function productively as civic participants. As a result, the future viability of our democratic culture is truly put at risk, since, as "theorists of democracy from Aristotle to Bryce have stressed . . . democracies are maintained by active citizen participation in civic affairs, by a high level of information about public affairs, and by a widespread sense of civic responsibility."[4] I also argue that the schools' inability to prepare students to meet the challenges of capable citizenship in the twenty-first century can be overcome only by the involvement of the federal and state courts, both of which have declared that preparing students for capable citizenship is a prime responsibility of the schools, in enforcing those pronouncements.

For America's founders, preparing young people to be capable citizens was the primary reason to establish a public school system. Harvard historian Alan Taylor summarized the founders' perspective as follows: "Schools needed to produce well-informed protectors of republican government. 'If the common people are ignorant and vicious,' [Benjamin] Rush concluded, 'a republican nation can never be long free.' . . . They also needed enough education to distinguish worthy from treacherous candidates for office—lest the republic succumb to those reckless demagogues or would-be aristocrats. As Jefferson put it, 'Ignorance and despotism seem made for each other.'"[5] The nation's founders believed that the profound experiment in republican government that they were initiating "depended on citizens' ability to participate in public life and to exhibit civic virtues such as mutual respect and prudent judgment."[6]

Over the past half century, however, most American schools have substantially neglected their responsibility to prepare students for civic participation. In 2000, when the annual PDK/Gallup poll on schooling last asked questions about education for citizenship, respondents chose "prepar[ing] people to become responsible citizens" as the least important purpose of schooling, behind such goals as "enhanc[ing] people's happiness and enrich[ing] their lives."[7] Policy makers and educators have tended to downgrade the teaching of social studies and civics, focusing in recent decades on basic reading and math instruction and emphasizing the economic value of education to individual students. The professional development of teachers in civics education has also been largely disregarded.[8] Consequently, "Americans have entered the twenty-first century, an epoch punctuated by debates over immigration, religious tolerance, and the role of government, with their schools devoting remarkably little attention to the formation of sound democratic citizens. A focus on academic performance, along with concerns about provoking controversy, have in many places demoted talk of citizenship to assemblies, ceremonies, or the occasional social studies lesson."[9]

The result of decades of neglect of the civic purposes of education has meant that, among other things, only 23 percent of a national sample of eighth graders performed at or above a "proficient" level on the civics exam administered by the National Assessment of Educational Progress (NAEP) in 2014,[10] participation in civic organizations has plunged,[11] most social studies classes do not discuss social problems and controversial ideas,[12] and most people avoid entering into political discussions with those who have opposing political views.[13] Opportunities for students to participate in extracurricular activities, service learning, and actual and simulated political experiences are inadequate and tend to be cut back or eliminated in times of fiscal constraint.[14]

Many parents and scholars are concerned that the schools are not sufficiently exposing students to appropriate civic values.[15] Many young people express deep skepticism and cynicism toward elections and the democratic political process.[16] In addition, there is a substantial and worrisome gap in civic knowledge, civic skills, and civic dispositions between most white students and both students from low-income backgrounds and students of color.[17]

Most schools have also failed to help students apply critical thinking to their use of new media, a pattern that does not bode well for the ability of our future voters to deal effectively with the one-sided presentation of information, the distortion of facts, and circulation of fake news stories through the Internet. The disturbing tendency to engage only with news sources and social media that confirm one's preexisting perspectives predated the 2016 election campaign and has affected liberal and conservative voters alike: "In fact, consistently liberal voters are most likely to block, un-follow, or defriend someone on social media because they disagreed with that person's political stance. Meanwhile, consistent conservatives do the same and tend to receive their news from one conservative source, FOX News."[18]

The Stanford History Education Group recently administered a series of assessments that gauge "civic online reasoning" to approximately eight thousand secondary school and college students across twelve states. The overall conclusion: "Young people's ability to reason about the information on the Internet can be summarized in one word: *bleak*."[19] In one of these Stanford exercises, the researchers sent high school and college students to MinimumWage.com, a website that purported to be a fair broker of information on the relationship between minimum-wage policy and employment rates. The site links to reputable sources like the *New York Times* and is identified as a project of the Employment Policies Institute, a nonprofit organization that describes itself as sponsoring nonpartisan research. In fact, however, the site is a front for an industry public relations firm that poses as a think tank.

Only 9 percent of high school students in an Advanced Placement history course were able to see through the language used on Minimum Wage.com language to determine that its reporting was biased. Among college students the results were actually worse: 93 percent of students were fooled. The simple act of Googling "Employment Policies Institute" and the word "funding" would have turned up a host of articles and other sources that exposed the deceptive practices of this site. Most students never moved beyond the site itself.[20] Another study revealed that students tend to focus on the first site that pops up in an Internet search, blindly trusting the search engine to put the most reliable results first.[21]

Although parents, educators, and policy makers have, in general, downplayed the significance of educating students for citizenship in recent decades, the state courts have not. In a remarkable series of decisions issued over the past fifty years, courts in almost half the states have issued rulings that have interpreted their state's constitution to require governors and legislators to provide adequate and/or equitable educational opportunities to all students. To reach these conclusions, they have examined the meaning of constitutional clauses that appear in almost all of the state constitutions that guarantee all students a "thorough and efficient education," a "sound basic education," or a "high quality" or "adequate education."

Most of these constitutional provisions were drafted as part of the common school movement that established the American public school system during the nineteenth century; some, especially in the New England states, actually date back to the post–Revolutionary War era of the eighteenth century. Not surprisingly, the text and the legislative history of these clauses reflect the strong commitment of the nation's founders and of the architects of the common schools to the need to ensure that all students be prepared to function as capable citizens in a democratic society.[22] As the Wyoming Supreme Court wrote in analyzing the history of that state's constitutional education article: "At the time these clauses were used in the wording of the education article at Wyoming's constitutional convention in 1889, similar education provisions were found in every State constitution, reflecting the contemporary sentiment that education was a vital and legitimate state concern, not as an end in itself, but because an educated populace was viewed as a means of survival for the democratic principles of the state."[23]

State courts interpreting and applying these clauses today have also consistently emphasized the continuing importance of educating students to be effective citizens. The New York Court of Appeals held that the purpose of public education is to provide students the skills they need to "function productively as civic participants capable of voting and serving on a jury."[24] The Kentucky Supreme Court, using language that has also been followed by eight other states' highest courts, specifically held that constitutional goals included the development in each and every child of the following:

1. Sufficient oral and written communication skills to enable students to function in a complex and rapidly changing civilization;
2. Sufficient knowledge of economic, social, and political systems to enable the student to make informed choices;
3. Sufficient understanding of governmental processes to enable the student to understand the issues that affect his or her community, state, and nation.[25]

The U.S. Supreme Court famously proclaimed in its landmark school desegregation decision, *Brown v. Board of Education*: "Today, education is perhaps the most important function of state and local governments. . . . It is the very foundation of good citizenship."[26] The Supreme Court has also reiterated in a variety of cases that "[the schools] are educating the young for citizenship,"[27] that "schools are where the 'fundamental values necessary for the maintenance of a democratic political system' are conveyed,"[28] and that "Americans regard the public schools as a most vital civic institution for the preservation of a democratic system of government."[29]

Overall, the highest courts in at least thirty-two states have explicitly stated that preparation for capable citizenship is the prime purpose or a primary purpose of the education clause of their state constitutions. (This does not mean that the other eighteen state highest courts have denied this proposition; rather, they have not spoken on the issue.) These courts have not, however, assiduously enforced these understandings. The primary focus of the judges in these cases, and of the parties who have appeared before them, has been to ensure that state funding is sufficient to allow for schools to provide meaningful educational opportunities to all students in a general sense, and their remedial decrees have not focused at all on education for citizenship.

Although by and large the education adequacy cases have resulted in substantial increases in educational funding, it is clear that states and school districts have not used these increased resources to improve preparation for civic participation. As discussed already, school districts have reduced, rather than increased, the opportunities for civic preparation they offer students over the forty-five years that state courts have been issuing their adequacy decisions.

The trauma of the 2016 election campaign has led some educators to propose using this experience as a "Sputnik moment"[30] for the schools to "restore the foundation that our public schools were founded on . . . to promote civic engagement and deliberative skills—skills that our democracy depended on to survive and thrive."[31] This will not, however, be an easy task. Politicians and educators have for years given lip service to the need for civic education, but they have failed to deliver on their abstract commitments. The courts need now to enforce their pronouncements regarding the primacy of education for citizenship in order to ensure that the schools actually meet effectively their civic preparation obligations.

One of the major reasons for the contemporary neglect of civic preparation in the schools is that policy makers and school officials have discouraged or even barred teachers from dealing with controversial issues, and many teachers also feel that they have not been trained in how to teach students to apply critical analytic skills to their use of the Internet and social media. The continuing political polarization that plagues our society is likely to perpetuate these trends—unless the schools are impelled to shift decisively their approach to civic education by judicious directives from the courts. In short, if students are to receive the civic knowledge, skills, experiences, and values that they will need to be capable citizens who are responsive to the contemporary challenges to our democratic system, then the courts will need to play an active role in inducing the schools to carry out their constitutional responsibilities in this area.

Preparing students to function as civic participants in a meaningful way in the twenty-first century requires a new approach to education, an approach that understands and incorporates contemporary cultural realities. For civic education to succeed, schools must create an environment that harnesses diversity and individualism; provides equal educational opportunities; forges common contemporary civic values; adopts pedagogical approaches that promote deliberation, critical inquiry, and participatory experiences; and capitalizes on the positive possibilities of the Internet and social media. These initiatives will undoubtedly require strong leadership, parental support, and additional resources, but they can be achieved.

The state and federal courts are uniquely positioned to induce the schools to adopt these kinds of policies and practices. Although judicial appointments, especially at the Supreme Court level, have become more politicized in recent years, the courts nevertheless remain the least polarized and most respected branch of American government. Their basic institutional functioning requires reliance on evidence, reasoned discussion, analysis of controversial issues, and respect for those who hold different viewpoints—many of the core skills that students will need to develop if they are to be effective citizens who exercise good judgment in dealing with policy issues. The state court equity and adequacy decisions, and the U.S. Supreme Court's past supportive statements, can provide important precedents for judicial action to enforce a right to meaningful education for citizenship. The equity and adequacy rulings have been issued by judges in red states and blue states, and they have expanded educational opportunities to students of color, to immigrants, and to children of white working-class families.

Many of the changes that are necessary for effective civic preparation will involve the dissemination and adoption of practices and activities that are already being carried out successfully in certain places. For example, some schools are already engaging students in deliberative examinations of controversial issues, teaching them how to use critical analysis to assess the validity of information on the Internet and social media, and providing students with the types of extracurricular and experiential activities that are critical for developing civic participation skills. These important practices need to become the norm in all schools, not just in a few exceptional schools. Judicial decisions and remedial orders can make this happen.

Would judicial advancement of improved civic preparation in the schools constitute inappropriate "judicial activism"? Although this term is often used in a pejorative sense in political contexts, the fact is that both the federal and the state courts have taken on an active role in many areas, often in coordination with the legislative and executive branches, for the past half century. They have been involved in formulating major policies not only in school funding but also in school desegregation, special education, school discipline, gender equity, and many other areas of educational policy. Similarly, outside of education, the courts have profoundly affected public policy in areas like housing, mental illness, and prison reform. Issues of separation of powers need to be looked at from a broad perspective. Instead of interpreting the involvement of courts in enforcing social and economic rights as somehow usurping the powers of the legislative and executive branches, we need to realize that progress can be made in complex, critical areas like preparation for citizenship only through the active involvement of all three branches of government.

As already noted, the U.S. Supreme Court, other federal courts, and a majority of the state supreme courts have repeatedly held that a primary purpose of the public schools is to prepare students to function productively as civic participants. The courts now need to focus directly on requiring states and school districts to carry out their civic preparation responsibilities and to make education for effective citizenship in today's world a high priority. The role of the courts is not to micromanage what is going on in the classrooms but to induce states and schools to carry out their traditional constitutional responsibilities in ways that meet society's contemporary civic needs.

This book describes what the schools need to do and the role that the courts need to play to reinvigorate preparation for civic participation in the schools. Chapter 1 delves into the reasons civic education held such meaning for the nation's founders and for the proponents of the common schools. It then documents how civic instruction in the schools—and civic participation in society at large—has markedly declined since the 1950s. It describes how the neglect of education for citizenship has resulted in our young people becoming increasingly ignorant of the basic institutions of American government, ill-equipped to engage in deliberative discussions, and increasingly unmotivated to engage in basic civic activities like voting, volunteering, and attending public meetings.

An additional dimension of the civic engagement crisis is that many students of color and white students from working-class and low-income families are even more alienated from the nation's civic culture and even less prepared for civic participation than are the majority of more affluent white students. The first chapter also documents the ways that our nation's education systems have been unable or disinclined to respond to these students' needs. It concludes by developing an argument for why judicial intervention is needed to induce them to do so.

Chapter 2 explores how historically the U.S. Supreme Court has emphasized the role that schools should play in preparing their students to be capable citizens. The chapter focuses in particular on the implications of the U.S. Supreme Court's 1925 ruling in *Pierce v. Society of Sisters*[32] that the state has the right to insist that all schools, including private schools, teach "studies plainly essential to good citizenship." Despite that clear holding, however, neither the Supreme Court nor the lower federal courts have taken steps to ensure that all public and private schools do, in fact, provide the kind of education that is "essential to good citizenship."

Importantly, in its 1973 holding in *Rodriguez v. San Antonio Independent School District*,[33] the Supreme Court held that education is not a "fundamental interest" under the federal constitution, but the justices did agree that education is essential for the effective practice of First Amendment freedoms and to the intelligent exercise of the right to vote. The Court declined to order the school-funding equity improvements sought by the plaintiffs in that case, but it indicated that it might reconsider in a future case whether there is a fundamental interest under the U.S. Constitution to ensure that all students receive the level of education necessary for them to function as capable citizens.

The Supreme Court's rejection of the fiscal equity claims of the *Rodriguez* plaintiffs shut the doors of the federal courthouses to advocates of reforming inequities in state education finance systems, most of which stem from the states' reliance for school funding on local property taxes, which inherently favors affluent communities. As a result, advocates of equity in school funding turned to the state courts; since 1973, litigation regarding the equity and adequacy of educational funding has been brought in forty-five of the fifty states. These court decisions and their implications for establishing a right to an adequate education for civic participation are the subject of chapter 3.

Plaintiffs have won the large majority of these cases in state courts.

As discussed earlier, in recent years, numerous state courts have specifically held that preparing students to function productively as civic participants is a primary purpose of public education. Some of the cases have discussed in detail what an education for citizenship should entail and the essential resources that would be needed to provide effective civic education for all students. However, largely because plaintiff attorneys have not asked the courts to enforce these precedents, the decrees that the courts have issued to date have not specifically mandated reforms related to civic preparation.

Precisely which school-based changes are needed to promote the development of capable citizens is the subject of chapters 4 and 5. Chapter 4 explores the political theory and educational policy literature relevant to providing the civic knowledge, skills, experiences, and values necessary for a diverse contemporary democratic society. It draws on this literature to develop a conceptual framework that delineates the main challenges that need to be considered. The framework emphasizes the need to provide all students with (1) broad-based civic knowledge that includes a strong grounding in civics, history, and economics, as well as in science, arts, and other humanistic subjects; (2) cognitive and verbal skills, as well as the critical analytic skills needed for democratic deliberation; (3) school governance experiences, extracurricular activities, and involvement in school-connected community service programs; and (4) basic character values like responsibility, honesty, work ethic, and self-discipline, as well as important democratic values like tolerance, equality, due process, respect for the rule of law, and support for the fundamental political institutions of our society. The chapter posits that preparing American students for civic participation necessitates recognizing and embracing our communities' increasing diversity. It also requires taking aggressive steps to establish equal educational opportunities for students in poverty and students of color.

Chapter 5 advances specific proposals, based on research and best practices, for carrying out the reforms that are called for in chapter 4. Civics and social studies classes that provide students with a deep understanding of how governmental institutions actually function and that emphasize both the accomplishments and the shortcomings of American democracy, past and present, should be required in all schools. Schools also need to provide all students with access to a broad, humanistic curriculum and to a full range of co-curricular and extracurricular activities. Teachers must help develop in their students higher-order thinking skills and critical analytic approaches. Chapter 5 shows how schools can accomplish these aims, offering specific examples of policies and techniques that some pioneering schools and educators have already implemented on issues like instructing students on how to deliberate respectfully with others on controversial issues and how to apply critical analysis to their use of the Internet and social media.

Schools also need to be able to provide all of their students with experiences that contribute to their civic preparation, including, but not limited to, involvement in community service and school and community improvement experiences, and online games and other simulated political activities. The chapter demonstrates how the character values and democratic values that are critical for civic preparation and agency can be taught effectively in an ideologically neutral manner.

In chapters 6 and 7, I propose specific, feasible actions that both the state and the federal courts can and should take to enforce the schools' constitutional responsibility to prepare students to function productively as civic participants. Chapter 6 explores additional remedies that the state courts that have issued school-funding equity and adequacy decrees can develop in order to implement the civic participation standards they have already articulated but have not yet enforced. It also discusses the kinds of decrees that courts that have ruled against plaintiffs in past equity and adequacy cases should now consider in response to the urgent need for civic preparation. State courts could issue general remedial decrees mandating greater attention to civic preparation needs but vesting in state officials substantial discretion to develop and implement appropriate standards for civic education, to provide necessary resources, and to assess the results of their efforts.

In the alternative, or in addition, some state courts might issue more specific remedial orders, depending on the strength of the evidence in particular cases. Examples of such decrees include requiring schools to instruct students in how to apply critical analytic skills to their use of social media and ensuring that all schools offer all students an appropriate range of extracurricular activities and opportunities for involvement in community activities. A discussion of the actions that state courts can take to promote increased diversity, desegregation, and inclusion and to ensure that all schools have sufficient resources to provide meaningful educational opportunities to all of their students concludes this chapter.

Chapter 7 argues that it is also important for the federal courts, and, in particular, the U.S. Supreme Court, to promote preparation for civic participation. Although the state courts can do much to ensure that all schools, public and private, fulfill their responsibility to provide all students with the necessary learning opportunities, the federal constitution has enhanced moral and political standing in our culture. A strong pronouncement from the U.S. Supreme Court would be the most effective way to ensure that all students in all states actually receive meaningful preparation for civic participation.

In chapter 7, I also propose a detailed legal strategy to respond to the Supreme Court's indication in *Rodriguez* that it might consider establishing a federal right to effective civic preparation in a future case. In addition, I discuss further legal theories for establishing a federal right to education based on the privileges and immunities clause of the Fourteenth Amendment and the republican guarantee clause of article 4 of the U.S. Constitution. Consideration is also given to whether the Court should issue a declaratory decision that leaves the development of the specifics of how the right should be implemented to the states and the lower federal courts and/or a specific order that mandates that the schools take action in certain priority areas like teaching students how to deliberate respectfully with people who hold different views from their own and how to develop critical analytic skills to deal effectively with information on the Internet and social media.

The book concludes in the final chapter with reflections on two major concerns that some readers are likely to express. First, is this approach legitimate? That is, under our system of separation of powers, is it appropriate for courts to intervene in issues of education policy and administration? Second, is this approach plausible? Would judges agree to take on such an active role in promoting preparation for civic participation in the schools, and would policy makers, educators, and the public accept such a stance? I also offer some concluding observations on the profound impact that a decisive stance on education for capable citizenship by the state and federal courts could have for the continued integrity of American democratic culture and the American political system.

CHAPTER ONE

The Civic Participation Crisis—and the Civic Empowerment Gap

We live today in a polity . . . that lacks the civic resources to sustain self-government.
—Lorraine Smith Pangle and Thomas L. Pangle

The American Revolution was not only a war for independence from England; it was also the catalyst of an unprecedented experiment in democratic government and civic participation. The war gave new impetus to concepts of liberty, freedom, and democracy that had inspired the colonists; it involved many more people in thinking about those ideas, and it compelled citizens of the states to enter into weighty conversations about how to create effective local and national political structures to guide the new nation.[1] The nation's founders also realized that to maintain and expand this fledgling democracy, they would need to create a new civic ethos, and schooling would need to play a central role in "the deliberate fashioning of a new republican character, rooted in the American soil . . . and committed to the promise of an American culture."[2]

Schools were already playing a larger role in the American colonies than they had in Europe.[3] But the founding fathers understood that for the kind of active democratic culture they sought, *all* citizens would need to obtain the knowledge and skills needed to make intelligent decisions. As John Adams wrote: "A memorable change must be made in the system of education and knowledge must become so general as to raise the lower ranks of society nearer to the higher. The education of a nation instead of being confined to a few schools and universities for the instruction of the few, must become the national care and expense for the formation of the many."[4] Similarly, Thomas Jefferson said that each citizen would need "to know his rights, to exercise with order and justice those he retains; to choose with discretion the fiduciary of those he delegates; and to notice their conduct with diligence, with candor and with judgment."[5]

The founding fathers' overall perspective on the purposes of education was clearly civic. While they valued the teaching of basic academic skills, they placed greater emphasis on developing citizens who would protect and nurture the new democracy. For example, reading was important, they thought, not as an abstract skill but mainly because it would "teach good political judgment, allow learning from prior generations' mistakes and successes, and inculcate honesty, integrity and compassion."[6]

Benjamin Franklin and James Madison attempted to include some form of public funding for education in the U.S. Constitution, but their proposals fell victim to fears that the national government was already gaining too much power under the constitutional scheme.[7] An emphatic commitment to public education was, however, clearly reflected in language that was written into the constitutions of most of the thirteen original states. Thus, the Massachusetts Constitution proclaims the critical importance of education to a democracy and commits the state to "cherish" education in perpetuity: "Wisdom and knowledge, as well as virtue, diffused generally among the body of the people, being necessary for the preservation of their rights and liberties; and as these depend on spreading the opportunities and advantages of education in the various parts of the country, and among the different orders of the people, it shall be the duty of legislatures and magistrates, in all future periods of this Commonwealth, to cherish the interests of literature and the sciences, and all seminaries of them; especially the . . . public schools and grammar schools in the towns."[8] For the drafters of the state constitutions, "virtue," by which they meant the "capacity to transcend their diverse self-interests by favoring the common good of the political community,"[9] was "an urgent necessity, a matter literally affecting the survival of the new Republic."[10] As Moses Mather put it in 1775, "The strength and spring of every free government is the virtue of the people; virtue grows on knowledge, and knowledge on education."[11]

In the late eighteenth century, schools in rural areas (where 95 percent of the people lived) were typically organized by the locality and financed by a combination of property taxes, fuel contributions, tuition payments, and state aid.[12] After the revolution, some states initially responded to the heightened interest in civic education, reflected in the state constitutions, by requiring local towns to found schools and sometimes by providing some financial support for them. For example, the Pennsylvania Constitution of 1776 provided that "a school or schools shall be established in each county by the legislature,"[13] and a Massachusetts statute enacted in 1789 required each town to maintain a school and directed schoolmasters to instruct children in the "virtues which are the basis upon which the republican Constitution is structured."[14] The Massachusetts law did not provide any state funding for education, but some other states did. For example, in 1795, the New York legislature appropriated $50,000 a year to be divided among local school committees that agreed to match at least half of their state allotment with local funds.[15]

The vitality unleashed by the revolution led not only to renewed interest in educating students for citizenship but also to a blossoming of civic involvement by citizens in general. The country's federal structure and its continued expansion encouraged the proliferation of new civic associations and diverse forms of civic engagement: "The number of [voluntary] associations in Boston went from 14 before 1760 to 121 between 1760 and 1830 (a roughly 760 percent increase). However, the number in the rest of Massachusetts/Maine went from 24 before 1760 to 1,281 between 1760 and 1830—an increase of more than 5,000 percent."[16]

The American experience of civic participation that developed during the post-Revolutionary era was powerful, as the French aristocrat Alexis de Tocqueville noted during his travels here in the early nineteenth century: "Americans of all ages, all stations in life, and all types of disposition are forever forming associations. There are not only commercial and industrial associations in which all take part, but others of a thousand different types—religious, moral, serious, futile, very general and very limited, immensely large and very minute. . . . In every case, at the head of any new undertaking, where in France you would find the government or in England some territorial magnate, in the United States you are sure to find an association."[17] In short, involvement in the life of the community was a vital part of every citizen's daily life; preparing the next generation for such a civic life was the schools' primary mission.

The Establishment of Common Schools

By the 1830s, the combination of rapid industrialization, population growth, mobility, and immigration fueled a broad-based movement to implement a free public school system dedicated to moral education and good citizenship.[18] The "common school" movement that began in New England spread rapidly to other states. The common school was an attempt to educate in one setting all the children living in a particular geographic area, whatever their class, religious, or ethnic background. Such a school "would be open to all and supported by tax funds. It would be for rich and poor alike, the equal of any private institution."[19] The term "common" in this context had a dual meaning: the schools would provide an education to students from all strata in one common setting, and this would be accomplished by centralizing administration of the schools under the auspices of a single education department in each state.

These common schools would replace the prior patchwork of town schools partially supported by parental contributions, church schools, "pauper schools," and private schools with a new form of systematic, statewide democratic schooling. For Horace Mann, the founder of the common school movement: "Education must be universal. . . . With us, the qualification of voters is as important as the qualification of governors, and even comes first, in the natural order. . . . The theory of our government is—not that all men, however unfit, shall be voters—but that every man, by the power of reason and the sense of duty, shall become fit to be a voter. Education must bring the practice as nearly as possible to the theory. As the children now are, so will the sovereigns soon be."[20]

The primacy of preparation for citizenship among the goals of schooling persisted throughout the nineteenth and most of the twentieth century. As one school superintendent put it in 1862, "The chief end is to make GOOD CITIZENS. Not to make precocious scholars . . . not to impart the secret of acquiring wealth . . . not to qualify directly for professional success . . . but simply to make good citizens."[21] During the Progressive Era at the turn of the twentieth century, public education became compulsory as policy makers sought to assimilate and acculturate the waves of new immigrants who were populating America's cities. A new curriculum approach, known as social studies, was developed by Progressive educators in the 1930s to "reflect the emerging social sciences (economics, sociology, etc.) as it attempted to address the pressing social problems of a rapidly industrializing nation."[22]

John Dewey, the leading progressive educator at the time, advocated an additional civic role for the schools. He saw them as miniature communities in which students should be active participants in democratic processes rather than passive recipients of abstract information.[23] Dewey sought to shape both the educational environment and the formal curriculum to enhance students' ability to participate in the political life of the community, broadly defined.[24] During the 1930s, 1940s, and 1950s, the schools' civic preparation role was infused with an extra dimension of patriotic ardor in order to meet the challenges of the Depression era and to support the national effort to save the world for democracy. As noted in an influential 1938 report: "If schools are to help in the defense of the democratic ideal, their purposes must be defined in terms of that ideal. . . . Those who administer and teach in the schools must regard the study of democracy as their first responsibility."[25]

Civic Participation Today

Beginning in the second half of the twentieth century, the schools' predominant civic focus began to erode. Today, education for citizenship no longer permeates the school curriculum, and "civic education" has come to be a discrete and diminishing component of the schooling experience. The U.S. Department of Education has itself acknowledged this reality. In a report issued in 2012, it stated: "Unfortunately, civic learning and democratic engagements are add-ons rather than essential parts of the core academic mission in too many schools and on too many college campuses today. Many elementary and secondary schools are pushing civics and service-learning to the sidelines, mistakenly treating education for citizenship as a distraction from preparing students for college-level mathematics, English and other core subjects."[26]

As a result of this neglect, American students' knowledge of basic political facts is pitifully low. For example, on the civics exam administered in 2014 by the National Assessment of Educational Progress (NAEP)—known as "the nation's report card"—only 23 percent of a national sample of eighth graders scored at or above a "proficient" level.[27] The depth of ignorance that these scores reflect were further highlighted in a recent report on the schools' civic mission that recounted the following:

- Less than one-third of eighth graders could identify the historical purpose of the Declaration of Independence, and less than a fifth of high school seniors could explain how citizen participation benefits democracy.
- In 2006, in the midst of both midterm elections and the Iraq [W]ar, fewer than half of Americans could name the three branches of government, and only four in ten young people (aged 18 to 24) could find Iraq on the map.
- Only one in five Americans between the ages of 18 and 34 read a newspaper, and only one in ten regularly click on news web pages.[28]

Other recent surveys have revealed that although the main political stake in the 2014 midterm election was control of the Senate and House of Representatives, only 38 percent of the public knew that the Democrats controlled the Senate before the election, and the same percentage knew the Republicans controlled the House. In one survey, only 20 percent knew that the poverty rate is closer to 15 percent than to 5 percent, 25 percent, or 35 percent, and only 17 percent knew that the percentage of the federal budget spent on foreign aid is less than 5 percent.[29]

With this level of ignorance of civic matters, if most native-born Americans were required to take the citizenship test that is administered to those seeking to become naturalized American citizens, they would fail.[30] There are also disturbing patterns in these surveys: "Men are more informed than women; whites are more informed than blacks; those with higher incomes are more informed than those with lower incomes, and older citizens are more informed than younger ones."[31]

This lack of basic political knowledge and the widespread political apathy associated with it can have serious political consequences. As Michael Delli Carpini and Scott Keeter point out, political knowledge promotes civic virtues like political tolerance, encourages active participation in politics, helps citizens construct stable and consistent opinions on a broad array of topics, aids them in identifying their true interests, and allows them to link their attitudes with their participation so that their participation serves their interests.[32]

Given the level of political ignorance and apathy, though, it is not surprising that relatively few Americans actually bother to vote. In the 2016 presidential election only 56.8 percent of Americans eligible to vote chose to do so. This means that nearly one hundred million Americans failed to go to the polls.[33] In the 2014 midterm elections, turnout was even worse: only 36.7 percent of eligible voters cast ballots that year.[34]

These percentages are consistent with the general trend of voter turnout for presidential and midterm elections for the past seventy years.

America's youngest voters in particular have become less engaged over time. The voting rates for eighteen through twenty-four-year-olds dropped from 50.9 percent in 1964 to 38 percent in 2012.[35] The norms "that a good citizen pays attention and votes have been weakening with each generation," said Rutgers political science professor Cliff Zukin. "So by now most people see it as a choice rather than a duty. Most feel there are few if any affirmative obligations of citizenship."[36]

Those who bother to vote sometimes do not really know what they are voting for. Many Florida voters—perhaps enough to shift the outcome of the 2000 presidential election—failed to understand the voting instructions and so cast their votes for a candidate whom they did not mean to endorse.[37] Similarly, on a recent Colorado anti–affirmative action referendum, many voted against affirmative action even though they meant to support it because of their confusion over the description of the intent of the ballot initiative.[38] There are also increasing signs that citizens are shirking civic obligations that are essential to the maintenance of a democratic political order. For example, about 30 percent of those summoned for mandatory jury duty in 2014 in California's Los Angeles and San Diego Counties simply failed to show up.[39]

Americans rank 139th in voter participation out of 172 world democracies.[40] Among citizens who do not vote, there is also a tendency not to participate—in any sustaining way—in other political or community civic activities.[41] There is a clear link between involvement in civic organizations and political participation; the one feeds on the other.[42] Not surprisingly, therefore, with the dramatic decline in recent decades in involvement in civic associations, parent-teacher associations, and religious organizations, overall social bonds have atrophied.

Robert Putnam, in his classic volume *Bowling Alone*,[43] documented that between 1973 and 1994, the number of people who served as an officer of a club or organization, worked for a political party, served on a committee, or attended a public meeting on town or school affairs declined by more than 42 percent.[44] These trends were consistent in all parts of the country—urban, suburban, and rural—and affected all classes of the population.[45] Putnam pinpointed the decline of traditional civic spirit as starting around the 1960s. He described a striking difference in civic involvement of the generation born in the 1920s and the generation born in the 1960s: "Controlling for educational disparities, members of the generation born in the 1920s belong to almost twice as many civic associations. . . . They vote at nearly double the rate of the most recent cohorts (80–85 percent vs. 45–50 percent). The grandparents are . . . twice as likely to work on a community project . . . they are almost three times as likely to read a daily newspaper (75 percent vs. 25 percent)."[46]

Putnam's findings have aroused considerable interest and some controversy. For example, other studies have found that while unions, fraternal organizations, sports-related groups, and Greek organizations experienced decreased levels of participation from 1974 to 1994, other group types—church-related organizations, hobby clubs, literary groups, professional associations, and school-related groups—saw increases in membership during the same period.[47] There also appears to have been substantial growth in membership in national organizations like the Sierra Club and Greenpeace USA since the 1960s.[48] Danielle Allen claims that Putnam ignored the impact of U.S. Supreme Court decisions that outlawed gender discrimination in associations like the Jaycees and Rotary clubs, and that membership in such organizations may have fallen because of these antidiscrimination mandates and not for the reasons he posits.[49]

Other studies, however, appear to have confirmed Putnam's findings. Recent federal data, for example, show declines in sixteen of twenty indicators of civic health, including falling rates of volunteerism and engagement with community organizations and flagging trust in public institutions.[50] Similarly, extensive survey data indicate dramatic changes between 1985 and 2004 in core networks, with substantially more people stating that they discuss important matters with no one or only with spouses and parents, and have fewer contacts through voluntary associations and neighborhoods.[51] A particularly disturbing recent study on democratic values found that when asked to rate on a scale of 1 to 10 how "essential" it is for them "to live in a democracy," 72 percent of those born before World War II chose 10, the highest value, but among millennials, only about 30 percent accorded maximal importance to living in a democracy.[52]

Although analyses of a decline in social capital over time are difficult to compare because of different definitions of social capital and variations in data,[53] it does appear that in recent decades there have been substantial qualitative and quantitative changes in Americans' involvement with community groups that engage in civic affairs.[54] Notable in this regard is that membership in civic organizations today is marked more by affiliation with large national organizations, which involves paying dues and signing petitions, or in local affinity groups that involve less time commitment and interpersonal bonding activities than did involvement with civic associations in the past.[55]

The Civic Empowerment Gap

The decline in civic knowledge and civic participation affects all students attending school today, but the gaps in civic knowledge and civic participation are particularly acute for African American students and students living in poverty, creating what Harvard professor Meira Levinson has called a "civic empowerment gap."[56] African American students on average have lower verbal achievement scores, as well as lower scores in civics and history than white students. For example, on the 2015 NAEP reading assessments, 46 percent of white eighth graders achieved proficiency scores, compared with 16 percent of black students.[57] On the 2014 NAEP test in civics, while 32 percent of white eighth graders performed at or above the proficient level, only 9 percent of black students did the same, while in U.S. history, 26 percent of white students performed proficiently, as compared with 6 percent of black students.[58]

The basic opportunity gap in programs and services that are available to African American and other minority students, as well as to students living in poverty, directly affects their civic education. For example, a recent study of the classroom experiences of African American and Latino students in California revealed that African American students had fewer civic-oriented government classes, current event discussions, and experiences in an open classroom climate than did white students, and Latino students reported fewer opportunities to participate in community service, simulations, and open classroom climates than did white students. The authors of this study also report that an additional study they undertook found that students in classes with an average lower socioeconomic status were roughly 50 percent less likely than students in classes with higher socioeconomic status to report having studied how laws are made or to have participated in service activities.[59]

Seth Andrew, the founder of Democracy Prep, a group of charter schools in the Harlem area of New York, describes why students from poverty backgrounds tend to exhibit a civic gap: "Low-income adults tend to participate in politics at much lower rates than more affluent citizens, trust government less, and have a weaker sense of political efficacy. Because low-income parents often lack these prerequisites for engaged civic life, they are less likely to pass on expectations for active citizenship and political participation to their children. What is more, less active parents may even pass on a real mistrust of government and sense of powerlessness, both of which can depress any attachment to civic life in their children."[60] For many African American students, the causes of the gap are even more deep rooted.

But the civic engagement gap goes deeper than disparities in test scores and opportunities for civic learning. The combined impact of the legacy of slavery, the contemporary realities of segregation, discrimination, and poverty, and explicit or implicit bias and low expectations from their teachers have left many African American students disillusioned, cynical, and largely indifferent to civic issues.[61] David Yaeger and his colleagues describe the vicious cycle that results from these factors: "Racial and ethnic minority youth, experiencing and perceiving bias, may generalize from specific interactions to a mental representation of the institution as an abstract entity. Youth may then demonstrate lower compliance with institutional policies, accelerating a self-reinforcing cycle of punishment and loss of trust. . . . Thus, [they] may be twice-harmed by institutional injustices: they both receive the lion's share of the initial punishment, and then may be required to psychologically adapt, through a loss of trust, in a way that prevents them from profiting from instruction and relationships."[62]

Regarding the civic empowerment gap, Levinson, an associate professor at Harvard Graduate School of Education who previously taught for eight years in all-black middle schools in Atlanta and Boston, tells of the reaction of her eighth-grade students when they heard of the attack on the World Trade Center on September 11, 2001, illustrating the implications of this profound distrust of basic American institutions: The students' immediate response to the attack was "I bet George Bush is behind this. . . . Bush doesn't care about anybody except rich people, and he wants to go to war with Iraq to take revenge for what his Saddam Hussein did to his dad."[63] Levinson relates how she was completely taken aback by this response: "Up until now, I've taken my students' questions in stride: their naiveté about the Pentagon, their confusion about their relationship between Manhattan and New York. . . . But this vitriol against Bush, and their almost sanguine assumption that the president of the United States might choose to and be capable of killing 5,000, maybe 10,000 American citizens[,] simply on a whim—I find it breathtaking in its combination of utter ignorance and absolute cynicism."[64]

Levinson then reflected on the implications of these attitudes on her desire to orient these students toward civic participation: "How on earth could I convince them to become civically and politically engaged—simply to vote, let alone to contact government officials, write letters, volunteer for campaigns, or even run for office themselves—if they believed their elected officials might readily murder 10,000 Americans on a whim."[65]

This "chasm" in trust in government institutions also affects children of many immigrant families. Levinson reports, for example, that many second-generation Arab students consistently use the term "Americans" to refer not to themselves but to other citizens.[66] The rhetoric of the 2016 election campaign has, of course, substantially increased this sense of anxiety and alienation among students from immigrant families.[67]

It is not surprising, therefore, that African Americans and Latinos consistently rank lower on indices of civic participation. African American voter participation rates are somewhat below those of whites, and Hispanic voter participation rates are substantially lower. In the 2014 congressional races, 45.8 percent of eligible whites voted, compared with 40.6 percent of blacks and 27 percent of Hispanic voters.[68] In terms of income disparities, a recent survey found that higher-income families were

- Four times as likely to be part of campaign work;
- Three times as likely to do informal community work;
- Twice as likely to contact elected officials; and
- Six times as likely to sit on a board.[69]

Demographers project that, over the next forty-five years, the proportion of the nonwhite U.S. population in the age category of zero to eighteen (i.e., the school-aged population) will grow from 43 percent to 64 percent.[70] This means that, unless the civic empowerment gap is ameliorated, as society becomes more diverse, apathy regarding "civic virtues" may become even more pronounced, and the maintenance of a vibrant democratic culture may become even more endangered.

Causes of Decline

Robert Putnam cited a number of factors for the decline in civic participation that he described in *Bowling Alone*, including the feminist movement, suburbanization, electronic entertainment, the cultural revolt against authority and Vietnam and Watergate. Although Putnam estimates that the surge in women working full-time has contributed no more than 10 percent to the diminution of community involvement,[71] other writers have seen a much greater causal connection between the decline in civic participation because of the impact of feminism and changes in the traditional family structure.

Mary Ann Glendon contends, for example, that families historically have been "first and foremost" among the "seedbeds of republican virtues,"[72] and she contends that "the weakening of child-raising families and their surrounding and supporting institutions constitutes our culture's most serious long-term problem."[73] In 2012, more than 40 percent of all births occurred out of wedlock,[74] and "for the children who are born into an intact family, the odds that their parents will stay together are lower in American society than in any other industrial nation."[75] This growing family instability has significant negative consequences, according to William Damon, for political and cultural socialization: "Families without at least a modicum of stability and continuity cannot establish the household routines that provide children with opportunities to learn virtues such as industry, self-control, and obligation. Families without the presence of dependable adults cannot provide children with examples of virtues they can emulate, nor can they offer the regular occasions needed to explain the nature and importance of virtuous behavior in the often-confusing social world that the child is entering."[76]

However, not all commentators accept the view that feminism and the change in family dynamics in recent decades necessarily undermine the "seedbeds" of civic virtue. For example, Linda McClain believes that new attitudes toward gender roles in the family help turn youth into capable, responsible, and self-governing citizens.[77] Others cite research that indicates that the development, adjustment, and well-being of children raised by lesbian and gay parents do not differ markedly from those of children with heterosexual parents.[78]

Damon also laments that, since Vietnam War era, "the idea of devotion to one's country . . . has been out of fashion in American cultural life."[79] Public confidence in American governmental institutions has shown marked declines from historical averages. Recent Gallup polls indicate that only 32 percent of those surveyed expressed "quite a lot" or a "great deal" of confidence in the U.S. Supreme Court, compared with a 44 percent historical average. Only 33 percent reported confidence in the presidency, as compared with 43 percent in the past. Only 8 percent reported confidence in Congress, a sharp decline from a 24 percent historical average.[80]

Others have claimed that a decline in commitment to organized religion has detrimentally affected civic engagement in recent decades.[81] According to a series of 2016 Gallup polls, 54 percent of Americans surveyed claimed to be members of a church or synagogue, while nearly 70 percent claimed the same in 1992.[82] Although a majority of Americans continue to have some religious affiliation, the extent of their participation in the institution's affairs has declined, as has public confidence in religious leaders.[83]

Indisputably, in many parts of the United States there has been a weakening of traditional family, religious, and patriotic values and of confidence in many traditional institutions since the 1960s; it is, however, far from clear that these factors are the major causes of the apparent decline in civic participation since that time. Much of the discussion of these changes is imbued with nostalgia for a golden age that never existed, and such recollections of the past often overlook the patterns of racial segregation, gender discrimination, and authoritarianism that previously existed and that most people today would be loath to reinstate. Russell Dalton has argued that citizenship norms are changing, from a "duty-bound" citizenship to an "engaged citizenship" marked by protest, tolerance, support for social policy, and less trust in government.[84] The stark attitudinal alienation from many traditional civic institutions that many African American and other students of color express is largely because the civil rights era created a new awareness of rights and opportunities, but, in the decades since, those expectations and aspirations have remained unfulfilled. The impact of globalization and the loss of solid middle-class jobs have also alienated many white middle-class families from their faith in traditional institutions.

Much of what has been described as a decline in civic participation can, therefore, also be seen as a societal failure to marry the continuing need for all citizens' vibrant civic participation in a democratic society with the new values, new rights, rapid technological change, and eightened expectations—and failure to fulfill those expectations—that have become important realities in the twenty-first century. How to infuse the individual rights, cultural diversity, rapid technological change, high expectations, and new types of communication into an informed, stable form of civic participation that is supportive of democratic values is the core challenge today.

The rapid changes in communications technology since the 1960s exemplify how traditional modes of civic engagement have been undermined, but at the same time, these changes have created vast potential new opportunities for civic participation. Robert Putnam described at length the effect on civic involvement of the impact of new modes of communications (largely television at the time he was writing).[85] He noted that in 1900, "music lovers needed to sit with scores of other people at fixed times listening to fixed programs," and that, "as late as 1975, Americans nationwide chose among a handful of television programs."[86] Today, of course, electronic technology allows us to consume tailored entertainment in private rather than in group or communal settings.

Putnam also described how newspaper readership, which he believed to be a major mark of civic engagement, had plunged during the second half of the twentieth century,[87] and he claimed that those who rely on TV news are less civically involved than newspaper readers.[88] The decline in newspaper readership has, of course, become even more pronounced in the years since his book was published, given the exponential growth of the Internet and social media.[89] In 2013, most people younger than age fifty said that the Internet, rather than television, was their main source of news, and close to 80 percent of people aged eighteen to twenty-nine said they check the news in spurts throughout the day instead of tuning in at a regular time, like for the five-o'clock news.[90] The percentage of Americans between the ages of eighteen and twenty-five who consistently follow the news in election years fell from 24 percent in 1960 to 10 percent in 2004 (a slight improvement over the nadir in 2000).[91]

Although Putnam and others believe that technological changes in communications have had a detrimental effect on civic awareness and civic participation, the explosion in use of electronic media, especially among the young, also has potentially enormous positive implications for civic participation. Blogs, online news stories with comment threads, wikis, and Twitter exchanges have removed the hierarchy of knowledge dissemination and democratized participation; they challenge the concentration of information and opinion in newspapers and television outlets, which increasingly have come to be controlled by a few corporations and wealthy individuals. Computers, cell phones, Facebook, and Twitter allow for many more voices to be heard and for information to be broadly disseminated, and they have enabled rapid mobilization for direct political action. People can be quickly mobilized to support political stances and to initiate and organize boycotts, demonstrations, and rallies. Indeed, the massive political movements in 2011 that came to be known as the Arab Spring were created and sustained largely by Internet and cell-phone contact among youthful activists.[92]

But there also is a downside to this cultural shift. Political activism engendered through the Internet and social media can be ephemeral rather than sustained. Joining a social movement does not necessarily commit anyone to becoming part of an organization or to working to maintain the enterprise. Rather, these movements "mobilize people sporadically and spontaneously and allow easy exit."[93] The pervasive use of laptops, cell phones, and other electronic devices can also undermine interpersonal relations in more profound ways: "As we instant message, e-mail, text, and Twitter, technology redraws the boundaries between intimacy and solitude. . . . Teenagers avoid making telephone calls, fearful that they 'reveal too much.' They would rather text than talk. Adults, too choose keyboards over the human voice. It is more efficient they say. Things that happen in 'real time' take too much time. Tethered to technology, we are shaken when the world 'unplugged' does not signify, does not satisfy."[94]

Furthermore, as the 2016 election campaign dramatically demonstrated, much of the discussion of issues that takes place on the Internet is superficial, one-sided, and false, and does not foster deliberation and debate. The enormous number of blogs, talk radio shows, and cable news outlets increases partisanship and often impedes, rather than promotes, civic dialogue. The growth of new media has been accompanied by a reduction in the numbers of professional reporters and investigative staff, and often the information transmitted through the Internet, the blogosphere, and social media is highly repetitive or represents entertainment news rather than current events or political information.[95] A recent search involving six major news topics found that "83 percent of the articles and blog posts repeated the same material—sometimes with commentary—and more than half of the original text came from paid print media."[96]

In short, then, how to harness the enormous positive potential of the new technologies—as well as the positive aspects of individual rights, cultural diversity, and globalization—and overcome their drawbacks, rather than lament putative positive aspects of days gone by, is the real challenge for civic preparation in the twenty-first century. Even if the civic education offered in the mid-twentieth century was adequate for the highly structured and somewhat hierarchical civil society of that time, it won't suffice for a world of much flatter networks and more individualized choice.

Directions for Civic Renewal

The greatest problem in reinvigorating civic participation in America today is the extreme polarization of views on major cultural and political issues. A decade ago, Ronald Dworkin, a noted legal and political philosopher, summarized the current political scene in terms that reverberate even more intensely today: "American Politics are in an appalling state. We disagree, fiercely, about almost everything. We disagree about terror and security, social justice, religion in politics, who is fit to be a judge and what democracy is. These are not civil disagreements: each side has no respect for the other. We are no longer partners in self-government; our politics are rather a form of war."[97] Despite his blunt, realistic description of the current scene, Dworkin thought it possible and important to put forward an analysis of shared principles on major issues of the day including abortion, gay marriage, and tax policy that he believed could make "a national political debate possible and profitable."[98]

Articulating shared principles that could possibly form the basis for a meaningful national debate is one thing; getting the warring parties to agree to actually take part in such an enterprise is, of course, a much more daunting challenge. The key question is, as Amitai Etzioni has stated, not only how rational people are but also how rational the social institutions are in which they function.[99] Dworkin seemed to agree. At the end of his book, he put forward three important proposals for institutional change that, though difficult, he thought should be pursued: radical reforms in education, in elections, and in the role of the courts.[100]

Before his death, Dworkin provided only a bare sketch of what reforms of these institutions would look like. In regard to education, he called for a mandatory contemporary politics course in every high school that would take up the most contentious political controversies of the day. In regard to elections, he proposed the creation of two special public broadcasting channels during each presidential election period and strict limits on election advertising and campaign spending by all candidates. His invocation of the courts in this context was based on the courts' unique role in shaping societal values and the fact that the judiciary is the only institution that has "the practical power to check this serious threat to American values and freedom"[101] posed by the current culture wars and political polarization.

I agree with Dworkin's conclusion that major institutional changes in schools, elections, and courts are needed to spark and sustain a revitalization of public dialogues on major issues in the twenty-first century. I also concur with his insightful assessment of the constructive role that both schools and courts can play in creating possibilities not only for political dialogue but also for broader forms of civic engagement. A number of strategic educational and judicial initiatives can go far toward countering the decline in civic spirit and civic engagement among our youth and in establishing the conditions necessary to support the kinds of communal dialogues that could ease the extreme polarization that infects our current politics.

Improvement in election procedures is also important, and Dworkin was right to highlight the merits of strongly regulating political advertising, the structure of candidate debates, and campaign financing. He recognized when he made these suggestions, however, that they flew in the face of what was then First Amendment law as enunciated by the U.S. Supreme Court. He made a number of strong arguments for why these precedents should be reconsidered to allow for the kind of genuine political dialogue and substantive free speech that his proposals would engender. Since the time Dworkin made these proposals, however, the U.S. Supreme Court did revisit the issue of the constitutionality of political speech under the First Amendment, but it did not move in the direction that Dworkin had advocated. On the contrary, in *Citizens United v. Federal Election Commission*,[102] the Court removed all limits on campaign advertising by corporations and unions and indicated that any further attempts to regulate political speech would not likely pass constitutional muster.

Not only in regard to regulating candidate advertising and campaign finance, but also in many other ways, our political institutions today discourage broad citizen participation, induce partisan confrontation, and allow affluent elites to dominate the political process. Stephen Macedo and a group of distinguished political scientists analyzed these problems in depth and highlighted a number of causal factors, in addition to campaign finance issues, that discourage broad-based participation of citizens in the political process: the presidential primary process is long and boring, our systems of redrawing district boundaries strongly favor incumbents, safe congressional seats empower the ideological bases of the two parties at the expense of moderates, and our metropolitan political institutions encourage residential segregation and defy the premise of common public institutions and a sense of shared fate.[103]

To remedy these problems, Macedo and his colleagues proposed a number of far-reaching institutional reforms.[104] However desirable these reforms might be, however, the likelihood of all, many, or even any of them actually being adopted in the current intensely partisan political environment is practically nil. Indeed, since the political scientists published their proposals a decade ago, the structural ills that they seek to change have become even more pronounced. Registration and voting have become more difficult as a growing number of states have adopted rigorous voter identification laws,[105] and the gerrymandering of district boundaries has become even more pervasive.[106] Legislators are highly unlikely to enact far-reaching political reforms, most of which would be contrary to their electoral self-interest.

Especially in light of the continuing gridlock in our political system, it seems clear that schools, which have long been the primary locus for political socialization,[107] constitute the best arena for focusing efforts to promote civic engagement. If there is to be a thoroughgoing revitalization of civic engagement, that effort will need to begin by systematically imbuing the next generation of citizens—that is, our children and grandchildren—with experiences and values that motivate them to become civically engaged, and with knowledge and skills that will allow them to do so effectively. In other words, if schools can better educate students on the workings of political institutions, train them to engage in substantive dialogues on controversial political issues, and instill in them the values and skills they need to be effective political participants, in time a new generation of activist voters may be capable of bringing about the types of sensible changes that Dworkin and Macedo and his colleagues advocated.

Despite their current difficulties in preparing students for capable citizenship, schools today, as in the past, are the most critical institution for promoting civic participation. Schools are the foremost place in our society where people from diverse political backgrounds come together in a setting that prizes and rewards rational discussion and understanding of different views. If oppositional attitudes are to be countered or defused, this is likely to occur only in a venue where diversity is valued and young people at a formative age are encouraged to deal with differences through tolerance and respect.

Some argue that "mandates and expectations [on the schools] are already burdensome, and [that] . . . jamming more into the already crowded mission statement of the public school system" will not be productive.[108] However, as we have seen, imbuing students with civic knowledge and civic purpose has always been a prime purpose of the schools, and if the school day needs to be lengthened or if drivers' education or extensive test preparation have to be truncated to allow more time for schools to again fulfill their civic preparation mission, that should be the first priority. There is no escaping the simple reality that "Americans must invest more time and effort in civic education . . . because other educative institutions have lost the capacity or will to recruit young citizens into public life."[109]

Thus far, however, despite numerous calls for more emphasis on civic education, and dozens of specific proposals on how schools might be more effective in preparing students for civic engagement, contemporary schools by and large have not proved capable of the task. For example, more than a decade ago, the Carnegie Corporation and the Center for Information and Research on Civic Learning & Engagement (CIRCLE) issued a widely cited report that called on schools to establish civic education curricula based on six promising pedagogical approaches, including offering more instruction in government, history, law, and democracy; incorporating discussions of current events into the classroom; offering more extracurricular activities; promoting community service opportunities; encouraging student participation in school governance; and promoting student participation in simulations of democratic processes and procedures.[110] These and similar recommendations have been endorsed and reiterated by other commissions and political leaders.[111] Nevertheless, in recent years, school activities and efforts have, if anything, moved in an opposite direction from those called for in these reports.

The primary concern of most parents today appears to be ensuring that their children have a competitive edge in preparation for the job market. As David Labaree has shown, the "well-defined set of republican ideals [that] drove the creation of the American system of common schools" has given way in twenty-first-century American schools to a market-oriented view "emphasizing job skills and individual opportunity."[112] Students also increasingly view education as a means for obtaining high-paying employment opportunities and less as a broad-based preparation for civic involvement and individual fulfillment.[113] As Danielle Allen has aptly noted, "Our public discourse about education, our articulations of our collective goals, routinely leave out the civic."[114]

Less time is spent on instruction in government and social studies in schools today than in the past. Whereas three separate courses in democracy, civics, and government were common in the 1950s, in states where formal civic education still exists these days, it usually consists of only a single-semester course in government or civics. Moreover, this single course tends to describe and analyze American government from a distance, usually without any explicit discussion of the citizen's role and rarely with any attention paid to the animating principles lying behind our political and legal system.[115]

Since the enactment of the No Child Left Behind Act of 2001, which mandated high-stakes tests in reading and math but not in social studies, significant amounts of instructional time have been shifted from social studies and other subjects to math and English,[116] a pattern that has particularly affected students of color and students in poverty. In 2014, New York City schools chancellor Carmen Farina candidly admitted, "Because there was no test, a lot of schools dropped social studies from their curriculum."[117] In addition, in times of fiscal constraint, courses and activities that are directly related to civic preparation skills appear to be the first to be sacrificed; following the 2008 recession, student opportunities for involvement in extracurricular activities, school governance, and simulated democratic processes were substantially reduced, especially in many high-need schools.[118]

Is there any way to turn this situation around? Can the calls for renewed emphasis on preparing students for active civic participation that have been ignored in the past be heeded in the future? Peter Levine, the director of CIRCLE, who has studied these issues in depth, concluded that these fundamental problems can be solved only if "an outside power . . . appl[ies] leverage to change the priorities of schools and colleges."[119] The "outside power" that Levine had in mind was "the government or a social movement." But Levine and others have been petitioning governors, legislatures, and state education departments for years to take affirmative actions to promote civic engagement in the schools, with limited success. Nor is there any strong social movement on the horizon that is likely to heed Levine's call.

There is, however, such an "outside power" that can apply the necessary leverage to turn this situation around—the judiciary. Both the federal and the state courts have repeatedly issued strong statements on the important role of the schools in preparing students to function productively as civic participants. In many cases, judges have held that the schools have a constitutional responsibility to carry out this role. The courts have not, however, acted on their pronouncements by issuing decisions or orders that would require the schools to carry out their mission effectively.

The premise of this book is that the pressing need for schools to properly prepare students to be capable citizens requires both the federal and the state courts to induce the schools to make civic education a high priority. Judicial declarations of rights and responsibilities and court orders can inspire and motivate state policy makers and educators to prepare their students to confront and surmount the serious challenges to democratic functioning that our students—and all Americans—face today.

The judicial branch has a comparative institutional advantage in terms of staying power. Court decisions and court-ordered remedies, especially when grounded in constitutional obligations, cannot be lightly set aside according to periodic changes in politics or personalities. If the U.S. Supreme Court declares that educational opportunities to prepare students for civic participation constitute a constitutional right, that principle becomes a permanent, foundational feature of educational policy and planning throughout the country. Congress, state legislatures, and state and local school boards can develop comprehensive programs and policies and implement them on a sound basis without fearing that their successors will radically change course and wipe out their accomplishments.

The discussion of how schools can revitalize civic education to meet contemporary needs and how the courts can ensure that they do so will begin in the next chapter with an analysis of the judicial precedents that have established a firm constitutional basis for the courts to take on this role.

CHAPTER TWO

Civic Participation and the Federal Courts

Schools are where the "fundamental values necessary for the maintenance of a democratic political system" are conveyed. — U.S. Supreme Court, *Plyler v. Doe*, 1982

The founding fathers thought it essential for the maintenance of their new experiment in democracy to establish schools that would ensure that all voters have the basic literacy, calculating, and analytic skills needed to engage successfully in the political process. But by the 1830s, with the rapid expansion of the new nation, the founders of the common school movement had broader aims. They viewed the mission of the common schools not only as instilling academic and political skills but also as inculcating patriotic and moral values in an increasingly diverse population. Because of the "fast-paced urbanization, immigration, and industrialization of the period . . . [m]orality was the most important goal of common education."[1] Horace Mann, the initiator of the common school movement, expressed these character-building ideals in visionary terms: "Let the common school be expanded to its capabilities, let it be worked with the efficiency of which it is susceptible, and nine-tenths of the crimes in the penal code would become obsolete; the long catalogue of human ills would be abridged; men would walk more safely by day; every pillow would be more inviolable by night; property, life and character held by strong tenure; all rational hopes respecting the future brightened."[2]

The values imparted by the nineteenth-century common schools included traditional virtues like honesty and charity, distinctive American needs like individualism and self-reliance, work-related attributes like discipline, self-control, and industriousness, and democratic values like patriotism and civic responsibility. The kinds of values conveyed by the common schools were reflected in the McGuffey Readers, the widely used elementary school primer that sold more than 122 million copies between 1836 and 1920, and, by one estimate, guided the minds of four-fifths of the nation's schoolchildren during that era.[3] Through reading passages with titles such as "The Greedy Girl," "Advantages of Industry," and "George and the Hatchet," the McGuffey Readers well conveyed the basic character, discipline, and democratic values of "middle class, conventional" nineteenth-century America.[4]

The common schools were also expected to convey fundamental spiritual values of love of God, piety, and respect for religious institutions—as reflected in the McGuffey Reader entitled *Religion, the Only Basis of Society*.[5] Common school advocates expected there to be "daily readings of the Bible, devotional exercises, and the constant inculcation of the precepts of Christian morality in all the public schools."[6] To be sure, Mann and the other leaders of the common school movement did not want the common schools to engage in the type of sectarian, religious indoctrination that had prevailed in the local church schools they sought to replace. On the contrary, they considered one of their major reforms to be the common schools' nondenominational orientation; they emphasized "natural theology" and explicitly rejected liturgical practices and sectarian doctrines. On the goal of non-denominationalism, the Unitarian minister Charles Brooks stated in 1837, "The primary goal should be Christian, but neither Protestant nor Catholic. They should not lean to any particular form of worship nor teach any positive dogmas; but should be of that kind that Jews might attend them without inconvenience to their faith."[7]

Many orthodox Protestants objected to this approach to religious instruction; they decried the emphasis on nondenominational natural theology divorced from ritual and the teachings of revelation. Even more substantial opposition came from Catholic leaders who saw the common school curriculum and especially the "nondenominational" readings from the King James Bible as serious threats to the integrity of their faith. A number of attempts were made to negotiate methods that might allow common schools with Catholic majorities to use a different Bible or to otherwise assert their own religious perspectives, but these proved abortive. Part of the problem was doctrinal: common school leaders wanted the schools to be as nonsectarian as possible, while Catholic leaders wanted to keep "Catholic children on the Catholic path."[8]

In addition, the Catholic response also "had something to do with the beleaguered and defensive nature of American Catholicism: as a poor immigrant church, it was subject to significant hostility and discrimination."[9] Consequently, Catholic leaders decided early on to establish a separate parochial school system.[10]

The early common schools guaranteed access to education for all children in the community, but it was left to parents to decide whether to send their child to the local public school, a Catholic school, a private school, or no school at all. At the end of the nineteenth century most states began to adopt compulsory education laws, and by 1918, education was compulsory in every state in the union.[11] The move toward compulsory education was impelled by the inherent logic of the public purposes of the common schools, a desire to assimilate the large numbers of immigrants arriving in the nation's urban areas during the late nineteenth and early twentieth centuries and by the progressives' desire to limit the patterns of abusive child labor that were associated with rapid urbanization at the time.

The *Pierce* Compromise

Some also saw compulsory education as a way to enforce social controls, which traditionally had been exercised informally in smaller and more homogeneous communities, among the bulging immigrant populations in many urban areas.[12] Xenophobia aroused by World War I and a continuing fear of Bolsheviks drove the compulsory education movement in some places. Nativist groups sought to expand the scope of the compulsory education laws to require all students to attend only public schools in order to ensure that "proper" American values were fully inculcated.

One such effort culminated in a ballot initiative that was adopted in Oregon in 1922 to mandate that every child aged eight to sixteen attend a *public* school. The sanctions for noncompliance were draconian: if parents did not send their child to a public school, they were subject to fines and to a jail term of two to thirty days for each day of delinquency.[13] The campaign for the compulsory education initiative in Oregon had actually been led by the Ku Klux Klan, which had appropriated the inculcation of patriotic values in the public schools to advance their own agenda. It was somewhat ironic that they choose Oregon as the locale for this effort, since 95 percent of Oregon students were already enrolled in public schools and the state had few immigrants, few urban slums, virtually no black residents, and only a small complement of Catholics (8 percent). Tyack, James, and Benavot speculate that "it was because Oregon did approximate the ideal WASP society that partisans like the Klansmen chose it as a test case for compulsory education: there were so many of US and so few of THEM."[14]

The Oregon law was quickly challenged by two private schools, one run by a group of Catholic sisters and the other, a military academy. The U.S. Supreme Court upheld the challengers' position in its 1925 ruling in *Pierce v. Society of Sisters.*[15] *Pierce* declared that the law was unconstitutional and enjoined its enforcement before it could take effect. Although the Court's order to invalidate the Oregon statute was clear, the reasoning behind the decision and its precedential impact was quite complex.

The case presented the Supreme Court with a difficult dilemma. On the one hand, the state clearly had a legitimate interest in ensuring that immigrant children receive an education that would prepare them to function productively as American citizens. On the other hand, Catholics or other minorities had a strong claim that they are entitled to continue to promote their own religious and other values by educating their children in schools that emphasized doctrinal issues they considered vital for forming and maintaining their children's attitudes and beliefs.

The Court reached a Solomonic resolution of the basic dilemma. It upheld the right of parents to send their children to private schools but at the same time served notice that the state could impose basic regulations on such schools: "No question is raised concerning the power of the state reasonably to regulate all schools, to inspect, supervise and examine them, their teachers and pupils; to require that all children of proper age attend some school, that teachers shall be of good moral character and patriotic disposition, that certain studies plainly essential to good citizenship must be taught, and that nothing be taught which is manifestly inimical to the public welfare."[16] Mark Yudof described the subtle balance involved in this "*Pierce* compromise" as representing "a reasonable, if imperfect, accommodation of conflicting pressures": "The state may make some demands of private schools in satisfaction of compulsory schooling laws, but those demands may not be so excessive that they transform private schools into public schools managed and funded by the private sector. The integrity of the communications and socialization processes in private school and families remains intact, while the state's interest in producing informed, educated and productive citizens is not sacrificed."[17]

The precise legal rationale for the so-called *Pierce* compromise was, however, far from clear. The stated constitutional basis for the Court's holding was the parents' liberty right under the due process clause of the Fourteenth Amendment to "direct the education and upbringing of children under their control."[18] The parents, however, were not the plaintiffs in *Pierce*. Those challenging the law were private schools that claimed that their businesses would be ruined if their clients—that is, the children—were prohibited from attending their facilities. Although the Court held that corporations "cannot claim for themselves the liberty which the Fourteenth Amendment guarantees,"[19] the Court did uphold the plaintiffs' position in this case because of the nexus of the parents' liberty interest to the survival of the businesses.[20]

The interest of the Catholic Church and of groups operating other private schools was, therefore, established through an indirect link to the parents' due process right to "liberty." But what was the basis for the other side of the balancing equation: the state's right to regulate private schools? The lower court had referred in general terms to the state's inherent police power to issue regulations related to "the safety, health, morals, and general welfare of the public."[21] The Supreme Court, however, specified in much more substantial terms the precise type of regulations that could be imposed on private schools, including the power to "supervise" the schools and to ensure that "teachers shall be of good moral character and patriotic disposition, that certain studies plainly essential to good citizenship must be taught and that nothing be taught which is manifestly inimical to the public welfare." Since the state's police powers clearly are subordinate to constitutional due process guarantees,[22] it is not self-evident that the state has an inherent authority to limit parental liberty rights by regulating private schools to the extent that the Supreme Court did in *Pierce*.

The affirmative regulatory powers that the Supreme Court articulated in *Pierce* could, however, have been justified by a declaration that the state's police powers and/or an implicit right to education in the federal constitution supports the state's responsibility to promote civic education for all students in all schools. Such an explicit constitutional basis for the state's regulatory authority over private schools would have been consistent with the original intent of both the founding fathers and the proponents of the common schools who considered schooling essential for maintaining a democratic culture. *Pierce* provided an opportunity for the Court to address the core questions of which values are necessary to sustain a democratic society in the twentieth century and which knowledge, skills, and experiences schools should be transmitting to immigrant children—and to all children—to promote those values.

The Court did not, however, seize this opportunity. It did not set forth any constitutional rationale for why the state had a right to regulate private schools to ensure that they prepared students to be good citizens, or for the studies "plainly essential for good citizenship" that the schools should be teaching. Nor did the Court indicate what type of instruction might be "manifestly inimical to the public welfare." Rather than explicating these fundamental issues, the Supreme Court simply stated: "No question [was] raised concerning the power of the state reasonably to regulate all schools."

Two years earlier, in *Meyer v. Nebraska*,[23] the Supreme Court had invalidated a Nebraska statute that would have outlawed the teaching of foreign languages in any school in the state. Here, as in *Pierce*, the Court based its ruling on constitutional due process, in this case, the "liberty" right of a teacher of German to pursue his profession. In *Meyer*, the Court also alluded in general terms to the state's inherent authority to inculcate civic values in its children, but again it cited no specific constitutional basis or provided any explanation for this assumption: "That the state may do much, go very far, indeed, in order to improve the quality of its citizens, physically, mentally and morally, is clear; but the individual has certain fundamental rights which must be respected."[24]

The Limited Implementation of the *Pierce* Compromise

Since *Pierce* explicitly authorized the state to "inspect, supervise and examine" private schools, to ensure that "teachers shall be of good moral character and patriotic disposition," and to determine that "certain studies plainly essential to good citizenship must be taught, and that nothing be taught which is manifestly inimical to the public welfare," one might have expected a series of follow-up federal decisions closely examining what these phrases meant and pinpointing the knowledge, skills, experiences, and civic values that all schools, public and private, would be expected to impart to students. This has not, however, been the case. Although the *Pierce* compromise has remained in effect for almost a century now, the tenuous balance of interests at its core, and especially the extent of the state's authority and obligation to educate students for civic participation, has never been closely examined and the constitutional basis for the state's authority in this area is still unclear.

The Supreme Court has cited *Pierce* in several cases over the years, including the liberty interest in access to contraceptives in *Griswold v. Connecticut*,[25] and on a woman's right to abortion in *Roe v. Wade*,[26] but it did not use any of those occasions to explain specifically the basis for, and extent of, the state's interest in preparing students for civic participation that underlay the state's authority to regulate private schools as established in the *Pierce* compromise.[27] Two years after *Pierce*, the Court invalidated a Hawaiian statute that sought to strangle, not merely regulate, Japanese-language schools. The statute required foreign-language schools to pay annual registration fees, and to submit the qualifications and proof of patriotism of their teachers to state review; the statute also regulated all subjects taught, limited the hours children could attend, and required the schools to use only state-approved textbooks. The Court summarily held that the statute violated the plaintiffs' due process liberty interests and cited *Pierce*, but without any further discussion of the civic preparation dimension of the *Pierce* compromise.[28]

Since *Pierce*, there have been a number of lower federal court and state cases that have dealt with specific issues involved in the states' regulation of private schools. Like the Supreme Court, however, the judges in these cases have simply assumed (often relying on general citations to *Pierce*) that the state has the right to regulate private schools without endeavoring to explain the basis for that authority. The state court cases that have arisen in this area generally involve fundamentalist church schools that seek to resist virtually all regulation. The issues in these cases have involved health and safety regulations,[29] teacher certification or minimum competence standards,[30] and requirements that some basic secular studies be taught.[31] These decisions tend to focus on whether the right of the parents and/or the school to the free exercise of religion under federal and state constitutional doctrines has been compromised; they generally discuss the applicable free exercise of religion issues without addressing with any specificity the legal basis for the state's authority to regulate private schools.

The Supreme Court summarized the post-*Pierce* case law in this area in 1968, again without providing any explication of the basis for, or extent of, the state's power to regulate civic education in the private schools:

> Since *Pierce*, a substantial body of case law has confirmed the power of the States to insist that attendance at private schools, if it is to satisfy state compulsory-attendance laws, be at institutions which provide minimum hours of instruction, employ teachers of specified training, and cover prescribed subjects of instruction. Indeed, the State's interest in assuring that these standards are being met has been considered a sufficient reason for refusing to accept instruction at home as compliance with compulsory education statutes. These cases were a sensible corollary of *Pierce v. Society of Sisters*: if the State must satisfy its interest in secular education through the instrument of private schools, it has a proper interest in the manner in which those schools perform their secular educational function.[32]

Although some state legislatures have enacted statutes requiring minimal hours of instruction, the teaching of core subjects, and teacher certification at private schools, many other states have not enacted such statutes.[33] Most states that have enacted specific minimal requirements have not established effective monitoring and accountability systems to make sure that private schools are, in fact, teaching "studies plainly essential to good citizenship," even though almost all of the states' constitutions and statutes proclaim that preparing students for civic participation is a prime purpose of education.[34] In some states, authorities are explicitly prohibited from monitoring the content of the curriculums in private schools or the qualifications of their teachers. For example, the Kentucky Supreme Court has ruled that the state constitution bans any attempt to monitor private schools other than through standardized achievement tests.[35]

A recent survey of forty-seven states found that twenty-one of them did not require private schools to register with the state or to be accredited in any way, thirty-eight either did not require teacher certification at all or required it only for schools seeking voluntary accreditation or approval, and eighteen states imposed no curriculum requirements whatsoever on private schools or on schools that have not voluntarily registered.[36] For example, in North Carolina, private schools are (1) not required to be accredited by the State Board of Education or any other state or national institution; (2) not required to employ teachers or principals who are licensed or have any particular credentials, degrees, experience, or expertise in education; (3) not subject to any requirements regarding the curriculum they teach; and (4) not required to provide a minimum amount of instructional time.[37]

Many of the states that have enacted statutes or regulations that call for regulatory oversight rarely exercise this authority in practice. For example, a New York statute provides that "instruction given to a minor elsewhere than at a public school shall be at least substantially equivalent to the instruction given to minors of like age and attainments at the public schools of the city or district where the minor resides."[38] In theory, this is a far-reaching statute: it empowers state officials to ensure that, among other things, to whatever extent knowledge, skills, experiences, and values that prepare students to be capable citizens are being taught in the public schools, similar instruction must be provided to students in all private schools. In fact, however, the local school boards and superintendents who are responsible for enforcing this law have generally failed to do so,[39] and private schools in New York State have been free to choose teachers and adopt curricula with virtually no state oversight. As a result, some religious schools have totally downgraded the teaching of secular subjects like history, English, and math.

Former students of ultra-Orthodox Jewish schools in New York City recently notified local school authorities that the schools they attended had failed to provide them any instruction in basic secular subjects like social studies and science and very limited and inadequate instruction in English and math. The leader of the student group in New York City told the *New York Times*:

> The state's Education Department requires the city's nonpublic schools to teach a curriculum that is "substantially equivalent to that provided in the public schools," and requires local school superintendents to ensure the standards are met. Mr. Moster says those standards are not being met.
>
> So he sat down with three superintendents in New York whose districts have large Hasidic populations. "Two of them had no idea it was their responsibility to enforce the law," he said. "In one case I was pointing out the regulations online."[40]

The chancellor of the New York City Public Schools promised in July 2015 to undertake an investigation of what is actually being taught in a number of Orthodox Jewish schools in the city in response to the group's threat to file a lawsuit.[41] Although the chancellor assured Mr. Moster's group that she would provide a report of her investigation within about a year, two years later no report regarding any such investigation had been issued.[42]

The states' failure to monitor proactively the preparation that students are receiving for civic participation in private schools indicates that the *Pierce* compromise in practice is out of balance. Most parents of children who attend such schools are well aware of their constitutional right under *Pierce* to attend private schools that affirm their values and their preferred educational approaches, but state policy makers and public school officials seem far less clear on the extent of their authority under *Pierce* to insist that private schools properly prepare students for civic participation and on their obligation to monitor these schools' effectiveness in doing so.

Wisconsin v. Yoder

Fifty years after its decision in *Pierce*, the Supreme Court focused for the first time on justifications for compulsory education. Although this analysis provided the Supreme Court an opportunity to expand on its cryptic references in *Pierce* as to why and how "studies plainly essential to good citizenship must be taught," it failed to do so in *Wisconsin v. Yoder*.[43] In fact, instead of clarifying and bolstering the state's authority to ensure that students are being adequately prepared to function as civic participants in our contemporary democratic culture, *Yoder* actually clouded the issue and raised more questions on this point than it answered.

The legal question in *Yoder* was whether Amish children who had attended public school through the eighth grade should be exempted from the state's requirement that all children attend school until age sixteen because of their religious beliefs. The Court summarized the plaintiffs' position as follows:

> They object to the high school, and higher education generally, because the values they teach are in marked variance with Amish values and the Amish way of life; they view secondary school education as an impermissible exposure of their children to a "wordly" [*sic*] influence in conflict with their beliefs. The high school tends to emphasize intellectual and scientific accom-

plishments, self-distinction, competitiveness, worldly success, and social life with other students. Amish society emphasizes informal learning-through-doing; a life of "goodness," rather than a life of intellect; wisdom, rather than technical knowledge; community welfare, rather than competition; and separation from, rather than integration with, contemporary worldly society.[44]

Chief Justice Burger's majority opinion for the Court was sympathetic to the Amish perspective. Citing *Pierce*, he first stated, "There is no doubt as to the power of a State, having a high responsibility for education of its citizens, to impose reasonable regulations for the control and duration of basic education."[45] Furthermore, in alluding to the education provided "in a privately operated system," Burger stated that the education must be "equivalent."[46] He did not elucidate what he meant by the term "equivalent," but presumably this assumes that basic curricula in English, mathematics, science, history, civics, and so on will be taught and will be "substantially equivalent" to the curricula being taught in the public schools.

Although the decision in *Yoder* did not further clarify the extent to which a state could or should regulate private schools, the Court did provide some basic justifications for the state's imposition of compulsory education: "The State advances two primary arguments in support of its system of compulsory education. It notes, as Thomas Jefferson pointed out early in our history, that some degree of education is necessary to prepare citizens to participate effectively and intelligently in our open political system if we are to preserve freedom and independence. Further, education prepares individuals to be self-reliant and self-sufficient participants in society. We accept these propositions."[47] Nevertheless, after accepting these justifications for compulsory education as a general proposition, the Court went on to make an exception to their application to the Amish plaintiffs in this case:

An additional one or two years of formal high school for Amish children in place of their long-established program of informal vocational education would do little to serve those interests. Respondents' experts testified at trial, without challenge, that the value of all education must be assessed in terms of its capacity to prepare the child for life. It is one thing to say that compulsory education for a year or two beyond the eighth grade may be necessary when its goal is the preparation of the child for life in modern society as the majority live, but it is quite another if the goal of education be viewed as the preparation of the child for life in the separated agrarian community that is the keystone of the Amish faith.[48]

The Court emphasized that it was allowing the plaintiffs' right to free exercise of their religion to prevail over the state's authority to enforce its compulsory education laws in this case because of the clear religious sincerity of the Amish and their profound commitment to a traditional agricultural lifestyle. The Chief Justice stressed that the holding in this case was based on a "convincing showing, one that probably few other religious groups or sects could make."[49] Still, there are a number of troubling statements in the *Yoder* opinion that raise questions regarding the Court's views of what preparation for "good citizenship" involves in the twenty-first century.

In upholding the Amish claim that they be exempted from compulsory education during the high school years, but not elementary school, Chief Justice Burger stated that Jefferson's ideal of democracy was premised on a society of "yeoman farmers" and that the successful social functioning of the Amish in this country for more than two hundred years at the time constituted "strong evidence that there is at best a speculative gain, in terms of meeting the duties of citizenship, from an additional one or two years of compulsory formal education."[50] He also referred to the fact that "the origins of the requirement for school attendance to age 16, an age falling after the completion of elementary school but before completion of high school, are not entirely clear. But to some extent such laws reflected the movement to prohibit most child labor under age 16."[51]

These references could be read to support a position that elementary-level education is sufficient to prepare students adequately for "good citizenship."[52] If that is the message the Court meant to convey in *Yoder*, it is strikingly inconsistent with the Court's ringing endorsement two decades earlier of the enhanced importance of education in contemporary times, in its landmark *Brown v. Board of Education* decision outlawing racial segregation in the public schools. In *Brown*, the Court had strongly proclaimed:

Today, education is perhaps the most important function of state and local governments. Compulsory school attendance laws and the great expenditures for education both demonstrate our recognition of the importance of education to our democratic society. It is required in the performance of our most

> basic public responsibilities, even service in the armed forces. It is the very foundation of good citizenship. Today it is a principal instrument in awakening the child to cultural values, in preparing him for later professional training, and in helping him to adjust normally to his environment. In these days, it is doubtful that any child may reasonably be expected to succeed in life if he is denied the opportunity of an education. Such an opportunity, where the state has undertaken to provide it, is a right which must be made available to all on equal terms.[53]

One can, of course, argue that there is no inconsistency between the Court's strong statements about the paramount importance of education in modern times and its minimizing the significance of "advanced," high school education in *Yoder*. The *Yoder* Court did emphasize that the Amish history of maintaining an Old World, rural way of life isolated from the demands of modernity is extremely rare. Therefore, the exception provided to this tiny Amish community was *sui generis* and the Court has not extended it to any other groups or individuals since. Presumably, then, *Yoder* has no bearing on the situation of all other students in public and private schools throughout the United States. The vast majority of students do need a full grounding in the knowledge and skills that they will need to function productively in modern society, including, of course, an "advanced" high school–level education.

Nevertheless, because there is arguably inconsistency between some of the language in *Yoder* and the emphasis on the importance of education for our modern democratic society in *Brown*, the Supreme Court needs to clarify its understanding of the level of education that preparation for civic participation and compulsory education laws require in today's America. In a number of other cases in recent decades beyond *Pierce* and *Yoder*, the Court has alluded to "the importance of public schools in the preparation of individuals for participation as citizens."[54] It has also repeatedly referred to the schools' critical role in educating for citizenship:

> [The schools] are educating the young for citizenship.[55]

> Schools are where the "fundamental values necessary for the maintenance of a democratic political system" are conveyed.[56]

> Americans regard the public schools as a most vital civic institution for the preservation of a democratic system of government.[57]

> The process of educating our youth for citizenship in public schools is not confined to books, the curriculum, and the civics class; schools must teach by example the shared values of a civilized social order.[58]

But aside from giving lip service to the importance of civic preparation, in none of these cases has the Court spelled out what "educating our youth for citizenship in public schools" means.

In other words, in each of the above-cited situations, the Court dealt piecemeal with the validity or invalidity of a single aspect of the schools' civic preparation authority but did not analyze the full scope of that authority. Thus, in these cases the Court upheld the state's specific authority to require teachers to be American citizens,[59] a school's authority to prohibit use of lewd and obscene language in a student's speech before a school assembly,[60]and a school's authority to prevent a student from wearing a black armband to protest the Vietnam War.[61] It also ruled that a state could not deny access to education to children of undocumented immigrants.[62] In none of these cases, however, did the Court place these particular issues in the larger framework of the full scope of the schools' authority and responsibility to provide a meaningful and effective program of civic preparation.

San Antonio Independent School District v. Rodriguez

The Court did have another opportunity to directly confront this issue a number of years ago in the case of *San Antonio Independent School District v. Rodriguez*.[63] The issue in *Rodriguez* was whether substantial fiscal inequities in the financing of education violated the equal protection clause of the U.S. Constitution. The plaintiffs, who were largely parents of low-income Latino students, lived in a school district that was able to spend only about half as much *per capita* on their education as was being spent on their more affluent peers in a neighboring district. The prime cause of this disparity was that in Texas, as in almost every other state, much of money used to fund the schools derives from local property taxes; even though residents of the plaintiffs' district paid a higher property-tax rate, the amount they were able to raise in taxes was substantially less because of the enormously higher property values in the neighboring district.

Although the Supreme Court acknowledged the impact of this inequity, it held, by a 5–4 vote, that this pattern was not unconstitutional. Its reasoning was that local control of education was a rational state policy,[64] and it would not closely scrutinize state policy unless education was a "fundamental interest" under the federal Constitution.[65] Despite the importance of education, the majority held that education was not a fundamental interest because "the importance of a service performed by the State does not determine whether it must be regarded as fundamental for purposes of examination under the Equal Protection Clause."[66]

Justice Marshall, in a strong dissent, took issue with this position. Even though education is nowhere directly mentioned in the Constitution, he argued that education must be deemed a fundamental interest because of "the unique status accorded public education by our society, and by the close relationship between education and some of our most basic constitutional values."[67] Specifically, he stressed the importance of education for exercising First Amendment rights, "both as a source and as a receiver of information and ideas," and for exercising the constitutional right to vote and to participate in the political process.[68]

Justice Powell, writing for the majority, accepted Justice Marshall's basic perspective. Summarizing the dissenters' arguments on this point, he stated: "Specifically, they insist that education is itself a fundamental personal right because it is essential to the effective exercise of First Amendment freedoms and to intelligent utilization of the right to vote. . . . A similar line of reasoning is pursued with respect to the right to vote. . . . The electoral process, if reality is to conform to the democratic ideal, depends on an informed electorate: a voter cannot cast his ballot intelligently unless his reading skills and thought processes have been adequately developed."[69] He then indicated that he had no disagreement with this perspective, stating, "*We need not dispute any of these propositions*,"[70] because the plaintiffs who had focused on the tax-based inequity issues had not presented evidence that any students were not receiving such an adequate education: "Even if it were conceded that some identifiable quantum of education is a constitutionally protected prerequisite to the meaningful exercise of either right, we have no indication that the present levels of educational expenditures in Texas provide an education that falls short. . . . [In the present case] no charge fairly could be made that the system fails to provide each child with an opportunity to acquire the basic minimal skills necessary for the enjoyment of the rights of speech and of full participation in the political process."[71]

In short, then, in *Rodriguez*, the Justices all seemed to agree that some basic level of education is necessary for students to obtain the essential knowledge and skills they need for "full participation in the political process." Because plaintiffs in that case had not specifically raised that issue, though, and had not presented arguments or evidence on what that basic level of education should be, the majority decision did not confront those issues. A number of years later, the Court specifically reiterated that it still had not definitively settled the question of whether a minimally adequate education is a fundamental right and whether a statute alleged to infringe that right should be accorded heightened equal protection review.[72]

Since *Rodriguez* was decided in 1973, a large number of state court decisions have held that there is a right to an "adequate" or "sound basic" education under their state constitutions and that a primary purpose of such an education is to prepare students to function productively as civic participants. These cases have consistently held that many schools today are failing to provide students an adequate basic education. I discuss these state cases in detail in the next chapter. The cases are important in their own right, but they also could provide a strong evidentiary and doctrinal basis for the U.S. Supreme Court to revisit the issue left open in *Rodriguez* and to consider the specific knowledge, skills, experiences, and values that students need in order to effectively exercise their First and Fifteenth Amendment rights under the federal constitution. I return in chapter 7 to a more detailed discussion of the significance of a potential Supreme Court holding that there is indeed a federal right to civic education, and to litigation strategies that might be advanced to convince the Court to issue such a decision, as well as recommendations for how such a decision might be implemented. Before doing so, however, we need to explore in the chapters that follow the relevant state court decisions and consider in detail what an education that prepares students for civic participation should look like in the twenty-first century.

CHAPTER THREE

Civic Participation and the State Courts

Productive citizenship means more than just being qualified to vote or serve as a juror, but to do so capably and knowledgeably. . . . An engaged, capable voter needs the intellectual tools to evaluate complex issues, such as campaign finance reform, tax policy, and global warming, to name only a few. —Justice Leland DeGrasse, *Campaign for Fiscal Equity v. State of New York*

In the 1970s, most states spent only half as much *per capita* on the education of their students with the greatest needs as they did on those students' peers in nearby affluent communities. This pattern, reflected in the Supreme Court's ruling in the *Rodriguez* case discussed in the previous chapter, prevailed not only in Texas but also throughout most of the United States.[1] A federal commission appointed by President Richard Nixon at that time took note of these facts and recommended strong steps to remedy them, but neither Congress nor state legislators paid any heed to their suggestions.[2]

Given the breadth, depth, and durability of these funding inequities, after *Rodriguez* shut the doors of the federal courthouses to civil rights attorneys, they turned to the state courts. They filed suits with little expectation of major success, however, because the state courts historically had not been pacesetters on constitutional civil rights issues. Moreover, from a practical point of view, state courts had fewer resources than the federal courts to deal with these complicated decisions. Surprisingly, though, most of the state courts did prove amenable to taking on this challenge. In fact, their involvement with education finance litigation has been the most active and creative area of constitutional jurisprudence in the 225-year history of the state courts.

Shortly after the U.S. Supreme Court issued its decision in *Rodriguez*, the California Supreme Court held that even if education is not a fundamental interest under the federal constitution, it clearly was under the California constitution.[3] Courts in New Jersey, Connecticut, and West Virginia also declared unconstitutional their state's systems of financing education.[4] Overall, over the past four decades, litigations challenging the "equity" or "adequacy" of state education finance systems have been filed in forty-five of fifty states.[5] Although plaintiffs' primary motivation in these cases was to obtain increased funding for their under-resourced schools, these cases—many of which are currently pending—also have enormous significance for the issue of preparation for civic participation.

The Primacy in State Constitutions of Preparation for Civic Participation

State constitutions use different language to describe the education to which all children in the state are entitled: in some states, it is called a "sound basic education,"[6] in others, a "thorough and efficient" education,[7] or a "basic system of free quality public elementary and secondary schools."[8] Regardless of the precise terminology, there is broad consensus on the core meaning of these constitutional provisions among the courts that have applied these concepts.[9] Virtually all these state courts have agreed that the aim of the drafters of these constitutional clauses was to ensure that the state would establish and maintain public schools that would develop in students the skills they needed to function capably as citizens and to compete effectively in the global labor market.

For example, the Vermont Supreme Court explained that the state's education clause "assumes paramount significance in the constitutional frame of government established by the framers: it expressed and incorporated that part of republican theory which holds education essential to self-government and which recognizes government as the source of the perpetuation of the attributes of citizenship."[10] Similarly, the Wyoming Supreme Court defined the core constitutional requirement in terms of providing students with "a uniform opportunity to become equipped for their future roles as citizens, participants in the political system, and competitors both economically and intellectually."[11] New Jersey's Supreme Court held that the constitution requires the state to provide "that educational opportunity which is needed in the contemporary setting to equip a child for his role as a citizen and as a competitor in the labor market";[12] and the New York Court of Appeals declared that the state must provide all students a "sound basic education" that will prepare them to "function productively as civic participants . . . qualified to vote or serve as a juror . . . capably and knowledgeably," as well as inculcate in them "the ability to obtain competitive employment."[13]

Most of the controversy that has arisen in these cases has centered on determining the amount of money that is needed to provide a constitutionally adequate education, and whether it is appropriate for the courts to deal with these issues. The majority of the state courts have held that the courts do have a responsibility to enforce these constitutional rights, and many of them have issued orders requiring the states to increase educational funding and/or to take other remedial actions.[14]

To determine the level of resources needed to provide students an "adequate" education, the courts generally have considered it necessary first to articulate the goals of a public education system; for this reason they have gone to great lengths to analyze the purposes of education and—virtually unanimously—have determined that those purposes are to prepare students for citizenship and for competitive employment. Typically, judges have approached this task either by looking to the intent of those who drafted the constitutional language, usually a century or two ago, or by analyzing the purposes of education in contemporary times. Both of these approaches have consistently led to substantial discussion of the importance of preparing students for civic participation.

Most of the education clauses in the state constitutions were written during the nineteenth century by proponents of the common school movement.[15] Next to abolition, the battle to establish common schools constituted the most contentious political issue of the nineteenth century.[16] In some states, the convening of state constitutional conventions that adopted these constitutional clauses helped advance the common school cause during legislative battles. In other situations, common school advocates codified their legislative victories by inserting clauses into state constitutions that would ensure that future legislatures could not revoke the system of broad access to public education. As the New York Constitution put it, the legislature must permanently "maintain a system of free common schools in which all the students in the state may be educated."[17] Many states. like New York, have not changed the language of these clauses over the past century or two; they have retained unchanged in their constitutions the historical but somewhat archaic phrase "common schools" rather than the more contemporary "public schools."

In their efforts to determine the intent of the drafters of these clauses, many state courts have dug deeply into the debates at the constitutional conventions where these provisions were adopted. The court decisions have highlighted, with approval and with assertions of their continued relevance, the many references to the civic purposes of the common schools.

For example, section 183 of the Kentucky Constitution, originally adopted in 1890, reads, "The General Assembly shall, by appropriate legislation, provide for an efficient system of common schools throughout the State." To understand the meaning of the somewhat opaque phrase "an efficient system of common schools," the Kentucky Supreme Court, in its 1989 decision in *Rose v. Council for Better Education*,[18] focused on the intent of the drafters of this provision by reviewing the debates at the constitutional convention of 1890. It emphasized the comments of a convention delegate Beckner, who set out four justifications for, and characteristics of, state-provided schools:

1. The education of young people is essential to the prosperity of a free people.
2. The education should be universal and should embrace all children.
3. Public education should be supervised by the State, to assure that students develop patriotism and understand our government.
4. Education should be given to all—rich and poor—so that our people will be homogeneous in their feelings and desires.

The *Rose* decision continues:

> As if these powerful words were not sufficient to show the purpose of Section 183, consider those of delegate Moore—
>
> "Common schools make patriots and men who are willing to stand upon a common land. The boys of the humble mountain home stand equally high with those from the mansions of the city. There are no distinctions in the common schools, *but all stand upon one level*." *Id.* at 4531 (emphasis added).[19]

For the Kentucky Supreme Court, then, the right to "an efficient education" set forth in the state constitution follows directly from the clear intent of the nineteenth-century advocates of the common school systems: "Delegates Beckner and Moore told their fellow delegates and have told us, what this section means."[20]

Most of the other constitutions that were written during the nineteenth century also expressed the prevalent view that education was vital to the functioning of American democracy. For example, the constitution of Indiana, first written in 1816, declared, "Knowledge and learning, generally diffused throughout a community, [are] essential to the preservation of a free government";[21] the Minnesota Constitution written in 1857 and the Idaho Constitution of 1890 both state: "The stability of a republican form of government depending mainly upon the intelligence of the people, it is the duty of the legislature to establish a general and uniform system of public schools";[22] and the North Dakota Constitution of 1889 declares that the legislature shall establish a public school system because "a high degree of intelligence, patriotism, integrity and morality on the part of every voter in a government by the people [is] necessary in order to insure the continuance of that government and the prosperity and happiness of the people."[23]

In most of the New England states, the education clauses in the state constitutions harked back to the eighteenth century. Thus, the language of the New Hampshire Constitution, using much of the verbiage originally adopted in 1789 by Massachusetts discussed in chapter 1, states:

> Knowledge and learning, generally diffused through a community, being essential to the preservation of a free government; and spreading the opportunities and advantages of education through the various parts of the country, being highly conducive to promote this end; it shall be the duty of the legislators and magistrates, in all future periods of this government, to cherish the interest of literature and the sciences, and all seminaries and public schools[,] . . . to countenance and inculcate the principles of humanity and general benevolence, public and private charity, industry and economy, honesty and punctuality, sincerity, sobriety, and all social affections, and generous sentiments, among the people.[24]

In its decision in the 1993 case on school-funding adequacy, *Claremont School District v. Governor of New Hampshire*, the New Hampshire court held that, despite its archaic language, this constitutional provision was still highly relevant to the current needs of the state's public school students:

> We do not construe the terms "shall be the duty . . . to cherish" in our constitution as merely a statement of aspiration. The language commands, in no uncertain terms, that the State provide an education to all its citizens and that it support all public schools.
>
> * * *
>
> Given the complexities of our society today, the State's constitutional duty extends beyond mere reading, writing and arithmetic. It also includes broad educational opportunities needed in today's society to prepare citizens for their role as participants and as potential competitors in today's marketplace of ideas.[25]

Overall, thirty-one of the fifty states still have education clauses in their constitutions that date back to the eighteenth or nineteenth century. Three of the four states that entered the union in the twentieth century also included in their constitutions the standard nineteenth-century common school language regarding the legislature's duty to "establish and maintain" a statewide school system open to all, although by that time the term "public school system" was substituted for the archaic "common school" language.[26] The drafters of these early twentieth-century constitutional clauses, like the drafters of state constitutional provisions in the eighteenth and nineteenth centuries, also clearly saw preparation for civic participation as the main purpose of public education. As the Arizona Supreme Court, discussing the intent of the framers of the state's 1911 constitution, put it: "The conventioneers believed that an educated citizenry was extraordinarily important to the new state. . . . The conventioneers believed these were more than mere words. By 1910, they had witnessed the most intense immigration in the history of America. They were keenly aware that education was responsible for preserving America's unity while wave after wave of peoples arrived from other countries. As the heated debates about education as a requirement for voting show, the conventioneers believed that a free society could not exist without educated participants. *See Records* at 564–69."[27]

Fifteen states revised their constitutions during the twentieth century for a variety of reasons. Many retained much of the language from the former constitution that expressed the framers' strong civic purposes. For example, article 9, section 1, of the Missouri Constitution of 1945 carried over the language of the state's original 1812 constitution: "A general diffusion of knowledge and intelligence [is] essential to the preservation of the rights and liberties of the people"; similarly, article 9, section 1, of the North Carolina Constitution of 1971 repeated language from the 1868 constitution: "Religion, morality, and knowledge being necessary to good government and the happiness of mankind, schools, libraries, and the means of education shall forever be encouraged."[28]

The retention of post–Revolutionary War and common school language in the current education clauses in the vast majority of state constitutions explains why the courts that have explored the original intent behind these clauses have emphasized preparation for citizenship as a primary, if not *the* prime, constitutional purpose of the public schools. It is also significant, however, that courts in other states that have adopted more contemporary language in their constitutional provisions have also agreed that educating students to maintain democratic institutions is of paramount importance. For example, Connecticut first adopted an education clause in 1965, and the words it chose were short and simple: "There shall always be free public elementary and secondary schools in the state."[29] Nevertheless, the Connecticut Supreme Court, when it interpreted this phrase, discussed at length the references to the history of education at the constitutional convention and concluded: "Although the proponents of article eighth, § 1, did not articulate a substantive standard, they emphasized the historical importance of education to Connecticut in the context of its role in fostering meaningful civic participation in a representative democracy."[30]

In other situations, where the constitutional text was opaque and there was no clear record of the framers' intent, state courts have analyzed the purposes of education solely from a contemporary perspective; these courts have also agreed that a prime purpose of the constitution's education clause is to ensure that students are prepared to be capable citizens. For example, in interpreting the constitutional language adopted in 1945, "The legislature shall provide for the maintenance and support of a thorough and efficient system of free public schools," the New Jersey Supreme Court focused on contemporary needs, holding, "The Constitution's guarantee must be understood to embrace that educational opportunity which is needed in the contemporary setting to equip a child for his role as a citizen and as a competitor in the labor market."[31] The court noted that in the nineteenth century, a high school education was not widely available, but "today, a system of public education which did not offer high school education would hardly be thorough and efficient."[32]

Overall, the highest courts in at least thirty-two states—twenty-six in education adequacy and fiscal equity decisions,[33] and six in the course of other types of decisions[34]—have explicitly stated that preparation for capable citizenship is the primary purpose or a primary purpose of the public education clause of the state constitution. This does not mean that the other eighteen state highest courts have denied this proposition; rather, they just have not spoken to the issue. In other words, 100 percent of the courts that have considered the purposes of public education have agreed that preparing students for capable citizenship is a primary goal of public education. In fact, the courts that have affirmed that preparation for democratic citizenship is a primary purpose of public education include six cases in which plaintiffs have not prevailed in equity or adequacy cases[35] (largely for separation-of-powers reasons).[36]

Judicial Analyses of the Specific Skills Students Need for Civic Participation

Some of the state courts, recognizing the enhanced importance of education for contemporary needs, have gone beyond both examining the intent of the eighteenth- and nineteenth-century drafters of the education clauses in their constitutions and emphasizing the continuing need to prepare students to be capable citizens. These courts have focused specifically on the particular knowledge and skills that students will need to function productively as citizens in the contemporary world.

Noteworthy in this regard is the 1989 decision of the Kentucky Supreme Court, whose discussion of the purposes of education has been especially influential—its analysis of the goals of public education has been followed by the highest courts in at least eight other states.[37] In *Rose v. Council for Better Education*,[38] the Kentucky court defined a constitutionally acceptable education as one that has as its goal the development in each and every child of the following seven capacities:

1. Sufficient oral and written communication skills to enable students to function in a complex and rapidly changing civilization;
2. Sufficient knowledge of economic, social, and political systems to enable the student to make informed choices;
3. Sufficient understanding of governmental processes to enable the student to understand the issues that affect his or her community, state, and nation;

4. Sufficient self-knowledge and knowledge of his or her mental and physical wellness;
5. Sufficient grounding in the arts to enable each student to appreciate his or her cultural and historical heritage;
6. Sufficient training or preparation for advanced training in either academic or vocational fields so as to enable each child to choose and pursue life work intelligently; and
7. Sufficient levels of academic or vocational skills to enable public school students to compete favorably with their counterparts in surrounding states, in academics or in the job market.

The Kentucky court's compendium begins with the insight that well-developed verbal skills are foundational for both civic participation and competitive employment. These skills have "a dramatic impact on the ability of individuals to gather information on a variety of subjects, organize facts meaningfully and efficiently process additional and related knowledge."[39] A solid set of verbal skills "not only provides individuals with the specific competence necessary to perform duties within a given profession but also enhances more generalizable skills that are applicable to understanding the political world."[40] But to apply these skills properly in political and civic arenas, the *Rose* criteria also emphasized that a student needs "sufficient knowledge of economic, social, and political systems to enable the student to make informed choices," and "sufficient understanding of governmental processes to enable the student to understand the issues that affect his or her community, state, and nation."[41]

Justice John Erlick of the Washington Superior Court explored in some detail the specific knowledge and skills and values citizens need for effective citizenship in discussing why that state's constitutional education clause established education as the state's highest priority and declared it the "paramount duty" of state government:

> For a citizen of this State to participate meaningfully in this State's democratic process and intelligently cast his or her vote on the broad array of State and local government offices and ballot measures noted above, that citizen must be meaningfully equipped to learn about, understand, and evaluate the candidates, ballot measures, positions, and issues being debated and decided in that election . . .
>
> Having an educated citizenry is also vital to the operation of this State's justice system. For example, the jury system upon which this State's justice

> system is based depends upon each juror being meaningfully equipped to read, understand, comprehend, and debate the evidence, issues, and arguments presented to the jury for decision.
>
> Having an educated citizenry also plays a vital role in preserving the cohesiveness of this State's pluralistic society as a whole. For example, broad public education provides each member of this State's citizenry a shared knowledge and understanding of the common history, common values, and common ideals that all citizens in this State share. This unifying awareness and understanding is especially important to maintain the cohesiveness of a widely diverse society like the one in this State. . . .
>
> Education also plays a critical civil rights role in promoting equality in our democracy . . . [by] equipping citizens born into the underprivileged segments of our society with the tools they need to compete on a level playing field with citizens born into wealth or privilege. . . .
>
> Education also plays a critical role in building and maintaining the strong economy necessary to support a stable democracy—one that is free and independent from outside power and influence.[42]

Justice Leland DeGrasse, the trial judge in the New York litigation on school-funding adequacy, probed in depth the verbal skills and specific knowledge of economic, social, and political systems and government processes that students today need to be capable citizens. In *Campaign for Fiscal Equity v. State*,[43] the state's highest court, the New York State Court of Appeals, had articulated as a "template" definition that a "sound basic education" meant that students should be provided an opportunity for an education that would provide them with the skills they would need "to eventually function productively as civic participants capable of voting and serving on a jury."[44] They then sent the case back for a trial to determine the types of skills students would need to function productively as civic participants and whether the New York City public schools were, in fact, providing students with an opportunity to develop those skills.

Justice DeGrasse had an insightful strategy for examining these issues. He first instructed the parties to have their expert witnesses analyze a charter referendum proposal that was on the ballot in New York City while the trial was in progress. The specific question posed was whether graduates of New York's high schools would have the knowledge and skills needed to comprehend that document. The attorneys for the parties were also asked to have their witnesses undertake similar analyses of the judges' charges to the jury and certain documents put into evidence in two complex civil cases that had recently been tried in the local state courts.[45]

Plaintiffs' witnesses closely reviewed the charter revision proposal and identified the specific civic knowledge and reading and analytical skills that an individual would need to understand the document.[46] They then related these skills to the particular standards for English language arts, social studies, mathematics, and sciences that were set forth in the Regents learning standards that had been recently adopted by New York State.[47] They also described the types of knowledge and skills a juror would need to comprehend and apply concepts like preponderance of the evidence and showed how the specific types of knowledge and skills needed to undertake this complex reasoning process were also cultivated by the New York State learning standards.[48]

The defendants introduced polling data indicating that the vast majority of American voters obtain their information from radio and television news and make up their minds on how to vote for candidates and propositions before they enter the voting booth.[49] Their implicit argument was that voters do not require high-level knowledge and cognitive skills to understand the political issues as discussed on radio and television news programs, and since most voters do not actually read complex ballot propositions, they do not need the level of knowledge and skill necessary to comprehend such documents.[50] They also claimed that dialogue among members of the jury could substitute for a lack of understanding of particular points by some of the individual jurors.[51]

Overall, the implied premise of the defendants' position was that citizens do not actually need to function at a high skill level and do not need to be capable of comprehending complex written material, so long as the subjects dealt with in the material are regularly discussed in the mass media, or so long as citizens can obtain assistance from others in carrying out their civic responsibilities. Justice DeGrasse's decision resoundingly rejected this position:

> An engaged, capable voter needs the intellectual tools to evaluate complex issues, such as campaign finance reform, tax policy, and global warming, to name only a few. Ballot propositions in New York City, such as the charter reform proposal that was on the ballot in November 1999, can require a close reading and a familiarity with the structure of local government.
>
> Similarly, a capable and productive citizen doesn't simply show up for jury

> service. Rather she is capable of serving impartially on trials that may require learning unfamiliar facts and concepts and new ways to communicate and reach decisions with her fellow jurors. To be sure, the jury is in some respects an anti-elitist institution where life experience and practical intelligence can be more important than formal education. Nonetheless, jurors may be called on to decide complex matters that require the verbal, reasoning, math, science, and socialization skills that should be imparted in public schools. Jurors today must determine questions of fact concerning DNA evidence, statistical analyses, and convoluted financial fraud, to name only three topics.[52]

The New York court's analysis of the level of knowledge and skills citizens need to exercise their civic responsibilities and constitutional rights is important. It makes clear that although society may have accepted unreflectively a wide gap between its democratic ideal and the actual functioning level of its citizens in the past, when the issue comes to the fore, its implications cannot be avoided. Our society cannot knowingly perpetuate a state of affairs in which voters cannot comprehend the ballot materials about which they are voting or in which jurors cannot understand legal instructions or major evidentiary submissions in the cases they are deciding. To function productively in today's complex world, citizens need a broad range of civic knowledge and substantial cognitive skills that will allow them to function capably and knowledgeably, not only as voters and jurors but also in petitioning their representatives, asserting their rights as individuals, participating in civic affairs and otherwise taking part in the broad range of interchanges and relationships involved in civic engagement.

The Courts' Remedial Orders

The New York Court of Appeals generally affirmed Justice DeGrasse's findings on these issues,[53] but its remedial order focused on ensuring sufficient levels of funding and did not call for any assurances that students would actually develop the particular civic knowledge and skills emphasized at the trial. The state's response to the decision was to adopt extensive reforms to its educational finance system and to commit to substantial increases in education spending, especially for New York City and other high-need school districts.[54] But few changes were made in the state statutes or regulations, and no actions were taken to ensure that schools were properly preparing students for civic participation.[55] Similarly, in Kentucky, a state that has adopted probably the most sweeping set of reforms in response to an adequacy litigation of any state in the nation, the state has "reformed its school finance system, reformed its school governance process, updated and improved its core required curriculum, and implemented a statewide assessment and accountability system,"[56] but despite the *Rose* court's emphasis on ensuring that students are well prepared "to understand the issues that affect his or her community, state, and nation," it has taken no steps to ensure that sufficient resources for civic preparation are available in the schools or that the accountability standards sufficiently emphasize civic preparation goals.[57]

What the courts have done in these cases is to require states to determine "the actual cost" of a "sound basic education,"[58] or to increase education spending by a stated amount,[59] or to establish accountability systems to determine whether substantially equal curricula and substantially equal facilities for an adequate education are being provided.[60] In essence, the courts have operated with an implied assumption that, given adequate resources, the schools would be able to provide the programs, services, and activities that students need to develop the requisite civic participation skills.

Certainly, money is a *sine qua non* for providing the full range of courses, services, and schooling experiences to prepare students for effective civic participation.[61] The education adequacy cases have, in fact, resulted in substantial increases in educational funding,[62] but it is clear that states and school districts have not substantially utilized these increased resources to improve preparation for civic participation. As discussed in chapter 1, school districts appear to have reduced, rather than increased, the opportunities they offer students for civic preparation over the forty-five years that state courts have been issuing adequacy decisions. Nor, in their follow-up compliance hearings, have courts examined whether the state has, in fact, taken any action to promote better preparation for civic participation or whether, as a result of the ordered funding increases, students are better prepared to be capable citizens.[63]

How, then, have these funds been used if not to promote civic participation skills? In most cases, the funds have been allocated to bolster student achievement in basic skills in reading and math and in attempts to reduce the racial achievement gaps in these areas. Plaintiffs' success in winning 60 percent of the adequacy cases since 1989 stemmed not only from the new rights-based legal theory they developed from the long-dormant clauses on common schools and civic virtue in the state constitutions, but also from the simultaneous emergence of a then-new education policy initiative known as "standards-based reform."[64] The availability of definitive standards that set forth the state's expectations regarding the academic content of an appropriate education substantially aided the courts' ability to craft effective remedies in these cases.[65]

However, the emphasis on standards also put a premium on quantifiable outcomes in core academic areas, such as scores on annual state achievement exams and graduation rates. The federal No Child Left Behind Act of 2001 magnified the significance of the state standards by compelling the states to implement annual standardized testing in reading and math in grades three through eight and once in high school and placing considerable weight on these annual test scores in enforcing the act.[66] Achievement in social studies or development of civic virtues and interpersonal skills that are more difficult to assess tended to take a back seat to this focus on basic skills.

Teachers' decisions on how they use instructional time often tend to be driven by whether a subject area is going to be tested.[67] As former U.S. Supreme Court justice Sandra Day O'Connor noted, No Child Left Behind "effectively squeezed out civics education because there is no testing for that anymore and no funding for that."[68] Consistent with O'Connor's contention, a 2007 survey of 349 American school districts by the Center on Education Policy revealed that, on average, the schools had increased time devoted to reading and/or math by 62 percent since the enactment of No Child Left Behind, and decreased time devoted to other subjects by a total of 145 minutes per week; specifically, 36 percent of the elementary schools in these districts had reduced instruction in social studies by an average of 76 minutes per week.[69] The reduction in teaching time for social studies also appeared to be widening the civic empowerment gap: for example, in New York's schools serving mostly nonwhite children, 38 percent of elementary schools reported decreasing the time devoted to social studies, compared with 17 percent in schools serving mostly white children.[70]

In 2015, Congress replaced the No Child Left Behind Act with the Every Student Succeeds Act (ESSA).[71] Although the newer law eliminates sanctions on schools and school districts that do not make sufficient progress on standardized achievement tests by a certain date, an emphasis on test-based accountability has been retained in the new law.[72] Most states have now adopted as their overall educational objective that all students graduate high school "college and career ready," the goal set forth in the Common Core standards.[73] But given the strong constitutional mandates in most states for schools to maintain the historical emphasis on civic preparation, the clarion call for state standards needs to be "college, career *and citizenship* ready."[74] Oklahoma has, in fact, adopted a "College, Career, and Citizen Ready (C3) goal and seven other states now include citizenship within the context of what it means to be prepared for postsecondary education and workforce training."[75] These states need to vigorously adopt similar goals, and judicial mandates that focus on this issue can require or encourage them to do so.

Facing the Future: The Need for Higher-Level Civic Skills

As discussed earlier, the perceived link between education and the maintenance of a viable democratic system motivated the drafters of the education clauses in the state constitutions that have supported the contemporary educational adequacy movement. The drafters of the education clause in Indiana's constitution in 1890 expressed in quantifiable terms why the state's constitution needed to guarantee all children an effective education:

> Sir, we have forty thousand voters in our State, who cannot read the ballots which they use. . . . Yes sir, and thirty thousand mothers who are rearing our successors and destitute of the very first elements of education. We have, sir, according to the latest census . . . seventy-three thousand two hundred and ninety-nine persons over the age of twenty years, who cannot read and write.
>
> * * *
>
> If the present Constitution be correct in asserting that "knowledge and learning generally diffused through a community, (is) essential to the preservation of a free government," what have we a right to expect from the state and condition of learning among us?[76]

Today, the challenge in maintaining a vibrant democracy requires much more of education than the minimal system the drafters of the education clauses in the eighteenth and nineteenth centuries had in mind. Those constitutional provisions arose in an era when the scope of public discussion was limited and when both the franchise and access to education were restricted largely to upper-income white males. Throughout most of America's history, women, people of color and other minorities and many working-class men were excluded from the franchise and from exercising most of the rights of citizenship.[77]

During the nineteenth century, the franchise was slowly extended to working-class men, then to newly freed black citizens, and early in the twentieth century to women. Yet stratagems like overly technical registration rules, poll taxes, and literacy tests effectively precluded many of these newly eligible citizens from actually voting.[78] It has only been in the past few decades, after the enactment of the Twenty-Fourth Amendment to the Constitution in 1964, the passage in 1965 of the Voting Rights Act,[79] and the implementation of that act that substantial numbers of African American and Latino citizens have actually begun to vote.

Thus, today, as full access to the ballot and other forms of political participation have been extended to virtually all citizens, the nation's founders' insight that all citizens in a democracy must be well educated if the polity is to flourish has taken on even greater practical significance. Voting and other aspects of civic participation now place greater demands on all citizens. The rise of technology, the Internet, and the information age in general all have increased the level of cognitive skills and knowledge of political and social systems that individuals need to vote and to undertake other forms of civic participation. Civic engagement today requires not only the ability to understand and act on one's political, economic, and social interests, but also the capacity to sort and analyze the continuing stream of information that confronts all of us daily, to make sense of an ever-changing world.

The issue of the level of skills that people need to function productively as contemporary civic participants came to a head dramatically in the 1980s in the debate in legal circles about whether so-called blue-ribbon juries, composed only of highly educated and accomplished citizens, should be permitted to decide complex litigations in areas like product liability, antitrust, and environmental regulation. This issue arose after a number of scholars questioned whether substantial numbers of citizens who were sitting on juries in such cases were capable of understanding complex statistical, scientific, and technical data,[80] and whether they could understand even legal instructions.[81]

In 1979, the former chief justice of the U.S. Supreme Court Warren E. Burger stated that jurors of the day were not capable of comprehending technical evidence in complex cases.[82] He said that "Jefferson would be appalled at the prospect of a dozen of his yeomen and artisans trying to cope with some of today's complex litigation in a trial lasting many weeks or months."[83] A fiery debate then ensued among legal scholars and federal judges on whether juries in complex cases should be limited to college graduates,[84] or whether the Seventh Amendment's guarantee of right to a trial by jury should be reinterpreted to exclude complex cases.[85]

This call for elite juries actually amounted to a return to the historical practice of convening blue-ribbon juries in important cases, a practice that had been prevalent throughout the United States before the passage of the federal Jury Selection and Service Act in 1968,[86] and before a series of Supreme Court cases that banned the systematic exclusion of women and people of color from jury panels.[87] The incompatibility of such blue-ribbon panels with basic democratic principles was scathingly set forth by U.S. Supreme Court Justice Frank Murphy, who dissented in a 1948 case that upheld the verdict of a blue-ribbon jury operating in accordance with a New York state statute—since repealed—that permitted such elite jury panels:

> The vice lies in the very concept of "blue ribbon" panels—the systematic and intentional exclusion of all but the "best" or the most learned or intelligent of the general jurors. Such panels are completely at war with the democratic theory of our jury system, a theory formulated out of the experience of generations. One is constitutionally entitled to be judged by a fair sampling of all one's neighbors who are qualified, not merely those with superior intelligence or learning. . . . Any method that permits only the "best" of these to be selected opens the way to grave abuses. The jury is then in danger of losing its democratic flavor and becoming the instrument of the select few.[88]

The outcome of the scholarly and judicial debate on the use of blue-ribbon juries in complex cases was a rejection of the proposal and a reaffirmation of the importance of juries being selected from the population at large.[89] This result has largely confirmed the historical understanding that juries should be selected from one's peers and should be representative of the broad community. There remain, however, persistent concerns about the ability of juries to function effectively, especially in complex civil cases.[90] Although empirical studies of jury functioning in the past had shown that "the jury does by and large understand the facts and get the case straight,"[91] many contemporary studies "buttress the contention of lay jury incompetence in complex cases."[92]

The recent literature on jury functioning, therefore, bears out both the testimony in the *CFE* litigation that students need to develop higher-level cognitive skills if they are to function productively as civic participants in today's complex society and the repeated calls of the authors and commissions cited in chapter 1 for the schools to prepare students more effectively for their civic responsibilities. The widespread rejection of the suggestion that blue-ribbon juries be reinstated in complex cases makes clear that the accepted understanding of democracy in the twenty-first century entitles and requires all citizens to participate fully in America's democratic institutions. Integral to the American concept of democracy is a belief that all citizens have equal worth and value, and that participation in voting, jury duty, exercise of First Amendment freedoms, and active engagement in civic affairs is important both for the dignity of individuals and for the effective functioning of political institutions and civic society. Accordingly, for American democracy to succeed and to thrive, it is unacceptable that the graduates of many high schools lack the knowledge, skills, experiences, and values they need to be civically engaged in a meaningful way in voting, serving on juries, or engaging in any of the other forms of civic participation.

It is quite striking that despite the broad consensus on the importance preparing all students for capable citizenship, none of the many state courts that have held that state education systems are constitutionally inadequate thus far has taken any specific steps to ensure that this preeminent constitutional purpose is, in fact, being honored. As discussed earlier, the primary focus of the courts in these cases, and of the parties who have appeared before them, has been to obtain sufficient state funding to allow for schools to provide meaningful educational opportunities to all students. Because of the schools' continuing neglect of effective civic preparation and the persistence of the civic empowerment gap, however, plaintiffs in future adequacy cases need to request that remedial decrees include specific provisions to ensure that states and schools carry out their constitutional responsibilities in this area. The U.S. Supreme Court also needs to reconsider its rulings in *Rodriguez*, *Pierce*, and other relevant cases and clearly assert that states and schools have a constitutional responsibility to prepare all students to function effectively as civic participants.

In the next two chapters, I discuss in more detail the knowledge, skills, experiences, and values that students need to function productively as civic participants in the twenty-first century, how schools can effectively help students acquire them, and the resources they need to do so. In the concluding chapters, I then return to the issue of the specific ways that both the state and the federal courts can induce states and schools to take meaningful actions to prepare students for capable citizenship.

CHAPTER FOUR

A Conceptual Framework for Preparing Students for Civic Participation

Our destiny is fashioned by what all of us do, by the deeds and desires of each citizen, as one tiny drop of water after another ultimately makes a big river. — President Lyndon Johnson, September 5, 1966

The shift in emphasis from "equity" to "adequacy" in the state court cases described in the previous chapter required judges to reflect on the purposes of public education. That quest led them to explore the original intent of the drafters of the state constitutional clauses and to recognize that historically the prime purpose of public education has always been to prepare students for democratic citizenship.

This search for constitutional roots also tended, however, to orient the courts to think about civic participation in overly historical terms. Most of the references in the state court adequacy cases have consisted of platitudes about the virtues of the common schools and the historical importance of education for democracy. There has been little forward-looking discussion about the kind of schooling that is needed in the twenty-first century to maintain and advance our democratic culture. Similarly, for the federal courts, invocation of the civic value of education has been a backdrop for the development of constitutional doctrines on racial discrimination, freedom of religion, free speech, and other issues that often have their locus in the schools, but the judges have given little consideration to the civic knowledge, skills, experiences, and values that contemporary schools actually should be imparting.

Federal and state policy makers have also largely avoided facing the challenges of providing meaningful education for civic preparation in recent decades. They have focused instead on improving basic academic skills, overcoming achievement gaps in reading and math, and on college and career readiness. These are important educational goals, but pursuing them does not necessitate or justify the widespread neglect of preparation for civic participation that has prevailed in American schools for the past half century.

Despite abstract agreement on the importance of civic participation, school officials, policy makers, and judges have made few real efforts to deal with its decline in recent decades. Certainly, preparing students for civic participation under contemporary conditions is a formidable challenge. Schools today operate in a rapidly changing society that is ideologically polarized and is confronting continuing racial inequality, accelerating economic gaps, rapid demographic shifts, and changing social norms. Our traditional concepts of education for citizenship were formed in simpler times, when society's values and expectations were relatively clear and when the challenges of change affected schools at a more manageable pace. Educators and policy makers have been unsure of how to deal with the complex challenges of today, especially when they fear that any proactive stances they take may generate legal confrontation or potential political backlash.

This institutional paralysis is precisely why the courts can and should play an important role in dealing with contemporary issues of civic preparation. The articulation of clear constitutional principles regarding the importance of preparation for civic participation can raise awareness and motivate school officials and policy makers to make preparation for civic participation a high priority. Remedial orders issued by the courts, where necessary and appropriate, can require state and school officials to identify and pursue effective methods for preparing students for civic participation and ensure that sufficient resources are directed toward that end. The courts' institutional orientation toward encouraging people with sharply different positions to find common ground and settle their disputes can counter the climate of intense polarization in which most policy issues are discussed these days.[1] It can promote meaningful discussions on how schools should deal with the challenging and sometimes contentious issues that are involved in active civic preparation efforts.

For courts to accomplish these tasks, however, judges need to understand the depth of challenges in this area, and they need to be convinced that there are judicially manageable standards and techniques available to help solve them. This chapter and the one that follows analyze the contemporary challenges involved in educating students for civic preparation and set the stage for a detailed discussion in chapters 6 and 7 of how judicial decisions and remedial orders can help meet them. In this chapter, I first propose a conceptual framework that delineates the main challenges that need to be considered in preparing students for civic participation under contemporary demographic, economic, political, and cultural conditions. Because critical aspects of diversity and equality must also be addressed if our schools are truly to prepare all of their students for civic participation, this chapter also includes a discussion of the political and legal steps that need to be taken to promote inclusive school communities and equal educational opportunities.

Then, in the next chapter, I discuss specific educational and policy approaches that schools can use to respond to each of these challenges. Later chapters set forth litigation strategies and specific proposals for how courts can ensure the effective implementation of the kinds of reforms discussed in the conceptual framework and the diversity and equity reforms that are needed to fully put them into effect.

A Conceptual Framework for Preparation for Civic Participation

One of the obstacles to developing good policy and practices for civic preparation is the range of seemingly different views that Americans hold about what it mean to be a "capable" civic participant or a "good" citizen. Some emphasize as the hallmarks of citizenship traditional traits and actions like being respectful to authority, helping neighbors in times of need, and voting. Others think of citizenship in more active terms, such as working on community projects and taking action to improve society and its institutions. Joel Westheimer and Joseph Kahne have articulated three analytic categories that they believe encapsulate the range of contemporary perspectives on defining a "good" citizen on the basis of their analysis of a number of programs designed to prepare students for democratic citizenship. These are the "personally responsible citizen," the "participatory citizen," and the "justice-oriented citizen":

1. The *personally responsible citizen* acts conscientiously in the community by, for example, picking up litter, giving blood, recycling, and otherwise volunteering to help fellow community members. He or she works and pays taxes, obeys laws, and helps those in need during crises such as snowstorms or floods. Educational programs that seek to develop personally responsible citizens work to build the values and dispositions of personal responsibility by emphasizing honesty, integrity, self-discipline, hard work, and being considerate to others.
2. The *participatory citizen* takes part actively in the civic affairs and social life of the community. While the personally responsible citizen would contribute cans of food to the local homeless shelter, the participatory citizen might organize a food drive. Programs designed to develop participatory citizens focus on the skills and dispositions involved in building relationships, common understandings, trust, and collective commitments. They teach students about how government and community-based and faith-based institutions work and about the importance of planning and participating in organized efforts to care for those in need.
3. The *justice-oriented citizen* critically assesses social, political, and economic structures and considers collective strategies for change that challenge injustice and, when possible, address root causes of problems. Educational programs designed to prepare justice-oriented citizens are less likely to emphasize the need for charity and volunteerism as ends in themselves and more likely to teach about social movements that challenge structural causes of poverty and how to effect systemic change. Although educators promoting justice-oriented citizens may well employ curricula that make political issues more explicit than those who emphasize personal responsibility or participatory citizenship, the focus on social change and social justice does not necessarily imply an emphasis on particular political perspectives, conclusions, or priorities.[2]

Educators and policy makers concerned with preparation for civic participation tend to emphasize one or another of these approaches. For example, Character Counts! promotes personally responsible citizenship by advocating the teaching of the "six pillars of character": "trustworthiness, respect, responsibility, fairness, caring and citizenship."[3] Robert Putnam and others who are concerned that citizens not "bowl alone" stress the need to develop in future citizens more participatory skills and civic involvement. Proponents of the "new civics" tend to advocate a justice-oriented approach.[4]

Westheimer and Kahne appear to believe that these three approaches are distinct and that there are inherent conflicts among those who emphasize aspects of the differing categories.[5] They acknowledge that they personally favor the justice-oriented approach and are critical of some who espouse the "personally responsible citizen" perspective because the emphasis on respect for authority and for existing institutions in this approach "works against the kind of critical reflection and action many assume are essential in a democratic society."[6] They cite in this regard the Nebraska State Board of Education's limited and disengaged response to the 2001 terrorist attacks on the World Trade Center: "Nebraska's State Board of Education specified that the high school social studies curriculum should 'include instruction in . . . the benefits and advantages of our government, the dangers of communism and similar ideologies, the duties of citizenship, and appropriate patriotic exercises, that middle-grade instruction should instill a love of country,' that the social studies curriculum should include 'exploits and deeds of American heroes, singing patriotic songs, memorizing the Star Spangled Banner and America, and reverence for the flag.' "[7] Some of those in the personally responsible citizen camp are also sometimes critical of the justice-oriented approach: "[T]oday there is an enormous emphasis on getting students to develop a critical view of this country: its values, activities and leaders. Students are encouraged to question 'myths.' . . . Patriotism is unfashionable and receives little expression. . . . There is an emphasis on the value of ethnic pluralism, but no balancing emphasis on patriotism or nationalism. . . . Boys Clubs, 4H and such groups retain an older form of citizenship training, but they do not reach those young people who are most disaffected."[8]

Such statements tend to respond to specific issues that arise at particular times. Although various groups and individuals often talk about citizenship primarily through one or another of these three lenses, I believe that there is, nevertheless, substantial agreement on many of the underlying aspects of the civic knowledge, skills, values, and experiences that schools need to impart to students to prepare them to be effective citizens under any of the definitional categories. Most people who emphasize personally responsible citizenship do not deny the importance of developing critical analytic skills that will allow students to advocate for the political and social positions that they support, and, similarly, those who emphasize justice-oriented citizenship do not deny the importance of character traits like responsibility and integrity.

For example, Thomas Lickona, a leading voice in the character education movement, writes in regard to controversial issues like abortion that "education has a role to play here . . . [in trying] to add, however modestly, to our capacity for reasoned public dialogue about this important public policy issue."[9] He also thinks that "students should know that all over the world, people are taking effective action to alleviate suffering, and restore hope and dignity to the poor and oppressed."[10] Similarly, adherents of the participatory and social justice perspectives like Meira Levinson agree on the importance of "moral and civic virtues such as concern for the rights and welfare of others, social responsibility, tolerance and respect, and belief in the capacity to make a difference."[11]

A major 2011 report, *Guardian of Democracy: The Civic Mission of the Schools*, reflects a broad national consensus on the elements of good citizenship in the twenty-first century.[12] The report was produced by the Campaign for the Civic Mission of Schools, headed by former Supreme Court justice Sandra Day O'Connor and former congressman Lee Hamilton in partnership with a number of university centers, and a division of the American Bar Association; its steering committee included seventy organizations that spanned the ideological spectrum on citizenship issues.[13] The report defines the traits of "competent and responsible" citizens in terms that incorporate all of the three perspectives identified by Westheimer and Kahne. Specifically, it defines good citizens as people who are "informed and thoughtful," "participate in their communities," "act politically," and exhibit "moral and civic virtues."[14]

The *Guardian of Democracy* report—like most scholars and educators who are concerned about these issues—states that effective preparation of students for civic participation requires (1) basic civic knowledge in government, history, law and democracy; (2) verbal and critical reasoning skills; (3) social and participatory experiences; and (4) responsible character traits and acceptance of democratic values and dispositions.[15] This consensus understanding demonstrates that schools can effectively prepare students from a broad range of cultural backgrounds and ideological orientations for capable citizenship in the twenty-first century. To motivate schools to do so, and to convince courts to encourage such efforts, requires, however, that the justifications for why educational initiatives need to be undertaken in each of these categories and the reforms that need to be put into effect be spelled out in much greater detail. The comprehensive conceptual framework for civic preparation that follows attempts to meet that need.

The Core Elements of Preparation for Civic Participation

Civic Knowledge

In 1983, *A Nation at Risk*, the report of the National Commission on Excellence in Education, warned that mediocre schools could undermine the country's ability to compete in a global marketplace. In this context, it pointed to the importance of a well-informed citizenry: "For our country to function, citizens must be able to reach some common understandings on complex issues, often on short notice and on the basis of conflicting or incomplete evidence. Education helps form these common understandings, a point Thomas Jefferson made long ago in his justly famous dictum: 'I know no safe depository of the ultimate powers of the society but the people themselves; and if we think them not enlightened enough to exercise their control with a wholesome discretion, the remedy is not to take it from them but to inform their discretion.' "[16] Peter Levine and Kei Kawashima-Ginsburg interpret this as support for "broader and deeper approaches to education,"[17] in contrast to the "back to basics" reforms that have been in favor in recent years. By "broader," they "mean opportunities to explore not only reading, mathematics, and science but also fields like the social studies, arts, and [world] languages, as well as interdisciplinary inquiry." And by "deeper," they mean "efforts to master not just core academic content (which is certainly important) but also . . . critical thinking and problem solving, collaboration, effective communication, [and] self-directed learning."[18] They argue that "deeper learning" can promote civic engagement and that greater attention within schools to preparing students for civic participation can foster deeper learning.

Danielle Allen agrees that students need a broad general knowledge base to understand and evaluate the wide range of issues that citizens of a democracy need to consider. She describes the type of education students require to become capable citizens in terms of "participatory readiness" and "democratic knowledge."[19] Allen asserts that there is a "humanistic baseline"[20] for educating citizens for democracy to which schools need to adhere. That baseline requires a solid grounding in history, economics, world languages, science, and the arts, all of which are necessary to produce, as Martha Nussbaum has put it, "complete citizens who can think for themselves, criticize tradition, and understand the significance of another person's sufferings and achievements."[21]

These calls for "broader and deeper approaches to education" and a "humanistic baseline" are clearly on point.[22] Today the range of knowledge citizens need to flourish in a democratic society is much greater than it was in the past. Successful deliberation in our complex and enormously diverse contemporary culture requires, for example, understanding of the history and culture of "the varied subgroups (ethnic, national, religious, gender based) that comprise one's own nation, their achievements, struggles, and contributions," and also "contributions and similarly complex knowledge about nations and traditions outside one's own."[23] For this reason, the Council for Basic Education argues for a well-rounded liberal arts education for everyone:

> Life in the twenty-first century has become very complex, and the educational requirements for success have grown accordingly. . . . Because the liberal arts span the domains of human experience, they afford the best foundation for the diverse challenges that confront us in this rapidly evolving world. At the same time, a liberal arts education returns us to first principles, fostering an understanding of what it means to be human, an understanding that transcends limiting conceptions of occupation, social class, race, or nationality. An education once reserved for the most privileged students has therefore become a necessity for all students.[24]

This runs counter to recent educational trends and to most contemporary definitions of the knowledge necessary for civic preparation.

Most efforts to promote civic education today emphasize a more limited knowledge base. For example, the National Assessment Governing Board, the division of the U.S. Department of Education that oversees the National Assessment of Educational Progress (NAEP), has delineated what it considers the key elements of civic education.[25] The NAEP framework identifies five major areas of civic knowledge covering America's political institutions, political values, and role in international politics:

1. What are civic life, politics, and government?
2. What are the foundations of the American political system?

3. How does the government established by the Constitution embody the purposes, values, and principles of American democracy?
4. What is the relationship of the United States to other nations and to world affairs?
5. What are the roles of citizens in American democracy?[26]

Unfortunately, the "high-quality education" to which our national educational policy purports to be committed does not currently emphasize even the limited range of civic knowledge that the NAEP framework describes, let alone the broad, humanistic base that Levine, Kawashima-Ginsberg, and Allen advocate. The educational priorities that were established in No Child Left Behind and that have been perpetuated by ESSA stress competency in basic literacy and mathematical skills, especially for low-performing schools, which many students living in poverty attend. For example, ESSA requires each state to implement "high-quality student academic assessments" in mathematics, reading or language arts, and science, but not in civics, history, world languages, social studies, economics, or the arts.[27] As was discussed in chapter 1, particularly in schools with constrained resources, what gets tested tends to be what gets taught; the lower status of civics, history, social studies, economics, and the arts has, in fact, meant that schools have in recent years substantially reduced the time students spend in instruction in these areas.[28] Rosemary Salomone aptly summarized the self-defeating nature of this substantial retreat from a broad, humanistic curriculum:

> Most fundamentally, the almost single-minded fixation on productivity undercuts Brown's legacy guaranteeing an effective, appropriate, and meaningful education. It runs the risk of denying students—especially the most disadvantaged—the means of self-realization through a broad-based curriculum including the arts and literature. At the same time, it fails to equip them with the knowledge and skills needed to compete in a global economy. What seems to be lost on Washington is the reality of why other nations consistently outrank the United States on the Programme for International Student Assessment (PISA) exam: those nations provide students not simply with standards but with a comprehensive, content-rich education in the liberal arts and sciences.[29]

In sum, to become engaged citizens who seek meaning and act with purpose to achieve the conditions they desire in their own and others' lives, all students need not only solid grounding in literacy and mathematical skills but also meaningful access to a full range of courses in civics, history and social studies, science, world languages, and the arts.

Civic Skills

VERBAL AND COGNITIVE SKILLS Effective political participation requires well-developed verbal and cognitive skills because "political struggles in democracy are waged in public arguments, amidst the rhetoric of political debate. Because politics is largely concerned with the utilization and manipulation of language, *verbal cognitive ability* . . . is the most relevant aspect of cognitive ability in relation to democratic citizenship."[30] The NAEP framework reflects this understanding: the skills it deems most important for students to acquire for civic preparation are those that help citizens identify, describe, explain, and analyze information and arguments; in addition, civic participants should be able to evaluate, take, and defend positions on public policies.[31]

Danielle Allen expands on the requisite intellectual skills by discussing the importance of "verbal empowerment," by which she means both "interpretive and expressive skills." These are critical, she argues, because "civic and political action must begin from a diagnosis of our current situation and move from that diagnosis to a prescription for a response. Such interpretive work . . . can be done only in and through language. . . . Moreover, success at the movement from diagnosis to prescription requires not merely the verbal skills embodied in actions of interpretation but also expressive skills. For these social diagnoses to become effective, one must convince others of them. The verbal work involved in civic agency extends well beyond our usual focus on deliberation to include also adversarial and prophetic speech."[32] In other words, citizens in a democracy need a substantive set of cognitive skills not only to understand written and spoken words but also to be able to analyze their meaning critically and to be able to express persuasively their own opinions on the important issues of the day.

CRITICAL ANALYTIC SKILLS AND DELIBERATIVE DEMOCRACY Many other scholars speak more broadly in terms of the skills required for "democratic deliberation." Democratic deliberation is "a talk-based approach to political conflict and problem solving—through arguing, expressing, demonstrating, and persuading"[33] that emphasizes critical reasoning, thoughtful discussion, openness to plural aims, respect for the legitimacy of decisions taken purposefully, and the mutual recognition of the deliberative capacities of the participants.[34] For most philosophers and political theorists who are concerned about civic participation, the ability to engage effectively in democratic deliberation is the essence of what it means to be a capable citizen.

Contemporary interest in deliberative democracy stemmed from a prominent group of political theorists in the 1990s who, in reaction to what they perceived as inappropriate emphasis on individualism and materialism in American society, advocated an approach to civic renewal based on "civic republicanism."[35] For civic republicans, sharing in self-rule involves more than pursing individual goals: "It means deliberating with fellow citizens about the common good and helping to shape the political community. . . . It requires knowledge of public affairs and also a sense of belonging, a concern for the whole, a moral bond with the community whose fate is at stake."[36]

Civic republicans believe that a reconciliation of individual and communal perspectives can be achieved through an emphasis on "public dialogue"[37] that can create a "dialogic community."[38] They assert that open, honest interchange can lead to new understandings, not only of the opponent's position but also of one's own.[39] Even if agreement is not reached, participants can formulate positions that others can accept, without feeling that they have abandoned their own basic beliefs.[40]

Political philosopher John Rawls's concept of public reason also substantially informs current thinking about deliberative democracy. Public reason is the idea that "citizens' reasoning in the public forum about constitutional essentials and basic questions of justice . . . [is] guided by a political concept of principles and values of which all citizens can endorse,"[41] and is, as far as possible, "independent of the opposing and conflicting philosophical and religious doctrines that citizens affirm."[42] In other words, although people will have different values and concepts of how to lead a good or proper life, as participants in a democratic polity, they can nevertheless deliberate in a spirit of mutual respect and reach agreement on a set of principles and processes that are important to the system's basic functioning.[43]

While desirable in theory, democratic deliberation is hard to achieve in practice. Diana C. Mutz, a professor of political science and communication at the University of Pennsylvania, closely examined several extensive national surveys on Americans' networks of political discussion and concluded that most people tend to avoid entering into political discussions with those who have opposing political views and tend to seek out like-minded people, both in choosing their residences and communal associations and in their interpersonal conversations.[44] She contends that this type of political activism leads to partisanship and polarization because "the best social environment for cultivating political activism is one in which people are surrounded by those who agree with them, people who will reinforce the sense that their own political views are the only right and proper way to proceed."[45] Mutz agrees, however, that it would be desirable to promote more heterogeneity in people's personal networks and more opportunities for democratic deliberation because when people are put into situations where they are exposed to "cross-cutting ideas," they do develop greater awareness of rationales for opposing viewpoints and greater tolerance.[46]

The highly partisan and polarized current state of American politics is far from the deliberative democracy ideal, and it may make talk of creating a "dialogic community" seem abstract and perhaps far-fetched. This polarization has been generated, to a large extent, by major structural political changes, such as party realignments since the 1960s that have resulted in Democrats becoming increasing liberal and Republicans increasingly conservative, as well as to closer elections and increasing inequality.[47] It is compounded by "affect" polarization that leads members of political parties not only to dislike members of the other party but also to attribute negative traits to rank-and-file members of the other party. Shanto Iyengar and his colleagues found that from 1960 to 2010, the percentage of Democrats and Republicans who said that members of their own party were more intelligent than those in the opposition party grew from 6 percent to 48 percent, and the percentage describing members of the opposition party as "selfish" rose from 21 percent to 47 percent.[48]

Other writers who are skeptical of the possibilities for deliberative democracy cite studies that indicate that increased education has only a modest effect on tolerance and on willingness to consider views that differ from one's own. Karen Stenner concludes from a range of worldwide studies that the effect of the superior knowledge and cognitive skills that stem from education is only a very modest decrease (between 3 percent and 8 percent) in intolerance.[49] Joseph Kahne and Benjamin Bowyer also describe the difficulty of promoting democratic dialogue in a digital culture that transmits unprecedented amounts of misinformation:

> When individuals are guided by directional motivation (the desire to justify conclusions that align with prior beliefs), information that is consistent with one's prior preferences tends to be accepted uncritically and judged positively, whereas information that runs contrary to one's preconceptions is subjected to greater scrutiny and judged less positively. . . . By contrast, when motivated by accuracy goals, "[Individuals] expend more cognitive effort on issue-related reasoning, attend to relevant information more carefully, and process it more deeply, often using more complex rules[.]" . . . Scholars find that directional motivation is especially common in the processing of political information.[50]

These cautionary findings do not, however, mean that efforts to promote deliberative democracy in the schools are futile. On the contrary, they support greater efforts by educators to deal strategically with the growing problem of misinformation. Significant in this regard are the results of the recent study that Kahne and Bowyer undertook of the impact of media literacy experiences among a subset of more than two thousand young people who took the Youth Participatory Politics Survey, a nationally representative survey of young people between the ages of fifteen and twenty-seven. They found that "individuals who reported high levels of media literacy learning opportunities were considerably more likely to rate evidence-based posts as accurate than to rate posts containing misinformation as accurate—even when both posts aligned with their prior policy perspectives."[51] Although further studies of this type are needed to pinpoint more precisely those educational techniques that can promote deliberative democracy most effectively, these findings are important because they indicate that education for deliberation—and specifically efforts involving the use of critical analytic skills with media, "can matter a great deal for its success."[52]

The bottom line is that we don't know how great an impact focused instruction in deliberative democracy techniques may have on students' civic behavior. We do know that other methods for dealing with the growing influence of false information on public discourse and political decision making are even less likely to succeed.[53] The critical importance of expanding students' tolerance and use of critical analytic skills in political thinking and political discourse would argue, therefore, for maximizing efforts to promote instruction in media literacy and deliberative democracy in the schools. Simply put, the cost-benefit returns for this investment are extremely high, and the downsides are virtually nonexistent.

Civic Experiences

As John Stuart Mill aptly noted, preparing citizens for civic participation is like teaching someone to ride a horse or to swim: both require the formation of habits through exercise.[54] In addition to civic knowledge and civic skills, therefore, students also need exposure to experiences that show them how politics and government actually work and how civic participation can influence social and political outcomes.[55] Involvement in student government, service-learning activities, speech and debate, civic action projects, participatory action research, and other actual and simulated civic and political activities provide important opportunities for developing civic skills and dispositions. These activities also provide students understanding of how civic and political institutions function and of tactical skills for active civic and political involvement later in life.

John Dewey recognized almost a century ago how much the school environment influences the habits, dispositions, and social attitudes of children; as a result, he called for schools to give students experiences in democratic processes and practices to the maximum extent possible.[56] Allowing students a voice in the operations of their own schools and classrooms develops specific listening, speaking, organizing, and petitioning skills that they will need to be active civic participants later in life. In addition, these experiences stimulate interest in civic and political participation, and help students develop a sense of agency and the ability to affect their environment as well. The schools' role in providing students with experiences to develop concrete democratic skills such as organizing a meeting and mobilizing support for a cause is probably even more important today than it was in Dewey's time because, as Peter Levine has noted, "citizens can no longer count on unions, churches, or fraternal associations to recruit and train most of the nation's youth."[57]

Through civic experiences like student council, student elections, active assemblies, and schoolwide forums, students practice using the interpersonal skills necessary to bridge racial, ethnic, political, and cultural differences in a diverse society. In deliberating and working out acceptable positions on issues that directly affect their lives and those of their peers, students learn to respect others, gain valuable experience in understanding and accepting different perspectives, and build trust. Positive results in these areas can best be achieved in schools in which administrators and teachers have established a supportive school climate. A recent study found that regardless of their racial or ethnic background, adolescents were more likely to believe that America was a just society and to endorse democratic goals if they felt that their teachers were fair to and respected students.[58]

An extensive body of research also holds that extracurricular activities and active community service experiences have a significant positive impact on long-term civic involvement. Extracurricular activities promote frequent and fruitful interactions among students of varied income, racial, religious, and ethnic groups. The experience of working closely together for extended periods of time on athletic teams, drama productions, band and choir concerts, school newspapers, clubs, debate teams, and the like, afford students the kind of experiences that are most conducive to overcoming stereotypes, breaking down cultural barriers, and facilitating meaningful communication among people from dissimilar backgrounds.

Robert Putnam writes that school-based extracurricular activities emerged roughly a century ago as part of the progressive educational reform movement precisely "to use extra-curriculars to diffuse among all classes what we now call 'soft skills'—strong work habits, self-discipline, teamwork, leadership and a sense of civic engagement."[59] These noncognitive skills have been directly linked with increased civic participation in later life. For example, a longitudinal analysis of the experiences of a sample of twenty thousand students found that the likelihood of involvement in civic engagement activities eight years after graduation was approximately 50 percent greater for students who had participated in high school extracurricular activities for one year than for students who had not, and that students who had participated for two years evidenced even greater rates of civic engagement.[60] Participation in extracurricular activities also has been found to promote increased voting,[61] and it is associated with educational success, higher lifetime earnings, and occupational attainment.[62] Extracurricular activities that explicitly articulate their relationship to civic participation are likely to be even more consequential in terms of ultimate civic outcomes.[63]

Studies have also shown that both voluntary and school-required community service activities, as well as involvement in extracurricular activities, are strong predictors of adult voting and volunteering.[64] Participation in community service activities directly acquaints students with community problems and political issues with which they may not have been aware or were aware only in the abstract, and it provides a network of people with whom to discuss civic issues.

Service learning, an approach that combines community service with classroom discussions and analysis of community service experiences, has been found to have a large effect on later civic participation, even when controlling for a range of neighborhood, school, and family characteristics.[65] As of 2011, twenty states had state standards related to service learning.[66] An effective service-learning program works well because "it not only enhances students' skills and interests, but changes their fundamental identities so that they become—and see themselves as—active citizens."[67] Service learning also can be a factor in promoting trusting relations among students in a diverse school community: "Ideally, reflection [on service] includes participants from a variety of racial, ethnic, and socioeconomic backgrounds, so that it reduces barriers and builds bonds between students who might not otherwise engage in dialogue, nor see commonalities, because they are from different backgrounds and/or because of prejudice. When students come to 'identify with' the act of being of service, thus becoming closer to others also serving, as well as with those served, they become more likely to engage in perspective-taking and experience an enhanced sense of connection with others."[68] And in building deliberative democracy skills, "meaningful communication between students about their effort to make a difference also increases social discourse on service at this micro-level, paving the way for more broad-based civic dialogue over time."[69]

In sum, school governance experiences as well as extracurricular activities and school-connected community service activities substantially advance motivation and develop important participatory skills for electoral and civic involvement later in life. It is, therefore, essential that all schools provide students a reasonable range of experiences in school governance, extracurricular opportunities, and community service activities.

Civic Values

CONTEMPORARY CONSENSUS VALUES The drafters of state constitutions in both the post–Revolutionary War and the common school eras believed that certain moral and civic values were vital to the successful functioning of a democratic society; for this reason, they specifically included references to "virtue" and other moral dispositions and character traits in their education clauses.[70] As James Madison wrote, "To suppose that any form of government will secure liberty or happiness without any virtue in the people, is a chimerical idea."[71] Most state constitutions adopted in the nineteenth century and the early part of the twentieth century also declared that schools needed to inculcate "morality" and religion as well as knowledge in their students.[72] John Dewey succinctly explained why virtue and morality are essential to a stable democratic order: "Democracy is more than a form of government, it is a mode of associated living. . . . Since a democratic society repudiates the principle of external authority, it must find a substitute in voluntary disposition and interest."[73]

Most contemporary educators who are concerned about civic preparation agree that schools today also need to promote certain character values and civic dispositions, in addition to providing access to civic knowledge, skills, and experiences.[74] The nineteenth-century common schools sought to inculcate values like patriotism, religious faith, hard work, responsibility, honesty, altruism, and courage.[75] Contemporary proponents of civic character endorse most of these personal values, although they do not allude to religious values (at least not in the public schools). They emphasize that democratic citizens need to be responsible, honest, hardworking, and caring, and to have the courage to do what is right and just, even in difficult circumstances.[76] The nation's experiences with abolition, Jim Crow, immigration, fighting totalitarianism, and terrorism have also led most contemporary educators and policy makers to emphasize additional significant democratic values like tolerance, equality, due process, and respect for the rule of law.[77]

The NAEP civic framework, discussed earlier, agrees that "traits of private character such as moral responsibility, self-discipline, and respect for individual worth and human dignity are essential to the well-being of the American nation, society, and constitutional democracy."[78] At the same time, it emphasizes additional "traits of public character, such as public spiritedness, civility, respect for law, critical-mindedness, and a willingness to listen, negotiate, and compromise, are indispensable for the nation's well-being."[79] Jennifer Hochschild and Nathan Scovronick have summarized the common set of democratic values on which Americans of all backgrounds and political positions agree and that schools should convey as follows:

> loyalty to the nation, acceptance of the Declaration of Independence and Constitution as venerable founding documents, appreciation that in American constitutionalism rights sometimes trump majority rule and majority

> rule is supposed to trump intensive desire, belief in the rule of law as the proper grounding for a legal system, belief in equal opportunity as the proper grounding for a social system, willingness to adhere to the discipline implied by rotation in office through an electoral system, and . . . economic and social values such as work ethic, self-reliance, and trustworthiness.[80]

In short, wherever families and individuals stand on the ideological spectrum, there is broad agreement in America today that the schools should instill in students basic character values like responsibility, honesty, work ethic, and self-discipline, and basic democratic values like tolerance, equality, due process, respect for the rule of law, and support for the fundamental political institutions of our society.

TOLERANCE AND CRITICAL ANALYTIC REASONING For Stephen Macedo, in a diverse, liberal society tolerance is a logical necessity, and so "the one theme that schools can rally around is *tolerating* differences."[81] In many areas, large public high schools are "microcosms of the diversity of society as a whole," and tolerance of differences is necessary for the maintenance of a peaceful coexistence. Thus, this environment presents unique opportunities for teaching moments on the meaning and importance of tolerance.[82]

Macedo is clearly correct in positing the importance of promoting tolerance in a diverse society. But the pedagogical demands of schooling also raise significant questions about whether schools also need to place limits and restraints on how critical analytic reasoning is taught and applied in the school setting. How far should the spirit of tolerance extend? Must the school authorities and teachers defer to families with strong religious or ideological positions that resist critical appraisals of their fundamental beliefs? For example, some fundamentalist religious groups take the position that exposing their children to ideas such as secularism, atheism, feminism, and value relativism is inconsistent with the family values they espouse and undermines their ability to inculcate in their children their beliefs in the sacred, absolute truth of the Bible.

Amy Gutmann directly confronts this concern. She argues that a democratic society cannot be either a "family state" that seeks to impose common values and "virtues" on all its citizens, as Plato and Aristotle would have done in ancient Athens, or a "state of families" that places educational authority exclusively in the hands of parents and allows them to "insulate their children from exposure to ways of life or thinking that conflict with their own."[83] Gutmann does not deny the parents' right to impart their values to their children, but she asserts that a democratic state must nevertheless be committed to "allocating educational authority in such a way as to provide its members with an education adequate to participating in democratic politics."[84]

This means that schools must not only teach children to tolerate other people's values and lifestyles; they must also instill in their students critical-thinking skills that will allow them to evaluate competing positions and enter into the public reasoning and deliberative processes that are at the core of democratic functioning. Families will, of course, substantially shape their children's values and outlooks, but, according to Gutmann, if our democracy is to thrive, the schools must also be able to develop in children "the deliberative capacity to evaluate competing conceptions of good lives and good societies."[85] This process may, of course, result in some young people ultimately choosing a life path and adopting values that differ from those of their parents.

Macedo agrees. He reasons that because "public power is held in common by us all, . . . we should exercise it together based on reasons and arguments that we can share in spite of our differences."[86] He also states: "Children must at the very least be provided with the intellectual tools necessary to understand the world around them, formulate their own convictions, and make their own way in life."[87] Essentially, living in a democratic society requires "bilingual"-type skills:[88] children must learn that they can adhere to their own heritage or deep-seated worldviews and at the same time develop a critical capacity in their civic role in order to, as Macedo puts it, "exclude appeals to *any* authority impervious to critical assessment from a variety of reasonable points of view."[89]

Some other thinkers, however, have a different view of how the relationship between tolerance and critical thinking should be implemented in practice, especially in regard to dealing with families with deeply held fundamentalist religious beliefs. For example, William Galston, although agreeing that schools must promote tolerance and critical thinking, does not believe that it is necessary to encourage children to question strongly held family values:

> Civic tolerance of deep differences is perfectly compatible with unswerving belief in the correctness of one's own way of life. It rests on the conviction that the pursuit of the better course should (and in many cases must) result from persuasion rather than coercion. . . . Civic deliberation is also compat-

> ible with unshakable personal commitments. It requires only that each citizen accept the minimal civic commitments . . . without which the liberal polity cannot long endure. In short, the civic standpoint does not warrant the conclusion that the state must (or may) structure public education to foster in children skeptical reflection on ways of life inherited from parents or local communities.[90]

Michael McConnell pushes this perspective even further. He agrees that schools need to develop tolerance and critical thinking in students, but he argues that this is best done through a pluralistic concept of schooling in which the state allows parents to choose from a range of schools, including government schools, private schools, and religious schools, that receive state financial support; these schools would then decide how to best combine the teaching of democratic values along with their own particular perspectives.[91]

Rob Reich rejects McConnell's proposal because its "view of democratic citizenship is threadbare and ignores the child's interest in autonomy."[92] He attempts to cut a pathway through the thick and thin perspectives on the state's role in democratic education:

> Democratic citizenship and autonomy can be fostered only when children become aware of the existence of other ways of life, and moreover, when they engage intellectually with such value diversity. The liberal state should be wary of parents whose choices are made solely on the basis of shielding them from any and all competing views. . . . [The state] must make it possible for children to make decisions about the kind of lives they wish to lead. This does not imply the ridiculous claim that children deserve to be able to lead any life possible, or that the state should seek intentionally to increase the chance that children will be skeptical of their parents' deepest convictions.[93]

In other words, for Reich, there is a viable middle ground that exposes all students to competing perspectives but does not attempt to limit the parents' ability to convey strongly their own values to their child. Of course, exactly how a fair balance of this type can be achieved on any particular issue in any particular school cannot be determined in the abstract.

In sum, then, to foster the kind of deliberative discussions needed to prepare students for civic participation in a diverse democratic society, schools must promote the values of tolerance and critical thinking, but they need to do so in a manner that is as inclusive as possible. This might mean, as Harry Brighouse and Adam Swift have noted, not only exposing children from sheltered religious environments to possibilities of other lifestyles but also exposing religious traditions, commitments, and practices to children whose parents seek to shield them from such experiences.[94] How much further public (or private) schools need to go to accommodate the views of fundamentalists or others who hold absolutist perspectives is a matter that courts and legislatures need to consider further. For our present purposes, it is important to stress that democratic deliberation and the significant "bridging" experiences that flow from it can be developed only in schools that instill in students the verbal and cognitive skills necessary for critical reasoning and that promote the value of tolerance.

In his recent book *Civics Beyond Critics: Character Education in a Liberal Democracy*, Ian MacMullen raises a further question as to whether promoting critical analytic skills in the schools is inconsistent with inculcating certain of the basic values that most people agree the schools should promote.[95] He asserts that many "orthodox" political theorists who promote deliberative democracy, including Gutmann, Macedo, and Galston, narrowly constrict the range of values that should properly be inculcated by the schools. In particular, he claims that their strong emphasis on critical thinking, personal autonomy, and tolerance preclude instilling in students the values of "law-abidingness, civic identification and support for the fundamental political institutions of one's society."[96]

MacMullen makes the case that maintaining a well-functioning society that can promote the values of tolerance, critical thinking, and personal autonomy necessarily requires a stable political order that allows for people to plan and execute their affairs in a reasonable manner.[97] Predisposing students to identify civically with current political institutions is necessary to maintain these institutions over the long run, he explains, and critical reasoning needs are satisfied if the polity allows citizens to express opposition to those institutions freely.[98]

It is far from clear, however, that adherents of the "orthodox" view would really dispute the validity of the three major civic values with which he is concerned. For example, Galston agrees that "every community creates a complex structure of law and regulations in the expectation that they will be accepted as legitimate, hence binding, without recourse to direct threats or sanctions. . . . Law-abidingness is therefore a core social virtue, in liberal communities and elsewhere."[99] Gutmann also believes that patriotic dispositions are not incompatible with critical reasoning since "people, quite naturally, value the specific cultural and political orientations of their society and family more than those of others, even if they cannot provide objective reasons for their preferences. The fact that these cultural orientations are theirs is an adequate (and generalizable) reason."[100] And Macedo emphasizes that "a system of free self-government needs to encourage . . . the patterns of social life that support [it.]"[101]

In essence, then, the orthodox political theorists do support the civic values stressed by the NAEP standards and other educators and policy makers, including law-abidingness, patriotism or "civic identification," and respect for the fundamental political institutions of the society. There is, indeed, a general consensus that these basic character and democratic values can and should be promoted in all American schools. Specific ways that schools can effectively promote these values, as well as civic knowledge, civic skills, and civic experiences, are the subject of the next chapter.

Diversity and Equality

Most political and educational discussions of the knowledge, skills, experiences, and values needed for civic participation omit or minimize the larger policy context in which schools operate. They ignore the reality that many of our schools do not provide environments in which students from diverse races, ethnicities, religions, sexual orientations, and socioeconomic backgrounds can thrive together. They do not take steps in the classroom and throughout the school environment to give students a sense of efficacy and engagement, and they do not seek to ensure that sufficient resources for many of the building blocks for civic preparation that they recommend are actually available. The stark fact is that in the absence of diverse school settings and equal and sufficient resources, "common" schooling that can truly prepare students for democratic functioning will remain a vision rather than a reality. Schools are capable of preparing today's students to function productively as civic participants, but they cannot fully accomplish that goal unless our society focuses major attention on promoting effective pedagogy for civic preparation and on the legal and policy context in which schools operate.

Horace Mann and the other founders of the common school movement had sought to minimize cultural and economic differences among citizens in a democratic republic by bringing together the children of the rich and the poor in a single, state-supported public school system. But that vision and the manner in which it was implemented also reflected an underlying assumption that, despite having differing class backgrounds, all Americans should agree on the core values of "republicanism, Protestantism and capitalism."[102] Thus, although much of the common school rhetoric spoke in terms of inculcating shared values, one of the impetuses for the adoption and expansion of the common schools was apprehension about the values that new immigrants were bringing into the country.

In the first half of the nineteenth century, there was broad-based concern about the influx of Irish Catholics to the East Coast, then about the arrival of Germans and Slavs in the Midwest, and, toward the end of the century, to the large numbers of immigrants arriving from Southern and Eastern Europe. Ellwood Cubberley, former dean of the Stanford Education School and an otherwise enlightened advocate of many progressive education reforms, summed up the prevalent nineteenth-century view in these words: "Everywhere these people tend to settle in groups or settlements, and to set up here their national manners, customs, and observances. Our task is to break up these groups or settlements, to assimilate and amalgamate these people as part of our American race, and to implant in their children, so far as can be done, the Anglo-Saxon conception of righteousness, law and order, and popular government, and to awaken in them a reverence for our democratic institutions, and for those things in our national life which we as a people hold to be of abiding worth."[103] The common school leaders were willing to consider adjustments on the fringes to accommodate Catholics and other minorities, but they were not inclined to entertain fundamental modifications to their core principles and to the mission of the schools as they conceived it. Rather than entering into a dialogue with Catholic leaders, they essentially shunned them, resulting in their creation of an entirely separate parochial school system.[104]

Today, the diversity in school populations throughout the country dwarfs the cultural differences experienced by nineteenth-century common schools. Schools bring together children from different races and ethnicities, with diverse cultures and home languages, with a range of intellectual and physical disabilities, with different family configurations and different sexual orientations. African Americans, who were excluded from the common schools, Latino or Hispanic, and Asian students now make up 45 percent of the student population nationally,[105] and they are projected to be a majority of the entire student population nationwide by 2020.[106] Students with identified disabilities constituted approximately 13 percent of the student population in 2012–2013,[107] and students who self-identify as gay constituted 5 percent of the student population.[108]

Changes in immigration laws and the arrival of refugees from throughout the world in recent decades have vastly expanded the diversity of cultures represented in the American school population. In 2013, New York City Department of Education reported that more than 41 percent (438,131) of students enrolled in New York City public schools speak one of 151 languages other than English at home,[109] and in the Los Angeles public schools 93 languages other than English are spoken.[110]

These new demographic trends are not limited to major urban areas. In rural schools, as of 2010, 10 percent of students were African American and 13 percent Hispanic,[111] and in rural and small town areas, the Hispanic population increased by 1.9 million, or 46 percent, between 2000 and 2010.[112] In 2017 in Lincoln County, Nebraska, students came from 115 different countries and spoke 96 different languages.[113]

Mexican Americans and other immigrants from Central and South America and the Caribbean who constitute a majority (52 percent) of all immigrants in the United States today tend to maintain continuing ties to their homelands.[114] They, as well as many immigrants from Europe, Asia, and Africa, often travel regularly to their countries of origin to visit relatives and reconnect with their ancestral roots. All of these factors related to immigrants and to racial and ethnic diversity, combined with society's broad acceptance today of the need to accommodate students with disabilities, and its increasing sensitivity to the needs of LGBTQ students, render all the diversity issues faced by contemporary schools substantially more complex than those faced by schools during the nineteenth century and even most of the twentieth century.

There is also a significant qualitative dimension to the diversity challenges American schools face today compared with years past. Although many of the European immigrants who arrived in the nineteenth century experienced some degree of discrimination from nativists and aggressive assimilationists, they were not burdened with the harsh history of slavery and Jim Crow segregation that follows African American students into the classroom. The growing economic gulf between the haves and the have-nots and increasing political polarization have created enormous cultural chasms among various groups in our society. For example, it has resulted in, among other things, many white students from low-income or working-class backgrounds becoming highly pessimistic and cynical about civic involvement.[115]

Given these realities, America's historical assumption of the melting pot—that immigrants and minority groups of diverse backgrounds can or should readily be assimilated into the dominant culture—no longer applies. Public schools today need to combine durable American institutions, traditions, and important democratic values with values and mores drawn from the vast array of sometimes conflicting practices and perspectives that heterogeneous population groups can contribute. As Eamon Callan has put it, schools today need to "offer a learning environment that is genuinely hospitable to the credal and cultural diversity the society exhibits."[116] To prepare students to function productively as civic participants in this dynamic, increasingly varied American society, schools today need not merely to tolerate diversity but also to embrace it and to provide students with knowledge, skills, experiences, and values appropriate to that task.

The U.S. Supreme Court's landmark 1954 decision in *Brown v. Board of Education*[117] provided a unique opportunity to develop affirmative, creative responses to racial and other forms of diversity by fully integrating public schools throughout the country. As Harvard law professor and former dean Martha Minow has noted, the integration ideal is "a crucial element of preparing individuals for successful and productive lives as workers, parents, and civic participants in a pluralistic, democratic society" because "social integration at its best (1) overcomes and prevents stereotyping and dehumanizing; (2) promotes not just tolerance for those who are different but mutual engagement, mutual appreciation, and the ability to take the perspective of another; (3) assists individuals in relating well to diverse others and in working together in mixed groups to solve problems and perform other tasks; (4) advances the resource of social capital and networking across different groups; and (5) reduces conventional lines of division through the creation and support of crosscutting groups."[118]

The Supreme Court initially appeared to be leading the country in this direction by insisting on effective and thoroughgoing racial integration of the public schools.[119] Its decisions from the mid-1970s to the present, however, have moved in the opposite direction. The federal courts' retreat from enforcing integration began with the U.S. Supreme Court's ruling in 1974 in *Milliken v. Bradley.* In that case, it ruled that extensive patterns of urban segregation, marked by largely black city schools and overwhelmingly white suburbs, could not be remedied unless the plaintiffs demonstrated that the suburban school districts had acted intentionally in ways that promoted racial segregation in the city's schools.[120] In the 1990s, a series of cases encouraged federal district courts to terminate desegregation decrees if the "vestiges" of desegregation had been ameliorated "to the extent practicable"[121]—even if racial integration had not been fully achieved and even if many of the black children in these districts were still were performing at low academic levels.[122]

This trend culminated in the Supreme Court's 2007 ruling in *Parents Involved in Community Schools v. Seattle School District No. 1.*[123] Although a majority of the Court agreed that racial integration of the schools is a compelling state interest, the scope for promoting integration was narrowly drawn, and, in the particular case, racial integration plans that local school boards had adopted with strong community support were invalidated. As a result of that ruling, local school districts are substantially constrained from implementing *voluntary* school desegregation plans. The dramatic shift in Supreme Court jurisprudence since the 1970s has resulted in a trend toward resegregation in public schools throughout the country. Indeed, Justice Stephen Breyer, dissenting in *Parents Involved*, noted that in 2000, more than 70 percent of all black and Latino students attended predominantly minority schools, a higher percentage than thirty years earlier. Furthermore, between 1980 and 2003, the percentage of white students in schools attended by the average black student fell from 45 percent to 29 percent.[124]

Looking to the future, however, demographic trends and resultant political pressures may motivate policy makers to accept the realities of racial diversity and induce schools to develop more efficacious policies to deal with them. As James E. Ryan, dean of the Harvard Graduate School of Education, has written: "Change, nonetheless, is coming—not from legislatures or courts, but from demographics and changes in attitudes about the most desirable places to live and about diversity itself. . . . [T]hese demographic changes are bringing racial and socioeconomic diversity to the suburbs and greater opportunities for racial and socioeconomic diversity within schools and school districts. Attitudes and behaviors among young adults aged eighteen to twenty-nine push in the same direction. This generation has embraced diversity as none has before it, which bodes well for future housing patterns. These changing demographics will inevitably shape the politics of educational opportunity."[125] Jennifer Hochschild, Vesla Weaver, and Traci Burch have delineated these trends in depth. They conclude that extensive intermarriage, immigration, changing definitions of race and ethnicity, genomics, a fluidity in the racial classifications of individuals, shifting relative positions within and among groups, shifting attitudes among the younger generation, and changes in social relations among groups are all creating a new racial social order.[126]

I agree that these patterns are likely to lead to greater racial and socioeconomic diversity in the schools and can have positive implications for building common civic perspectives. I also think, however, that these demographic trends will need proactive support from the courts to ensure that they actually result in diverse, egalitarian environments that are conducive to effective civic preparation. Moreover, the effects of these demographic changes won't be felt equally everywhere, and those places where they are least likely to be felt may be most in need of proactive steps to address these issues.[127]

Studies on the effects of racial integration provide some indication of how thoroughgoing school integration can improve cross-racial understanding and the reduction of racial prejudice. For example, a meta-analysis of 515 studies showed that intergroup contact typically reduces intergroup prejudice; it found that the optimal conditions for prejudice reduction are equal status between groups in the situation, common goals, intergroup cooperation, and the support of authorities, law, or custom.[128] A survey of more than fifteen thousand students in fifty-eight large urban high schools indicated that students of all racial groups who attend more diverse schools have higher levels of comfort with individuals from racial groups other than their own, a greater desire to live and work in settings with multiple racial groups, and an increased sense of civic engagement.[129] Integration also has positive effects on achievement of both minority and majority students.[130]

A hospitable, inclusive climate is necessary to establish the social trust that, as Danielle Allen has explained, is an essential prerequisite for both successful school desegregation and effective civic participation.[131] The general sense of social trust has declined markedly in the United States, having fallen from 58 percent in 1960 to 32 percent in 2008.[132] The level of social trust among young people also appears to have declined markedly in recent years.[133] Meira Levinson reminds us of how deeply the legacy of slavery, segregation, and continuing racial and class inequities impinge on the schooling environment and how hard it will be to build the feelings of efficacy and empowerment that are necessary for civic engagement and for creating the kind of trust that Allen espouses among large segments of the public school population.[134] Robert Putnam reports that a lack of basic trust in societal institutions is associated not only with racial minorities but also with students from low-income families.[135]

Allen decries the missed opportunity for creating positive interpersonal relations and trust that the initial period of implementation of the *Brown* desegregation decree could have provided. She emphasizes, however, that practical tools are available for building the necessary level of social trust among students in a diverse setting by teaching students to develop skills that will allow them to "bond with those who are like us so as to help us bridge even with those who differ from us."[136] Contemporary schools can help develop students' self-confidence and a sense of efficacy by building pride in their own group's culture and contributions to American society, and this self-confidence can help to foster trust by constructing positive "bridging" relationships with other groups in the school and in the society at large.

For positive intergroup relations to flourish, however, Allen reminds us that students "must feel that their relationship rests on equality: each must believe that the relationship's benefits and burdens are shared more or less equally."[137] This kind of relationship cannot exist in schools where students are treated unequally or among students who are resentful of the fact that their schools lack important opportunities that students who attend other schools regularly enjoy.

For more than a decade, the stated educational policy of the United States has been "to ensure that all children have a fair, equal, and significant opportunity to obtain a high quality education and reach, at a minimum, proficiency in meeting challenging state academic achievement standards and state academic assessments."[138] Similar commitments to high-quality education for all students constitute the prime educational policy goal of most of the states.[139] But, of course, the reality in America's public schools today falls far short of that equitable ideal. As the national Equity and Excellence Commission recently put it: "While some young Americans—most of them white and affluent—are getting a truly world-class education, those who attended schools in high poverty neighborhoods are getting an education that more closely approximates school in developing nations. . . . With the highest poverty rate in the developed world, and amplified by the inadequate education received by many children in low-income schools, the United States is threatening its own future."[140]

Plaintiffs' victories in the majority of the educational equity and adequacy cases discussed in the previous chapter have made a significant dent in this problem, and they demonstrate that litigation can result in increased funding and more equitable distribution of resources. Nevertheless, much more still needs to be done, especially since equity and adequacy litigations have not succeeded in all states, and the remedies ordered by the courts in many of the states where plaintiffs have prevailed have not confronted the depth of the problems involved. I discuss in detail what both the state and the federal courts need to do in this regard in chapters 6 and 7.

CHAPTER FIVE

Education for Civic Participation in the Twenty-First Century

We need schools to do their job, which is to make democracy work. — Diana E. Hess

As of May 2017, fifteen states had enacted laws that require high school students to pass some version of the hundred-question multiple-choice test on the U.S. Constitution and the rights and responsibilities of U.S. citizens that is given to individuals applying to become naturalized citizens.[1] The organization that is sponsoring this initiative aims to have it adopted by all fifty states.[2]

Most educators believe, however, that rote learning of this type is "insufficient for achieving the goals of truly moving young people to participate meaningfully and effectively in democratic civic and political life."[3] They assert that students today can be motivated to become active citizens only through a much more ambitious and dynamic approach to civic participation.[4] The conceptual framework for preparation for civic participation set forth in the preceding chapter spelled out in detail the kinds of dynamic educational initiatives that need to be adopted to prepare students effectively for capable citizenship in the twenty-first century. In this chapter, I describe the degree to which current practices fall short of the recommendations set forth in conceptual framework and propose specific, practical ways to implement effective approaches for imparting civic knowledge, civic skills, civic experiences, and civic values to all students.

Many of the "best practices" that I recommend in this chapter assume that schools striving to truly prepare all of their students for civic participation will have created a positive "ethos," a sense of mission and community that is a major factor in producing positive civic outcomes.[5] They also assume that the school has created a welcoming and supportive climate for students from diverse backgrounds,[6] and that adequate and equal resources are available to meet the needs of all students. These conditions obviously do not exist in many schools today. Therefore, in this chapter and the next, I suggest policy initiatives and judicial actions that can ameliorate some of these inequities and promote positive interactions among diverse populations in the schools.

Implementing the Conceptual Framework for Civic Preparation

Civic Knowledge

CIVICS AND GOVERNMENT COURSES The framework for civic education promulgated by the National Assessment for Educational Progress (NAEP), discussed in the previous chapter, delineates five major aspects of civic knowledge that schools should impart.[7] The actual state of the teaching of civics and government, however, falls far short of providing students meaningful opportunities to reach the NAEP expectations.

In the mid-twentieth century, three civics-related courses were common in high school: civics, problems of democracy, and American government. The traditional civics course used to emphasize the rights and responsibilities of citizens and the ways that they could work together and relate to government. Courses in "problems of democracy" involved discussions of public policy issues. The government class (which remains common today) describes and analyzes government in a distant way, often with little explicit discussion of a citizen's role. Today, civics and problems of democracy courses have largely disappeared, and generally only a one-semester course in American government is required.[8]

The Center for Information and Research on Civic Learning & Engagement (CIRCLE) reports that, as of 2012–2013,

- 21 states required a state-designed social studies test. This is a dramatic reduction compared with 2001 when 34 states conducted regular assessments on social studies subjects.
- Only nine states require students to pass a social studies test in order to graduate from high school.
- Eight states have statewide, standardized tests specifically in civics/American government. Only two of these (Ohio and Virginia) require students to pass this test to graduate from high school.

- Social studies assessments have shifted from a combination of multiple-choice and performance tasks to almost exclusively multiple-choice exams since 2000.[9]

The marked decline in emphasis on required testing in civics and social studies in recent years may be related to the fact that since the enactment of No Child Left Behind in 2001, states have shifted educational resources away from social studies and toward English language arts, mathematics, and science, the subjects that are included on federally mandated statewide assessments.[10]

All states do have standards for social studies, a broad category that includes civics and government, along with other disciplines such as history, economics, and geography. In 1999, the Policy Research Project on Civic Education Policies and Practices at the University of Texas at Austin undertook a comprehensive analysis of these standards. They found that, on average, the civics content in states' social studies standards overemphasized the lower-order skills of identifying and describing a position rather than the more challenging skills of explaining and analyzing the position.[11] They also noted: "Civics statements requiring students to evaluate, take, and defend positions—the highest order level of thinking—are the least prevalent in most state standards."[12]

In recent years, many educators and policy organizations have urged states to adopt standards that emphasize higher-order thinking skills and critical analytic approaches to civics and other social studies topics. In 2013, fifteen national professional organizations—including the American Bar Association, the American Historical Association, the National Council for the Social Studies, the Campaign for the Civic Mission of Schools, and the Center for Civic Education—collaborated on the College, Career, and Civic Life (C3) Framework for Social Studies State Standards.[13] The C3 standards recommend that by the end of twelfth grade, students should, among other things, be able to do the following:

- Analyze the role of citizens in the U.S. political system, with attention to various theories of democracy, changes in Americans' participation over time, and alternative models from other countries, past and present.
- Explain how the U.S. Constitution establishes a system of government that has powers, responsibilities, and limits that have changed over time and that are still contested.

- Evaluate citizens' and institutions' effectiveness in addressing social and political problems at the local, state, tribal, national, and/or international level.
- Apply civic virtues and democratic principles when working with others.
- Use appropriate deliberative processes in multiple settings.[14]

Most states, however, do not seem to have been substantially influenced by these standards. Many state social studies standards still largely reflect an approach to civic knowledge that emphasizes structure and function rather than critical analysis and active civic participation. Although factual knowledge of functions and structures is a necessary prerequisite for a deep understanding of social, political, and civic issues, a limited functional approach is not likely to stimulate strong student interest in civic issues or develop their critical analytic skills. In addition, "civics classes that emphasize the mechanisms of a functional and essentially fair and democratic system will . . . be rejected as irrelevant or worse" by many African American and low-income students who "think that government doesn't work—at least for them or anyone they know."[15]

An example of such a mechanistic, formalistic approach is provided by Georgia's standards for high school social studies, which contain only the following limited types of expectations:

- The student will demonstrate knowledge of the organization and powers of the national government.
  a. Describe the structure and powers of the legislative, executive, and judicial branches.
  b. Analyze the relationship between the three branches in a system of checks and balances and separation of powers.
- The student will demonstrate knowledge of the federal system of government described in the United States Constitution.
  a. Explain the relationship of state governments to the national government.
  b. Define the difference between enumerated and implied powers.
  c. Describe the extent to which power is shared.
  d. Identify powers denied to state and national governments.
  e. Analyze the ongoing debate that focuses on the balance of power between state and national governments.
  f. Analyze the supremacy clause found in Article VI and the role of the U.S. Constitution as the "supreme law of the land."
  g. Explain the meaning of the Pledge of Allegiance to the flag of the United States.

- The student will describe how thoughtful and effective participation in civic life is characterized by obeying the law, paying taxes, serving on a jury, participating in the political process, performing public service, registering for military duty, being informed about current issues, and respecting differing opinions.[16]

Some states, however, have adopted the more probing, critical analytic approach to civics and government themes that the C3 standards recommend. For example, the section on civics in Kentucky's high school social studies standards among other things requires students to

- examine ways that democratic governments do or do not preserve and protect the rights and liberties of their constituents (e.g., U.N. Charter, Declaration of the Rights of Man, U.N. Declaration of Human Rights, U.S. Constitution)
- evaluate the relationship between and among the U.S. government's response to contemporary issues and societal problems (e.g., education, welfare system, health insurance, childcare, crime) and the needs, wants and demands of its citizens (e.g., individuals, political action committees, special interest groups, political parties); examine conflicts within and among different governments and analyze their impacts on historical or current events
- investigate the rights of individuals (e.g., Freedom of Information Act, free speech, civic responsibilities in solving global issues) to explain how those rights can sometimes be in conflict with the responsibility of the government to protect the "common good" (e.g., homeland security issues, environmental regulations, censorship, search and seizure), the rights of others (e.g., slander, libel), and civic responsibilities (e.g., personal belief/responsibility versus civic responsibility)[17]

It was, of course, the Kentucky Supreme Court that developed the demanding *Rose* standards, discussed in chapter 3, that were subsequently adopted by many other state courts. The fact that Kentucky has adopted rigorous civics and social studies standards raises the interesting question of whether more generally there is a correlation between the issuance of court orders in education adequacy cases and a state's adoption of more rigorous standards.

To shed some light on this question, I compared the current civics and government sections of the social studies standards issued by six of the approximately twenty-five states in which courts had ruled in favor of plaintiffs in education adequacy cases with the current standards in six of the states in which courts had ruled for the defendants or in which no cases have been litigated. To randomize the sample, I chose every third decision in the alphabetical listing for each category. Given the small sample size, readers should not generalize the results of this analysis or consider them definitive. Nevertheless, the results were illuminating and suggestive.

In all the studied states where courts enforced students' right to an adequate education (Arkansas, Kansas, Maryland, New Hampshire, New York, and South Carolina), the social studies standards did emphasize critical analytic thinking and active civic participation to a greater or lesser extent; four of the states (Kansas, Maryland, New York, and New Hampshire) also specifically alluded to the C3 framework.[18] By way of contrast, in five of the six states where courts declined to enforce the constitutional right to an adequate education or where no cases had been litigated (Indiana, Nebraska, and Pennsylvania declined; Iowa and Utah have not litigated), critical analytic themes were not emphasized in the social studies standards.[19] In one of the states where defendants prevailed (Colorado), the standards emphasize functions and structures of government but also require students to "research, formulate positions, and engage in appropriate civic participation to address local, state, and national issues or policies."[20]

This analysis indicates that the judicial emphasis on civic participation may have had a positive impact on social studies standards in states where plaintiffs have prevailed, but it is far from clear that students actually receive the type of education that the standards call for. Because civics instruction is generally packed into a single semester, teachers are pressed for time to cover more than the basic function and structure of government. Even if they are inclined to engage students in active projects and civic involvement, they simply lack the time to do so.

Meira Levinson, a noted advocate of active civic instruction, acknowledges that when she taught eighth grade: "I skipped over almost every one of the sidebars, insets and pages emphasizing active citizenship because they did not fit into my curriculum calendar. It is hard to see how and why other teachers might be led to make a different choice."[21] Furthermore, textbooks generally are written for national markets and not individually for states that emphasize active citizenship in their standards; not surprisingly, therefore, most textbooks emphasize the structure-and-function approach to civics education.[22] Finally, high-quality professional development that enables teachers to prepare students for civic participation is almost nonexistent in American schools today.[23]

ACCESS TO A BROAD LIBERAL ARTS CURRICULUM In addition to the superficiality of much of the civics instruction in schools today, the breadth and depth of students' exposure to the broader liberal arts are also on the decline. A national survey undertaken by the Council on Basic Education revealed "ample evidence of waning commitment to the arts, foreign language, and elementary social studies."[24] This decline has been accelerated by the accountability emphasis that federal laws have imposed for reading, math, and science, but not for other basic subjects, over the past fifteen years.

Of particular concern in this regard is that this impoverishment of the curriculum and course offerings disproportionately affects students of color and students living in poverty. As the Council for Basic Education found, "the greatest erosion of the curriculum is occurring in schools with high minority populations—the very populations whose access to such a curriculum has been historically most limited."[25] Because of inequities in funding, most of the schools these students attend provide less access to broad and deep opportunities for learning than do schools attended by more affluent students.

A recent nationwide analysis undertaken by the Office of Civil Rights of the U.S. Department of Education found that "eighty-one percent of Asian-American high school students and 71% of white high school students attend high schools where the full range of math and science courses are offered (Algebra I, geometry, Algebra II, calculus, biology, chemistry, physics). However, less than half of American Indian and Native-Alaskan high school students have access to the full range of math and science courses in their high school. Black students (57%), Latino students (67%), students with disabilities (63%), and English language learner students (65%) also have less access to the full range of courses."[26] State regulations play an important role in permitting these disparities to exist. In New York State, for example, high schools are not required to offer courses in chemistry or physics, and the regulations call for only one year of instruction in a language other than English, and that instruction may be in only one foreign language.[27] Schools in lower-wealth communities often lack the means to provide more than these minimum requirements. A survey conducted in 2008, even before the school budget cuts of the recession that year, found that 55 percent (164 of 298) of New York City high schools surveyed did not offer physics as a subject; this means that approximately 23 percent of the city's public high school student population, disproportionately students living in poverty and students of color, did not have access to any physics course in high school.[28]

The systematic denial of access to a full range of courses to students of color and students in poverty is inconsistent with the premise that all students can learn at high cognitive levels and the professed national commitment to provide all students meaningful educational opportunities. To ensure educational equity and as a foundation for preparation for civic participation, all public high school students should have access to a full college- and career-preparatory curriculum, and schools should be required to offer or ensure "reasonable access"[29] to courses in biology, chemistry, and physics; to advanced mathematics and a reasonable range of world languages; and to English language arts, history and social studies, art, music, and physical education.

An additional concern, discussed in more detail in chapter 2, is that in at least eighteen states, there is no regulation of the content of the curriculum taught in private schools,[30] including the increasing number of states in which students now receive public funding through vouchers or tax-credit programs.[31] Therefore, many of the approximately five million students who currently attend private schools may be receiving a curriculum that imparts even less of the knowledge, skills, and disposition needed to be prepared for civic engagement than even the most minimal state standards require.[32]

Civic Skills

The skills students need for civic engagement start with basic verbal and math skills that provide "the intellectual tools to understand complex issues."[33] Although most American students attain satisfactory literacy and mathematical skills, substantial gaps still exist for students living in poverty and for students of color.[34] Development of basic literacy and computational skills, though, is not the end of the matter. Many American students who have developed these basic skills have not sufficiently learned the critical reasoning and deliberation skills that, as discussed in the previous chapter, are essential for students to analyze effectively one-sided or false information, assess policy alternatives, and enter into fruitful conversation with persons who hold opposing views.[35]

Imbuing students with the skills they need for deliberative democracy is a major challenge. Even schools that have diverse student populations do not necessarily provide a supportive environment for effective student interchanges. Some research has found that mere attendance at a racially pluralistic school is actually associated with a reduced likelihood of future political and civic engagement; significantly, however, discussion of controversial current issues in social studies classes reduces this negative correlation.[36] School-based discussion is particularly important for young people who attend pluralistic schools but do not participate in political discussion at home.[37]

DISCUSSION OF CONTROVERSIAL TOPICS Developing skills for deliberative democracy begins with exposing students to controversial ideas in the classroom. As Diana Hess nicely put it: "Democratic education without controversial issues discussion would be like a forest without trees or fish without water, or a symphony without sound. Why? Because controversy about the nature of public good and how to achieve it, along with how to mediate among competing democratic values, are intrinsic parts of democracy. If there is no controversy, there is no democracy. It is as simple as that."[38]

The teaching of controversial subjects instills in the students a sense of the complexity of issues, an understanding of positions different from those the students are likely to encounter at home or among friends, and some idea of what a conscientious and respectful argument over these issues might be like.[39] It also emphasizes the importance of accurate facts, since students "cannot meaningfully engage in necessary political debates *about* the facts . . . unless they learn to accept the facts themselves."[40] It accentuates the significance of Senator Daniel Moynihan's famous quip that "each of us is entitled to our own opinions—but not to our own facts."[41]

Unfortunately, most American middle schools and high schools are not even attempting to promote active classroom discussion of controversial topics. According to one study, almost 80 percent of social studies classes do not even discuss social problems and controversial issues,[42] and the teaching of civics and social studies in many schools has become "bland, homogeneous, ethically numb. . . . In this marketplace of ideas, the shelves are mostly stocked with pabulum."[43] The lack of adequate training in school for democratic deliberation may explain in part why recent national surveys indicate that only 18 percent of Americans had recently engaged—either face-to-face or online—in discussions to determine solutions to problems with people who held different views, and only 23 percent of adults in the United States had participated in "crosscutting" political talk.[44]

Of course, handling controversial subjects in the classroom is not easy; it requires that teachers exercise balance and sensitivity. As Judith Pace explains, "Classrooms are charged spaces filled with tensions that are intensified by contemporary forces in schools and society, from accountability pressures to heightened awareness of racism to presidential campaigns. . . . [C]lassroom discussion can move in unpredictable directions and may trigger anxiety for teacher and students when homophobia, racism, or other provocations emerge."[45] For these reasons, "good facilitation requires understanding the subject matter, thorough preparation, tolerance for conflict, reflection on ethical dilemmas, and a variety of teaching skills. Teachers must be able to listen carefully and connect student questions and comments to curricular knowledge. On top of all that, educators must learn how to deal with speech that challenges civil discourse."[46] Even though dealing with controversial subjects in the classroom is especially difficult in the highly charged political atmosphere that now envelops America, confronting charged issues in a fair and balanced manner under current conditions may actually be the most effective way to help students develop the skills they need to surmount polarization and engage constructively in democratic dialogue.

Many African American students and students from low-income or working-class families have no motivation to take seriously the civics instruction they receive in the schools, or to vote and become civically involved when they grow older, because they feel that society does not take their views and needs seriously. As one of Meira Levinson's students put it: "No matter what you vote for, not matter how much you vote, it ain't gonna be in our hands. Whatever is going to happen is going to happen."[47] Creating in these students a sense of "political efficacy" can go far toward overcoming this innate cynicism and mistrust, and well-conceived classroom experiences can help build such a sense of efficacy and empowerment.[48]

Shira Eve Epstein provides an example of how well-designed classroom exercises can encourage students both to understand their own racial, ethnic, and religious backgrounds better while simultaneously feeling empowered and capable of engaging and building trusting relations with students in the class from other backgrounds. She advocates a three-stage methodology for engaging students in potentially controversial social problems: problem identification, problem exploration, and action.[49]

During the initial problem-identification stage, a teacher can organize an open forum in which students present problems that bother them;[50] this allows students to express their personal interests, concerns, and aspirations in a safe environment. After hearing these varied views and experiences, the class as a whole selects a problem or a set of problems, does research on them, and determines action to take to affect the problem or problems. These phases allow students to work together to understand a complex issue and take joint action to change it.

Classroom projects of this type can provide opportunities to build the "bonding" experiences that create self-esteem and self-confidence among minority groups and allow them to establish successful "bridging" experiences with students from other backgrounds.[51] Another promising approach for engaging disaffected youth is the program Youth Participatory Culture Research, which asks young people to use their academic skills to address real social problems that are affecting their lives—like zero-tolerance discipline problems, the impact of inadequate state funding on equal educational opportunity in the public schools, and the proliferation of charter schools—instead of having them engage in hypothetical or abstract exercises.[52]

Diana Hess and Paula McAvoy offer another example of a pedagogical approach that promotes successful empowerment and engagement. They describe a classroom discussion of affirmative action issues involved in recent U.S. Supreme Court cases concerned with college admissions. The teacher emphasized the importance of "democratic participation" and "active listening," then asked the class to consider the constitutional issues raised by these cases. The discussion quickly focused on whether race or class should matter more in affirmative-action policies in college admissions:

> [Many students] question whether race is really the most relevant issue. Students draw upon a variety of evidence, including some of the readings from class and their personal experiences. Many of the White students are leaning toward caring more about social class, but Tonya, an African American student who had participated in a college access summer program at the nearby university for the past several summers, argues that racial considerations matter. . . .

> Following [her] comment, others continue to defend the view that social class matters more than race in admissions, but the discussion also pivots to talk about the value of diversity and what all schools can do to help students learn to talk about race.[53]

Judicial rulings have had a substantial impact on the schooling environment in recent decades in a wide range of areas, including school discipline, free speech, patriotic exercise, and equity issues involving race, gender, English-language learners, and students with disabilities. Many of these decisions relate to important civic preparation issues. Therefore, these cases provide significant opportunities for discussing with students why courts have taken certain stands on important issues that directly affect their lives, and the interplay between majority and dissenting opinions exemplify how differences of opinion can be properly expressed and provide substantial factual information and analytic perspectives that may constitute effective teaching tools.

Development of the skills to provide the kind of instruction needed to deal with controversial issues requires effective professional development, and "most teachers did not learn, or at least did not have adequate time to master, the kinds of high-leverage pedagogies that are so critical to quality civic education."[54] As a result, "teachers appear uncertain about what the precise content of a proper civic education should be."[55] Effective professional development for civic preparation, especially with controversial political issues, should promote deep subject-matter knowledge, techniques for presenting the issues in a fair and balanced manner, "active learning" that encourages teachers to become engaged in meaningful discussion, planning and practice, and sensitivity and responsiveness to the context in which individual teachers work.[56] In addition, "the support of school administrators is key."[57]

Some teachers avoid dealing with certain issues because of "a fear of criticism or even litigation if they address topics that may be considered controversial or political in nature."[58] School boards need to develop and promulgate clear policies that encourage teachers to deal with controversial topics. Many school boards do have such policies, and professional organizations such as the National Council for Social Studies encourage their adoption.[59] While explicitly favoring teaching controversial subjects, effective policies can also identify specific topics that should be avoided because they might raise particular sensitivities among students, school board members, or the local community. Because there are a broad range of controversial issues that can fruitfully be discussed in a class, it might be prudent to steer clear of any issues that might unnecessarily arouse significant parental or community opposition.[60]

APPLYING CRITICAL ANALYTIC SKILLS TO USE OF THE INTERNET Widespread use of the Internet and social media present both major challenges and major opportunities for educators seeking to develop critical reasoning and deliberation skills in students. As of 2015, 92 percent of teens used the Internet daily, and 76 percent of young people were active participants in social media, including Facebook, Twitter, Instagram, and Snapchat.[61] On the one hand, the Internet and social media may make it more difficult to motivate and equip students for civic participation if students use these tools primarily for socializing, entertainment, and consumer pursuits. On the other hand, the digital age has the potential to create a dynamic new public square that motivates young people to engage more deeply with political issues and to develop more sharply honed research and deliberative skills.

Surveys undertaken by Joseph Kahne and his colleagues have found that substantial numbers of youth are engaging in political life through "participatory politics" that address issues of public concern through peer-based interactive means.[62] They and others cite the Arab Spring of 2010, as well as the political successes of the Obama and Sanders campaigns, to illustrate how large numbers of young supporters can be mobilized to support significant political causes through digital means. These examples demonstrate how digital media have unprecedented power for communicating quickly and cheaply with thousands, and even millions, of people; they indicate that when particularly inspiring messages go viral, they can move huge numbers of people to take immediate civic or political action.

Others, however, have expressed concern about the depth of digital participatory politics and the extent to which youth involvement through these means can be sustained. Malcolm Gladwell argues that online social networks consist of weak ties between large numbers of virtual friends with whom one has little meaningful contact. He asserts that these contacts cannot substitute for the bonds of close friendship and solidarity that have been integral to the success of previous social movements like the civil rights protests.[63]

His point was borne out by a recent study of ninety U.S. sites aimed at youth civic engagement of various sorts (including cause activism, community service, and community engagement); it found that online involvement tended to encourage personal expression without much systematic follow-up effort to learn more or to channel that expression into forming groups, or coordinated political action.[64] Organizations like MoveOn.org that heavily utilize digital media are very different from the traditional membership organizations that Putnam described in *Bowling Alone*.[65] Participation in these digitally organized groups "is defined less through dues payments and clear boundaries between membership and non-membership and more through flows of communication and networked actions."[66]

Rapid-response political participation through social media also tends to focus efforts and resources on relatively minor issues, or to present the issues in an emotional, one-sided manner that avoids analysis and deliberation.[67] Kahne and Middaugh report that teens often believe that "if a search engine provides information, then it must be reliable and that many youth do not fact-check their online sources and are unable to recognize bias and propaganda."[68] Howard Gardner points out that, on the Internet, "it has become extremely difficult for all but the most informed to make needed distinctions among claims of quality."[69]

A further problem with the digital revolution is that it can exacerbate the civic empowerment gap. Putnam writes that even though children in low-income households are coming to have equal physical access to the Internet, "they lack the digital savvy to exploit that access in ways that enhance their opportunities." Young people from high-income backgrounds, in contrast with their poorer counterparts, are "more likely to use the Internet for jobs, education, political and social engagement, health and news gathering and less for entertainment or recreation."[70]

A contributing factor to this continuing gap is the lack of access to skilled library media specialists in many of the schools attended by students of color and students living in poverty. School libraries these days are major sources not only of traditional access to books but also of the full range of online information sources and media literacy skills that students need for civic participation.[71] For example, New York State regulations require all middle and high schools to provide students with access to certified school library-media specialists.[72] Nevertheless, a study of high-need schools in New York State that my colleagues and I undertook in 2012 revealed that more than half of the middle and high schools (thirteen of twenty-three) did not meet the minimum library staffing requirements; moreover, eight schools lacked adequate computers and two had no libraries at all.[73]

The key question for educators at this point, therefore, is to how to develop curricula and instructional practices that enable and motivate all students to make use of the potential of the Internet to develop lifelong critical reasoning skills and to use those skills to engage in "deliberative dialogue" on the Internet. As Harold Rheingold, a media communication writer and lecturer at Stanford University, has stated, "Education could play a pivotal role by equipping today's digital natives with historical knowledge, personal experience, rhetorical skills and a theoretical framework for understanding the connection between their power to publish online, their power to influence the circumstances of their own lives, and the health of democracy."[74] Kahne and Bowyer's findings on the substantial impact that media literacy instruction can have on students' ability to distinguish accurate information they receive on the Internet and social media from misleading information is especially significant in this regard.[75]

A number of programs already have responded to these possibilities. Student Voices is one such example. Taught over the course of ten weeks as a supplement to existing civic education curricula, Student Voices combines classroom discussions of political and social issues with online activities. At computer terminals that are provided in the classrooms,

> Students can read daily news coverage of their city and state, locate their state officials and their district's city council member, and research their positions on issues of relevance to them. The Web site also promotes interaction with other Student Voices participants by providing the opportunity to vote in "click polls" on current issues and communicate with students from other classrooms by posting their own opinions on controversial topics.[76]

A study of the implementation of this program in twenty-two Philadelphia high schools found that the strongest predictor of positive outcomes was effective classroom political discussions.[77]

Rheingold has suggested that teachers should instruct students to (1) write a blog post that takes a position on an issue and uses links to other relevant sites to support the position, (2) ask probing questions about the assumptions, assertions, and logic of the arguments on a selected Internet site, and (3) use wikis to develop collaborative communities that can share knowledge and coauthor documents on topics of mutual interest.[78] Others have proposed that teachers provide students the opportunity and tools to undertake high-quality investigations through multiple sources and tap social networks to engage in dialogue with people with diverse perspectives;[79] promote "digital dialogues" that develop argumentative skills, including the understanding of opposing positions and the need for substantive evidence to justify one's own position;[80] and encourage students to create "digital portfolios" in which they post writings, videos of activities, and examples of their civic and political analyses and actions.[81] These portfolios, and other products resulting from students' digital efforts, might merit "digital badges" that reward students for accomplishing a given task or demonstrating a particular skill.[82]

The MacArthur Foundation, through its Youth and Participatory Politics Research Network, has also established a number of projects to support and highlight new media practices that promote youth civic and political engagement, such as engaging platform designers to improve their ability to engage youth in participatory politics, and working with educators and youth to develop a framework of core participatory political practices that articulate a new vision for civic education.[83] Ernest Morrell, a professor at Teachers College, Columbia University, and his colleagues are also promoting a "critical media pedagogy" that aims to make high school students "more explicitly aware of their relationships with the media and . . . imparts the skills they need to powerfully consume and produce new media."[84] This approach motivates students to improve their academic skills and to develop a sense of empowerment by producing videos and other media content that analyzes important issues that affect their own lives and that are built from their own experiences.

In short, then, a number of educators have developed a range of programs and techniques for developing in students the critical reasoning and deliberative skills they need to function productively and participate civically through the Internet and social media. Promising practices like these need to be implemented much more broadly, and doing so will require much more emphasis on these needs in teacher training and professional development programs,[85] as well as consistent administrative support.

Civic Experiences

EXTRACURRICULAR ACTIVITIES Extracurricular activities provide an effective training ground for the development of the interpersonal skills and experiences that students need to function productively as civic participants, as the discussion in the preceding chapter demonstrated. Most schools do provide a range of extracurricular opportunities to students most of the time. However, a good number of schools that are populated predominantly by students living in poverty and students of color lack the resources to provide a reasonable range of extracurricular activities. For example, a recent study of all high schools in North Carolina found that school size and poverty levels significantly influence the number and types of activities available, with larger schools and those schools with more affluent student bodies offering more activities.[86]

An additional problem is that many schools tend to consider these activities of secondary importance, and as a result, they are readily disposable in times of recession or fiscal constraint. For example, following the 2008 recession, schools throughout the country eliminated field trips to legislatures, art museums, and local historical sites,[87] and also dropped middle school sports, cut back on interscholastic competitions, and eliminated spelling bees and drama clubs.[88] The Center for Educational Equity's study of the impact of budget cuts on thirty-three high-need schools in New York City and seven other school districts throughout New York State found that "budget cuts had forced most of the high schools in our study to eliminate their civics-related afterschool offerings, including community service programs, student government, school newspaper, and programs like Model UN and Moot Court."[89]

Another practice that a growing number of schools utilize during times of financial constraint is a "pay-to-play" policy, which requires students who want to engage in such activities as playing on an athletic team, participating in a drama club, or writing for a school newspaper to pay a fee. For example, in recent years, students in Arlington, Massachusetts, were required to pay $720 to play ice hockey or participate in gymnastics, and $408 to be on the cheerleading squad; in Lake Villa, Illinois, it cost $150 to join the chess club; in Shannon, New Jersey, the fee to write for the literary magazine was $200, and in Medina, Ohio, students were charged $660 to play a high school sport, $200 to join the concert choir, and $50 to act in the spring play.[90]

Needless to say, these policies disproportionately exclude students from low-income households, many of whom are students of color. The California Supreme Court has explicitly banned such practices as an unconstitutional infringement on the right to a free public education,[91] the Kansas Supreme Court has held that "extracurricular functions of the k–12 system . . . are vital to the achievement of the [state] standards,"[92] and the federal district court in Montana ruled that "the right to attend school includes the right to participate in extracurricular activities."[93] In other states, however, courts have held that extracurricular activities are not integral aspects of education, and they have allowed these practices to continue.[94]

In schools where a range of extracurricular activities are available, students from low-income backgrounds and students of color tend to be substantially underrepresented in these activities:

> Poor kids are three times as likely as their nonpoor classmates to participate in *neither* sports *nor* clubs (30 percent to 10 percent) and half as likely to participate in *both* sports *and* clubs (22 percent to 44 percent.)
>
> Even more distressing is the fact that extracurricular participation rates in recent decades display the familiar scissors gap. One study found that during the past 15 years, activity levels in out-of-school clubs and organizations rose among affluent youth and fell among poor youth. From 1997 to 2012, the "extracurricular gap" between poor kids and nonpoor kids aged 6–11 nearly doubled, from 15 to 27 percentage points, while the comparable gap among kids aged 12–17 rose from 19 to 29 points.[95]

Generally, blacks and Latinos are also less likely than whites to participate in all types of extracurricular activities and vocational activities.[96]

Work obligations, child care and other domestic responsibilities, and discouraging teacher attitudes are some of the reasons for these marked disparities in extracurricular participation by low-income students and students of color. In some situations, perverse school policies prevent students from being involved in extracurricular activities; for example, some schools require students to maintain a minimum grade-point average to participate in certain extracurricular activities. Others revoke students' right to participate in extracurricular activities or student government as a sanction for infractions.

For example, students have been barred from running for class secretary for a year because of writing a blog post with inappropriate language;[97] from a school's academic team, choir, show choir, and marching band for drug use;[98] and from playing sports for a year because of alcohol use.[99] Some state policies encourage school authorities to use such bans on participation from extracurricular activities as a sanction for misconduct. A recently enacted Massachusetts regulation, for example, states that "the principal may remove a student from privileges, such as extracurricular activities and attendance at school-sponsored events, based on the student's misconduct" without even holding a hearing or pursuing regular disciplinary procedures.[100]

Students of color and students living in poverty are, of course, more likely to be affected by such sanctions because they are punished in schools at highly disproportionate rates. Black students are suspended and expelled at a rate three times that of white students. On average, 5 percent of white students are suspended, compared with 16 percent of black students.[101] The enactment in many states of so-called zero-tolerance discipline policies beginning in the late 1990s has exacerbated these trends.[102] Studies of school suspension have also consistently documented the overrepresentation of low-socioeconomic-status students in receiving disciplinary sanctions.[103]

The critical importance of extracurricular activities to preparing students for civic participation should impel state policy makers and school administrators to consider ways to deal with disciplinary issues that promote, rather than obstruct, civic preparation. For example, an increasing number of schools are adopting restorative justice programs that use mediation and conferencing among those who have been affected by an offense, rather than punishing only the wrongdoer, to find a mutually acceptable way forward.[104] The restorative justice approach builds on and helps advance a sense of community and an ethos that is conducive to civic preparation.[105]

In sum, then, state policy makers and school authorities need to rethink current policies that relegate extracurricular activities to a second-class status and consider them expendable in times of fiscal constraint. Resources need to be provided to schools to ensure that a reasonable range of extracurricular activities are available in all schools at all times and greater efforts should be made to encourage low-income students and students of color to take full advantage of these opportunities. Pay-to-play policies need to be banned. If school authorities and state policy makers are unwilling to take these actions, the courts should compel them to do so.

COMMUNITY SERVICE AND SCHOOL AND COMMUNITY IMPROVEMENT EXPERIENCES Service learning and participation in school-based or out-of-school community improvement activities also provide important opportunities for civic preparation. An example of an effective service learning or community improvement program is the Madison County Youth Service League, as described by Joel Westheimer.[106] Students in this program took a standard government course during the first semester, then in the second semester worked on engaging, nonpartisan public service projects in their county's administrative offices. One group of students investigated whether citizens in their community wanted curbside trash pickup. Another group helped develop a five-year plan for the fire and rescue department. For each project, students had to collect and analyze data, interact with government agencies, write a report, and present their findings in a formal hearing before the county's board of supervisors. After evaluating this program, Westheimer concluded that the program had a powerful impact on students' capacity for and commitment to civic participation: "Students could detail the skills they used (e.g., conducting polls, interviewing officials, making presentations, reading legislation) as well as the knowledge they gained about how government works. Survey measures of students' sense of personal responsibility to help others, their vision of how to help, and their leadership efficiency showed significant improvements. Especially notable from both the surveys and interviews was the change in students' confidence that they had the knowledge or 'social capital' to make things happen in the community."[107]

A broad experiment in participatory school governance was instituted in 2003 in Hudson, Massachusetts. The high school there launched a comprehensive civic engagement initiative by organizing the school into clusters of 100–150 students that were structured around areas of student interest such as communications and media, science and the environment, business and engineering, and public policy and service. The clusters meet for one hour each week to discuss and decide on service projects and other issues that the cluster would pursue, as well as school governance and other school-related issues. An initial evaluation indicated that, although there were growing pains, the experience increased measures of community service and political knowledge throughout the student body, and that changes were larger for disenfranchised youth and students who initially scored lower on civic measures.[108]

An example of even more extensive student involvement is the program in Hampton, Virginia, that promotes active participation of high school students in a broad range of significant municipal responsibilities. Hampton has created an influential youth commission with twenty-four youth commissioners, as well as a new city office to work with them. Under the commission's purview are community service programs that involve most of the city's youth: empowered principals' advisory groups in each school, a special youth advisory group for the school superintendent, paid adolescent planners in the planning department, and youth police advisory councils whom the police chief contacts whenever a violent incident involves teenagers. Young people are encouraged to climb this pyramid from service projects toward the citywide commission, gaining skills and knowledge along the way.[109] All of these activities prepare students both for active citizenship and for college and/or career success.

Some schools have encouraged students to engage in actual political activities, in a nonpartisan manner. One example is the Get Out the Vote campaign that Democracy Prep High School in New York City sponsors each Election Day. Students stand on street corners, wearing T-shirts and handing out flyers that read "I Can't Vote, but You Can!" The school claims that over the past five years, they have encouraged more than fifty thousand Harlem voters to go to the polls.[110] Other schools have used the Internet and social media to involve students in petitioning city officials on important political issues. For example, students in a civics class in Chicago who were concerned about gun violence in the community initiated a campaign to raise awareness and mobilize support for providing youth with summer jobs: "Students worked in groups to create a class Twitter account, an Instagram account and a Facebook page which all drew attention to an online petition on Change.org that included information and research on violence in the city and urged people to write to Chicago's mayor to convince him to expand a summer jobs program for youth. Students also gathered signatures, accumulated followers on Twitter . . . and followed people and groups . . . that were working to prevent youth violence in the city."[111] The students' teacher explained: "It was empowering for them to see . . . the people who had gone online to sign the petition because they weren't all people that they knew. They were starting to see the links between different people and the circles that connect people."[112]

A cost-efficient complement, but not a substitute, for these participatory experiences is the use of online games that provide students virtual experiences in running for political office, legislating, deciding legal cases, and administering public institutions. An example of such a set of games in wide use is the iCivics games, which sponsored an organization established by former U.S. Supreme Court justice Sandra Day O'Connor.[113] To maximize the effectiveness of the students' usage of these games, the games should be integrated into social studies lessons with appropriate teacher guidance.

Civic Values

Most Americans agree that to be capable citizens today, young people need to be imbued with certain core civic values, traits, and dispositions. As Richard Weissbourd writes: "American public schools were originally . . . intended chiefly to cultivate in children a certain degree of character. . . . Today that expectation is again widespread and deep. The American public, deeply concerned about the failure of children to absorb key values from their parents, sees schools as the next best hope. Polls show that 70 percent of parents want schools to teach 'strict standards of right and wrong,' and 85 percent want schools to teach values."[114] Picking up on this sentiment, President Bill Clinton, in his 1996 State of the Union message, said, "I challenge all our schools to teach character education, to teach good values and good citizenship."[115] A burst of character education programs were adopted in the schools during the 1990s, but most were narrow and superficial,[116] and studies by the U.S. Department of Education and others generally found them to be ineffective.[117] Many contemporary proponents of teaching character in the schools recognize that the approach needs to be "re-energized and retooled"[118] to include a broader range of civic values, and to infuse the advancement of these values into broader civic preparation efforts.[119] Nevertheless, many states have retained much of the past superficial approach to character education in their civic preparation statutes.

For example, North Carolina requires that "each local board of education shall develop and implement character education instruction" that must "address the following traits": courage, good judgment, integrity, kindness, perseverance, respect, responsibility, and self-discipline.[120] We can all agree that these values are unobjectionable. The problem, though, with this simple listing of character traits is that it stresses only character values, neglecting broader democratic values and the traits and dispositions that students need to act responsibly and effectively in today's society. As one commentator has aptly noted:

> The failure to achieve a just and equal society outside of school must be confronted in schools, especially when addressing the character of children. It is difficult to demand that students believe in this program that values high ideas, when, at the same time, their lives are being affected by economic, tax, and social policies that do not reflect the beneficence of the character traits that are to be required of them in their lives as students and budding citizens. Students are aware of the palpable injustice they are confronted by when they enter deteriorating schools and are taught by overburdened and underprepared teachers.[121]

Students, unsurprisingly, reject one-dimensional approaches to civic values. An illuminating study of student reactions to a superficial character education program elicited such comments as

> I think we know what honesty is, and it teaches what honesty is about but it's not going to make us be honest. Just because we know what the right thing to do is, doing the right thing is a personal decision, and it can't be affected by a character education program like this.

* * *

> We mock the program. Like if Mrs. Smith tells us that we should do something then we will exaggerate it times ten. We all beat it to death. If we are learning compassion or something we will be so nice to each other until it is over and out of her sight. We just make fun of it.[122]

As with conveying civic knowledge and civic skills, an effective approach to instructing students about civic values—certainly for secondary school students—must be one that strikes them as dealing forthrightly with issues that affect their lives and their perceptions of what is really happening in the environment in which they live.[123] Traits like honesty, compassion, and responsibility continue to be important, but so are dealing with difference, confronting injustice and inequities, and responding to the full range of moral issues with which productive citizens of a contemporary democratic society must grapple. Students can best develop positive civic values, traits, and dispositions within a regime of civic preparation that effectively combines character values and democratic values within a holistic ethos that pervades the entire schooling environment. Students should develop and hone their civic values as they wrestle with the realities of diversity and equality; deliberate about controversial political, social, and moral issues; and work with others on school-based and community service and political activities.

Scott Seider, an assistant professor of education at Boston University, provides a number of examples of schools that have successfully created an ethos that implements such a holistic approach. The three Boston-area schools he studied combined courses that conveyed civic knowledge, advisories that pressed students to grapple in a balanced manner with controversial political and social issues, and school community meetings and assemblies that dealt with important school governance issues. For example, students at Roxbury Prep engaged in exercises like writing letters to students in their school who were being bullied,[124] then reflected on their reactions to the expulsion of half a dozen of their classmates for drug dealing in school through performing a speech, a poem, and a rap before a schoolwide assembly.[125] At the nearby Pacific Rim School, discussions focused on such issues as whether racism existed in Boston and how the numbers of students who were sent to the principal's office break down by gender, race, and grade, and how those patterns compare to law enforcement patterns outside the school.[126]

Traditional values like patriotism can also be taught in a way that rings true to contemporary issues and contemporary values. According to Diane Ravitch, historically American schools probably emphasized patriotism more extensively than the schools of other nations because "other nations are based on ties of blood or religion, but the United States is a social creation evolving . . . from a shared adherence to the democratic ideology embedded in the Declaration of Independence and the Constitution."[127] During the nineteenth century, American schools taught "an old fashioned patriotism" that emphasized "the glory of the United States, the greatness of democracy and the blessings of American liberty."[128] Beginning in the 1890s, assimilation of growing immigrant populations became a dominant concern, and after World War I, textbooks became "strongly nationalistic. . . . There was little criticism of American characteristics or activities."[129] These trends began to shift after World War II, and especially after "patriotism" became a contentious issue during the Vietnam War era, as many students and teachers viewed the war and the government as immoral: "The Vietnam war had instilled in them the belief that to criticize the political system was the most important goal they could pursue."[130]

The terrorist attack on September 11, 2001, however, precipitated a renewed sense of a "shared fate"[131] among American's diverse citizens and has led many schools to adopt a more balanced approach of "democratic patriotism" rather than "authoritarian patriotism."[132] This approach emphasizes that "patriotism has three parts that educators should address: (1) felt attachment to society and to the ideals that the United States has traditionally espoused; (2) willingness to criticize and change aspects of the country that do not live up to those values; and (3) commitment to make personal sacrifices, when necessary, for those ideals and for the common good."[133] Teaching "democratic patriotism" is a constructive way to promote a sense of efficacy and engagement, as well as bonding and bridging skills within a diverse classroom. Students from different racial, ethnic, and religious backgrounds can be encouraged to take pride in their groups' contributions to the development of American democracy. From these perspectives, a teacher can then stimulate meaningful discussions of the progress and the failures that America has experienced and is experiencing in implementing the values and visions of the Declaration of Independence and the Constitution. Patriotism taught in this way "acknowledges and promotes visions of shared histories, struggles, institutions, languages, and value commitments."[134] Such an approach to patriotism—and to most other civic values, traits, and dispositions, if properly taught—can "bridge the gap between political knowledge and motivation while recognizing that each school's capacity to introduce visions of good citizenship is continually challenged by the particular population it serves."[135]

Students can also learn in a concrete, productive way about values of tolerance and caring through school-based efforts to respond to bullying incidents. According to the U.S. Department of Education, 22 percent of all students aged twelve to eighteen reported being bullied at school in 2013, and about 7 percent reported being victims of cyberbullying.[136] Rising teen suicide rates and a spate of mass shootings in schools by students who were victims of bullying practices led legislatures in all fifty states in recent years to pass anti-bullying statutes.[137] Although many of these laws merely exhort school districts to adopt anti-bullying policies, laws and policies in some states, like New Jersey, require school districts to deal proactively with incidents of bullying and harassment. This means not only conducting thorough investigations and imposing sanctions on perpetrators but also organizing focus groups, providing training, and creating schoolwide safety teams that motivate students, staff, administrators, and parents to take tangible actions to improve the school climate and promote intergroup communication and understanding to prevent bullying.[138] Proactive initiatives of this type can effectively instill in students a deep understanding of, and commitment to, values of tolerance, and empathy for the "other."

CHAPTER SIX

Advancing Civic Preparation through the State Courts

We all share one common interest: a future where democracy in our state continues to thrive and flourish. We all understand that the common vehicle to achieve that future is civic learning. — Tani G. Cantil-Sakauye, Chief Justice, California Supreme Court

Prior chapters have documented the substantial decline over the past half century in the schools' efforts and effects in carrying out their responsibility to prepare students for civic participation. They have also proposed a framework and specific policies and practices that schools could adopt to fulfill that responsibility in the twenty-first century. Politicians and educators have for years given lip service to the need to upgrade civic education in the schools, and it is possible that the trauma of the current challenges to the viability of our democratic institutions will shock them into taking potent action to do so. In this polarized age, however, I remain skeptical that they will. Accordingly, barring the prompt emergence of serious sustained efforts by Congress, state legislators, and education leaders to revitalize civic preparation in the schools, it is incumbent on the courts to take steps to ensure that the states and the federal government carry out their constitutional responsibilities to prepare all students to be capable citizens.

The state courts are already on record regarding the importance of doing so. The highest courts in thirty-two of the fifty states have proclaimed that preparation for civic participation is the primary purpose, or one of the primary purposes, of the education clause in their state's constitution. However, not one of these courts has issued any remedial decree that would specifically advance this goal.[1] This does not mean that these judges should not, could not, or would not take such actions or issue such orders. The simple fact is that the judges have not acted to enforce civic preparation objectives because no one has asked them to do so.

Although there has been extensive litigation regarding the financing and adequacy of public education in most of the states, the chief aim of plaintiffs and their attorneys in these cases has been to obtain additional funding for some or all of the state's schools. For all the reasons discussed in the preceding chapters, however, the time has come for litigants to ask the state courts to issue appropriate remedial orders aimed specifically at the schools' responsibility to prepare all students to be capable citizens. The substantial knowledge gaps about basic governmental institutions among American students, the low voting rates (especially among younger citizens), the sharp decline in participation in civic affairs, and the large civic empowerment gaps between racial and socioeconomic groups constitute compelling evidence of the need for remedial action. The substantial agreement among educators, policy makers, and researchers on the nature of the necessary reforms provide a workable basis for the courts to design effective judicial decrees that can ameliorate these problems.

Litigation Approaches

A claim that substantial numbers of students in a particular state are not being properly prepared for civic participation can be raised under the education clauses that exist in virtually all state constitutions. Since most courts have already declared preparation for civic participation to be the primary purpose or a prime purpose of the state constitution's education clause, proof that a substantial number of students are not properly being prepared to become capable citizens should, *ipso facto*, constitute a denial of a student's right to an adequate (or a "sound basic," "thorough and efficient," "ample," or "high quality"[2]) education as guaranteed by the state's constitution. In those states that have already entertained adequacy claims, the civic preparation arguments can be presented as a request for further relief, or possibly for compliance if the case is still pending. Or if the litigation has terminated, plaintiffs may file a new litigation based on the prior adequacy precedents.

Plaintiffs may also consider bringing such claims in states where prior adequacy cases have not been successful. The majority of those cases were decided on justiciability or separation-of-powers grounds.[3] Since the political questions raised and the potential remedial standards at issue in a civic preparation case would differ substantially from the claims raised in an education adequacy case focused on financial needs, courts in these states may now be more receptive to considering the constitutional issues. For example, in a state like Georgia, which rejected education adequacy claims in the past but where the state supreme court has declared that an "adequate" education at a minimum requires the state to provide each child the basic skills needed for "full participation in the political process,"[4] plaintiffs may now be able to convince the court that there are indeed judicially manageable standards for meeting this objective.

A key issue in any adequacy case is the plaintiffs' obligation to establish a causal link between the state's actions or inactions and undesirable student outcomes. The fact that many schools in a large number of states have reduced the amount of time students spend on civics and social studies instruction, and their failure to include civics-related items in high-stakes tests, to equip and encourage teachers to provide proper instruction in media literacy, to ensure an appropriate range of extracurricular and experiential opportunities, and to inculcate values of tolerance and other essential democratic values—as well as the glaring neglect of the civic empowerment gap—would provide strong and sufficient evidence of the necessary causal link.

The requisite correlation here is between deficient school practices and students' lack of appropriate civic knowledge, skills, experiences, and values. Although it is reasonable to expect that in the long run students who are well educated in these areas will vote more often and more intelligently, and that they will engage in more civic activities, proof of whether or not they actually do will require focused longitudinal studies extending over many years that rarely exist at present. This type of evidence need not, however, be available for plaintiffs to prevail now in this type of case. If states have failed to adopt reasonable regulations and/or schools have not implemented existing regulations or adopted acknowledged best practices to prepare students for capable citizenship, then plaintiffs will likely have met their burden of proof.

The more difficult challenge in these cases will be determining the content and contours of the remedy that a court might issue if the evidence were to establish that students were not being properly prepared to function as civic participants. The potential remedies that might be sought in these can usefully be discussed under four major headings: enforcement of already-articulated constitutional standards, issuance of a general remedial order, issuance of a specific remedial order, and additional remedies needed to overcome inequities in the availability of basic resources to eliminate the civic empowerment gap.

Enforcement of Already-Articulated Constitutional Standards

At least thirteen of the states that have acknowledged the constitutional primacy of civic preparation have also set forth constitutional standards that define what they believe civic preparation entails. The most notable of these was the Kentucky Supreme Court's delineation of the seven "capacities" that a constitutionally acceptable education should attempt to provide to all students. These include four "capacities" relating specifically to civic preparation: "sufficient oral and written communication skills to enable students to function in a complex and rapidly changing civilization"; "sufficient knowledge of economic, social, and political systems to enable the student to make informed choices"; "sufficient understanding of governmental processes to enable the student to understand the issues that affect his or her community, state, and nation"; and "sufficient grounding in the arts to enable each student to appreciate his or her cultural and historical heritage."[5] These constitutional standards are especially significant because they were adopted not only by the Supreme Court of Kentucky but also in whole or in part by the highest courts in eight other states: Alabama, Arkansas, Kansas, Massachusetts, New Hampshire, North Carolina, South Carolina, and Texas.[6] West Virginia also articulated a constitutional standard similar in several respects to the Kentucky standards.[7]

Kentucky's constitutional capacities were not cut from whole cloth by the justices; rather, they emerged from an extensive public engagement process.[8] After the trial judge declared the state's educational finance system to be unconstitutional, he appointed a select committee to advise him on the contemporary parameters of the education system that the framers of Kentucky's state constitution had envisioned. The select committee held five large-scale public meetings around the state to invite input on these issues, and the committee's recommendations centered on civic participation issues.[9] These hearings were covered extensively by the press.[10] The committee's recommendations were then accepted by the judge and formed the basis for most of the seven capacities that he articulated and that were subsequently affirmed by the Kentucky Supreme Court.

The New York Court of Appeals also articulated substantive constitutional standards. It held that students are entitled to a "meaningful high school education" that prepares them to "eventually function productively as civic participants capable of voting and serving on a jury."[11] The trial court further defined the knowledge and skills students need to function productively as voters in terms of "the intellectual tools to evaluate complex issues, such as campaign finance reform, tax policy, and global warming," and as jurors in terms of being able to "determine questions of fact concerning DNA evidence, statistical analyses, and convoluted financial fraud, to name only three topics."[12]

The New York standards were also developed through a process that involved substantial input from both educational experts and the public at large. In its first *Campaign for Fiscal Equity* (*CFE*) opinion, the Court of Appeals articulated a "template" definition of sound basic education and made clear that it would revisit the issue when the case returned on appeal after the trial.[13] The final definition would be determined after a factual record, based on documentary evidence and expert testimony, was developed at trial. The trial judge's explication of the kinds of knowledge and skills students would need to act capably as voters and jurors resulted from extensive expert testimony on this precise issue. The final definition of a "sound basic education" was also influenced substantially by a multiyear, statewide public education process that the plaintiffs initiated that allowed thousands of parents, students, teachers, school board members, business leaders, and the media to weigh in on these issues.[14]

A third example of constitutional civic preparation standards was articulated by the Washington Supreme Court. It held that the state had a constitutional duty to provide an "education" that "must prepare our children to participate intelligently and effectively in our open political system to ensure that system's survival. It must prepare them to exercise their First Amendment freedoms both as sources and receivers of information; and, it must prepare them to be able to inquire, to study, to evaluate and to gain maturity and understanding."[15] The trial court judge expanded on this statement by also specifying that students must "be meaningfully equipped to learn about, understand, and evaluate the candidates, ballot measures, positions, and issues being debated and decided in that election"; be "meaningfully equipped to read, understand, comprehend, and debate the evidence, issues, and arguments presented to the jury for decision"; and obtain "knowledge and understanding of the common history, common values, and common ideals that all citizens in this State share."[16] The Washington standards were informed by the court's analysis of the legislature's responses over several decades to a prior court order that the legislature develop detailed concepts concerning what a "basic education" must entail.[17]

In sum, then, the highest courts in Kentucky, New York, Washington, and ten other states have already adopted remedial standards that, if enforced seriously, would require schools to revamp and upgrade their civic preparation efforts substantially so that students obtain extensive civic knowledge, develop critical analytic and deliberation skills, be exposed to meaningful civic experiences, and learn and appreciate common civic values and ideals. The attorneys for plaintiffs in past education adequacy cases—myself included—did not, however, ask the courts to issue remedies that would deal with these matters; they asked the courts only to issue orders that would increase state spending for education. The implied assumption behind plaintiffs' remedial requests was that with sufficient additional resources, the states would substantially improve educational opportunities generally, and, among other things, presumably meet the courts' stated expectations for civic preparation.

The extra funds that resulted from many of these cases do not, however, appear to have been used to improve schools' capacity to prepare students for civic participation. As noted by Deborah Meier, a distinguished New York educator, thirteen years after the verdict in the *CFE* case, "Democracy has dropped out of sight in most of the discourse about education reform. . . . [N]othing has changed."[18] A recent analysis undertaken by the Center for Information and Research on Civic Learning and Engagement (CIRCLE) at Tufts University found that there was no correlation between states in which plaintiffs prevailed in education adequacy cases and seven indicators of civic preparation that the center tracks (i.e., state-required civics course, civics test, state social studies assessment, test plus course required, social studies standards, number of years of required social studies, and service learning).[19] In other words, the fact that plaintiffs prevailed in the litigation and the fact that the state may have substantially increased its spending on education did not make any evident difference in whether or not the state took the seven specific actions to enhance civic preparation that CIRCLE tracked.

If the lawyers in Kentucky and in the nine other states that adopted standards similar to the *Rose* standards had asked their state supreme courts to order the state to take steps to ensure that all students were, in fact, being provided meaningful opportunities to obtain "sufficient knowledge of economic, social, and political systems to enable the student to make informed choices," the court might have ordered the state to enhance its civics and social studies requirements and assessments. All of the state's schools might also have had to offer a full "humanistic base line" of courses needed "to enable each student to appreciate his or her cultural and historical heritage."

Similarly, the New York courts might have ordered the state to ensure that students received meaningful opportunities to develop the critical thinking and deliberation skills necessary "to evaluate complex issues, such as campaign finance reform, tax policy, and global warming," and to adopt validated assessments to ensure that they did develop those skills. The Washington court might have ordered the state to provide students a range of in-school and out-of-school activities and experiences that would allow them to be "meaningfully equipped to learn about, understand, and evaluate the candidates, ballot measures, positions, and issues being debated and decided in [an] election" and to understand the "common values, and common ideals that all citizens in [that] State share."

Although plaintiffs in past cases did not ask the courts to issue these types of remedial orders, plaintiffs in future cases certainly could. If a set of indisputable facts about the schools' failure to provide meaningful opportunities for students to develop the skills called for in the constitutional standards is established, an order might be obtained relatively quickly on a motion for summary judgment. The kinds of indisputable facts that could trigger such a rapid order might include lack of a required civics course, insufficient state social studies standards, a failure to train teachers to instruct students in democratic deliberation and media literacy techniques, and lack of access to a reasonable range of extracurricular activities, service learning, and in-school and out-of-school civic experiences. Such evidence would be especially compelling if statistical data were to indicate that these deficiencies had a disparate impact on the civic knowledge or skills of particular groups of students, such as students living in poverty, students of color, and English-language learners.

Since the constitutional standards that would form the basis for these decrees would be phrased in general terms, they would allow governors, legislatures, and school boards substantial discretion to determine the actual programs and educational strategies that should be implemented to enhance civics or social studies standards, improve teacher preparation, develop critical thinking skills, and provide access to a reasonable range of extracurricular activities to meet the court's stated objectives.[20] Presumably, therefore, school districts or schools that favor "justice-oriented" approaches to civic participation could implement civic and political activities aimed at effecting social change, whereas those that are wary of such approaches could emphasize service-learning activities that are "participatory" but not "justice oriented."

This implicit deference to the political branches is likely to both lessen political resistance to the court orders and enhance judges' willingness to issue them. The fact that these constitutional standards were developed after extensive public discussion and input means that public opinion presumably will respond favorably to remedial decrees based on them. Governors and legislators are not likely to take a stance against steps to improve civic functioning, and public opinion will also bolster their motivation to faithfully implement such orders. As Professor Gerald Rosenberg has acknowledged, "Courts, then, may be producers of significant social reform when their decisions are announced in a political context of broad elite and popular support for the issue or right in controversy."[21]

A definitive judicial stance would undoubtedly make civic preparation a much higher legislative and educational priority, and it would also engender substantially increased attention by the media and the public at large.[22] It could thereby motivate some states to adopt even more extensive reforms than a court might actually have ordered. For example, in Kentucky, although the court ordered reforms only of the state's education finance system, the state not only radically revamped its funding formulas but also totally transformed the entire statewide education system by overhauling its governance procedures, reorganizing school structures, adopting an innovative accountability system, and hiring a new commissioner of education.

To maximize the likelihood that the state will conscientiously comply with its remedial order, the court should require the governor and/or the legislature to file an annual report with the court that documents actions taken and progress achieved in each of the areas covered by the constitutional standards.[23] This would provide a formal mechanism for understanding the actions the state has taken to implement the order, reviewing the resources that have been devoted to these reforms, assessing results achieved to date, and revealing the state's plans for further progress. Scrutiny of the annual report by scholars, researchers, the media, and the public at large will help ensure that the state officials fulfill their compliance responsibilities.

Issuance of a General Remedial Order

In states where courts have ruled for plaintiffs but have not articulated constitutional standards regarding civic preparation—and in states where the courts previously ruled for the defendants—plaintiffs can now ask the courts to articulate such standards or seek a general remedial order that would require state officials to develop civic preparation standards, provide necessary resources to allow districts and schools to implement them effectively, and assess the results of that process.

Such a general remedial order might, for example, require the state to do the following:

1. Establish appropriate standards for ensuring that schools provide all of their students meaningful opportunities to learn and acquire civic knowledge, skills, experiences, and values.[24]
2. Ensure that all schools properly implement these standards.[25]
3. Adopt a system of accountability to ensure that the state is making reasonable progress toward achieving its civic preparation goals.[26]

Response to such an order may well be prompt and effective. A number of states currently have statutory standards that relate to civic preparation or have guidelines or recommended approaches for promoting civic education that have emerged from commission or task force reports. For example, California's Task Force on K–12 Civic Learning that the chief justice of the state supreme court had established issued a report that includes many of the best practices for civic preparation discussed in chapter 5. It explicitly rejects the state's current approach to civics education that centers on a single civics course usually taught in the twelfth grade, and it incorporates the main principles of the *Guardian of Democracy* report.[27] It sets forth the following far-reaching recommendations:

- Revise the California History–Social Science Content Standards and accompanying curriculum frameworks to incorporate an emphasis on civic learning starting in kindergarten, so all students acquire the civic knowledge, skills and values they need to succeed in college, career and civic life.
- Integrate civic learning into state assessment and accountability systems for students, schools and districts. This will enable periodic reporting to the legislature and the public on the state of students' civic learning.
- Improve professional learning experiences for teachers and administrators to help them implement civic learning in schools. Connect professional learning in civics to Common Core State Standards professional learning experiences.
- Develop an articulated sequence of instruction in civic learning across all of K–12, pegged to revised standards. At each grade level, civic learning should draw on the research-based Six Proven Practices listed [in the *Guardian of Democracy* report] and include work that is action-oriented and project-based and that develops digital literacy.
- Establish a communication mechanism so community stakeholders can easily connect with teachers and students on civic education and engagement. Students need to get out of the school building to practice civic engagement, and civic leaders need to come into schools to engage students.
- Provide incentives for local school districts to fund civic learning in Local Control Accountability Plans.[28]

The Illinois Civic Mission Coalition, an affiliate of the national Campaign for the Civic Mission of Schools, has developed a creative Democracy Schools initiative that requires schools to thoroughly assess the state of civic learning in the school and submit a detailed plan for future schoolwide civic learning commitments; so far, twenty-two schools have been recognized as "democracy schools."[29]

As the California and Illinois examples demonstrate, in some states, there already is creative thinking about and interest in improving civic preparation. Other states can look to these examples, to the *Guardian of Democracy* report, or to other useful model programs like the State Civic Education Policy Framework issued by the Education Commission for the States.[30]

In short, there is no dearth of appropriate programmatic thinking about how to move forward in preparing students for civic participation. The real challenge is that existing standards and commission recommendations are not being implemented or enforced.[31] This is precisely why judicial orders mandating that positive steps be taken to ensure that the schools adequately prepare students for civic participation are important: they can induce the states to implement and enforce the programs and activities that many policy makers and educators have already concluded should be put into effect.

In many ways, the impact of such an order would be similar to that of an order based on already-articulated judicial constitutional standards discussed in the previous section. Like those judicial standards, these remedial orders would be phrased in general terms, and they would leave broad areas of discretion to governors, legislatures, and school boards to determine the specific programs, activities, and resources that would meet the stated objectives. The proposed general remedial standards might, however, be more comprehensive in some cases than the already-articulated judicial standards, since if they were based on evidence in trials that closely examined the practices that are actually needed for effective civic preparation, they might specify areas of particular concern that the state needs to address to put into effect meaningful opportunities for civic participation for all students.[32]

As with an order enforcing judicially developed constitutional standards, courts might issue such a remedial order quickly in response to a summary judgment motion if undisputed evidence demonstrates manifest inadequacies in major areas affecting civic preparation. The judicial focus provided by a general remedial order would also make civic preparation a much higher legislative and educational priority, and would possibly lead to more extensive reforms than the court actually orders. And again, the state should be expected to file an annual public report with the court that would track progress and encourage compliance.

Issuance of a Specific Remedial Order

Because the general remedial order is phrased in broad terms, a state could comply by adopting and implementing a limited number of civic preparation programs but without dealing effectively with some of the most important reforms that should be undertaken. The lack of specificity in the constitutional standards upon which such general orders would be based might also mean that assessing compliance and results might be difficult. Therefore, in some circumstances, where evidence of deficiencies in particular areas is particularly strong, plaintiffs should consider seeking a remedial order that would require the state to rectify those specific problems.

A relevant precedent is provided by the extensive order issued by the New Jersey Supreme Court in the *Abbott v. Burke* litigation.[33] Following hearings regarding programs that "at risk" children needed to succeed academically, the New Jersey Supreme Court ordered the state to implement specifically, among other things, whole-school reforms, full-day kindergarten, half-day preschool programs, on-site health and social services, and summer and after-school programs. Depending on the relevant evidence, in a civic preparation case, a specific remedial order might include some of the items discussed in the following sections.

ACQUISITION OF CIVIC KNOWLEDGE Ten states currently do not require students to take a course in civics or American government.[34] If evidence were to show that students in these states have inadequate knowledge of civics and governmental functioning, a court might order the state to require all students to take a civics course or a sequence of courses as a graduation requirement or to receive focused instruction in civics and government in required courses throughout their educational careers.

In those states, or in any other states where the evidence establishes that many students have blatantly inadequate civic knowledge, a court might also explicitly order the state to adopt and implement the College, Career, and Civic Life (C3) Framework for Social Studies State Standards,[35] or similar standards that can reasonably ensure that, by the end of grade 12, students are able to demonstrate knowledge in areas such as the following:

- Analyzing the role of citizens in the U.S. political system, with attention to various theories of democracy, changes in Americans' participation over time, and alternative models from other countries, past and present.
- Explaining how the U.S. Constitution establishes a system of government that has powers, responsibilities, and limits that have changed over time and that are still contested.
- Evaluating citizens' and institutions' effectiveness in addressing social and political problems at the local, state, tribal, national, and/or international level.

- Applying civic virtues and democratic principles when working with others.
- Using appropriate deliberative processes in multiple settings.[36]

If the court found that adequate civic preparation required students to be exposed to a broad curriculum in the area of civics, history, world languages, social studies, economics, and the arts, and that substantial numbers of students were being denied reasonable access to some of these subjects, or that the instructional time being devoted to some of these subject areas was unreasonably truncated, the judges might also require the state to take appropriate steps to remedy these shortcomings.

ACQUISITION OF CIVIC SKILLS Especially in these times of inordinate political polarization, if the judges were convinced that students need to develop the kinds of deliberative skills that will enable them to engage in discussions about important issues with people with whom they disagree, they might also order the state to require school districts to adopt appropriate policies and programs for promoting values of tolerance, teaching students to deal with controversial issues, and instructing them in how to identify misleading facts and false information, especially when using the Internet and social media. They might also specifically direct states to ensure that teacher training and professional development programs adequately deal with these issues. Because of the importance of the Internet and social media to the practice of such skills today, the court might also order the state to ensure that all students have access to adequately stocked libraries and computer labs and receive adequate instruction and experience in using the Internet and social media to develop appropriate research and critical reasoning skills.

ACCESS TO CIVIC EXPERIENCES The research findings set forth in chapter 4 demonstrated that students who receive service-learning opportunities and participate in extracurricular activities will be better prepared for civic participation. Yet many states do not consider extracurricular activities to be required subjects, and many schools, especially in low-income areas, do not offer a reasonable range of extracurricular opportunities. In times of fiscal constraint, these activities tend to be the first to be cut back or eliminated.

Courts in many states have not as yet recognized the importance of these opportunities for developing interpersonal relationships and skills needed for civic engagement. For example, the Idaho Supreme Court has held that "extra-curricular activities are not necessary elements of a high school career."[37] Most of the litigation that has considered extra-curricular activities in the past has done so in the context of whether or not fees can be charged for these activities. No court has examined directly evidence of the strong causal links between extracurricular activities and civic participation.[38] When substantial proof of this connection is established in a future case, a court may indeed hold that extracurricular activities are integral components of public education that need to be available to all students. It might then order the state to ensure that at all times all students have access to a reasonable range of extracurricular activities such as student government, school newspapers, speech and debate, and other actual and simulated civic and political activities, as well as field trips to courts, state legislatures, city councils, and other experiential learning opportunities.

Twenty-eight states and the District of Columbia currently include some specific requirements or suggestions for service learning in their social studies or civics standards.[39] For example, Maryland requires that "students shall complete one of the following: (1) seventy-five hours of student service that includes preparation, action, and reflection components and that, at the discretion of the local school system, may begin during the middle grades; or (2) a locally-designed program in student service that has been approved by the State Superintendent of Schools."[40] A court might, therefore, appropriately make such specific service learning requirements mandatory or provide general guidelines for the state to develop and implement their own specific approaches to service learning.

DEVELOPMENT OF CIVIC VALUES If a judicial order ensures the development and implementation of mechanisms for providing all students effective instruction in civic knowledge and civic skills, as well as reasonable access to extracurricular activities and civic experiences, many of the civic values of responsibility, honesty, compassion, patriotism, tolerance, equality, and respect for the rule of law will implicitly be conveyed to students through their civic learning and civic experiences. Some judges may, however, be convinced that additional instruction in character values and in democratic values like the rule of law and democratic patriotism should be made mandatory.[41]

For example, all states now have anti-bullying laws, but most of these laws have little substance. As Justin Patchin of the Cyberbullying Research Center at the University of Wisconsin writes: "Lawmakers are simply passing legislation for the sake of showing their communities that they're concerned about bullying. . . . None of the state laws offer the resources to implement effective bullying prevention programs."[42] Judicial intervention in this area could be particularly helpful.[43] A court decree could require a state to implement meaningful anti-bullying procedures that instill values of tolerance and empathy in students and promote deliberative democracy by including such features as active student participation in the development of the policies and schoolwide forums to discuss the policies and training of students in their implementation. A court decree can also ensure sufficient and stable funding and monitoring to ensure that these programs are actually implemented and have the intended results.[44]

* * *

To ensure that the state's education system is actually providing students sufficient civic knowledge, skills, experiences, and values, courts should also consider including in their orders a requirement that the state require assessments of civic knowledge and civic skills as graduation requirements. As David Campbell has noted, "For all that scholars, policymakers, and the public know about performance in reading, math and science . . . they know very little about the civic dimension of K–12 education."[45] Such assessments would signal the importance of civic education and render this area a priority for both teachers and students. They would also provide the court with important data on the effectiveness of the steps the state has taken to comply with its civic preparation orders.

Currently only two states require students to pass a specific civics or government test, and only eight states require that students pass a test in social studies in order to graduate from high school.[46] More states should do so. Valid assessments of proficiency in civic knowledge and skills should go beyond a limited number of questions on a standardized format. The federal Every Student Succeeds Act adopted in 2015 encourages states to develop broader measures of student success such as student engagement, educator engagement, student access to advanced coursework, or other indicators that "allow[] for meaningful differentiation in school performance" and are "valid, reliable, comparable, and statewide."[47] These and other qualitative indicators should specifically relate to knowledge and competencies relevant to preparation for civic participation.

Appropriate civic preparation assessments could also possibly include assessments of students' analytic ability to deal with complex civic issues. An example of such a measure is the current Washington State examination that requires students to take a position on a complex subject, provide background and reasons for the position, and make explicit references in their paper or presentation to three or more credible sources.[48] Another approach, presently used in Alberta, Canada, is to conduct surveys of teachers, parents, and students to determine whether they are satisfied that students have learned the characteristics of active citizenship.[49] Courts might also assess the adequacy of the resources and opportunities that are actually being made available in the state by asking state defendants to answer questions like "How many [students] participated in dramatics and how many took part in service learning opportunities[?]"[50] or how many teachers have been trained to provide appropriate instruction in dealing with controversial issues?

Reducing the Civic Empowerment Gap

Extensive inadequacies in the resources provided to schools attended predominantly by students of color, English-language learners and students in poverty, together with historical and current discriminatory practices that result in feelings of alienation and disempowerment, have created what Meira Levinson has called the "civic empowerment gap."[51] Two important levers for reducing the civic empowerment gap and helping prepare all of America's students to function productively as civic participants are to ensure adequate school funding and to maximize the benefits of diversity through affirmative steps to overcome racial, ethnic, and socioeconomic isolation and alienation. State courts can be highly effective in both of these areas.

ADEQUATE SCHOOL FUNDING Adequacy and equity in the distribution of school resources are prerequisites both for ensuring the availability of programs and services needed for civic preparation in every school and for bringing all students up to "a standard of 'autonomy' that is necessary to respect the dignity of each person" and for ensuring they are prepared for civic participation.[52] Accordingly, the most obvious and feasible way that state courts can lessen the civic empowerment gap is to issue additional and more extensive decrees in education adequacy cases to ensure that states provide sufficient resources for the schools attended by large numbers of students of color, English-language learners, and students in poverty (including students living in rural areas and students growing up in depressed economic zones like the Rust Belt).

As Diana Hess writes, "It is one thing to say that students, especially poor students who are more likely to be students of color than White, need more and better democratic education. But . . . it is hard to expect that under-funded and under-supported schools and the students within them who are being attacked by the *hard bigotry* of inequality should do any better with respect to democratic education outcomes than they do with any other outcomes."[53] Money clearly matters. The schools attended by students in poverty and students of color offer substantially fewer of the programs and services that are essential for preparation for civic participation, such as access to a full range of courses, basic instrumentalities of contemporary learning like computers, teachers skilled in instilling deliberative skills and media literacy techniques, and availability of a full range of extracurricular, service-learning, and civic experiential opportunities. National data collected by the Office for Civil Rights of the U.S. Department of Education indicates that many schools attended by black and Latino students still do not offer basic courses like Algebra II, calculus, chemistry, and Advanced Placement courses, and that access to instructional materials and technology is also substantially lacking in many of these schools.[54]

In twenty-three states, state and local funding combined provides the poorest school districts fewer *per capita* dollars than it does to affluent school districts, even though these students have greater needs. In Pennsylvania, schools in the poorest areas receive on average 33.5 percent less *per capita* funding than schools in affluent areas; in Vermont, 18.1 percent less; in Missouri, 17 percent less; Illinois, 16.7 percent less; Virginia, 16.7 percent less; and Nevada, 15.3 percent less. For the United States as a whole, the disparity is 15.6 percent.[55] These inequities not only deny equal educational opportunity to the students in these schools; they also undermine possibilities for successful racial and class integration by communicating to affluent school communities that involvement with these schools and their students may imperil the educational opportunities of their own students.

The adequacy litigations discussed in chapter 3 have reduced, and in a few cases eliminated, disparities in funding between poor and affluent districts, and these cases have resulted in higher and more adequate funding levels in many states.[56] But although plaintiffs have won twenty-two of these litigations, defendants have prevailed in eighteen, and four have had mixed results.[57] It is perhaps not coincidental that five of the six states with the greatest disparities in funding between their affluent and poor districts listed above were states in which the plaintiffs lost (Pennsylvania, Missouri, Illinois, and Virginia) or in which no litigation had been brought (Nevada). Reconsideration by the courts in these states of their decisions to not even review the evidence of these funding disparities and their impact on students would go far toward ensuring the resource base necessary to prepare all of these students for civic participation.

To create meaningful opportunities for all students to be prepared for capable citizenship, schools actually need to provide not only equal funding but also additional services and supports to some students to overcome past deprivations and to counter the effects of poverty. Poverty creates a number of significant barriers to learning and school success, and the United States' child poverty rate—at 20 percent—ranks thirty-third of the forty-one European and North and South American countries analyzed by UNICEF's Office of Research.[58] (By way of contrast, the lowest poverty rates among these countries are 3.7 percent in Finland and 4.5 percent in Norway.)[59]

Fully overcoming the impediments to school success imposed by poverty would, of course, require substantial improvements in the social and economic conditions in which children and their families live, and eliminating the growing economic gaps between the haves and the have-nots in our society.[60] Although we are not likely to see poverty and the conditions that cause it eliminated in the foreseeable future, it is possible and feasible to ameliorate substantially the educational effects of poverty by taking affirmative steps to eliminate the impediments to learning created by conditions of poverty in the schools.[61] This would entail ensuring access to quality prekindergarten, after-school, and summer programs, as well as to health services and family engagement.[62] Schools that serve upper- and middle-class children can count on students coming to class with these needs met. To be effective in leveling the playing field for schools that serve students living in poverty, these resources must be of high quality and provided consistently and comprehensively. Access to these critical resources for the students who need them should be considered an integral part of the right to an adequate education.

Ensuring adequate funding for all schools, including extra resources for children who live in poverty, will undoubtedly require increased spending on public education, although serious efforts at cost-effectiveness could minimize these costs substantially.[63] America has, however, a long history of prioritizing education above all other areas of social welfare expenditures, as is exemplified by the fact that most state constitutions include specific clauses that establish positive rights to an adequate education but do not have comparable clauses in regard to health, housing, welfare, transportation, and other important services. The progress that has been made in the education adequacy cases to date indicates that courts, legislatures, and the public at large are more willing to accept increased funding for educational improvement, especially when they are convinced that the money will be spent well.

Education has had a favored status throughout American history, and it continues to do so today, because of its centrality to the "American dream" ideology to which most Americans have long subscribed. The American dream promises individuals an equal opportunity, in accordance with their individual talents and efforts, to advance materially or to develop their potential in whatever other ways they choose. Today, the "schoolhouse is the main engine to realize the [American] Dream."[64] The American dream is a core American ideology because it reconciles egalitarianism and capitalist individualism by proclaiming that if all children are provided an equal educational opportunity to prepare for life's competitive economic and social competition, then all should agree that the system is fair even though unequal material and status rewards will be the ultimate result.[65]

In recent years, there has been some waning of belief in the meritocratic aspects of the American dream,[66] because the rate of upward mobility for low-income families has substantially declined; in fact, there is less upward mobility in America today than there is in most European and Asian countries.[67] African Americans in particular seem to have been losing faith in the American dream.[68] Nevertheless, a majority of Americans still believe that "hard work, ambition, and education are important for getting ahead" in the United States,[69] and for many of the white working class whose material existence is worse than that of their parents, the American dream still "occupies a space in people's rhetoric reserved exclusively for the likes of Jesus Christ and George Washington."[70]

Schools can capitalize on and enhance that faith. Providing low-income minority students and children of disaffected working-class families schools with adequate facilities and sufficient resources can go far in building and revitalizing young people's belief in the American dream and in creating a sense of efficacy and empowerment and communities of hope, possibility, and trust within their schools.

Overall, commitment to equal educational opportunity remains strong in the United States. Support for publicly funded prekindergarten services, especially for children living in poverty, is growing,[71] and public backing for increases in educational funding continues, even as funding for other social services is on the decline.[72] For these reasons, as well as because of the higher priority that state constitutions give to public education, achieving the level of equal educational opportunity that is necessary for civic preparation is fully feasible.

RACIAL, ETHNIC, AND SOCIOECONOMIC INTEGRATION Federal desegregation law has placed significant roadblocks in the path of those seeking to promote thoroughgoing racial or ethnic integration in the schools.[73] There are, however, meaningful actions that state courts can still take to promote integration. Indeed, despite the fact that the U.S. Supreme Court has held that only intentional *de jure* segregation violates the federal constitution,[74] the Connecticut Supreme Court has ruled that *de facto* segregation resulting from housing patterns or any other factors is unconstitutional; it found that the schools in Hartford and twenty-four surrounding suburbs were unconstitutionally segregated. The parties then entered into a series of consent orders that have decreased racial isolation and improved diversity in the Hartford-area schools.[75]

Although language specifically banning all forms of segregation does not appear in any state constitutions other than those in Connecticut and Hawaii,[76] courts in other states, if convinced that diversity is essential for promoting civic preparation and overcoming the civic empowerment gap, could interpret the adequacy clauses in their state constitutions to require states to take steps to minimize racial isolation and maximize conditions for diversity. Such a reading of an adequacy clause is not implausible. In fact, the Washington Supreme Court has said as much: "Admittedly, we have never explicitly held that the state constitution requires racial integration. We have, however, been unwavering in holding that article IX [of the state constitution] imposes upon the State the paramount duty to provide an ample, general and uniform basic education to all children. Therefore, if it is determined that in a contemporary setting de facto segregated schools cannot provide children with the educational opportunities necessary to equip them for their role as citizens, then the state constitution would most certainly mandate integrated schools."[77]

As discussed in chapter 4, the U.S. Supreme Court decision in *Parents Involved in Community Schools v. Seattle School Dist. No. 1*[78] invalidated voluntary racial integration plans that took into account the race of individual students. However, race-conscious factors that do not depend on individual student assignments—like redistricting, school siting, revising school assignment zones, and promoting interdistrict school integration programs—are constitutional.[79] In addition, consolidation of school districts,[80] promoting inter-district transfer programs when there are empty seats in affluent suburban schools,[81] and promoting housing integration projects that create viable integrated communities[82] all remain viable racial integration strategies. The U.S. Department of Justice and Department of Education have jointly issued a detailed guidance letter to school districts on a range of productive actions that districts can take, consistent with current federal law, to promote diversity and reduce racial isolation in K–12 schools.[83] A state court that was convinced of the importance of civic preparation in the schools could issue an order requiring school districts to develop policies to promote racial, ethnic, and socioeconomic diversity within these parameters.

In addition, *Parents Involved* does not prohibit plans that take into account the socioeconomic status of individual students. This means that school districts can take extensive affirmative steps, including the use of numerical targets, to reduce socioeconomic isolation without running afoul of federal constitutional law. Such orders could have a significant impact in many areas,[84] not only in ensuring greater socioeconomic diversity but also in indirectly promoting racial and ethnic diversity, since students of color tend disproportionately to come from low-income households or communities.[85]

Developments in Jefferson County, Kentucky, one of the two school districts whose attempt to promote better racial balance in schools was invalidated in the *Parents Involved* case, illustrates what school authorities committed to diversity can still accomplish even under current legal strictures. Rather than abandon taking any further steps to promote diversity, the Jefferson County school board, with strong community support, has continued to maximize diversity in its schools within the limitations imposed by the U.S. Supreme Court decision. The board has done this by consulting with national diversity experts, holding public forums, reviewing research on school desegregation, and redrawing school attendance zones to maximize economic class balance.[86] By way of contrast, some other school districts that had in the past been successfully integrated have, in recent years, adopted policies that have promoted segregation.[87]

State courts' desegregation orders can also build on the fact that demographic trends are creating conditions that may be more conducive to successful desegregation than were the demographic patterns of past decades.[88] Current desegregation law was developed during a time when students in poverty and students of color primarily lived in urban areas and the surrounding suburbs were overwhelmingly white. Today more than half of minority students in large metropolitan areas attend suburban schools, and there are more low-income people living in suburbs than in cities.[89] Many of our urban complexes are multiracial, and "acceptance of interracial neighborhoods has clearly improved."[90] According to Erika Frankenberg and Gary Orfield, these changes "suggest that stable integration may be considerably more feasible now than in the past."[91]

Amy Stuart Wells and her colleagues have found that "opinion polls and interview data suggest a growing number of parents are paying attention to our 'demographic destiny' and seeking racially and culturally diverse public schools to prepare their children for a global society."[92] These attitudes are, however, clearly less prevalent among white working-class parents, many of whom articulate deep resentment of and anger toward people of color and immigrants.[93] Although the older generation of resentful working-class whites will probably retain these attitudes unless and until their economic conditions are improved and stabilized, affirmative interracial experiences in schools can have a positive effect on the attitudes of their children.

Justin Gest found in his research among white working-class populations in the United States and Britain that "listening closely to the statements of the youngest interviewees, a sort of post-racist politics is emerging."[94] He cited as examples the following statements of working-class millennials whom he interviewed: "We were brought up with different races, [one interviewee] said. There were just as many nationalities in school as white . . . students. It's the parents who don't want to adapt. . . . You got different types of people, [another] said. There are people like me who went to diverse schools, and are used to being around people of different backgrounds. But then there are people who not used to it and need to be. And third, you got some who never met a black person in their lives."[95]

These statements are consistent with the increasing body of research that demonstrates "the role that diverse schools play in preparing students to live in a multicultural society—particularly in terms of promoting interracial understanding and comfort, friendship building, and fostering civic and democratic engagement."[96] Policy makers can take advantage of the increasing diversity of our population and recent metro-area migration patterns to "lead this increasingly diverse nation toward a more equal and cohesive future"[97]—and courts can prompt them to do so.

The history of school desegregation in the United States has been a rocky road, both in terms of school districts' ability to maintain racial balances and in terms of whether political and educational leaders have actually sought to foster positive cross-racial relationships in the schools. Ansley Erikson's detailed analysis of the history of school desegregation in the Nashville area concluded that substantial "statistical desegregation" was achieved, but not true equality of opportunity or consistently positive cross-racial relationships.[98] Erikson notes, though, that "what was not tried was desegregation in the context of a robust commitment to equality of educational opportunity, with careful attention to the quality of students' experiences in schools and the continued effort toward desegregation alongside public recognition of and value for all of a metropolis' communities and children."[99] She further notes that school desegregation has rarely been "shaped by or measured for its potential impact on the making of democratic citizens."[100]

Past desegregation orders rose out of a bitter history of white resistance in the Deep South and of implementation of busing plans that often undermined educational programming, resulted in constant reassignments, and destabilized school-community relationships by requiring students to travel long distances at inconvenient times.[101] Courts that aim to promote racial, socioeconomic, and ethnic balancing as a necessary component of preparing students for civic participation can learn from these mistakes and forge a new path for integrating the public schools. The fact that most minority students and many immigrant populations today live in the suburbs also means that the mechanisms for effectuating racial and ethnic balancing, like busing, can be less complicated and less costly than in the past.

Over the past forty-five years, at the same time that the courts and society as a whole have retreated from promoting effective racial integration, there has been broad-based support for fully integrating students with disabilities into the public schools. Under the federal Individuals with Disabilities Act (IDEA),[102] children with disabilities must be educated with children who are not disabled, to the maximum extent feasible.[103] The preference for including students with disabilities in regular mainstream classes is so strong, "based on recognition of the non-academic value of such integration, [that it] is not overcome by a showing that a special education placement may be academically superior to placement in a regular classroom."[104] The vast majority of students with disabilities are, in fact, educated in regular classes, with extra supports and services, as necessary.[105]

The recent history of special education inclusion exemplifies how dramatically certain societal attitudes toward achieving true diversity in school settings can be changed through court orders and legislation, and that with support from courts, and the adoption of appropriate state laws and regulations, analogous gains in regard to racial and class diversity can be accomplished. To do so, judicial mechanisms to integrate the schools and continued efforts by policy makers and educators to overcome impediments to full inclusion of all students must be promoted and understood as critical components of creating a democratic school culture that will benefit all students and society at large.

Courts should also enforce positive action to promote diversity in the burgeoning charter school sector. From school year 1999–2000 to 2012–13, the number of public charter schools increased from 1.7 percent to 6.2 percent of all public schools, and the total number of these schools increased from 1,500 to 6,100.[106] This trend is continuing at an accelerating rate. Recent studies indicate that charter schools are more racially isolated than traditional public schools in virtually every state and large metropolitan area in the nation. In some regions, white students are overrepresented in charter schools, whereas in other charter schools, minority students predominate and have little exposure to white students.[107] Students with disabilities are also substantially underrepresented in charter schools.[108]

Many charter schools in urban areas now target only low-income students and students of color, arguing that they can provide a higher-quality education for these students than can the traditional public schools in their neighborhoods. Indeed, some charter schools emphasize that they are segregated and have "the highest octane mix of poor and minority kids," Frederick Hess notes, "even though just about every observer thinks that" integrated schools are "good for kids, communities and the country."[109] The data is mixed regarding whether these segregated charter schools do achieve better results in terms of scores on standardized achievement tests than traditional public schools.[110] Assessed by the diversity experiences needed for effective civic preparation, they clearly are dismal failures.

State courts can substantially ameliorate this situation. They can require states to ensure that their charter laws require these schools to take affirmative steps to attract a diverse body of teachers and students through their outreach and recruitment efforts and that they document these efforts. Charter schools, like all schools, should have as a central part of their missions not only improving students' academic outcomes but also making sure that students leave their schools well prepared to function productively as civic participants.

State courts can also require states to reconsider the draconian disciplinary policies some school districts have adopted, including zero-tolerance rules and aggressive policing in schools. These practices often create antagonistic relationships among students and staff, and impede the creation of positive school climates that promote civic preparation. Studies have found that young adults with a history of school suspensions are less likely than others to vote and volunteer in civic activities after high school, which suggests that suspension negatively affects the overall likelihood that youth will engage in future political and civic activities.[111]

* * *

In sum, then, state courts can substantially motivate and require states and school districts to fulfill their constitutional obligation to prepare students to be capable citizens. As warranted by the evidence and the particular circumstances, they can do so by doing the following:

A. Issuing remedial decrees to enforce judicial standards regarding civic preparation in the schools that many state courts have already articulated in past education adequacy cases.
B. Issuing general remedial orders promoting civic preparation in the schools both in states that have upheld rights to an adequate education in past cases and in states that previously have not. Such general decrees should
    1. Establish appropriate standards for ensuring that schools provide all of their students meaningful opportunities to acquire civic knowledge, skills, experiences, and values.
    2. Ensure that all schools properly implement these standards.
    3. Adopt a system of accountability to ensure that the state is making reasonable progress toward achieving its civic preparation goals.
C. Implementing specific remedial orders that might, among other things, require a state to
    1. Include a civics course or a sequence of courses as a graduation requirement, or ensure that all students receive focused instruction in civics and government in required courses throughout their educational careers.
    2. Adopt and implement the College, Career, and Civic Life (C3) Framework for Social Studies State Standards.
    3. Ensure that all schools provide appropriate programs and strategies to enhance students' critical analytic skills, especially in applying such skills to the Internet and social media.
    4. Issue standards and/or guidelines for promoting the value of tolerance and for the use of productive discussion of controversial issues in the classroom and ensure adequate teacher training and professional development of teachers to provide this instruction.
    5. Ensure that all students have access to adequately stocked libraries and computer labs.
    6. Ensure that all students have access to a reasonable range of extracurricular activities.
    7. Ensure that all students have opportunities to participate in student government and/or actual or simulated civic and political activities.
    8. Include requirements for completion of service learning experiences with opportunities for reflection in its social studies or civics standards.
    9. Adopt programs that effectively promote character values and democratic values.

D. Remedying inequities in opportunities for civic participation by requiring the state to
   1. Ensure that all schools have sufficient funding and resources to provide their students the opportunity for a sound basic education.
   2. Adopt specific remedies to promote racial, ethnic, and socioeconomic integration in all schools as necessary components of a school culture that prepares students for civic participation.

CHAPTER SEVEN

Advancing Civic Preparation through the Federal Courts

Every child in the land should receive a sufficient education to qualify him to discharge all the duties that may devolve upon him as an American citizen. — Congressman Samuel W. Moulton, 1866

State courts decrees can do much to advance civic preparation in the schools, but there is also a limit to what they can accomplish. Twenty-two state courts have issued rulings to promote funding equity and educational adequacy, especially for students of color and students in poverty. In contrast, courts in eighteen states have refused to accept jurisdiction or have otherwise declined to act to remedy educational inequities and/or inadequacies, and in the other ten states there were mixed decisions or no litigation has been pursued. And although the remedies issued in many of the states in which the plaintiffs have prevailed have resulted in enhanced educational opportunities and improved educational achievement, other state court remedial decrees have not proved successful.

Though students in many states have benefited substantially from state court rulings, their peers in many other places have not. For example, per-pupil expenditures in Philadelphia and Los Angeles, cities in states where courts have not enforced students' right to an adequate education, are only 50 percent of the per-pupil expenditures in New York City, where state courts have enforced the right to an opportunity for a sound basic education.[1] These spending disparities have real consequences: students in New York City score substantially higher than students in Philadelphia and Los Angeles in terms of their average reading and math scores on the National Assessment of Educational Progress (NAEP) examinations.[2]

Emphasizing civic preparation issues in education adequacy cases may induce more state courts to find for plaintiffs and issue appropriate remedial orders, as discussed in the previous chapter. The impact of such state court litigation and the long-term sustainability of court reforms is tempered, however, by the failure of the U.S. Supreme Court to declare that there is a national right to education. As Jonathan Kozol has put it, "No matter what the state in which a case takes place, the most important disadvantage advocates for equal education or for adequate education have to face is that attorneys are unable to incorporate within their pleadings claims deriving from the U.S. Constitution—the only constitution that has truly elevated moral standing in the eyes of most Americans—and cannot, as a consequence, defend the rights of children in these cases *as Americans*."[3] Historian Carl Kaestle adds, "Most people in America think one has a 'right' to equal educational opportunity,"[4] and "when you tell [them] that [education is not a fundamental right], they say, 'It should be.'"[5]

Many members of Congress agree. At the time of the passage of the No Child Left Behind Act (NCLB) in 2001,[6] a number of them stated explicitly that all children in the United States have a right to education:

> Every child in this country has the right to a free public education. Every child. That is an awesome responsibility, and one that should not have to be shouldered by local communities alone.[7]

> The proposal before the Senate represents an important step in the right direction by recognizing the right of every child to receive a high quality education.[8]

> Every child in America has a right to a world-class education. This bill enacts the reforms and provides the resources necessary to make this right a reality.[9]

Indeed, one of the prime stated purposes of the NCLB—which has been maintained in the current Every Student Succeeds Act (ESSA), its successor statute—is that "all children have a fair, equal, and significant opportunity to obtain a high quality education."[10] This language arguably may be read to indicate that there is an implied federal right to education, but neither Congress nor the courts have acted to implement and enforce it in that manner.[11]

Despite Congress's rhetorical support, no such federal right to education will be fully, fairly, and consistently enforced until and unless the Supreme Court definitively declares that such a right does exist under the U.S. Constitution. Although in the past the Court has declined to declare the existence of a federal right, it might be persuaded to do so if the issue were presented in the context of the schools' responsibility to prepare all students to function productively as civic participants.

A declaration by the U.S. Supreme Court of a federal right to an education that adequately prepares all students for civic participation would have wide-ranging effects. It would focus attention and stir a national discussion on the importance of preparing citizens to function productively as civic participants and to participate in the political process. It would also highlight the extent to which schools throughout the country are presently failing to prepare their students for these important responsibilities. As the Southern Education Foundation has noted, "An earnest national debate about the causes and consequences of education inequality in light of changing national demographics is long overdue. The American people need to become involved at every level in a searching inquiry about the value of a quality public education to individuals, families, communities, and the nation."[12]

The Supreme Court plays a unique role in American society. In our system, there is a special reverence for the Constitution and for the Supreme Court's role in interpreting it because many of its provisions derive from principles of higher law and natural law;[13] in addition, the Court has a distinctive "educative role"[14] in guiding the nation "with respect to those long-term 'value questions' that are so vital to the maintenance of a just political order."[15] The Court's status is also enhanced by "the realization that there may be no other basis for uniting a nation of so many disparate groups. The constitution thus becomes the *only* principle of order, for there is no otherwise shared moral or social vision that might bind together a nation."[16] The importance of the Supreme Court's role in articulating basic societal values has taken on greater significance in recent decades as political polarization has impeded the functioning of the congressional and the executive branches, and because for many people the values-influencing role of traditional religious, communal, and familial institutions has declined.

Contemporary Americans have come to look to the principled decision-making processes of the courts for considering fundamental societal issues like school desegregation,[17] legislative apportionment,[18] abortion,[19] the right to bear arms,[20] campaign finance reform,[21] gender equity,[22] and gay rights.[23] Even though all citizens may not agree on the Supreme Court's stance on these and other issues, the rulings tend to have significant moral suasion, and even those who are dissatisfied with a particular judicial stance look to the Court as the ultimate authority to change it. Although partisan politics certainly enters into the selection of judges, and judges' thought processes obviously are influenced by their personal values and experiences, institutionally courts are bound to consider issues from a principled perspective because they have to give explicit reasons, justified in terms of the constitutional text and legal precedents, for their decisions, and "this in turn requires norms or rules for determining what counts as a 'good' reason."[24]

The articulation and clarification of public values by the Supreme Court has in the past had a substantial impact on society's attitudes and mores.[25] For example, despite explosive initial resistance to the Court's 1954 school desegregation decision, over time, attitudes regarding racial integration have changed dramatically. The proportion of American whites who expressed approval when asked, "Do you think white students and Negro students should go to the same schools or to separate schools" rose from 30 percent in the years before the Supreme Court's decision to 49 percent in 1956 and 63 percent in 1963.[26] Attitudes on gay rights and marriage equality have also changed dramatically in recent years, at least partially because of major decisions of the U.S. Supreme Court and influential state court opinions in Hawaii, Massachusetts, and elsewhere. For example, between 2001 and 2016, the percentage of Americans in favor of gay marriage shifted from 57 percent opposed and 35 percent in favor to 55 percent in favor and 37 percent opposed.[27] On an issue like the right to education, and in particular on preparing students for civic participation, where there is likely to be scant opposition, a clear pronouncement from the Court about the direction the country needs to take and how to get there would likely be enormously influential.

Relitigating *Rodriguez*

As discussed in chapter 2, the U.S. Supreme Court has repeatedly affirmed that the schools "are educating the young for citizenship"[28] and that they are the places where the "fundamental values necessary for the maintenance of a democratic political system" are conveyed.[29] However, the Court has never explicated these references or articulated a coherent statement of what educating students for citizenship should mean. The Court did, however, indicate forty-five years ago in its decision in *San Antonio Independent School District v. Rodriguez* that in a future case it might consider whether some basic level of civic education should be considered a "fundamental interest" under the U.S. Constitution.[30] The time has now come for the Supreme Court to rethink *Rodriguez* and answer this critical question.

Constitutional claims that either involve discrimination against "suspect classes" like racial minorities or that involve "fundamental interests" like freedom of speech or voting rights, get "strict scrutiny" from the Court. Plaintiffs have almost always won such cases because the state must show a "compelling state interest"—a standard that rarely can be met—for the Court to deny the claim. Cases that do not involve suspect classes or fundamental interests are given less scrutiny, and defendants have generally prevailed in these cases if they can show a "rational relationship" between the state action at issue and any legitimate state interest. Plaintiffs lost in *Rodriguez* because the Court considered the Texas education finance system to be "rationally related" to the state's interest in promoting local control of education, even if the system did result in huge disparities in educational expenditures among school districts.

In their dissents in that case, Justices Marshall and Brennan argued that despite the absence of any specific references to education in the U.S. Constitution, education should nevertheless be considered a fundamental interest. They largely based this argument on the proposition that citizens could not properly exercise other fundamental constitutional interests like free speech and the right to vote unless they had acquired the basic skills "necessary for the enjoyment of the rights of speech and of full participation in the political process."[31] The majority of the justices did not dispute this proposition. They held, however, that the *Rodriguez* plaintiffs had claimed that the large funding disparities between their school district and other more affluent districts denied them equal protection of the laws, but they had not presented evidence as to whether their students were being denied the educational essentials they would need to exercise their free speech and voting rights.[32]

Effective exercise of First Amendment rights to free expression in the twenty-first century does require a high level of basic education. Clearly, those who are "verbally empowered" are more likely to feel confident about exercising those skills in politics and to be effective when they do.[33] As Alexander Meicklejohn succinctly put it, "Far deeper and more significant than the demand for the freedom of speech is the demand for education, for freeing of minds. These are not different demands. The one is a negative and external form of the other. We shall not understand the First Amendment unless we see that underlying it is the purpose that the citizens of our self-governing society shall be 'equally' educated."[34] And, similarly, education is critical to voting and the maintenance of a vibrant democratic system because "nonvoting results from a lack of knowledge about what government is doing and where parties and candidates stand, not from a knowledgeable rejection of government or parties. Further, it is not the poor performance of political institutions as much as ignorance of the institutions that is the source of many current discontents."[35]

Potential plaintiffs who are interested in bringing this issue before the Supreme Court now have ample evidence to make this case. Earlier chapters of this book have detailed the basic knowledge, skills, experiences, and values students need today to function productively as civic participants capable of exercising free speech, voting, and pursuing other fundamental constitutional interests and how the schools can prepare them for these important responsibilities. They also documented the extent to which in the decades since *Rodriguez* was decided, schools throughout the nation have increasingly failed to properly prepare students for successful citizenship and the extent to which the civic knowledge, skills, experiences, and values of American students have substantially deteriorated.

The Supreme Court has alluded to the importance of many of the specific kinds of knowledge, skills, experiences, and values that many schools are neglecting or are not conveying effectively. For example, the Court has emphasized the importance of basic knowledge of how our governmental institutions function,[36] and of exposing students to a marketplace of ideas, controversies, and opposing viewpoints.[37] It has also underscored that it is important for students to take part in authentic democratic experiences,"[38] and that schools need to inculcate basic civic values,[39] specifically including the values of tolerance and democratic deliberation.[40]

Potential plaintiffs who are able to offer concrete examples of specific shortcomings of their schools in all or many of these areas may well gain a positive response from the Supreme Court. Such school- and state-specific facts can often be found in the extensive evidence that has been developed in the forty-five states where equity and adequacy cases have been litigated (in some states multiple times). This trove of evidence includes concrete data on many of the particular educational policy questions the Court raised in *Rodriguez*. The decisions in these cases also contain a host of relevant legal doctrines the Court can consider, and a range of remedial mechanisms that it uses to respond to the problems in this area. The adequacy cases constitute a veritable "laboratory"[41] of the states from which litigants and the Supreme Court can extract enormously significant information.

Moreover, the very fact that, in the more than four decades since *Rodriguez* was decided, equity and adequacy cases have been litigated in forty-five states and that the majority of these courts that have reviewed the evidence have agreed that millions of students, and especially students in poverty and low-income students, are being denied an adequate education is in and of itself a convincing reason for the Supreme Court to revisit the issues left open in *Rodriguez*. As Yale professor Jack M. Balkin has explained, "When lots of different states from different parts of the country agree that these rights deserve protection, they are more likely to be rights with special constitutional value that all governments are supposed to protect."[42]

Balkin cites gay rights as an example of how developments in state courts can influence the Supreme Court's willingness to reconsider a constitutional issue that it had previously decided. In 1986, the Court held that Georgia's sodomy law that criminalized same-sex relations did not violate the fundamental rights of gay men and women.[43] At that time half the states criminalized same-sex relations. Seventeen years later, the Court essentially reversed this ruling, holding in *Lawrence v. Texas*[44] that a statute that prohibited sexual relations among homosexuals violated their right to liberty under the due process clause of the Fourteenth Amendment. By then only thirteen states criminalized same-sex relations, and the law was never enforced in criminal prosecutions.[45] In 2015, the Court went further, ruling that gay couples have a constitutional right to marry.[46] In that case, the Court explicitly referred to the significance of the fact that "there has been extensive litigation in state and federal courts," and it specifically listed in an appendix the dozens of cases that had discussed the issue.[47]

In the state court adequacy cases, the judges considered and resolved many of the specific educational issues that the Supreme Court in 1973 was reluctant to confront. Justice Powell, writing for the majority in

Rodriguez, explicitly stated that the Court did not want to venture into areas of educational policy on which scholarly opinion was substantially divided: "On even the most basic questions in this area the scholars and educational experts are divided. . . . In such circumstances, the judiciary is well advised to refrain from imposing on the States inflexible constitutional restraints that could circumscribe or handicap the continued research and experimentation so vital to finding even partial solutions to educational problems and to keeping abreast of ever-changing conditions."[48] Extensive state court litigation involving many of these issues has focused attention on these problems and spurred further research and analysis that has clarified and resolved some of these issues. The courts' handling of these issues has also demonstrated that judges can properly understand and rule on many of these complex issues of educational policy.

For example, the state courts have considered in depth one of the specific educational policy issues about which Justice Powell seemed most concerned. He stated in *Rodriguez* that "one of the major sources of controversy concerns the extent to which there is a demonstrable correlation between educational expenditures and the quality of education."[49] This question of whether "money matters" has, in fact, been extensively considered in virtually all of the state cases, and these litigations have sparked an extensive economics of education literature on the subject.[50] To a large extent, the judicial experience has resolved the core issue, with experts on both sides agreeing that, "of course, money matters—if it is spent well."[51] Some social scientists have acknowledged that the judicial process has clarified the issues and advanced scholarly understanding in this area: "Courts can navigate well through (disputed) social science arguments regarding educational outcomes, educational inputs (the education production function), and the deployment of teacher inputs. Moreover, rulings themselves can offer useful guidance to researchers on what fields of inquiry are important for resolving key public policy concerns, on what empirical evidence and which methodologies are deemed most valid, as well as indicate new areas for academic interest."[52]

In addition to the strong arguments that can be made for why the Supreme Court should consider whether the denial of an adequate education that prepares students for civic participation is a fundamental interest entitled to strict scrutiny review, there also is an important Supreme Court precedent for applying here an intermediate scrutiny test that falls short of strict scrutiny but is more demanding than a rational relationship. In *Plyler v. Doe*,[53] the issue was whether children of undocumented immigrants were entitled to a free public education: " [This law] imposes a lifetime hardship on a discrete class of children not accountable for their disabling status. The stigma of illiteracy will mark them for the rest of their lives. By denying these children a basic education, we deny them the ability to live within the structure of our civic institutions, and foreclose any realistic possibility that they will contribute in even the smallest way to the progress of our Nation."[54]

The Court held that in light of the long-term implications of the denial of education to these students, Texas's policy of barring them from enrolling in public schools would be considered unconstitutional unless the state could show that the exclusion policy furthered some "substantial goal" of the state.[55] It rejected the rationales for its exclusionary policy put forward by the state (preserving educational resources for its lawful residents, impact on other students, and the fact that these students might move out of state after receiving a state-funded education) as being "wholly insubstantial in light of the costs involved to these children, the State, and the Nation."[56]

Most states are now denying many students in poverty and students of color not only opportunities to develop basic literacy skills but also opportunities to obtain the knowledge, skills, experiences, and values they need to function productively as civic participants. In doing so, these states are failing to prepare these students to participate in our "civic institutions" and are impeding their ability to "contribute in even the smallest way to the progress of our nation." In light of this, the cost of compliance, local control of education, and other rationales that the state might put forward for denying adequate education for civic preparation to these students might well also be deemed "wholly unsubstantial"[57] and unacceptable reasons for perpetuating discrimination against these students.

The existence of a large civic empowerment gap between white students and students of color may also convince the Court to reconsider whether these students are being denied a right to an adequate education, even if rational relationship, the least demanding level of scrutiny that the Court applied in *Rodriguez*, is utilized in this situation. African American and Latino students and students living in poverty are disproportionately deprived of basic educational resources and of the opportunities they need to function productively as civic participants in specific areas such as lack of access to relevant courses and limited access to extracurricular activities.[58] As a result, these students have dramatically lower scores on the NAEP civics test and display more cynical attitudes toward political participation,[59] and they ultimately have substantially lower rates of participation in civic and political activities as adults. The fact that some students are being denied important services that are, at the same time, being provided to their peers might constitute evidence of a constitutional violation, even under the rational relationship test that the Supreme Court applies in cases that do not involve fundamental interests.[60]

In sum, then, under any of the three levels of scrutiny that the Supreme Court applies to claims brought under the equal protection clause of the Fourteenth Amendment, a strong case can be made that denial of an adequate education that properly prepares students for civic participation constitutes a violation of the federal constitution. Such a ruling by the Supreme Court would mean, in essence, that there is an enforceable federal right to such an adequate education even though education is not specifically mentioned in the U.S. Constitution.[61]

Rethinking Privileges and Immunities

The Fourteenth Amendment to the U.S. Constitution not only prohibits the denial to all persons of the "equal protection of the laws" but also states that "all persons born or naturalized in the United States are citizens of the United States" and that all of them are entitled to the "privileges and immunities" of the United States and of the state wherein they reside.[62] The Court has enforced this privileges and immunities clause only on rare occasions, but the need for a federal right to an education adequate for civic participation may provide a justification for the Court to reconsider the purpose and the contemporary relevance of this provision. Accordingly, the privileges and immunity clause may provide an alternate or additional constitutional basis for the Court to hold that there is a federal right to education.

The Fourteenth Amendment was enacted shortly after the Civil War, primarily to ensure constitutional protection for newly emancipated black citizens, although the amendment by its terms also clearly applied generally to all citizens.[63] On its face, the privileges and immunities clause seems to assume that all citizens possess certain inherent privileges or basic rights that should be considered "immune" from state abridgement.

According to Balkin, this is precisely what the Congress that adopted the amendment intended it to mean: "In 1868, 'privileges' and 'immunities' were both synonyms for rights. Generally speaking, a privilege was a right to do something; an immunity was protection against invasions of a legally protected interest."[64]

In a major decision issued shortly after the amendment was enacted known as *The Slaughter-House Cases*,[65] however, the Supreme Court interpreted the clause in very narrow terms. The 5–4 majority decision distinguished between citizenship of the United States and citizenship of a state. It deemed "citizenship of the United States" to include only the rights set forth in the federal constitution plus such matters as a citizen's right to be able to "come to the seat of government to assert any claim he may have upon that government, to transact any business he may have with it," and "the right to use the navigable waters of the United States, however they may penetrate the territory of the several States."[66]

The issue in the *Slaughter-House Cases* was whether granting a partial monopoly of the slaughtering business in New Orleans to a single company violated the right of employees of other companies to work in a profession of their choosing without unreasonable governmental interference. The majority's narrow reading of the privileges and immunities clause did not encompass this claimed right, and the Court held that whether the butchers in New Orleans had such right as citizens of Louisiana was a matter to be determined by the Louisiana state courts. Justice Stephen Field dissented. He argued that the privileges and immunities clause was intended to bring within the scope of federal constitutional protection all of the fundamental rights of "citizens of all free governments, and which have at all times been enjoyed by the citizens of the several states which compose the Union."[67]

Because of the very narrow ruling of the Supreme Court majority in the *Slaughter-House Cases*, the privileges and immunities clause has seldom been invoked by litigants in the federal courts. For the past 150 years, virtually all the major questions regarding the existence and extent of rights covered by the Fourteenth Amendment have been decided under the equal protection and due process clauses. Many scholars have, however, continued to criticize the narrow interpretation of privileges and immunities in the *Slaughter-House Cases*. Goodwin Liu, formerly a professor at University of California–Berkeley Law School and now an associate justice of the California Supreme Court, has argued that the drafters of the Fourteenth Amendment understood that they were creating new substantive national rights when they wrote the privileges and immunities clause.

Liu closely examined the history of the enactment of the Fourteenth Amendment and concluded, "Beyond granting legal status to newly freed blacks, the citizenship clause established a national political community and made allegiance to it the primary aspect of our political identity."[68] Steven Calabresi, a professor at Northwestern University Law School, and his student Sarah Agudo agreed that the privileges and immunities clause was intended to be read broadly to encompass all of the substantive rights that were generally considered fundamental for citizens in a democratic society in the nineteenth century. To understand exactly which rights were considered fundamental at the time, they examined all of the individual rights that were set forth in constitutions of the thirty-seven states in existence in 1868 when the Fourteenth Amendment was ratified. They found that three-quarters of those states "recognized a fundamental state constitutional duty to provide a public-school education as a matter of their formal, positive state constitutional law."[69] Their findings also indicated that 92 percent of all Americans in 1868 lived in states whose constitutions imposed this duty on state government. On the basis of these facts, they concluded that "the existence of such a duty on government could be said to create a right on the part of individuals."[70]

One of the current justices of the U.S. Supreme Court, Clarence Thomas, has also examined the history leading up to the passage of the Fourteenth Amendment, concluding that at the time "the terms 'privileges' and 'immunities' (and their counterparts) were understood to refer to those fundamental rights and liberties specifically enjoyed by English citizens and, more broadly, by all persons."[71] Justice Thomas has criticized the narrow reading of the privileges and immunities clause rendered by the Supreme Court in the *Slaughter-House Cases*, and he stated that the Court should be "open to reevaluating its meaning in an appropriate case."[72]

A claim to a right to an adequate education for civic preparation would constitute an appropriate vehicle for reevaluating the meaning of the privileges and immunities clause in the twenty-first century. The importance of education—and, in particular, its critical role in preparing students to function productively as civic participants—has long been recognized by the Supreme Court. If convincing evidence is presented to the Court indicating that large numbers of students are not being properly prepared for citizenship, then the Court might deem the privileges and immunities clause, which is directly tied in the constitutional language to the attributes of citizenship, to be the most appropriate constitutional provision for establishing a federal right to education adequate for civic participation. An additional consideration might be that establishing this right under the privileges and immunities clause would not raise the type of precedent for "slippery slope" accretions that concerned the Court in *Rodriguez*.[73]

Justices like Clarence Thomas who ground their interpretations of constitutional provisions in the original intent of those who drafted the language of the constitutional language at issue might also find convincing Calabresi and Agudo's findings that education had been well established as a fundamental right in the overwhelming majority of the states at the time the Fourteenth Amendment was enacted. The history of the common school movement, its emphasis on preparing students for citizenship in our democratic society, and espousal of that view by the drafters of most of the educational clauses in the state constitutions at that time would also support such an originalist interpretation.

Those justices who believe that the meaning of broad constitutional phrases necessarily must evolve in accordance with major changes in society's needs and values would undoubtedly take account of the immense importance of education in contemporary times. As a unanimous Supreme Court stated in *Brown v. Board of Education*: "Today, education is perhaps the most important function of state and local governments. Compulsory school attendance laws and the great expenditures for education both demonstrate our recognition of the importance of education to our democratic society. . . . It is required in the performance of our most basic public responsibilities, even service in the armed forces. It is the very foundation of good citizenship."[74] Liu writes that the framers of the Fourteenth Amendment "chose generic language sufficiently elastic to permit reasonable future advances through legislation and judicial interpretation."[75] He argues that the privileges and immunities clause properly understood and applied today "authorizes and obligates Congress to ensure a meaningful floor of educational opportunity."[76]

Balkin also believes that constitutional interpretation should take into account the evolution of needs, values, and public understanding, and that, therefore, the privileges and immunities clause should be reinvigorated to meet contemporary needs. He argues that the privileges and immunities clause would provide a stronger basis for asserting rights than the equal protection clause: "Instead of asking whether an interest is a fundamental right . . . the more natural and sensible question is whether it is a privilege or immunity of national citizenship, part of a basic template of rights that all citizens enjoy."[77] For present purposes, we need not go so far. There are strong arguments for declaring the existence of a right to education under both the equal protection and privileges and immunities clauses—and also under another long-neglected constitutional provision, the "republican guarantee" provision of article 4, section 4.

The Republican Guarantee Clause

Article 4, section 4, of the U.S. Constitution requires the federal government to guarantee each of the states a "republican form of government." In 1787, "republican government" connoted mainly a representative government based on popular sovereignty and majority rule in making and changing constitutions.[78] Some have also argued that James Madison promoted the clause to minimize the influence of self-interested factions by ensuring not only the forms of republican government, but also the kinds of deliberative processes that are needed to make it work properly.[79] In the nineteenth century, most of the states, embracing the common school movement, recognized that for the people to exercise their popular sovereignty effectively, republican government required the establishment of a public school system that would prepare students to be capable citizens. As Horace Mann put it, "Under a republican government, it seems clear that the minimum of this education can never be less than such as is sufficient to qualify each citizen for the civic and social duties he will be called to discharge."[80]

A prime justification for the compulsory education laws that most of the states adopted at the end of the nineteenth century was to ensure that all students receive the basic education that they need to function productively as republican citizens.[81] The constitutions that many of the states adopted at that time also directly linked education to the viability of a republican form of government. Thus, for example, the constitution of Minnesota, adopted in 1857, explicitly proclaims: "The *stability of a republican form of government depending mainly upon the intelligence of the people*, it shall be the duty of the legislature to establish a general and uniform system of public schools."[82]

The republican guarantee clause has been largely ignored for the past two centuries primarily because of the Supreme Court's 1849 holding in *Luther v. Borden*.[83] There, the Court was asked to validate the legitimacy of the sitting government in Rhode Island whose *bona fides* were being challenged. The Court held that it was for Congress, and not the federal courts, to determine the legitimacy of a state government.[84] This decision has sometimes been read to mean that all issues concerning the constitution's republican guarantee are "political questions" that are not suitable for judicial resolution. As Balkin has explained, however, the case does not actually stand for such a broad proposition.[85] Rather, it holds only that claims involving federal recognition of the legitimacy of a state government are best determined by the political branches.

The Supreme Court has avoided applying the republican guarantee clause in a number of other cases involving sensitive political questions regarding the structure and functions of state governments,[86] but the High Court also stated in 1992 that "perhaps not all claims under the Guarantee Clause present nonjusticiable political questions."[87] The Court has never focused squarely on the basic issue posed here as to whether the federal government has the authority and the responsibility under section 4 of article 4 to ensure that all students are being provided an education that will prepare them to exercise their First Amendment rights, vote knowledgeably, and otherwise carry out properly the civic responsibilities of a member of a republican community. It should do so now.[88]

The enhanced importance of education in the twenty-first century, combined with the extensive evidence that many of the states are not effectively carrying out their responsibilities to prepare students properly for citizenship, have added new significance to the republican guarantee clause. In modern times, the broad extension of the franchise beyond the limited domain of white male property owners that prevailed at the time the Constitution was enacted requires that all citizens be well prepared to vote intelligently, to understand and analyze critically the glut of information that they receive daily from the media and the Internet, and to participate actively in a range of civic affairs.

Congress itself has recognized the need for federal intervention to spur the states to improve the education they are providing to many students in enacting major education reform statutes like the Elementary and Secondary Education Act, NCLB, ESSA, and the Individuals with Disabilities Education Act (known as IDEA). These initiatives have obviously not solved the problems. Accordingly, the persistent, widespread failures by the states to provide an education adequate to prepare students for capable citizenship should justify a claim that in order to guarantee a republican government in all of the states in the twenty-first century, the federal courts and Congress must take appropriate action to ensure that all students are receiving an adequate education that prepares them to function productively as civic participants.[89]

* * *

In short, then, there is a strong case to be made that the Supreme Court should declare that there is a federal right to an education adequate to prepare students for civic participation under either the equal protection or privileges and immunities provisions of the Fourteenth Amendment or under the republican guarantee clause of article 4, section 4, or under all of these provisions.[90] One remaining issue that needs to be addressed is whether, under any of these rationales, it is constitutionally appropriate for the federal government to enforce a "positive" right to education by compelling the states to take certain actions to promote educational opportunities and civic participation.

All previous discussions of civic participation issues by the Court occurred in cases in which parents, students, or teachers were resisting state actions that they claimed were inconsistent with their constitutional rights. Thus, in *Pierce*,[91] parents were objecting to a state law that banned attendance at private schools; in *Tinker*,[92] students were opposing restrictions on their right to object to the war in Vietnam; in *Island Trees*,[93] parents were challenging the school board's decision to remove certain books from the school library; and in *Plyler*, the undocumented immigrant children were opposing a school exclusion policy.

In all of these situations, the Court was upholding the plaintiffs' rights to prevent state governments from taking actions that would harm them rather than enforcing a constitutional right that would require the government to act affirmatively to provide them substantive benefits. The Court's stance in these cases was consistent with the general understanding that "the Constitution is a charter of negative rather than positive liberties . . . ; [t]he men who wrote the Bill of Rights were not concerned that government might do too little for the people but that it might do too much to them."[94] Asking the court to hold that students have a right to an education that prepares them adequately for civic participation would involve a "positive" right that would require the states to act affirmatively to provide adequate programs and services to meet this need.

Does the federal constitution allow for positive rights? Although much of the Constitution is oriented toward "negative" rights, there clearly are exceptions. As Harvard Law professor Laurence Tribe has noted, "Even within our largely individualistic and negative constitutional scheme, however, there are exceptional rights that the constitutional text itself expresses in affirmative form. For example, the sixth amendment guarantees to 'the accused' the right to 'enjoy . . . a speedy and public trial, by an impartial jury.' . . . These commands obviously entail recognition of positive and not merely negative rights."[95] Tribe also cites the republican guarantee clause as an example of a constitutional clause that on its face sets forth a positive right.

Other scholars have also pointed out that positive rights to governmental assistance are implied in many traditional constitutional protections like the equal protection clause, and whether a right is perceived as involving action or inaction really depends on baseline assumptions about "the natural or desirable functions of government."[96] As Liu has concluded, "Neither the text nor the history of the Constitution forecloses a reading of its broad guarantees to encompass positive rights."[97]

Tribe delineates a number of areas in which individuals cannot exercise basic capacities without affirmative governmental support. He cites in this regard Supreme Court rulings that require affirmative government actions to enable citizens to exercise their right to vote, and that require assistance of counsel for those who cannot pay for a lawyer themselves in criminal cases or divorce proceedings.[98] He states that "access to basic education may well be of the same character."[99]

The Remedy

Were the Supreme Court to declare education a federal right either as a fundamental interest under the equal protection clause, or as a substantive right under the privileges and immunities, and/or republican guarantee clauses, it would then need to issue a remedy that would ensure that students in all states were being provided an adequate education to prepare them to function productively as civic participants. The main question at that point would be whether the remedy, at least in an initial case, should be a declaratory judgment that leaves it to Congress and the state legislatures to determine the specific steps that need to be taken to enforce the right or whether the Supreme Court itself should issue specific decretal requirements articulating particular actions that Congress and/or the states need to take.

Declaratory Remedy

If the Supreme Court were to hold that there is a right to education under the federal constitution, it might choose to issue a declaratory judgment, that is, one that proclaims there is such a substantive right but leaves to Congress and/or state legislatures the responsibility for developing the specific mechanisms for implementing the right. This approach would minimize the degree of judicial intervention and reduce the potential for federal-state or judicial-legislative confrontations.[100]

A relevant precedent in this regard is the U.S. Supreme Court's issuance of a declaratory judgment in a major education case involving the rights of English-language learners (ELLs) that precipitated extensive and effective remedial action by the political branches. In *Lau v. Nichols*, the Court held that the San Francisco school system's failure to provide instructional programs geared to meeting the linguistic needs of Chinese-speaking students denied them a meaningful educational opportunity.[101] The Court noted: "No specific remedy is urged upon us. . . . Petitioners ask only that the Board of Education be directed to apply its expertise to the problem and rectify the situation."[102]Accordingly, it remanded the case to the lower federal courts to supervise the development of a specific remedy. The school board, acting on the advice of federal officials, appointed the Citizens Task Force on Bilingual Education, which issued a report calling for bilingual and bicultural education wherever feasible. This plan, with some modifications, became the basis for a consent decree that was filed in October 1975.[103]

Although the Supreme Court set forth no specific remedy in *Lau*, its declaration that ELLs had a right to meaningful educational opportunities engendered a massive response from Congress, the U.S. Department of Health Education and Welfare (HEW), and the state legislatures over the following decades. The HEW's Office for Civil Rights issued a set of guidelines known as the "*Lau* Remedies."[104] The *Lau* Remedies required a school district to provide a remedial plan whenever it had twenty or more students of the same language group and described the range of remedial programs considered acceptable for these students. *Lau* also resulted in two immediate federal statutory revisions—of the Equal Educational Opportunities Act of 1974[105]and the Bilingual Education Act[106]—as well as numerous state legislative initiatives on bilingual education and programs for English-language learners, and follow-up litigation to enforce these statutory and regulatory provisions in the federal and state courts.[107]

A declaration of a right to an education adequate for civic participation that the Supreme Court might articulate could be something simple and straightforward as "All students are entitled to a meaningful opportunity to obtain the knowledge, skills, experiences, and values they need to function productively as civic participants in a democratic society." Or, building on language in NCLB, ESSA, and *Rodriguez*, it might read, "All students are entitled to a fair, equal and substantial education that prepares them adequately to vote, to serve on a jury, to express their opinions and to function capably as citizens in our democratic society."

Those suggestions are, of course, offered for illustrative purposes only. The exact language that the Supreme Court might choose to articulate for this right, and any guidelines on how it should be interpreted, would depend on the Court's findings and conclusions from the evidence presented in the case before it, its analysis of relevant precedents from its previous decisions and from the various state courts, and suggestions from the parties and amicus briefs.

The specific reforms that might be adopted to implement such a broadly stated right would be determined mainly by federal and state policy makers and the policies, practices, and needs in each state. As with the follow-up to the *Lau* decision, Congress and the U.S. Department of Education might choose to enact specific statutes, regulations, and/or guidelines to establish national priorities and recommended approaches regarding civic preparation and equal educational opportunity, which would then leave much of the development of specific remedies to the states.[108] The history of both NCLB and ESSA indicates that the determination of the civic preparation standards by which state efforts will be judged would probably be left largely to the states themselves,[109] although if a number of states set unreasonably low standards, over time there could be pressure for Congress to establish some basic national norms.

Compliance with the Supreme Court's declaratory judgment and with any statutes or regulations issues by the federal authorities would then be subject to review and interpretation by the state courts or lower federal courts. The Supreme Court's declaration of a federal right to education might also fuel increased interest and activity in state court adequacy litigations and spur state courts to issue the kind of specific remedies, tailored to local needs, which were discussed in the previous chapter.

A decision announcing a right to education for civic preparation is likely to be relatively well received, in contrast to the resistance that arose in many parts of the country after the Supreme Court's ruling in *Brown v. Board of Education.* As was discussed in the previous chapter, many states already have promulgated, though not enforced, educational standards and policies for preparing students for civic participation in the twenty-first century; in such situations, compliance with the Court order might entail no more than actually implementing state standards or commission recommendations that state authorities had already endorsed.

Federal funding for education for the past five years has averaged between 10 percent and 12 percent of total national educational expenditures.[110] Declaration of a federal right to education might increase that amount, since there could be substantial political and moral pressure for the federal government to assist states with low tax bases that lack the means to prepare their students properly for capable citizenship. Such action would be consistent with the proposition that a federal right to education is needed to ensure that all students throughout the nation, whether living in low-income or affluent areas, need to be educated to participate capably in the American democratic system.

Today, the annual per-pupil amount spent on elementary and secondary education varies substantially from state to state. It ranges from a low of $6,555 in Utah to a high of $19,918 in New York; the national average expenditure in 2013 was $10,700, and twenty-seven states spent less than that amount.[111] An "effort index," calculated in terms of each state's spending on education in relation to its economic productivity or gross state product, finds a range from a high effort level of 5.1 percent in Vermont and West Virginia to a low effort level of 2.3 percent in Delaware for 2012.[112] Some states, like Arkansas and South Carolina, have per-pupil expenditures below the national average,[113] although they rank high on the effort index.[114] Such states could make a strong case for a substantial increase in federal aid, and, historically, when federal funding has been increased for the needy, political pressures dictate that all other states get some increase as well.[115] It is likely that increased federal spending would also be accompanied by financial incentives for states to raise their education expenditure efforts; to ensure adequate funding, especially for school districts with large populations of students of color and students in poverty; and to meet appropriate civic preparation standards. States that fail to make such efforts might face financial or other sanctions.

Specific Remedies

If strong evidence of blatant inadequacies in certain areas essential to civic preparation is presented in a federal litigation, the U.S. Supreme Court could decide to issue a specific decree that delineates certain policies or practices that all states need to have in place in order to prepare students properly for civic participation. The number of remedial requirements that the Court might highlight would undoubtedly be limited, and they would likely be issued in addition to a broad declaration of a basic right to an adequate education for civic preparation. *Brown II*,[116] the remedial decision that the Court issued a year after its landmark 1954 desegregation ruling, is instructive in this regard.

In *Brown II*, the Court left to the lower federal courts the basic decisions about how to dismantle segregated school systems, but it also specifically advised them that they should consider "problems related to administration, arising from the physical condition of the school plant, the school transportation system, personnel, revision of school districts and attendance areas into compact units to achieve a system of determining admission to the public schools on a nonracial basis, and revision of local laws and regulations which may be necessary in solving the foregoing problems."[117] In a case on the federal right to education for civic preparation, the Court might consider emphasizing the importance of such issues as ensuring access to a full range of courses and extracurricular activities and encouraging service learning, as well as national service programs.[118] In light of the concerns raised during the 2016 election campaign, and continuing since, about the prevalence of misleading information and "fake news," and the continuing polarization of political discussion in this country, the Court may also deem it essential to underscore the schools' responsibility to teach students the importance of factual evidence and how to identify it, to help students develop critical analytic skills and how to apply these skills to information and issues they encounter in the media, and especially on the Internet and social media, and to inculcate the value of tolerance and the ability to discuss controversial issues with people who hold views different from their own.

A decision by the U.S. Supreme Court declaring that there is a federal right to an adequate education to prepare students for civic participation should also make clear that the right applies not only to traditional public schools but also to public charter schools and to private schools. It should stress that adequate civic preparation requires states to take active steps to overcome gaps in civic preparation and civic empowerment among subgroups of students.

As discussed in detail in chapter 2, in *Pierce v. Society of Sisters*,[119] the Court upheld parents' constitutional right to send their children to private schools but specified that in such schools, "studies plainly essential to good citizenship must be taught, and that nothing be taught which is manifestly inimical to the public welfare."[120] Neither in *Pierce* nor in any later decisions, however, has the Court explicated either in general or specific terms which type of studies are "essential to good citizenship." Partially because of this vacuum in constitutional direction, requirements regarding civic preparation in private and charter schools have often been minimal or nonexistent in some states, and in other states statutes and regulations that do speak to teacher competence and curriculum content in private schools and in charter schools have largely been unenforced.[121]

For this reason, the Supreme Court should set forth in broad terms the kinds of knowledge, skills, experiences, and values that it considers essential to good citizenship. It should require that states adopt and enforce appropriate statutes and regulations that apply those precepts to all schools, public and private. Specific details of the policies and practices that these statutes and regulations would require would, of course, be left to the states.

As *Pierce* made clear almost a century ago, although private schools may be exempted from most state regulations, they still must adhere to basic civic preparation requirements, because their students, like all students, must be in a position to contribute productively to the maintenance of our democratic society. This issue takes on added importance in light of the current policies of the Trump administration to expand school choice and to encourage greater use of vouchers and other mechanisms for increasing the numbers of students attending private schools.

This is not to say, of course, that many private schools are not currently doing an adequate or even a superior job in preparing their students for civic participation. Indeed, many Catholic schools and independent schools currently do better than the public schools in preparing students for civic participation.[122] Some charter schools also emphasize civic education in exemplary ways.[123] However, many other private schools and charters clearly do not.[124] In particular, some religious private schools neglect entirely instruction in civics and social studies,[125] and others inculcate values that conflict with basic constitutional norms.[126]

State statutes in this area need not be overbearing or interfere with the independent functioning of private schools and charters, but surely all private schools and charters must teach civics and social studies courses that are "substantially equivalent"[127] to these types of courses that are (or should be) taught in the public schools, and their students should take part in the kinds of extracurricular, community service, and experiential acvities that foster important civic skills. State regulations should not and need not interfere with the teaching of religious texts or religious values in private schools or with the ability of independent schools to provide instruction in accordance with their educational philosophies and priorities.

The Supreme Court should also specify that states have a constitutional responsibility to remedy gaps in civic preparation and empowerment among subgroups of students. Indeed, this is the stated national policy as set forth both in the past in the NCLB and currently in the ESSA statute. In light of the rapid demographic changes that are taking place in our schools and in the society at large, the future of our democratic system truly will be at risk if large segments of the population continue to be treated unequally and do not feel that they are part of a common culture and share a common destiny. Constitutional expectations to overcome the civic engagement gap need to emphasize both equality and inclusion.

In particular, the Supreme Court should consider emphasizing the states' duty to ensure that all schools, including schools in which students in poverty and students of color are enrolled in large numbers, and schools in areas that have been detrimentally impacted by large-scale job losses, receive sufficient funding to provide these students a meaningful opportunity for an adequate basic education. Access to relevant courses, participation in extracurricular and experiential activities, and teaching of critical analytic skills should be made available in all schools and to all students. The Court should also consider that if the opportunities promised by the American dream are to be realized, students in poverty must be provided critical additional services, like high-quality, publicly funded early childhood and prekindergarten programs.

Finally, the Court needs to convey a clear message to educators and to the population at large that racial integration and full inclusion of *all* students are critical components of the constitutional right to adequate education for civic preparation. This means, at the least, that states should take all actions permitted under existing school desegregation law to promote racial balance and positive intergroup relationships in the schools. The Court should also reconsider in light of current needs, and in light of the importance of preparing students for civic participation, its holdings in some of its past major school desegregation decisions like *Keyes v. School District No. 1*,[128] *Milliken v. Bradley*,[129] and *Parents Involved in Community Schools v. Seattle School Dist. No. 1*.[130] It should consider whether civic preparation considerations require states at this time to deal with problems created by both *de facto* and *de jure* segregation and whether the importance of preparing students to sustain our country's democratic values and institutions constitutes a compelling state interest and whether it outweighs the value of local control of education.

Positive statements and actions by the Supreme Court regarding the importance of integration and inclusion would spark fresh thinking and new solutions for promoting positive intergroup relations in the schools. A Supreme Court emphasis on the "commitment to public education as the center of a free society"[131] might also expand democratic dialogue in political discourse more generally and help mitigate the political polarization that stymies much of our politics today.

CHAPTER EIGHT

The Legitimacy of the Courts' Role

Civic education reform is, literally, essential to the continued vitality of American Constitutional government as we know it. — David Souter, retired U.S. Supreme Court Justice

The arguments I have made in previous chapters for both the state and federal courts to ensure that schools prepare their students properly to become capable citizens are likely to raise two immediate reactions from many readers: First, is this approach legitimate? Under our system of separation of powers is it appropriate for courts to intervene in issues of education policy and administration? Second, is this approach plausible? Would judges agree to take on an active role in promoting preparation for civic participation in the schools and would policy makers and the public accept such a stance and implement any such decrees appropriately? In this chapter, I will respond to both of these concerns.

Legitimacy

Judicial Involvement in Policy Making

FEDERAL COURTS My call for the courts to take action to confront the current crisis in civic preparation in the schools may come as a surprise to some readers. After all, the traditional understanding of the American principle of separation of powers is that the formulation and implementation of public policy in areas like education are the responsibilities of legislatures and executive agencies. Where then do the courts fit in? Is it legitimate for courts to weigh in on issues of educational policy?

A judicious policy-influencing role for the courts is not only legitimate, it is crucial. Ever since the U.S. Supreme Court issued its landmark decision outlawing racial segregation in the schools in *Brown v. Board of Education*,[1] the development of major policies in education and in a wide variety of other areas of social policy have been shaped not only by the legislative and executive branches but also by the courts. The Court's follow-up ruling in *Brown II*,[2] issued a year after the initial constitutional holding, authorized the federal district courts to oversee the implementation of school desegregation by local school districts. The strong stance of the federal courts on school desegregation in the 1960s helped fuel the civil rights movement.[3] *Brown v. Board of Education* also initiated a "new model of public law litigation,"[4] that has led both the federal and state courts over the past 60 years to expand their role beyond the traditional sphere of resolving private disputes between individuals and to issue broad remedial decrees that substantially affect the implementation of public policy.

The federal courts have promoted systemic improvements in public education not only in regard to desegregation but also in areas like bilingual education,[5] gender equity,[6] school discipline,[7] special education,[8] and immigrant rights.[9] They have also fostered reforms in other social policy areas, including the deinstitutionalization of services for the developmentally disabled,[10] employment discrimination,[11] housing integration,[12] and prison conditions.[13] *Brown* led not only to judicial intervention in a wide variety of educational and social policy domains, but also to the development of new judicial mechanisms for dealing with the complex administrative and policy issues that arise at the remedial stage of institutional reform litigations, such as the structural injunction,[14] the use of special masters,[15] and expanded class action procedures.[16]

To a large extent, this new judicial role emerged as an aspect of the broader expansion of governmental activities in the welfare-state era. As Malcolm Feeley and Edwin Rubin have explained: "[Judges] are part of the modern administrative state. . . . And they fulfill their role within that context. Under certain circumstances that role involves public policy makings; as our state has become increasingly administrative and managerial, judicial policy-making has become both more necessary for judges to produce effects and more legitimate as a general model of governmental action."[17] This "new model of public law litigation" has, in practice, modified traditional separation of powers concepts. It has become such an established part of the legal landscape that conservatives and liberals alike routinely look to the courts to remedy legislative or executive actions of which they disapprove. Indeed, if "judicial activism" is defined in terms of declaring legislative acts unconstitutional, the conservative Rehnquist Court was the most activist in American history. Until 1991, the United States Supreme Court struck down an average of about one congressional statute every two years. From 1994 to 2004, the Court struck down 64 congressional provisions, or about six per year. This invalidated legislation has involved civil rights, social security, church and state, campaign finance, and a host of other major social policy issues.[18] The Roberts Court appears to be continuing or even accelerating this trend. In recent years, it has undermined affirmative action in elementary and high school admissions policies,[19] opened the door to virtually unlimited support of political campaigns by wealthy individuals,[20] upheld the Affordable Care Act,[21] and given constitutional sanction to gay marriage.[22]

Although the U.S. Supreme Court has continued to take a stance on major policy decisions of the executive and legislative branches, it has in recent years tended to limit the scope of the lower federal courts' involvement in reviewing specific state policies and overseeing administrative compliance in the implementation of "new model" litigations. At the beginning of the desegregation era, the Court encouraged the federal district courts to supervise plans formulated by local school districts and to consider problems related to administration, facilities, personnel and revision of attendance areas.[23] Beginning in the 1970s, in the face of strong resistance to desegregation orders, and as desegregation cases moved from the South to the northern and western states, the Court substantially curtailed the extent of the federal courts' involvement in promoting thoroughgoing school desegregation.[24]

The Court has also adopted a cautious approach to federal oversight of remedial decrees and consent decrees with other types of institutional reform litigations, such as educational services for English-language learners.[25] Nevertheless, "the lower courts continue to play a crucial role in a still-growing movement of institutional reform in the core areas of public law practice Chayes identified: schools, prisons, mental health, police, and housing."[26] The Supreme Court has also continued to approve such arrangements where warranted by the facts and the need. For example, in a recent prison litigation, the Court affirmed a district court decision requiring the State of California to reduce its prison population to alleviate unconstitutional overcrowding conditions stating that

> Courts nevertheless must not shrink from their obligation to "enforce the constitutional rights of all 'persons,' including prisoners." . . . Courts may not

> allow constitutional violations to continue simply because a remedy would involve intrusion into the realm of prison administration.
>
> Courts faced with the sensitive task of remedying unconstitutional prison conditions must consider a range of available options, including appointment of special masters or receivers and the possibility of consent decrees. When necessary to ensure compliance with a constitutional mandate, courts may enter orders placing limits on a prison's population.[27]

An order from the U.S. Supreme Court that would prompt the schools to improve their civic preparation activities, as discussed in the previous chapter, would certainly be less intrusive into the domain of state policy making than was this California prison decree.

STATE COURTS Over the past half century, the state courts have also taken a "new model" approach on such policy issues as gay rights,[28] land use regulation,[29] special education,[30] and the constitutionality and funding of charter schools.[31] The area in which the state courts have been most active has been adjudicating challenges to the inequities and inadequacies of state educational finance systems under state constitutional provisions. As was discussed in more detail in chapter 3, since 1973, there have been litigations in 45 of the 50 states involving these issues, and in many states there have been multiple cases over this time period.[32]

As with the federal judiciary, the many state judges that have determined that constitutional or statutory provisions compel them to take stands on educational policy issues have also been accused of engaging in inappropriate "judicial activism." These charges are even less valid when applied to the state courts. Historically the pejorative use of this term arose from resistance to the role of the federal courts in school desegregation cases. The facile extension of criticisms of those federal court interventions to educational policy interventions by state courts is, however, fundamentally misguided.

State court cases do not involve the federalism issues that overlay separation of powers concerns in school desegregation and other federal cases. In contrast to federal judges, who were sometimes "pictured as 'outsiders,' rendering their controversial decisions subject to more resistance than an equally controversial decision handed down by the 'local' judge,"[33] state court judges are usually drawn from the local political elite and are well aware of the legal and political environment of the state scene. One of the reasons that state legislative leaders are more prone to comply readily with state court orders in major education policy litigations is that, as one observer of the reaction of state legislators to a state court decree in Texas stated, "Many former colleagues sat on the state supreme court . . . and the state court had to face the same electorate the legislature did, producing more of a 'comfort zone' on the part of the legislature."[34]

Judith Kaye, former chief judge of the New York Court of Appeals, also noted that state court judges have a firmer democratic pedigree: "State courts are generally closer to the public, to the legal institutions and environments within the state, and to the public policy process. This both shapes their strategic judgments and renders any erroneous assessments they may make more readily redressable by the People."[35] In contrast to federal judges who are appointed for life, state judges in 39 of the 50 states are chosen by the public either in garden-variety partisan elections or through a variant of a retention election.[36] Moreover, the constitutions that state judges are called upon to interpret can be amended relatively easily, rendering their decisions subject to a form of "majoritarian ratification."[37]

A final and highly significant distinction between federal courts and state courts is that in key areas of state responsibility like education, state constitutions clearly incorporate "positive rights" that call for the affirmative governmental action in contrast to the greater emphasis on "negative restraints" of the federal constitution. The implications of such positive rights in state constitutions have been explained as follows by NYU law professor Helen Hershkoff: "When the state constitution mandates a specific purpose and thus authorizes the government to carry out the stated goal, the legislature and the governor have a duty to achieve, or at least to help promote, the constitutional mandate . . . a positive constitutional right imposes an affirmative obligation on the state to realize and advance the objects and purposes for which . . . powers have been granted. . . . Judicial review in such a regime must serve to insure that the government is doing its job and moving policy closer to the constitutionally prescribed end."[38] The Washington Supreme Court, citing the Hershkoff article, acknowledged this distinction in its decision in the state's education adequacy decision: "This distinction between positive and negative constitutional rights is important because it informs the proper orientation for determining whether the State has complied with its [education adequacy] duty in the present case. In the typical constitutional analysis, we ask whether the legislature or the executive has overstepped its authority under the constitution. . . . This approach ultimately provides the wrong lens for analyzing positive constitutional rights, where the court is concerned not with whether the State has done too much, but with whether the State has done enough. Positive constitutional rights do not restrain government action; they require it."[39]

The fact that state courts in 60% of the education adequacy cases have issued rulings upholding plaintiffs' claims indicates that most state judges understand and accept their constitutional responsibilities to uphold positive constitutional rights in appropriate cases. This does not mean, however, that the judges are eager to engage in wide-ranging policy making in education or any other policy areas. As Albert Rosenblatt, former judge of the New York Court of Appeals stated, judges act when they believe that "there's a constitutional command" that is "not being honored by the legislators. . . . I would not call that 'social engineering.' I would call it fidelity to the constitutional command, and judges don't do it cheerfully."[40]

Consistent with Rosenblatt's dictum, state court judges have been reluctant to extend the precedents of the education equity and adequacy cases to issues beyond educational funding. Thus, in recent cases, state appeals courts have rejected equity or adequacy claims based on allegations that teacher tenure or seniority lay-off statutes had caused low-income and minority students to be taught by incompetent teachers,[41] that school segregation denies students an "adequate education,"[42] and that constitutional sound basic education rights apply to students in charter schools.[43] However, in light of the specific language in many state constitutions equating education with the preservation of democracy and the pronouncements of most state supreme courts that the prime purpose or a prime purpose of education is to prepare students for civic participation, state court judges may well deem adequate education for civic preparation to be "a constitutional command" to which they must affirmatively respond.

The Justification for Judicial Involvement in Policy Making

In the 1980s, my colleague Arthur R. Block and I undertook two major empirical studies to consider the competing arguments regarding the legitimacy of judicial involvement in educational policy matters. Focusing on comparative perspectives of institutional capacity, we studied instances of educational policy making by state courts, state legislatures, and a major administrative agency, the Office of Civil Rights in the U.S. Department of Health, Education and Welfare (OCR).[44] We concluded, among other things, that the evidentiary records accumulated in the court cases were more complete and had more influence on the actual decision-making process than did the factual data obtained through legislative hearings. The latter tended to be "window dressing" occasions organized to justify political decisions that had already been made.[45] Our study also found that judicial remedial involvement in school district affairs was both less intrusive and more competent than is generally assumed. School officials and experts representing both the plaintiffs and the state defendants generally participated in the formulation of reform decrees, with the courts serving as catalysts and mediators. The courts' "staying power" and their ability to respond flexibly to changed circumstances were also markedly more effective than the long-term responses of the legislatures and the administrative agency.[46]

One of the major fallacies of those who argue that courts lack the institutional capacity to deal with complex social policy issues is that they focus on the limitations of the judicial branch, while ignoring the comparable institutional shortcomings of the legislative and the executive branches. For example, Donald Horowitz, one of the foremost critics of the courts' involvement in policy issues, catalogued a bevy of examples of alleged judicial incompetence, ranging from receiving information in a skewed and inconsistent fashion to failing to understand the social context and potential unintended consequences of the cases before them.[47] As Neil Komesar has pointed out, however, Horowitz's critique was one-sided: "Horowitz's study can do no more than force us to accept the reality of judicial imperfection. By its own terms it is not comparative, and that is far more damning than Horowitz supposes. All societal decision makers are highly imperfect. Were Horowitz to turn his critical eye to administrative agencies or legislatures he would no doubt find problems with expertise, access to information, characterization of issues, and follow-up. Careful studies would undoubtedly reveal important instances of awkwardness, error and deleterious effect."[48] In the state court educational equity and adequacy cases, among the main criticisms of judicial intervention were that the courts failed to "require[e] the efficient or cost-effective use of funds."[49] As Komesar pointed out, however, none of these critics have even claimed that the other branches of government have been more effective than the courts in ensuring the productive use of educational funding.

Separation of powers issues need to be looked at in a different way. Instead of interpreting the active involvement of courts in enforcing social and economic rights as somehow usurping the powers of the legislative and executive branches, we need to realize that progress can only be made in complex, critical policy areas like preparation for citizenship through the active involvement of all three branches of government. In the rapidly changing political, economic, regulatory, and technological environment in which we now live, neither courts nor legislatures nor administrative agencies can resolve major social problems operating alone. Effective policy making frequently requires continuing interchanges and often continuing involvement of all three branches of government.

Successful advances in implementing educational opportunity have, in fact, generally occurred in the past in the United States when the judicial, legislative, and executive branches have managed to work together collaboratively. For example, in the late 1960s, extensive desegregation of southern schools was finally achieved after the courts developed detailed desegregation remedies, Congress enacted the Elementary and Secondary Education Act and Title VI of the 1964 Civil Rights Act, and the Office for Civil Rights actively enforced the court decrees and these statutes.[50] Similarly, Congress enacted the extensive Individuals with Disabilities Education Act (IDEA) to implement the rights of students with disabilities that had been articulated and developed by two of the federal district courts,[51] and the IDEA continues to be enforced actively by the federal administrative agencies and by the federal and state courts.

In considering the role of the courts in promoting effective preparation of students for civic participation, analysts should assess from a comparative institutional perspective what functions courts can best undertake, in collaboration with the other branches, to promote necessary changes and improvements. What is needed, therefore, is a "colloquy"[52] among the branches to accomplish this critical task. Such a colloquy should build on the realization that each of the three branches has specific institutional strengths and weaknesses in regard to social policy making and remedial problem solving. The focus, therefore, should be on how the strengths of each of the branches can best be jointly brought to bear on solving critical social problems.

The courts' principled approach to issues and their long-term staying power are essential for providing continuing guidance on constitutional requirements and sustained commitment to meeting constitutional goals. Legislatures, however, are better equipped to develop specific reform policies, and executive agencies are most effective in undertaking the day-to-day implementation tasks of explaining what is required, why it is required, and how it can be done well. When disputes arise on whether specific mechanisms are, in fact, meeting constitutional requirements, judicial fact-finding mechanisms should be invoked because they tend to be more extensive, more objective, and more probing than legislative or administrative fact-finding mechanisms. These were the essential principles that informed my recommendations in the two preceding chapters about the types of remedies state and federal courts should issue to enforce the states' constitutional responsibility to prepare students effectively for civic participation.

Plausibility

Although both state and federal judges do sometimes issue decisions and orders that directly affect policy decisions of the executive and legislative branches, most judges approach the prospect of issuing orders against the coordinate branches with some reluctance, and, as Judge Rosenblatt put it, they do not involve themselves in policy matters "cheerfully." How likely then, are federal or state judges to issue orders enforcing the schools' constitutional obligation to prepare students effectively to be capable citizens if asked to do so? And if they should agree to act in accordance with the types of proposals for judicial action that I recommended in chapters 6 and 7, would federal and state policy makers, educators, and the public at large be receptive to this new assertion of judicial authority?

Judicial Reactions

If presented with a well-conceived complaint and strong evidence justifying enforcement of the schools' constitutional obligation to prepare students to function productively as civic participants, I believe that most judges are likely to understand the issues and the need and to respond positively. Judges, because of their own professional responsibilities, probably have greater awareness of the importance of civic participation than most other people. Their decisions often call upon them to consider and rule upon the functioning of federal state and local public institutions, and they often witness firsthand the importance of competent and active civic participation in our democratic institutions. I came to understand how deeply many judges are concerned about civic participation from my own experience in serving as counsel for the plaintiffs in the *Campaign for Fiscal Equity* (*CFE*) litigation. I was surprised when the New York Court of Appeals, in its initial decision in this case, stated that the "sound basic education" required by the state constitution appeared to mean that the schools must prepare their students "eventually [to] function productively as civic participants capable of voting and serving on a jury."[53] As counsel for plaintiffs I had not suggested or requested such a definition.

Although other state courts had previously stressed the importance of civic participation, none had highlighted voting and jury service as synecdoche for civic participation. I then remembered that Judith Kaye, the chief judge of the New York Court of Appeals, had a particular interest in promoting jury service. Her first action upon attaining that office in 1993 had been to establish "The Jury Project," a reexamination of New York's entire jury system, from enlarging the jury pool to making more effective use of jurors' court time, improving juror compensation, and upgrading dilapidated juror facilities.[54] She had then pressed the legislature to adopt the thoroughgoing reforms that the members of her commission had recommended. The legislature responded by, among other things, eliminating automatic exemptions for doctors, lawyers, mothers, mayors, and governors[55] and making jury service a more satisfying experience for the vastly larger number of citizens who now do serve as jurors.

Judge Kaye had a firm belief that service on a jury was a prime civic responsibility in which all citizens should take part. After she had retired from the bench, I had an opportunity to ask her why the court had put such a strong emphasis on civic participation and on jury service in particular. She answered, "We used the examples of voting and serving on a jury to illustrate what it means to be a productive citizen . . . the concept of the jury is very clear from the civic engagement point of view."[56] One might also speculate that the Court of Appeals' judges had a particular interest in improving the educational preparation of jurors, since a significant part of their time is spent reviewing jury verdicts.

The judges of the New York Court of Appeals are not the only state jurists who are personally committed to promoting civic participation. Tani G. Cantil-Sakauye, Chief Justice of the California Supreme Court, recently established a statewide "civic learning initiative" in order to promote "a broad and far-reaching effort to improve civic awareness, learning, and engagement in California."[57] As part of this effort, she appointed a Task Force on K–12 Civic Learning[58] and a "Power of Democracy Steering Committee" that includes representatives of all three levels of the California courts, the state and local bar associations, as well as state and local education organizations that are also actively supporting the initiative.[59] Cantil-Sakauye also joined the State Superintendent of Public Instruction in establishing an annual Chief Justice's Civic Learning Award that recognizes public high schools for their achievements in civics education.[60]

Court systems in other states have created similar civics education initiatives. For example, the Alaska court system works with local bar associations and other groups to offer "educational programs that help students better understand our legal system and the rights and responsibilities of citizenship." Twice a year, the Arkansas Supreme Court organizes "appeals on wheels" where local students of all ages attend oral arguments and over 100 judges visit classrooms as part of a civics outreach program. Members of the Maryland judiciary take part three times a year in a Civics and Law Academy that engages young people of middle school and high school age in learning about law and civil society.[61] In Boston, students tackle age-appropriate legal issues regarding the Bill of Rights and how constitutional protections apply in public schools, and ultimately try cases in real courtrooms before federal or state judges and juries made up of community members.[62]

Federal judges also actively promote civic preparation. For example, Robert A. Katzmann, chief judge of the federal Second Circuit Court of Appeals, in his 2014 "state of the circuit" address proposed a circuit-wide program of public engagement and civic education designed to bring classes of schoolchildren and individuals of all ages, backgrounds, and experiences into the circuit's courthouses by offering innovative and educational programs and participatory events.[63]

Former U.S. Supreme Justice Sandra Day O'Connor, after retiring from the bench, established an institute that promotes young people's preparation for citizenship. She was motivated by her strong belief that "[s]ecuring the future of our democracy requires teaching the next generation to understand and respect our system of governance, and then passing that knowledge and passion along to the next generation."[64] The Sandra Day O'Connor Institute advances this goal through civics education and leadership development, debates, moderated public discussions, internships, and fellowships[65]—and through a widely distributed web-based education project disseminated by a sister organization created by O'Connor called iCivics. Among other tools, iCivics offers online games that are linked to clear learning objectives and integrated with lesson plans and support materials. The games teach students how the institutions of government work by having them step into the roles of a judge, a member of Congress, a community activist fighting for local change, or even the President of the United States.[66] U.S. Supreme Court Justice Sonia Sotomayor is now a member of the board of iCivics, and Justices Anthony Kennedy and Neil Gorsuch have also evidenced a deep interest in civic education.[67]

As these examples show, many judges have a special interest in promoting civic preparation and civic participation. This recognition may result from judges' regular involvement with cases that require them to think deeply about the functioning of governmental institutions and the importance of citizens' rights. In cases involving constitutional rights, regulatory authority, legislative intent, powers of public officials, voting issues and, of course, in reviewing jury verdicts, judges must constantly review the workings of the American democratic system. Courts' active sponsorship of civic outreach activities is one of judges' best opportunities to communicate to the public their often strongly held beliefs on civic matters. The emphasis on youth education in these programs demonstrates the judges' understanding of the importance of educating students at an early age about their civic opportunities and responsibilities.

Critics of judicial involvement in social policy making often emphasize that, in most of these situations, judges are "generalists" who lack sufficient knowledge and experience to make informed decisions in specialized policy areas.[68] In regard to matters of civic participation, however, judges are specialists by the very nature of their own daily professional experiences. As the broad scope and number of federal and state cases involving equal educational opportunity indicate, judges generally tend to be more involved with cases dealing with public education than with most other social policy areas. Education cases that focus on preparing students for civic participation are even more likely to attract judicial interest and understanding.

Policy Maker, Educator, and Public Reactions

The reactions of policy makers, educators, and the public at large obviously influence compliance with and the effectiveness of court remedies in cases that deal with public policy. The federal courts' attempt to implement *Brown v. Board of Education* during the initial desegregation era met fierce resistance from many policy makers, educators, and white parents.[69] Eventually, southern schools were largely desegregated, in spite of this resistance; however, the battle may have influenced the Supreme Court's subsequent reluctance to continue to press diligently to integrate public schools in the North and the West. State courts have met less resistance from educators and the public in their efforts to promote greater equity and adequacy in school funding, but, in some of these cases also, state legislators have delayed, resisted, or neglected compliance with the courts' orders.[70]

Judicial decrees that courts may issue in cases focused on civic preparation issues are less likely to generate official or public disapproval or resistance. As discussed in chapters 6 and 7, the substance of these decrees would likely be goals, policies, and practices to which most policy makers and most educators already subscribe but have failed to prioritize or to put into actual practice. Many of policy suggestions that I have set forth in this book are also recommended, for example, by the *Guardian of Democracy* report,[71] which has been endorsed by the American Bar Association's Division for Public Education, members of Congress, and a broad array of educators and civic groups. Judicial orders that motivate and oblige schools and states to put into effect policies and practices that they already support are not likely to engender strong opposition.

As noted in chapter 7, most Americans already believe that there is a right to education under the federal constitution. A declaration by the U.S. Supreme Court that makes that perception a legal reality in the context of ensuring schools adequately prepare their students for capable citizenship would likely be welcomed. The public at large strongly supports the concept of civic education,[72] and the constitutional imprimatur that preparation for citizenship would gain by affirmative declarations and enforcement actions by the U.S. Supreme Court and the state courts would energize many citizens to demand that policy makers and educators put in place the schooling reforms that are necessary to prepare all students properly for civic participation.

Throughout this book I have emphasized civic preparation policies and practices that relate directly to contemporary needs. I have also emphasized that schools and courts need to develop policies and practices that resonate with the experiences and civic needs of students from all races, religions, genders, economic classes, and sexual orientations, and that this can be done in a manner that respects, but transcends, ideological differences. Civic education that is implemented in this way can orient many more students to approach the kinds of political issues they will confront as voters with knowledge and critical judgment, and to engage with others who have differing views with greater understanding and empathy.

Strong judicial endorsements of civic values like tolerance of opinions with which one disagrees, the importance of deliberative democracy, and an emphasis on factual accuracy can positively affect the civic capacities of the current generation of students as they come of age. Such judicial action might also have an immediate ameliorative impact on political polarization and use of misleading and false information to further political ends by bringing to the fore the realization that democratic institutions cannot be sustained without their citizens' active, intelligent civic involvement and by inspiring the public to demand that the media and our politicians begin to act in accordance with these understandings. In this way, schools in our time could truly become, in the words of former Supreme Court Justice Felix Frankfurter, "the most powerful agency for promoting cohesion among a heterogeneous democratic people."[73]

A constructive dialogue on preparation for civic participation inspired by the courts might also lead to a broader understanding that to maintain our democracy the United States ultimately will have to confront "the importance of [eliminating] status hierarchies or significant disparities of resources."[74] A sustainable democracy must, to a large extent, be a well-functioning community. Meaningful civic participation requires that all citizens have the minimal economic means and the basic social supports they need to develop social trust and a sense of efficacy that enables and motivates them to participate effectively in political and civic affairs.[75] The huge economic gaps that currently exist between the haves and the have-nots in our society create economic instability and racial resentments and allow for a small elite to dominate political institutions. These patterns are incompatible with the maintenance of a viable democratic culture. Judicial decrees that promote provisions for civic preparation and the broader dialogues that they inspire may also cause many more citizens and political leaders to reflect and act upon these fundamental realities.

Notes

Introduction

1. Fake news was so prevalent during the presidential campaign that in the final three months, the top-performing fake election news stories on Facebook generated more engagement than the top twenty stories from major news outlets, such as *New York Times*, *Washington Post*, *Huffington Post*, and NBC News. Craig Silverman, *This Analysis Shows How Fake Election News Stories Outperformed Real News on Facebook*, BuzzFeed News (Nov. 16, 2016), https://www.buzzfeed.com/craigsilverman/viral-fake-election-news-outperformed-real-news-on-facebook?utm_term=.faXvML98g#.sx2WOgVv7. Reliance on false information and reluctance or inertia to overcome it has been a major factor in American politics for decades. *See* Jennifer L. Hochschild & Katherine Levine Einstein, Do Facts Matter? Information and Misinformation in American Politics (2015).

2. Justice Sandra Day O'Connor, foreword to Campaign for Civic Mission of the Schools, No Excuse: Eleven Schools and Districts That Make Preparing for Citizenship a Priority and How Others Can Do It Too 5 (2010), *available at* https://www.americanbar.org/content/dam/aba/migrated/publiced/LabReport_Booklet_August_2010.authcheckdam.pdf.

3. Remarks of Frederick Hess, director of education policy studies at the American Enterprise Institute at Teachers College symposium *Education: The Public Good or the Individual Good: A Conversation About the Next Four Years*, Teachers College, Columbia University (Mar. 24, 2017). For analyses of the plight and accumulated resentments of the white working class, *see* Justin Gest, The New Minority: White Working Class Politics in an Age of Immigration and Inequality (2016); J.D. Vance, Hillbilly Elegy: A Memoir of a Family and Culture in Crisis (2016); Arlie Russell Hochschild, Strangers in Their Own Land: Anger and Mourning on the American Right

(2016); THOMAS FRANK, WHAT'S THE MATTER WITH KANSAS: HOW CONSERVATIVES WON THE HEART OF AMERICA (2004).

4. GABRIEL A. ALMOND & SIDNEY VERBA, THE CIVIC CULTURE: POLITICAL ATTITUDES AND DEMOCRACY IN FIVE NATIONS 9 (1963).

5. Alan Taylor, *The Virtue of an Educated Voter*, AM. SCHOLAR, Autumn 2016, at 18–27, *available at* https://theamericanscholar.org/the-virtue-of-an-educated-voter/#.

6. Lorraine M. McDonnell, *Defining Democratic Purposes*, *in* REDISCOVERING THE DEMOCRATIC PURPOSES OF EDUCATION 1, 2 (Lorraine M. McDonnell, P. Michael Timpane & Roger Benjamin eds., 2000).

7. Quoted in STEVE FARKAS & ANN M. DUFFETT, HIGH SCHOOLS, CIVICS AND CITIZENSHIP: WHAT SOCIAL STUDIES TEACHERS THINK AND DO (AM. ENTER. INST., Sept. 2010), at 1, *available at* https://www.aei.org/wp-content/uploads/2014/09/High-Schools-Civics-Citizenship-Full-Report.pdf.

8. There has been a decline in the number and frequency of civics professional development programs that are available to civics educators and in funding both for teachers to attend and for providers to offer appropriate professional development programs. *See* REBECCA BURGESS, CIVIC EDUCATION PROFESSIONAL DEVELOPMENT: THE LAY OF THE LAND (AM. ENTER. INST., Mar. 2015), at 1, *available at* https://www.aei.org/wp-content/uploads/2015/03/Civics-Education-Professional-Development.pdf.

9. FARKAS & DUFFETT, *supra* note 7, at 3.

10. This performance level was not significantly different from the results in 2010. *See New Results Show Eighth Graders' Knowledge of U.S. History, Geography, and Civics*, THE NATION'S REPORT CARD, *available at* https://www.nationsreportcard.gov/hgc_2014/#.

11. *See, e.g.*, ROBERT PUTNAM, BOWLING ALONE: THE COLLAPSE AND REVIVAL OF AMERICAN COMMUNITY 254 (2000).

12. *See, e.g.*, DIANA E. HESS, CONTROVERSY IN THE CLASSROOM: THE DEMOCRATIC POWER OF DISCUSSION 35 (2009).

13. *See, e.g.*, DIANA C. MUTZ, HEARING THE OTHER SIDE: DELIBERATIVE VERSUS PARTICIPATION DEMOCRACY (2006).

14. *See, e.g.*, MICHAEL A. REBELL, JESSICA R. WOLFF & JOSEPH R. ROGERS, JR., DEFICIENT RESOURCES: AN ANALYSIS OF THE AVAILABILITY OF BASIC EDUCATIONAL RESOURCES IN HIGH-NEEDS SCHOOLS IN EIGHT NEW YORK STATE SCHOOL DISTRICTS (CAMPAIGN FOR EDUC. EQUITY, 2012), http://www.equitycampaign.org/publications/essential-and-deficient-resources/.

15. *See, e.g.*, RICHARD WEISSBOURD, THE PARENTS WE MEAN TO BE: HOW WELL INTENTIONED ADULTS UNDERMINE CHILDREN'S MORAL AND EMOTIONAL DEVELOPMENT 116 (2009); WILLIAM DAMON, FAILING LIBERTY: HOW WE ARE LEAVING YOUNG AMERICANS UNPREPARED FOR CITIZENSHIP IN A FREE SOCIETY (2011).

16. *See* Ioana Literati & Neta Kliger-Vilenchik, *Formative Events, Networked Spaces, and the Political Socialization of Youth*, *in* A NETWORKED SELF: BIRTH, LIFE, DEATH (Zizi Papacharissi ed., forthcoming 2018). *See also* HENRY JENKINS ET AL., CONFRONTING THE CHALLENGES OF PARTICIPATORY CULTURE: MEDIA EDUCATION FOR THE 21ST CENTURY 10 (2006), *available at* https://www.macfound.org/media/article_pdfs/JENKINS_WHITE_PAPER.PDF.

17. *See, e.g.*, MEIRA LEVINSON, NO CITIZEN LEFT BEHIND (2012).

18. Richard D. Kahlenberg & Clifford Janey, *Putting Democracy Back Into Public Education* 13 (CENTURY FOUND., 2016), *available at* https://s3-us-west-2.amazonaws.com/production.tcf.org/app/uploads/2016/11/10195924/Putting-Democracy-Back-into-Public-Education1.pdf (citing Pew Research Center findings). The authors also point out that the polarization among voters in the United States is becoming increasingly pronounced. In the presidential election of 1976, 27 percent of voters lived in so-called landslide counties—counties in which the winning presidential candidate won by twenty points or more. By the 2004 election, that number had reached 48 percent. *Id.* at 6. For an insightful discussion of the role Fox News has played in developing these tendencies, *see* Marc S. Tucker, *Trump, Fox News, and Educating the American Voter*, EDUC. WK., Sept. 21, 2016, at 20, 24. President Barack Obama quipped, "If I watched Fox, *I* wouldn't vote for me," quoted in David Remnick, *It Happened Here*, NEW YORKER, Nov. 28, 2016, 54, at 58.

19. STANFORD HISTORY EDUC. GRP., EVALUATING INFORMATION: THE CORNERSTONE OF CIVIC ONLINE REASONING 4 (2016).

20. *Id.* at 5. "Last year, Leu's New Literacies Research Lab at the University of Connecticut found that fewer than 4% of 7th graders could correctly identify the author of online science information, evaluate that author's expertise and point of view, and make informed judgments about the overall reliability of the site they were reading." Benjamin Herold, *Fake News' Bogus Tweets Raise Stakes for Media Literacy*, EDUC. WK., Dec. 8, 2015, at 12, *available at* http://www.edweek.org/ew/articles/2016/12/08/fake-news-bogus-tweets-raise-stakes-for.html. There also appears to be a substantial gap in online reading skills based on income inequality. *See* Donald J. Leu et al., *The New Literacies of Online Research and Comprehension: Rethinking the Reading Achievement Gap*, 50 READING RES. Q. 37–59 (2015).

21. Sam Wineburg & Sarah McGrew, *Why Students Can't Google Their Way to the Truth*, EDUC. WK., Nov. 1, 2016, at 11, 22, 28, *available at* http://www.edweek.org/ew/articles/2016/11/02/why-students-cant-google-their-way-to.html.

22. *See, e.g.*, N.D. CONST. art. VIII, § 1: "A high degree of intelligence, patriotism, integrity and morality on the part of every voter in a government by the people being necessary in order to insure the continuance of that government and the prosperity and happiness of the people, the legislative assembly shall make provision for the establishment and maintenance of a system of pub-

lic schools which shall be open to all children of the state of North Dakota and free from sectarian control." *See also* N.H. CONST. pt. 2, art. 83: "Knowledge and learning, generally diffused through a community, being essential to the preservation of a free government; and spreading the opportunities and advantages of education through the various parts of the country, being highly conducive to promote this end; it shall be the duty of the legislators and magistrates, in all future periods of this government, to cherish the interest of literature and the sciences, and all seminaries and public schools."

23. Campbell Cty. Sch. Dist. v. State, 907 P.2d 1238, 1259 (Wyo. 1995).

24. Campaign for Fiscal Equity, Inc. v. State, 801 N.E.2d 326, 332 (N.Y. 2003).

25. Rose v. Council for Better Educ., 790 S.W.2d 186, 212 (Ky. 1989). The California Supreme Court has also emphasized the importance of civic education in the electronic age: "With the rise of the electronic media and the development of sophisticated techniques of political propaganda and mass marketing, education plays an increasingly critical role in fostering 'those habits of open-mindedness and critical inquiry which alone make for responsible citizens, who, in turn, make possible an enlightened and effective public opinion. . . . Without high quality education, the populace will lack the knowledge, self-confidence, and critical skills to evaluate independently the pronouncements of pundits and political leaders." Hartzell v. Connell, 679 P.2d 35, 41 (Cal. 1984) (citations omitted).

26. Brown v. Bd. of Educ., 347 U.S. 483, 493 (1954).

27. Tinker v. Des Moines Indep. Sch. Dist., 393 U.S. 503, 507 (1969).

28. Plyler v. Doe, 457 U.S. 202, 221 (1982).

29. Sch. Dist. of Abington Twp. v. Schempp, 374 U.S. 203, 230 (1963) (Brennan, J., concurring).

30. KAHLENBERG & JANEY, *supra* note 18, at 14. "Just as Soviet technological advances triggered investment in science education in the 1950s, the 2016 election should spur renewed emphasis on the need for schools to instill an appreciation for liberal democratic values." *Id.*

31. Erika Kitzmiller, *Donald Trump and Teaching in a Democracy: Where Did We Go Wrong?* HECHINGER REP., Nov. 28, 2016, *available at* http://hechingerreport.org/donald-trump-teaching-democracy-go-wrong/.

32. Pierce v. Society of Sisters, 268 U.S. 510 (1925).

33. Rodriguez v. San Antonio Indep. Sch. Dist., 411 U.S. 1 (1973).

Chapter One

1. Theda Skocpol et al., *How Americans Became Civic*, *in* CIVIC ENGAGEMENT IN AMERICAN DEMOCRACY 27, 43 (Theda Skocpol & Morris P. Fiorina eds., 1999).

2. LAWRENCE A. CREMIN, AMERICAN EDUCATION: THE NATIONAL EXPERIENCE, 1783–1876 (1980).

3. For the original colonists, the move to the New World dislodged traditional cultural moorings, and education became less of a private family responsibility and more of a broad communal function. In traditional European society, grammar school education—limited generally to bourgeois and aristocratic families—was primarily the responsibility of the patriarchal family, and home education was the assumed educational mode. *See* Frank Musgrove, *The Decline of the Educative Family*, UNIVERSITAS Q. 377, 391–92 (1969).

4. DAVID MCCULLOUGH, JOHN ADAMS 364 (1995).

5. THOMAS JEFFERSON, *The University of Virginia*, *in* THE COMPLETE JEFFERSON 1097 (S. Padover ed., 1943) (1818).

6. RICHARD ROTHSTEIN, REBECCA JACOBSEN & TAMARA WILDER, GRADING EDUCATION: GETTING ACCOUNTABILITY RIGHT 14 (2008). *See also* Kevin Ryan, *Lost in the Cave: Citizenship and the Decline of Public Education*, 29 Vt. B.J. 7, 9 (2004) ("In general, the founders imagined political education to be more a matter of habituation, of character formation, than of intellectual training").

7. M.J. Hirschland & S. Steinmo, *Correcting the Record: Understanding the History of Federal Intervention and Failure in Securing U.S. Educational Reform*, 17 EDUC. POL'Y 343 (2003).

8. MASS. CONST. pt. 2, ch. 5, § 2.

9. Alan Taylor, *The Virtue of an Educated Voter*, AM. SCHOLAR, Autumn 2016, *available at* https://theamericanscholar.org/the-virtue-of-an-educated-voter/#.

10. Brigham v. State, 692 A.2d 384, 392 (Vt. 1997). *See also id.* at 393: "Thus understood, the Education Clause assumes paramount significance in the constitutional frame of government established by the framers: it expressed and incorporated 'that part of republican theory which holds education essential to self-government and which recognizes government as the source of the perpetuation of the attributes of citizenship."

11. MOSES MATHER, AMERICA'S APPEAL TO THE IMPERIAL WORLD (1775), *quoted in* GORDON S. WOOD, THE CREATION OF THE AMERICAN REPUBLIC, 1776–1787, 120 (1969).

12. KARL KAESTLE, PILLARS OF THE REPUBLIC: COMMON SCHOOLS AND AMERICAN SOCIETY 1780–1860, 13 (1983).

13. PA. CONST. of 1776, § 44. North Carolina and Vermont had similar language. *See* N.C. CONST. of 1776, § XLI, *and* VT. CONST. of 1777, ch. II, § XL.

14. An act to provide for the instruction of youth and the promotion of good education. Mass. Stats. 1789, c. 19. Similarly, during the eighteenth century, New Hampshire required every town with fifty households or more to provide a schoolmaster to teach children to read and write, and every town of one hundred households to maintain a grammar school. 2 LAWS OF N.H., Province Period, 336–37 (1702–1745).

15. Kaestle, *supra* note 12, at 10.

16. Skocpol et al., *supra* note 1, at 39.

17. Alexis de Tocqueville, Democracy in America 523 (J.P. Mayer ed., 1969) (1835).

18. Kaestle, *supra* note 12, at 23–25, 63–66, 69.

19. Cremin, *supra* note 2, at 138.

20. Horace Mann, Lectures on Education vii (1855). Mann and the other founders of the common school movement took note of developments at the time regarding state-administered school systems in the Netherlands and in Prussia. *See* Charles C. Glenn, The Myth of the Common School (1988), but the concept of a public school system rooted in republican values, operated through a local participatory structure, yet subject to overall state regulation was a uniquely American innovation.

21. Quoted in Michael C. Johanek, *Preparing Pluribus for Unum: Historical Perspectives on Civic Education*, *in* Making Civics Count: Citizenship Education for a New Generation (David E. Campbell, Meira Levinson & Frederick M. Hess eds., 2012), at 59.

22. *Id.* at 61.

23. John Dewey, Democracy and Education: An Introduction to the Philosophy of Education (1935).

24. John Dewey, *Social Purposes in Education*, *in* 15 The Middle Works, 1899–1924 (J. Boydston ed., 1983).

25. Educ. Poly's Comm'n, Am. Ass'n of Sch. Admins. & Nat'l Educ. Ass'n, The Purposes of Education in American Democracy 16 (1938). *See also* Tom Brokaw, The Greatest Generation (1998) (describing the patriotic and civic motivations of those who fought in World War II and shaped postwar cultural and educational goals).

26. U.S. Dep't of Educ., Advancing Civic Learning and Engagement in Democracy: A Road Map and Call to Action 1 (2012).

27. *New Results Show Eighth Graders' Knowledge of U.S. History, Geography, and Civics*, The Nation's Report Card, *available at* https://www.nationsreportcard.gov/hgc_2014/#. The NAEP civics assessment is designed to measure the intellectual and participatory skills students need to face the challenges of public life in a constitutional democracy. Central among these are the ability to describe, explain, and analyze information and arguments, and to evaluate, take, and defend positions on public issues. The third area of the assessment, civic dispositions and participatory skills, refers to the rights and responsibilities of citizens as members of society. *Id.* Students who are proficient "demonstrate solid academic performance and competency over challenging subject matter." In 2014, 51 percent of students functioned at a "basic" level of civic understanding on the NAEP exam. Both the "proficiency" and the "basic" statistics have not changed much since 1998.

28. CAMPAIGN FOR THE CIVIC MISSION OF THE SCHOOLS ET AL., GUARDIAN OF DEMOCRACY: THE CIVIC MISSION OF SCHOOLS 14 (2011). Another recent survey revealed the following:

- While little more than a third of respondents (36 percent) could name all three branches of the U.S. government, just as many (35 percent) could not name a single one.
- Just over a quarter of Americans (27 percent) know that it takes a two-thirds vote of the House and Senate to override a presidential veto.
- One in five Americans (21 percent) incorrectly thinks that a 5–4 Supreme Court decision is sent back to Congress for reconsideration.

Survey of 1,416 adults conducted by the Civics Renewal Network, released on Constitution Day, Sept. 17, 2014, *available at* http://cdn.annenbergpublicpolicycenter.org/wp-content/uploads/Civics-survey-press-release-09-17-2014-for-PR-Newswire.pdf. Similarly, a recent report of the New York State Bar Association reported that more than half of Americans asked (57 percent) couldn't name a single current justice on the U.S. Supreme Court, only 27 percent of Americans knew the Bill of Rights expressly prohibits establishing an official religion in the United States, and 75 percent of high school seniors were unable to name one power granted to Congress. N.Y. ST. BAR ASS'N, REPORT AND RECOMMENDATIONS OF THE LAW, YOUTH AND CITIZENSHIP COMMITTEE ON CIVIC EDUCATION (2013), *available at* http://www.nysba.org/LYCcivicsReport2014.

29. ILYA SOMIN, DEMOCRACY AND POLITICAL IGNORANCE: WHY SMALLER GOVERNMENT IS SMARTER 24 (2016).

30. Liav Orgad, *Creating New Americans: The Essence of Americanism Under the Citizenship Test*, 47 HOUS. L. REV. 1227, 1265 (2011).

31. MICHAEL X. DELLI CARPINI & SCOTT KEETER, WHAT AMERICANS KNOW ABOUT POLITICS AND WHY IT MATTERS 157 (1996).

32. *Id.* at 219. Other studies indicate that "the relationship between education and civic engagement is a curvilinear one of increasing returns. The last two years of college make twice as much difference to trust and group membership as the first two years of high school." Robert Putnam, *Tuning In, Tuning Out: The Strange Disappearance of Social Capital in America*, 28 POL. SCI. & POLS. 664, 667 (1995). *See also* Thomas S. Dee, *Are There Civic Returns to Education?,* 88 J. PUB. ECON 1697–720 (2004) (correlating years of schooling with voting, group membership, and attitudes toward free speech).

33. NAT'L VOTER ELECTION PROJECT, VOTER TURNOUT, *available at* http://www.electproject.org/home/voter-turnout/demographics.

34. *Id.*

35. THOMAS FILE, YOUNG-ADULT VOTING: AN ANALYSIS OF PRESIDENTIAL

Elections, 1964–2012, U.S. Census Bureau 2 (2014), *available at* https://www.census.gov/prod/2014pubs/p20-573.pdf.

36. Quoted in Ariel Edwards-Levy, *Millennials Really Don't Think Everybody Should Vote*, Huffington Post, May 8, 2015, http://www.huffingtonpost.com/2014/11/21/young-voters_n_6200852.html.

37. Brennan Ctr. for Justice, Better Ballots 9 (2008), *available at* http://www.brennancenter.org/sites/default/files/legacy/Democracy/Better%20Ballots.pdf (discussing the notorious "butterfly" ballots used in Florida in the 2000 presidential election and stating that not only on that occasion but "all too often," tens and hundreds of thousands of votes are miscast because of voters' failure to understand ballot instructions).

38. A.N. Farley, M.N. Gaertner & M.S. Moses, *Democracy Under Fire: Voter Confusion and Influences in Colorado's Anti-Affirmative Action Initiative*, 83 Harv. Educ. Rev. 432 (2013).

39. Bob Egelko, *Many Snub Call to Serve Jury Duty*, S.F. Chron., May 13, 2015, at D1.

40. McCormick Tribune Found., Civic Engagement in Our Democracy 6 (2007), *available at* http://documents.mccormickfoundation.org/publications/civicdisengagement.pdf.

41. *Id.*

42. "People who participate in organizations receive training for participation within the organization, and this training is then transferable to the political sphere." Gabriel A. Almond & Sidney Verba, The Civic Culture: Political Attitudes and Democracy in Five Nations 256 (1963).

43. Robert Putnam, Bowling Alone: The Collapse and Revival of American Community 254 (2000).

44. *Id.* at 45.

45. *Id.* at 46.

46. *Id.* at 254. Surveys of political interest and political knowledge reflect the same patterns of decline. For example, a study of first-year college students found that in 1998, 26.7 percent thought that "keeping up with political affairs" was very important, compared with 57.8 percent in 1966. *See* Henry Milner, Civic Literacy: How Informed Citizens Make Democracy Work 48 (2002).

47. Thomas Rotolo, *Trends in Voluntary Association Participation*, 28 Nonprofit & Voluntary Sector Q. 199 (1999).

48. Jeffrey M. Berry, *The Rise of Civic Groups*, in Civic Engagement in American Democracy, *supra* note 1.

49. Danielle Allen, *Social Capital and the Art of Association* (unpublished manuscript) (on file with author).

50. Megan O'Neil, *American's Engagement with Organizations Wanes, Report Says*, Chron. Philanthropy, Dec. 17, 2014, *available at* https://philanthropy.com/article/Americans-Engagement-With/152055. Note also that

between the late 1990s and 2017, membership in the Boy Scouts plummeted from nearly 4.6 million to 2.3 million. Alan Blinder & Mitch Smith, *After Trump Injects Politics Into Speech, Boy Scouts Face Blowback*, N.Y. Times, July 26, 2017, at A13.

51. Miller McPherson, Lynn Smith-Lovin & Matthew E. Brashears, *Social Isolation in America: Changes in Core Discussion Networks Over Two Decades* 71 Am. Soc. Rev. 353 (2006).

52. Roberto Stefan Foa & Yascha Mounk, *The Democratic Disconnect*, 27 J. Democracy 5, 7–8 (2016), *available at* http://www.journalofdemocracy.org/sites/default/files/Foa%26Mounk-27-3.pdf. This study also found that "in 2011, 24 percent of U.S. millennials (then in their late teens or early twenties) considered democracy to be a 'bad' or 'very bad' way of running the country." *Id.*

53. Pamela Paxton, *Is Social Capital Declining in the United States? A Multiple Indicator Assessment*, 105 Am. J. Soc. 88 (1999).

54. Alan Wolfe, *Is Civic Society Obsolete?*, *in* Community Works: The Revival of Civil Society in America 17, 22 (E.J. Dionne, Jr., ed., 1998). Wolfe notes that some of the change during this period stems from the dramatic expansion into the workforce of women, who traditionally carried out much of the work of civic associations. *Id.* at 20.

55. Theda Skocpol, *Don't Blame Big Government*, *in* Community Works: The Revival of Civil Society in America, *supra* note 54, at 37, 42–43.

56. Meira Levinson, No Citizen Left Behind (2012). Seth Andrew, founder of Democracy Prep, a group of charter schools in Harlem, agrees that there is such a gap. He describes the reasons for it as follows: "Low-income adults tend to participate in politics at much lower rates than more affluent citizens, trust government less, and have a weaker sense of political efficacy. Because low-income parents often lack these prerequisites for engaged civic life, they are less likely to pass on expectations for active citizenship and political participation to their children. What is more, less active parents may even pass on a real mistrust of government and sense of powerlessness, both of which can depress any attachment to civic life in their children." Quoted in Daniel Lautzenheiser & Andrew P. Kelly, Charter Schools as Nation Builders: Democracy Prep and Civic Education 4 (Am. Enter. Inst. 2013).

57. Nat'l Ctr. for Educ. Stats., *2014 National Assessment for Educational Progress* (2014), *available at* http://www.nationsreportcard.gov/reading_math_2015/#reading?grade=4.

58. Nat'l Ctr. for Educ. Stats., *2014 Civics Assessment: Achievement Levels* (2014), *available at* https://nationsreportcard.gov/hgc_2014/#civics/achievement. Hispanic students also scored at markedly lower levels. For example, only 12 percent achieved a proficient level in civics compared to 32 percent of white, non-Hispanic students, and only 8 percent reached proficiency in U.S. history, compared with 26 percent of white, non-Hispanic students. *See* Nat'l Ctr. for Educ.

STATS., *2014 History Assessment: Achievement Levels* (2014), *available at* https://nationsreportcard.gov/hgc_2014/#history/achievement.

59. Joseph Kahne & Ellen Middaugh, *Democracy for Some: The Civic Opportunity Gap in High School* (Ctr. for Info. & Res. on Civic Learning & Engagement, Working Paper No. 59, 2008). African American students also have less access to extracurricular activities that have an important influence in shaping civic participation skills. *See* Kaisa Snellman, Jennifer M. Silva, Carl B. Frederick & Robert D. Putnam, *The Engagement Gap: Social Mobility and Extracurricular Participation Among American Youth*, 657 ANNALS AM. ACAD. POL. & SOC. SCI. 194–207 (2015), *available at* http://ann.sagepub.com/content/657/1/194.full.pdf+html.

60. Quoted in DANIEL LAUTZENHEISER & ANDREW P. KELLY, CHARTER SCHOOLS AS NATION BUILDERS: DEMOCRACY PREP AND CIVIC EDUCATION (Am. Enter. Inst. 2013).

61. *See, e.g.*, SONYA HORSFORD, LEARNING IN A BURNING HOUSE: EDUCATIONAL INEQUALITY, IDEOLOGY AND (DIS)INTEGRATION (2011) (describing the continuing vestiges of segregation and failed experiences with desegregation); BARRY A. GOLD, STILL SEPARATE AND UNEQUAL: SEGREGATION AND THE FUTURE OF URBAN SCHOOL REFORM (2007) (study of impact on student achievement of negative administrator and teacher attitudes).

62. David Yaeger et al., *Loss of Institutional Trust Among Racial and Ethnic Minority Adolescents: A Consequence of Procedural Injustice and a Cause of Life-Span Outcomes*, 88 (2017). Gimpel and Pearson-Merkowitz also reported higher levels of cynicism about the government among African American and Latino youth: "Without question, much of the distrust and scorn of the system we have seen expressed stems from attitudes developed toward law enforcement authorities. Some of it was also anchored in the experience of unequal treatment by local government authorities when it came to public policy. . . . For many low-income minorities, even welfare program experience provide unpleasant points of reference from which to generalize about how government works." James G. Gimpel & Shanna Pearson-Merkowitz, *Policies for Civic Engagement Beyond the Schoolyard*, *in* ENGAGING YOUNG PEOPLE IN CIVIC LIFE 86–87 (James Youniss & Peter Levine eds., 2009).

63. LEVINSON, *supra* note 56, at 27–28. Skeptical or cynical reactions to the events of 9/11 were not limited to low-income African American students. Ta-Nehisi Coates, a distinguished African American writer, described his immediate reaction to the destruction of the twin towers in New York City on that day in the following terms: "I was out of sync with the city. I kept thinking about how southern Manhattan had always been Ground Zero for us. They auctioned our bodies down there, in that same devastated, and rightly named financial district. . . . I did know that Bin Laden was not the first man to bring terror to that section of the city." TA-NEHISI COATES, BETWEEN THE WORLD AND ME 86–87 (2015).

64. LEVINSON, *supra* note 56, at 28.

65. *Id.* at 37.

66. *Id.* at 41. Alienation of undocumented students also has a multiplier effect, since these students tend to serve as civic lifelines for their families who rely on public schools to develop their civic knowledge. *See* J. Rogers, M. Saunders, V. Terriquez & V. Velez, *Civil Lessons: Public Schools and the Civic Development of Undocumented Students and Parents*, 3 NW. J. SOC. POL'Y 203 (2008).

67. Madeline Will found shortly after the election that "educators have pointed out a 'Trump effect' in schools: a spike in anxiety among students of color, particularly immigrant students and students from immigrants families, which teachers have attributed to the Republican candidate's inflammatory words about Muslim and Mexican immigration." Madeline Will, *After Election, Students Express a Mix of Emotions*, EDUC. WK., Nov. 14, 2016, *available at* http://www.edweek.org/ew/articles/2016/11/16/after-election-students-express-a-mix-of.html.

68. Thomas File, *Who Votes? Congressional Elections and the American Electorate: 1978–2014* 4 (U.S. Census Bureau 2015), *available at* http://www.census.gov/content/dam/Census/library/publications/2015/demo/p20-577.pdf. In presidential years, the percentage of eligible Hispanics voting has also been consistently well below the non-Hispanic white percentage (48 percent versus 64.1 percent in 2012), but in the Obama election in 2012, the percentage of eligible blacks voting actually surpassed that of whites (66.2 percent versus 64.1 percent). In 2000, in contrast, 61.8 percent of eligible white voters went to the polls versus 56.8 percent of eligible blacks. Thomas File, *The Diversifying Electorate—Voting Rates by Race and Hispanic Origin in 2012 (and Other Recent Elections)* (U.S. CENSUS BUREAU 2013), *available at* https://www.census.gov/prod/2013pubs/p20-568.pdf.

69. Study quoted in Joseph Kahne & Ellen Middaugh, *Democracy for Some: The Civic Opportunity Gap in High School*, *in* ENGAGING YOUNG PEOPLE IN CIVIC LIFE 30 (James Youniss & Peter Levine eds., 2009).

70. SANDRA COLBY & JENNIFER ORTMAN, *Projections of the Size and Composition of the U.S. Population: 2014–2016* (U.S. CENSUS BUREAU 2015), *available at* https://www.census.gov/content/dam/Census/library/publications/2015/demo/p25-1143.pdf.

71. PUTNAM, *supra* note 43, at 277. Putnam also estimated that suburbanization, commuting, and sprawl explained 10 percent of the decline; electronic entertainment, 25 percent; and generational change (which appears to involve virtually all of the other factors already cited), 50 percent. *Id.* at 283.

72. Mary Ann Glendon, *Introduction: Forgotten Questions*, *in* SEEDBEDS OF VIRTUE: SOURCES OF COMPETENCE, CHARACTER & CITIZENSHIP IN AMERICAN SOCIETY 2 (Mary Ann Glendon & David Blankenhorn eds., 1995)

73. *Id.* at 3. *See also* CHRISTOPHER WOLFE, THE FAMILY, CIVIL SOCIETY, AND

THE STATE ix (1998) discussing the *substantial though indirect* effects of the quality of family life on the well-being of the nation").

74. Brady Hamilton, Joyce Martin & Stephanie Ventura, *Births: Preliminary Data for 2012*, NAT'L VITAL STATS. REP., Sept. 6, 2013, *available at* https://www.cdc.gov/nchs/data/nvsr/nvsr62/nvsr62_03.pdf.

75. WILLIAM DAMON, FAILING LIBERTY: HOW WE ARE LEAVING YOUNG AMERICANS UNPREPARED FOR CITIZENSHIP IN A FREE SOCIETY 30–31 (2011). *See also* MITCH PEARLSTEIN, FROM FAMILY COLLAPSE TO AMERICA'S DECLINE (2011).

76. DAMON, *supra* note 75, at ch. 2. *See also* ROBERT PUTNAM, OUR KIDS: THE AMERICAN DREAM IN CRISIS (2015) (setting forth case studies of the "troubled, isolated, hopeless" lives of working-class children growing up in dysfunctional contemporary families); RICHARD WEISSBOURD, THE PARENTS WE MEAN TO BE: HOW WELL-INTENTIONED ADULTS UNDERMINE CHILDREN'S MORAL AND EMOTIONAL DEVELOPMENT (2010) (arguing that parents' intense focus on their children's happiness undermines moral messages and is turning many children into self-involved, fragile conformists).

77. LINDA C. MCCLAIN, THE PLACE OF FAMILIES: FOSTERING CAPACITY, EQUALITY AND RESPONSIBILITY (2006).

78. William Meezan & Jonathan Rauch, *Gay Marriage, Same Sex Parenting, and America's Children*, 15 MARRIAGE & CHILD WELLBEING 97 (2005), *available at* https://www.princeton.edu/futureofchildren/publications/journals/article/index.xml?journalid=37&articleid=108§ionid=699&submit.

79. DAMON, *supra* note 75, at 65.

80. Jeffrey M. Jones, *Confidence in U.S. Institutions Still Below Historical Norms*, GALLUP (June 15, 2015), *available at* http://www.gallup.com/poll/183593/confidence-institutions-below-historical-norms.aspx. "Historical averages" are based on all years Gallup asked about attitudes toward institutions, which generally were from 1973 to 1993.

81. *See, e.g.*, Robert Wuthnow, *Mobilizing Civic Engagement: The Changing Impact of Religious Involvement, in* CIVIC ENGAGEMENT IN AMERICAN DEMOCRACY, *supra* note 1 at 331.

82. *Religion*, GALLUP, *available at* http://www.gallup.com/poll/1690/religion.aspx. Of those surveyed in 2016, 41 percent had "a great deal" or "a lot" of confidence in organized religion in 2016, compared to 66 percent in 1985. *Id.*

83. MARK CHAVES, AMERICAN RELIGION: CONTEMPORARY TRENDS (2011). Chaves notes that "religious involvement is softening because one of the most religiously involved demographic groups- married couples with children- is shrinking as a proportion of American society." *Id.* at 53.

84. RUSSELL DALTON, THE GOOD CITIZEN: HOW A YOUNGER GENERATION IS RE-SHAPING AMERICAN POLITICS (rev. ed. 2009).

85. PUTNAM, *supra* note 43, at 283.

86. *Id.* at 216.

87. *Id.* at 218. Henry Milner further substantiates the significance of the shift from newspaper reading to television viewing: "A number of studies have found that what is learned is qualitatively different in the two types of media. Studies have shown that adults remember more from a print account than from a comparable television presentation. More generally . . . a high amount of TV viewing is linked to low concentration and cognitive effort, and is thus inimical to learning." HENRY MILNER, CIVIC LITERACY: HOW INFORMED CITIZENS MAKE DEMOCRACY WORK 92 (2002).

88. *Id.* at 220.

89. Between 1990 and 2010, newspaper readership continued to decline, with the number of weekday readers dropping from 62.6 million to 44.1 million. PEW RESEARCH CTR., *The State of the News Media 2015* (2015), *available at* http://www.journalism.org/files/2015/04/FINAL-STATE-OF-THE-NEWS-MEDIA.pdf. "In local TV, . . . sports, weather and traffic now account on average for 40% of the content produced on the newscasts studied while story lengths shrink. On CNN, the cable channel that has branded itself around deep reporting, produced story packages were cut nearly in half from 2007 to 2012." PEW RESEARCH CTR., *The State of the News Media 2013* (2013), *available at* http://www.stateofthemedia.org/2013/overview-5.

90. Emma Green, *Young People Are Fleeing TV as a Main Source of News*, ATLANTIC, Aug. 16, 2013, *available at* http://www.theatlantic.com/business/archive/2013/08/young-people-are-fleeing-tv-as-a-main-source-of-news/278781.

91. Mark Hugo Lopez, Peter Levine, Kenneth Dautrich & David Yalof, *Schools, Education Policy, and the Future of the First Amendment*, 26 POL. COMM. 84, 86 (2009).

92. Catherine O'Donnell, *New Study Quantifies Use of Social Media in Arab Spring*, UNIV. WASH. NEWS, Sept. 12, 2011, *available at* http://www.washington.edu/news/2011/09/12/new-study-quantifies-use-of-social-media-in-arab-spring.

93. PETER LEVINE, THE FUTURE OF DEMOCRACY: DEVELOPING THE NEXT GENERATION OF AMERICAN CITIZENS 95 (2007).

94. SHERRY TURKLE, ALONE TOGETHER: WHY WE EXPECT MORE FROM TECHNOLOGY AND LESS FROM EACH OTHER 11 (2011). *See also* SHERRY TURKLE, RECLAIMING CONVERSATION: THE POWER OF TALK IN A DIGITAL AGE, (2015) (proposing methods to promote face-to-face conversation in the digital age).

95. Monica Anderson & Andrea Caumont, *How Social Media Is Reshaping News* (PEW RESEARCH CTR., Sept. 24, 2014), *available at* http://www.pewresearch.org/fact-tank/2014/09/24/how-social-media-is-reshaping-news/. The authors also note: "Visitors who go to a news media website directly spend roughly three times as long as those who wind up there through search or Facebook, and they view roughly five times as many pages per month."

96. PETER LEVINE, WE ARE THE ONES WE HAVE BEEN WAITING FOR: THE PROMISE OF CIVIC RENEWAL IN AMERICA 144 (2013).

97. Ronald Dworkin, Is Democracy Possible Here? Principles for a New Political Debate (2006).

98. *Id.* at 6.

99. Amitai Etzioni, The Moral Dimension: Toward a new economics 1986 (1988).

100. Dworkin, *supra* note 97, at 147–59.

101. *Id.* at 157.

102. Citizens United v. FEC, 558 U.S. 310 (2010).

103. Stephen Macedo et al., Democracy at Risk: How Political Choices Undermine Citizen Participation, and What We Can Do About It, 4 (2005).

104. Among other things, they would (1) simplify and facilitate registration and voting procedures; (2) use nonpartisan commissions to establish boundaries for congressional and state legislative districts; (3) give two electoral college votes to the statewide winner of the presidential election, and one vote to the winner of each congressional district; (4) encourage municipalities to provide a mix of housing; and (5) reconsider Progressive Era reforms, including city manager governance, at-large city council districts, and nonpartisan elections.

105. Wendy R. Weiser & Erik Opsal, *The State of Voting in 2014* (Brennan Ctr. for Justice, NYU School of Law, 2014), *available at* http://www.brennancenter.org/analysis/state-voting-2014.

106. Sam Wang, *The Great Gerrymander of 2012*, N.Y. Times, Feb. 2, 2013, *available at* http://www.nytimes.com/2013/02/03/opinion/sunday/the-great-gerrymander-of-2012.html.

107. *See, e.g.*, Richard E. Dawson et al., Political Socialization (1969).

108. James G. Gimpel & Shanna Pearson-Merkowitz, *Policies for Civic Engagement Beyond the Schoolyard*, *in* James Youniss & Peter Levine, Engaging Young People in Civic Life 85 (2009).

109. Peter Levine, *Education for a Civil Society*, *in* David E. Campbell, Meira Levinson & Frederick M. Hess, Making Civics Count: Citizenship Education for a New Generation 41 (2012). *See also* Public Agenda, Kids These Days: What Americans Really Think About the Next Generation 41 (1997) (national survey indicates that most of the public—67 percent—believes that improving the public schools is the best way to help young people); Goss v. Lopez, 419 U.S. 565, 593 (1975) (Powell, J., dissenting) ("In an age when the home and church play a diminishing role in shaping the character and value judgments of the young, a heavier responsibility falls upon the schools").

110. Carnegie Corp. Am. & CIRCLE, *The Civic Mission of Schools* (2003).

111. *See, e.g.*, Campaign for the Civic Mission of the Schools et al., *supra* note 28; U.S. Dep't of Educ., *For Each and Every Child—A Strategy for Education Equity and Excellence* (2013); Educ. Comm'n of the States, *State Civic Education Policy Framework* (2014), *available at* http://www.ecs.org/clearinghouse/01/16/12/11612.pdf.

112. DAVID F. LABAREE, SOMEONE HAS TO FAIL: THE ZERO SUM GAME OF PUBLIC SCHOOLING 15 (2010).

113. The rapidly growing economic divide between well-paid finance and high-tech jobs and low-paying liberal-arts and social-service jobs both reflects and heightens these trends. *See, e.g.*, Nelson G. Schwartz, *Gap Widening as Top Workers Reap the Raises*, N.Y. TIMES, July 25, 2015 (describing sharp increases from 2007 to 2014 in starting salaries for college graduates in engineering, computer science, and business, as compared to sharp decreases for entry-level positions in social work, teaching, and journalism).

114. DANIELLE ALLEN, EDUCATION AND EQUALITY 27 (2016).

115. CAMPAIGN FOR THE CIVIC MISSION OF THE SCHOOLS ET AL., *supra* note 28, at 5.

116. CTR. ON EDUC. POL'Y, *From the Capital to the Classroom: Year 4 of the No Child Left Behind Act*, tbl. 4-D, 96 (2006) (in 2006, 33 percent of diverse school districts in a nationally representative selection of 299 reported that they had reduced social-studies instruction—history, geography, civics—somewhat or to a great extent in order to devote more time to English and/or math, in response to NCLB accountability systems).

117. Beth Fertig, *Chancellor to Schools: Focus on Social Studies*, WNYC SCHOOLBOOK, Sept. 24, 2014, *available at* http://www.wnyc.org/story/carmen-farina-social-studies.

118. MICHAEL A. REBELL, JESSICA R. WOLFF & JOSEPH R. ROGERS, JR., *Deficient Resources: An Analysis of the Availability of Basic Educational Resources in High-Needs Schools in Eight New York State School Districts* (CAMPAIGN FOR EDUC. EQUITY 2012) (as a result of budget cuts, most of the high schools studied had eliminated their civics-related afterschool offerings, including community service programs, student government, school newspaper, and programs like model UN and moot court); *Field Trips Becoming History at Some Ohio Schools*, Oct. 8, 2012, *available at* http://www.northjersey.com/news/education/field-trips-becoming-history-at-some-ohio-schools-1.383829 (Ohio school districts substitute online virtual trips to save money and time for test preparation).

119. LEVINE, *supra* note 93.

Chapter Two

1. CARL F. KAESTLE, PILLARS OF THE REPUBLIC: COMMON SCHOOLS AND AMERICAN SOCIETY, 1780–1860 96 (1984).

2. HORACE MANN, COMMON SCHOOL JOURNAL III 15 (1841), *quoted in* LAWRENCE CREMIN, AMERICAN EDUCATION: THE NATIONAL EXPERIENCE, 1783–1876 137 (1980).

3. Richard Mosier, Making the American Mind: Social and Moral Ideas in the McGuffey Readers 168–69 (1947).

4. Henry Steele Commager, *Foreword* to McGuffey's Fifth Eclectic Reader (6th ed. 1962) (1879).

5. *Id.*

6. Horace Mann, *Eleventh Annual Report of the Secretary of the Board* 90–91 (1848), *quoted in* Charles Glenn, The Myth of the Common School 166 (1988).

7. *Quoted in* Glenn, *supra* note 6, at 38.

8. Stephen Macedo, Diversity and Distrust: Civic Education in a Multicultural Democracy 72 (2000).

9. *Id.* at 75.

10. For a detailed discussion of split between the common school and Catholic leaders on these issues and the origins of the separate Catholic school systems in New York City and California, *see* Diane Ravitch, The Great School Wars (1974); David Tyack, Turning Points in American History 90–91 (1967).

11. Gershon M. Ratner, *A New Legal Duty for Urban Public Schools: Effective Education in Basic Skills*, 63 Tex. L. Rev. 777, 823 (1985).

12. David Tyack, Thomas James & Aaron Benavot, Law and the Shaping of Public Education 1785–1954 155 (1987).

13. 1923 Ore. Laws, ch. 1, p. 9.

14. Tyack et al., *supra* note 12, at 179. The authors added: "A similar plan had failed in Michigan, but if the Oregon campaign proved successful, a dozen other states were next in line." *Id.*

15. Pierce v. Soc'y of Sisters, 268 U.S. 510 (1925).

16. *Id.* at 534.

17. Mark Yudof, When Government Speaks 230 (1982).

18. Pierce, *supra* note 15, at 534–35.

19. *Id.* at 535.

20. "Appellees asked protection against arbitrary, unreasonable, and unlawful interference with their patrons and the consequent destruction of their business and property. Their interest is clear and immediate, within the rule approved in . . . many other cases where injunctions have issued to protect business enterprises against interference with the freedom of patrons or customers." *Id.* at 536.

21. Soc'y of Sisters v. Pierce, 296 F. 928, 935 (D. Ore. 1924).

22. *See, e.g.*, Nixon v. Commonwealth, 839 A.2d 277, 286 (Pa. 2003) ("While the General Assembly may, under its police power, limit those rights by enacting laws to protect the public health, safety, and welfare, any such laws are subject to judicial review and a constitutional analysis"). *See also* People v. Ewer, 25 L.R.A. 794 (N.Y. 1894) (case discussing the balancing of the state's police power against parental liberty rights to "exhibit" a young child as a dancer in a Broad-

way theater). *Ewer* was cited generally in regard to the state's inherent police power by the lower court in *Pierce*, 296 F. at 936.

23. Meyer v. Nebraska, 262 U.S. 390 (1923).

24. *Id.* at 401. As in *Pierce*, the Court did discuss at length the importance of the constitutional "liberty" interest asserted by the plaintiffs: "The protection of the Constitution extends to all, to those who speak other languages as well as to those born with English on the tongue. Perhaps it would be highly advantageous if all had ready understanding of our ordinary speech, but this cannot be coerced by methods which conflict with the Constitution—a desirable end cannot be promoted by prohibited means." *Id.* As further examples of excessive state actions in inculcating societal values in the young, the Court also invoked Plato's suggestion that certain children be taken from their parents and raised in common by state officers as well as the Spartan practice of assembling males at age seven into barracks and entrusting their subsequent education and training to official guardians. *Id.* at 401–2.

25. Griswold v. Connecticut, 381 U.S. 479 (1965).

26. Roe v. Wade, 410 U.S. 113 (1972).

27. The Court's establishment of a due process right to liberty in *Pierce* and *Meyer* occurred during an era when the due process clause was given substantive as contrasted with procedural, content, mainly in cases involving the "liberty" of corporations to be free from economic regulation by the government. *See, e.g.*, Lochner v. New York, 198 U.S. 45 (1904) (striking down a state statute that prohibited bakers from working more than sixty hours per week). Although the use of substantive due process to counter economic regulation has fallen into desuetude since the 1930s, the substantive due right of individuals to resist unreasonable governmental imposition on their liberty interests established in *Meyer* and *Pierce* has survived in the sphere of personal liberties, as exemplified by *Griswold* and *Roe.*

28. Farrington v. Tokushige, 273 U.S. 284 (1927). The Court's terse analysis of the constitutional infirmity of this statute read as follows:

> The School Act and the measures adopted thereunder go far beyond mere regulation of privately supported schools, where children obtain instruction deemed valuable by their parents and which is not obviously in conflict with any public interest. They give affirmative direction concerning the intimate and essential details of such schools, intrust their control to public officers, and deny both owners and patrons reasonable choice and discretion in respect of teachers, curriculum and text-books. Enforcement of the act probably would destroy most, if not all, of them; and, certainly, it would deprive parents of fair opportunity to procure for their children instruction which they think impor-

> tant and we cannot say is harmful. The Japanese parent has the right to direct the education of his own child without unreasonable restrictions; the Constitution protects him as well as those who speak another tongue.

Id. at 298.

29. *See, e.g.,* City of Sumner v. First Baptist Church, 639 P.2d 1358 (Wash. 1982).

30. *See, e.g.,* Fellowship Baptist Church v. Benton, 815 F.2d 486 (8th Cir. 1987).

31. *See, e.g.,* Johnson v. Charles City Bd. of Educ., 368 N.W.2d 74 (Iowa 1985).

32. *Bd. of Educ. v. Allen*, 392 U.S. 236, 245–47 (1968). In *Allen*, the Court held that state expenditures for secular textbooks used in private religious schools did not violate the establishment clause of the First Amendment to the federal constitution. *See also* Lemon v. Kurtzman, 403 U.S. 602, 613 (1971) ("A State always has a legitimate concern for maintaining minimum standards in all schools it allows to operate").

33. For an overview of the laws and regulations in all fifty states regarding oversight of private schools, *see* U.S. DEP'T OF EDUC., STATE REGULATION OF PRIVATE SCHOOLS (2009).

34. These constitutional provisions and statutes are discussed in detail in the next chapter.

35. Ky. State Bd. for Elementary & Secondary Educ. v. Rudasill, 589 S.W.2d 877 (Ky. 1979).

36. Eric A. DeGroff, *State Regulation of Non-Public Schools: Does the Tie Still Bind?*, B.Y.U. EDUC. & L.J. 363, 382, 390, 393 (2003). *See also* U.S. DEP'T OF EDUC., *supra* note 33 (based on self-reporting, only four states require teacher certification of all private school teachers, and twenty-two states do not impose curriculum requirements on some or all of the private schools in the state).

37. *See* N.C. GEN. STAT. § 115C-562.1. A few states do have regulations containing substantial curriculum requirements for private schools. Maryland, for example, requires private schools to have an educational program in English language arts, mathematics, science, and social studies that is appropriate for students enrolled. MD. CODE REGS. 13A.09.09.07A(2). Those schools must also require at a minimum the following credits for secondary school graduation: four in English language arts, two in social studies to include at least one credit in U.S. history, six in science and mathematics (at least two credits in each), and nine additional credits in accordance with the school's written requirements. MD. CODE REGS. 13A.09.09.09.

38. N.Y. EDUC. LAW § 3204.2. New York law further specifically provides that private schools must "offer courses of instruction in patriotism, citizenship, and human rights and instruction in the Constitution of the United States and New York and the Declaration of Independence." *See also* N.Y. EDUC. LAW § 801.

39. *See* N.Y. State Educ. Dep't, Guidelines for Determining Equivalency of Instruction in Nonpublic Schools, *available at* http://www.p12.nysed.gov/nonpub/guidelinesequivofinstruction.html. These guidelines, which incorporate many of the specific curriculum requirements of the Regulations of the Commissioner, expect local school boards and superintendents to inspect new nonpublic schools and review their curricula, and to review the program and curricula at established schools if "a serious concern arises about equivalency of instruction." *Id.* at § III. Children attending nonpublic schools not providing equivalent instruction in accordance with these guidelines and regulations will be considered truants, and their parents will be notified to transfer them to either a public school or a nonpublic schools that is in compliance. *Id.* at §§ IB, III. Nonpublic schools are specifically required to teach all basic school subjects, including English, social studies, science, mathematics, music, and arts. Questions and Answers Relating to Determining Equivalency of Instruction in Nonpublic Schools (attached to Guidelines for Determining Equivalency of Instruction) § 24.

40. Jennifer Miller, *Yiddish Isn't Enough: A Yeshiva Graduate Fights for Secular Studies in Hasidic Education*, N.Y. Times, Nov. 14, 2014. Seven former students at an Orthodox Jewish school in Rockland County, New York, filed a federal lawsuit that asserts similar claims. *See* Amy Sara Clark, *Chasidic Parents, Yeshiva Grads Sue State for Ignoring Subpar Secular Ed*, Jewish Wk., Nov. 19, 2015, *available at* http://www.thejewishweek.com/news/new-york/chasidic-parents-yeshiva-grads-sue-state-ignoring-subpar-secular-ed#OfV151jeocCwZEG3.99.

41. Kate Taylor, *New York City Questions English, Math and Science Taught at Yeshivas*, N.Y. Times, July 31, 2015, *available at* http://www.nytimes.com/2015/08/01/nyregion/new-york-city-questions-english-math-and-science-taught-at-yeshivas.html.

42. Naftuli Moster, Testimony Before the N.Y. City Council (Mar. 23, 2017); Carmen Fariña (N.Y. City Dep't of Educ.), Testimony Before N.Y. City Council (May 16, 2016) (promising issuance of a report by June 2016), *available at* http://legistar.council.nyc.gov/LegislationDetail.aspx?ID=2702766&GUID=5BF6B5F1-C4FA-4272-BA3E-3A105D59B1B7&Options=Advanced&Search=.

43. Wisconsin v. Yoder, 406 U.S. 205 (1972).

44. *Id.* at 210–11. The Court also noted:

> The Amish do not object to elementary education through the first eight grades as a general proposition because they agree that their children must have basic skills in the 'three R's' in order to read the Bible, to be good farmers and citizens, and to be able to deal with non-Amish people when necessary in the course of daily affairs. . . . While Amish accept compulsory elementary education generally, wherever possible they have estab-

> lished their own elementary schools in many respects like the small local schools of the past. In the Amish belief higher learning tends to develop values they reject as influences that alienate man from God.

Id. at 212.

45. *Id.* at 213.

46. *Id.*

47. *Id.* at 221.

48. *Id.* at 222.

49. *Id.* at 235–36. He summarized the uniqueness of the Amish position in this case as follows:

> Aided by a history of three centuries as an identifiable religious sect and a long history as a successful and self-sufficient segment of American society, the Amish in this case have convincingly demonstrated the sincerity of their religious beliefs, the interrelationship of belief with their mode of life, the vital role that belief and daily conduct play in the continued survival of Old Order Amish communities and their religious organization, and the hazards presented by the State's enforcement of a statute generally valid as to others. Beyond this, they have carried the even more difficult burden of demonstrating the adequacy of their alternative mode of continuing informal vocational education in terms of precisely those overall interests that the State advances in support of its program of compulsory high school education.

Id. at 235. In fact, so far no other group has been able to qualify for the Amish exemption that the Court allowed in this case.

50. *Id.* at 225.

51. *Id.* at 228.

52. Three of the Justices filed a concurring opinion that contained additional language that can be read to disparage the importance of a high school level education: "Since the Amish children are permitted to acquire the basic tools of literacy to survive in modern society by attending grades one through eight and since the deviation from the State's compulsory-education law is relatively slight, I conclude that respondents' claim must prevail, largely because 'religious freedom—the freedom to believe and to practice strange and, it may be, foreign creeds—has classically been one of the highest values of our society.'" *Id.* at 238 (White, J., concurring, joined by Stewart, J., and Brennan, J.)

53. Brown v. Bd. of Educ., 347 U.S. 483, 493 (1954).

54. Ambach v. Norwick, 441 U.S. 68, 77 (1979).

55. Tinker v. Des Moines Indep. Sch. Dist., 393 U.S. 503, 507 (1969).

56. Plyler v. Doe, 457 U.S. 202, 221 (1982).

57. Sch. Dist. of Abington Twp. v. Schempp, 374 U.S. 203, 230 (1963) (Brennan, J., concurring).

58. Bethel Sch. Dist. v. Fraser, 478 U.S. 675, 683 (1986).

59. Ambach v. Norwick, *441 U.S. at 493*.

60. Bethel Sch. Dist. v. Fraser, 478 U.S. at 683.

61. Tinker v. Des Moines Indep. Sch. Dist., 393 U.S. at 507.

62. Plyler v. Doe, *457 U.S. at 221.*

63. San Antonio Indep. Sch. Dist. v. Rodriguez, 411 U.S. 1 (1973).

64. *Id.* at 49.

65. *Id.* at 29–30. Strict scrutiny would also have been applied if the plaintiffs were from a suspect class, like racial minorities, who also were entitled to strict scrutiny of their claims of discriminatory state action. The *Rodriguez* plaintiffs did claim that poor people should also be considered a suspect class, but the Court also rejected that claim. *Id.* at 18–28.

66. *Id.* at 30.

67. *Id.* at 111.

68. *Id.* at 113–14. *See also id.* at 63 (Brennan, J., dissenting): "Here, there can be no doubt that education is inextricably linked to the right to participate in the electoral process and to the rights of free speech and association guaranteed by the First Amendment."

69. *Id.* at 37.

70. *Id.* at 36 (emphasis added).

71. *Id.* at 36–37. In upholding the rationality of the local funding component of the Texas Education Finance system, Justice Powell also noted that "*while assuring a basis* [*sic*] *education for every child in the State*, it permits and encourages a large measure of participation in and control of each district's schools at the local level." *Id.* at 49.

72. Papasan v. Allain, 478 U.S. 265, 284 (1986).

Chapter Three

1. As of the 1969–70 school year, the differences in *per capita* expenditures between the highest- and lowest-spending school districts were as high as 56 to 1 in Texas, 24 to 1 in North Dakota, 11 to 1 in New York, 8 to 1 in California, and 6 to 1 in New Jersey. Overall, and excluding potential outliers, the maximum-minimum *per capita* ratio between school districts at the 95th percentile of spending of all districts in the state and those at the 5th percentile on average for all fifty states was 2.082 to 1. PRESIDENT'S COMM'N ON SCH. FIN., 2 REVIEW OF EXISTING STATE SCHOOL FINANCE PROGRAMS 13 (1972).

2. The commission recommended, among other things, that state finance sys-

tems be funded 90 percent or more by the state and no more than 10 percent by local school districts. They also proposed that the federal government provide incentive grants to the states to help them raise their share of educational funding and that it institute the Urban Education Assistance Program to provide matching grants to the states to overcome funding gaps between cities and suburbs. PRESIDENT'S COMM'N ON SCH. FIN., SCHOOLS, PEOPLE & MONEY: THE NEED FOR EDUCATIONAL REFORM (1972).

3. Serrano v. Priest, 557 P.2d 929, 949–52 (Cal. 1976).

4. Robinson v. Cahill, 303 A.2d 273 (N.J. 1973); Horton v. Meskill, 376 A.2d 359 (Conn. 1977); Pauley v. Kelly, 255 S.E.2d 859 (W. Va. 1979).

5. For a detailed discussion of this history, *see* MICHAEL A. REBELL, COURTS AND KIDS: PURSUING EDUCATIONAL EQUITY THROUGH THE STATE COURTS (2009); MICHAEL A. REBELL, COURTS AND KIDS: PURSUING EDUCATIONAL EQUITY THROUGH THE STATE COURTS (SUPP. 2017), *available at* http://press.uchicago.edu/ucp/books/book/chicago/C/bo8212990.html. For up-to-date information about the status of these cases, see the Schoolfunding.info website maintained by the Center for Educational Equity at Teachers College, Columbia University, at http://www.schoolfunding.info.

6. N.Y. CONST. art. XI, § 1. The specific language in this constitutional provision states that "the legislature shall provide for the maintenance and support of a system of free common schools, wherein all of the children of this state may be educated." The New York Court of Appeals has interpreted the concept of educated in this provision to mean "a sound basic education." Levittown Union Free Sch. Dist. v. Nyquist, 439 N.E.2d at 368–69 (1982). *See also* Campaign for Fiscal Equity v. State (CFE I), 655 N.E.2d 661, 665 (N.Y. 1995) (holding that the New York State Constitution's education clause requires "a sound basic education").

7. N.J. CONST. art. IV, § 1. Cf. IDAHO CONST. art. IX, § 1 (a "general, uniform and thorough system" of education.); KY. CONST. § 183 (an "efficient system of common schools throughout the state").

8. MONT. CONST. art. X, § 1.

9. Attempts to categorize the constitutional language in the state constitutions in terms of their relative strength have proved unavailing. For example, William E. Thro, in *The Role of Language of the State Education Clauses in School Finance Litigation*, 79 EDUC. L. REP. 19 (1993), set forth four basic categories related to the relative "strength" of the educational clauses: (1) seventeen states that simply mandate free public education; (2) twenty-two states that "impose some type of minimum standard of quality"; (3) six states that require a "stronger and more specific educational mandate" than the first two categories; and (4) four states that regard education as an "important, if not the most important, duty of the state." *Id.* at 23–24. His predictions regarding the likely outcome of court cases based on his categorizations have, however, been belied by the actual decisions. For example, following Thro's categorization, plaintiffs

should have won the cases in Maine, Rhode Island, and Illinois that they lost and plaintiffs should have lost the decisions in New York, North Carolina, and Vermont that they won.

10. Brigham v. State, 692 A.2d 284, 393 (1997).

11. Campbell Cty. Sch. Dist. v. State, 907 P.2d 1238, 1259 (Wyo. Sup. Ct. 2001). *See also* Claremont Sch. Dist. v. Governor, 703 A.2d 1353 (N.H. 1997) (defining the constitutional duty in terms of preparing "citizens for their role as participants and as potential competitors in today's marketplace of ideas").

12. Robinson v. Cahill, 303 A.2d 273, 295 (N.J. 1973).

13. Campaign for Fiscal Equity, Inc. v. State, 801 N.E.2d 326, 331 (N.Y. 2003). *See also* Conn. Coal. for Justice in Educ. Funding v. Rell, 990 A.2d 206, 253 (Conn. 2010) (The constitution entitles "students to participate fully in democratic institutions such as jury service and voting . . . [and to be] prepared to progress to institutions of higher education or to attain productive employment and otherwise contribute to the state's economy").

14. Specifically, plaintiffs have prevailed in 60 percent of the decisions in these cases. In most of the cases in which defendants prevailed, the outcome was based on separation of powers or other legal issues that precluded any decision on the merits of whether the current state education finance system was adequate. Details regarding the state court education adequacy cases can be found in REBELL, *supra* note 5.

15. *See* EMILY ZACKIN, LOOKING FOR RIGHTS IN ALL THE WRONG PLACES: WHY STATE CONSTITUTIONS CONTAIN AMERICA'S POSITIVE RIGHTS, ch. 5 (2013).

16. E.P. CUBBERLEY, PUBLIC EDUCATION IN THE UNITED STATES (1934).

17. N.Y. CONST. art. XI, § 1.

18. Rose v. Council for Better Educ., Inc., 790 S.W.2d 186, 205 (Ky. 1989).

19. *Id.* at 205–06.

20. *Id.* Other state courts that included extensive discussion of the original intent of the drafters of their constitutional clauses include Lake View Sch. Dist. No. 25 v. Huckabee, 91 S.W.3d 472, 491–92 (Ark. 2002); Roosevelt Elem. Sch. Dist. No. 66 v. Bishop, 877 P. 2d 806, 812 (Ariz. 1994); McDuffy v. Sec.'y of the Exec. Office of Educ., 615 N.E.2d 516, 523–45 (Mass. 1993); Claremont Sch. Dist. v. Governor, 635 A.2d 1375, 1378–81 (N.H. 1993); DeRolph v. Ohio, 677 N.E.2d 733, 736, 740–41 (Ohio 1997); Edgewood Indep. Sch. Dist. v. Kirby, 777 S.W.2d 391, 393–98 (Tex. 1989); Pauley v. Kelly, 255 S.E.2d 859, 866–69 (W. Va. 1979); and Seattle Sch. Dist. No. 1 v. State, 585 P.2d 71, 91 (Wash. 1978).

21. IND. CONST. art. VIII, § 1.

22. MINN. CONST. art. XIII, § 1; *see also* IDAHO CONST. art. IX, § 1.

23. N.D. CONST. art. VIII, § 1. *See also, e.g.,* ARK. CONST. art. XIV, § 1 (1874) ("Intelligence and virtue being the safeguards of liberty and the bulwark of a free and good government, the State shall ever maintain a general, suitable and efficient system of free public schools"). Some territories when they became

states adopted verbatim the language of the Northwest Ordinance: "Religion, morality, and knowledge, being necessary to good government and the happiness of mankind, schools and the means of education shall forever be encouraged." An Act to Provide for the Government of the Territory Northwest of the River Ohio, ch. 8, 1 Stat. 50, 52 n.(a) (1789). *See, e.g.*, KANS. CONST. of 1855, art. 3; MONT. CONST. of 1812, art. 3.

24. N.H. CONST. pt. 2, art. 83.

25. Claremont Sch. Dist. v. Governor, 635 A.2d 1375, 1378, 1381 (1993). The Court also dismissed the state's contention that the its failure to pay for education in the post-Revolutionary years was inconsistent with the founders' intent to provide all students a right to education:

> We are unpersuaded by the State's argument that the fact that no State funding was provided at all for education in the first fifty years after ratification of the constitution demonstrates that the framers did not believe part II, article 83 to impose any obligation on the State to provide funding. . . . "That local control and fiscal support has been placed in greater or lesser measure through our history on local governments does not dilute the validity" of the conclusion that the duty to support the public schools lies with the State. *McDuffy*, 415 Mass. at 606, 615 N.E.2d at 548. "While it is clearly within the power of the [State] to delegate some of the implementation of the duty to local governments, such power does not include a right to abdicate the obligation imposed . . . by the Constitution."

Id. at 1381.

26. *See* ARIZ. CONST. art. 11; N.M. CONST. art. XII, § 1; OKLA. CONST. art. XIII-1.

27. Roosevelt Elementary Sch. Dist. v. Bishop 877 P.2d 806, 812 (Ariz. 1994).

28. Michigan, when it revised its constitution in 1908, included the religion, morality and knowledge clause that had not appeared in its prior constitutions in 1835 and 1850. When the Constitution was again revised in 1963, this clause was retained in art. VIII, § 1.

29. CONN. CONST. art. 8, § 1.

30. Conn. Coal. for Justice in Educ. Funding, Inc., 990 A.2d at 246 (Conn. 2010).

31. Robinson v. Cahill, 303 A.2d 275, 295 (N.J. 1973).

32. *Id.*

33. Roosevelt Elementary Sch. Dist. v. Bishop 877 P.2d at 812 (Ariz. 1994); Lake View Sch. Dist. No. 25 v. Huckabee, 91 S.W.3d 472, 492 (Ark. 2002) (citing DuPree v. Alma Sch. Dist. No. 30, 651 S.W.2d 90, 93 (Ark. 1983)); Serrano v. Priest, 557 P.2d at 929; Conn. Coal. for Justice in Educ. Funding, Inc., 990 A.2d

at 253 (Conn. 2010); McDaniel v. Thomas, 285 S.E.2d 156, 165 (Ga. 1981); Comm. for Educ. Rights v. Edgar, 672 N.E.2d 1178, 1194 (Ill. 1996); Bonner v. Daniels, 907 N.E.2d 516, 522 (Ind. 2009); Gannon v. State, 319 P.3d 1196, 1226–27 (Kan. 2012); Rose, 790 S.W.2d at 186, 189–90 (Ky. 1989); McDuffy v. Sec.'y of the Exec. Office of Educ., 615 N.E.2d 516, 554 (Mass. 1993); Skeen v. State, 505 N.W.2d 299, 310 (Minn. 1993); Claremont Sch. Dist. v. Governor, 635 A.2d 1375, 1378, 1381 (N.H. 1993); Abbott v. Burke, 495 A.2d 376, 383 (N.J. 1985); CFE v. State, 801 N.E.2d 326, 330 (N.Y. 2003); Leandro v. State, 488 S.E.2d 249, 255 (N.C.1997); Bismarck Pub. Sch. Dist. v. State, 511 N.W.2d 247, 259 (N.D. 1994); DeRolph v. State, 677 N.E.2d 733, 736 (Ohio 1997); Abbeville Cty. Sch. Dist. v. State, 767 S.E.2d 157 (S.C. 2014); Davis v. State, 804 N.W.2d 618, 628 (S.D. 2011); Edgewood Indep. Sch. Dist. v. Kirby, 777 S.W.2d 391, 395–96 (Tex. 1989); Brigham v. State, 692 A.2d 384, 392–93 (Vt. 1997); Scott v. Commonwealth, 443 S.E.2d 138, 142 (Va. 1994); Seattle Sch. Dist. No. 1 v. State, 585 P.2d 71, 94 (Wash. 1971); Pauley v. Kelly, 255 S.E.2d 859, 877 (W.Va. 1979); Vincent v. Voight, 614 N.W.2d 388, 415 (Wisc. 2000); Campbell County Sch. Dist. v. State, 907 P.2d 1238, 1259 (Wyo. 2001).

34. Bush v. Holmes, 919 So.2d 392, 405 (Fla. 2006), Spears v. Honda, 449 P.2d 130, 134 (Haw. 1968), Sheridan Rd. Baptist Church v. Mich. Dep't of Educ., 396 N.W.2d 373, 380 (Mich. 1985), Concerned Parents v. Caruthersville Sch. Dist. 18, 548 S.W.2d 554, 558 (Mont. 1977), Citizens of Decatur for Equal Educ. v. Lyons-Decatur Sch. Dist., 739 N.W.2d 742, 760 (Neb. 2007), and LAW v. State, 348 P.3d 1005, 1009 (Nev. 2015).

35. As the Supreme Court of Indiana put it, the education clause "reflects a prevailing public sentiment in 1850 that a public education system was needed to eliminate illiteracy and to protect Indiana's democracy." Bonner v. Daniels, 907 N.E.2d 516, 522 (Ind. 2009). *See also* Comm. for Educ. Rights v. Edgar, 672 N.E.2d 1178, 1194 (Ill. 1996); Concerned Parents v. Caruthersville Sch. Dist. 18, 548 S.W.2d 554, 558 (Mont. 1977); Citizens of Decatur for Equal Educ. v. Lyons-Decatur Sch. Dist., 739 N.W.2d 742, 760 (Neb. 2007); Davis v. State, 804 N.W.2d 618, 628 (S.D. 2011); Scott v. Commonwealth, 443 S.E.2d 138,142 (Va. 1994). In addition, justices concurring or dissenting in cases in at least five other states have also noted the importance of the tie between education and democracy. *See* Lobato v. State, 304 P.3d 1132 (Colo. 2013) (Bender, C.J., dissenting, and Hobbs, J., dissenting); King v. State, 818 N.W.2d 1, 50–62 (Iowa 2012) (Appel, J., dissenting); Hornbeck v. Somerset Cty. Bd. of Educ., 458 A.2d 758, 802 (Md. 1983) (Cole, J., dissenting); Skeen v. State, 505 N.W.2d 299, 320–21 (Minn. 1993) (Page, J., concurring in part, dissenting in the judgment); Bd. of Pub. Educ. v. Intile, 163 A.2d 420, 446 (Pa. 1960) (Musmanno, J., dissenting).

36. The vast majority of states that have held for defendants have done so on justiciability or separation-of-powers grounds and have not heard evidence or had occasion to consider at length the purposes of public education. *See* Rebell,

supra note 5, at 22–29. Note that in two of the cases in which defendants prevailed, McDaniel v. Thomas, 285 S.E.2d 156, 165 (Ga. 1981), and Vincent v. Voight, 614 N.W.2d 388, 415 (Wis. 2000), the courts indicated that there is a right to an adequate education that would prepare students for capable citizenship, but that in the present litigations, plaintiffs had not demonstrated that the state was not providing such an education.

37. These standards have been explicitly adopted by courts in Kansas, Massachusetts, and New Hampshire. *See* Gannon v. State, 319 P.3d 1196 (Kan. 2014), McDuffy v. Sec.'y of the Exec. Office of Educ., 615 N.E.2d 516, 554 (Mass. 1993); Claremont v. Governor, 703 A.2d 1353, 1359 (N.H. 1997), and have substantially influenced the constitutional definitions adopted by the courts in Alabama, Arkansas, North Carolina, South Carolina, and Texas. *See* Alabama Opinion of the Justices, 624 So.2d 107 (Ala. 1993); Lake View Sch. Dist. No. 25 v. Huckabee, 91 S.W.3d 472 (Ark. 2002); Leandro v. State, 488 S.E.2d 249, 255 (N.C. 1997); Abbeville Cty. Sch. Dist. v. State, 515 S.E.2d 535 (S.C. 1999); Neeley v. W. Orange Cove Consol. Indep. Sch. Dist., 176 S.W.3d 746 (Tex. 2005).

38. Rose, 790 S.W.2d at 186.

39. NORMAN H. NIE, JANN JUNN & KENNETH STEHLIK-BARRY, EDUCATION AND DEMOCRATIC CITIZENSHIP IN AMERICA 41 (1996).

40. *Id.* at 41.

41. *See* E.D. HIRSCH, JR., THE MAKING OF AMERICANS: DEMOCRACY AND OUR SCHOOLS (2009) (emphasizing the importance of teaching students shared knowledge of American history, institutions and civic ideals).

42. McCleary v. State, 2010 WL 9073395 (Wash. Sup. Ct. 2010), *aff'd* 269 P.3d 227, 229 (Wash. 2012).

43. Campaign for Fiscal Equity (CFE) v. State, 655 N.E.2d 661 (N.Y. 1995). The author was counsel for plaintiffs in this case.

44. *Id.* at 666–67.

45. The expert testimony presented at the CFE trial was also substantially influenced by public input that plaintiffs had obtained through an extensive, multiyear public engagement process. Tom Sobol, the former commissioner of education who testified as an expert for the plaintiffs, and other witnesses took part in many of the public engagement forums and incorporated the consensus that emerged from those sessions in their testimony. For a discussion of the CFE public engagement process, *see* Michael A. Rebell, *Adequacy Litigations: A New Path to Equity, in* BRINGING EQUITY BACK: RESEARCH FOR A NEW ERA IN AMERICAN EDUCATIONAL POLICY (Janice Petrovich & Amy Stuart Wells eds., 2005).

46. Transcript of Record at 6484–89, 13452–60, CFE v. State, 719 N.Y.S.2d 475 (N.Y. Sup. Ct. 2001).

47. *Id.* at 6484, 6489.

48. *Id.* at 6516.

49. *Id.* at 16874, 16878–79, 16886, 16888–89; Defendants' Exhibits Nos. 19290, 19293, CFE v. State, 719 N.Y.S.2d 475 (N.Y. Sup. Ct. 2001).

50. Defendants also undertook a computerized "readability analysis" of various newspaper articles dealing with electoral issues, and of some of the jury documents that had been analyzed by the plaintiffs' experts; they concluded that only a seventh- or eighth-grade level of reading skills was needed to comprehend these materials. Transcript of Record, *supra* note 46, at 17182–83. The plaintiffs countered that this analysis relied on reading scales that focus on sentence length and other mechanical factors, rather than on the cognitive level of the materials being reviewed, and that by doing so they reached the implausible conclusion that *New York Times* and *New York Daily News* have essentially the same level of reading difficulty. *Id.* at 17185, 17201, 17215.

51. *Id.* at 17220.

52. CFE, Inc. v. State, 719 N.Y.S.2d 475, 485 (N.Y. Sup. Ct. 2001). Justice DeGrasse apparently meant that a capable voter or juror needs sufficient skills to follow arguments made by experts on complex subjects, not that voters and jurors necessarily need to master the intricacies of campaign finance reform or DNA themselves.

53. Specifically, the Court of Appeals held:

> Based on [Walberg's] testimony, the Appellate Division concluded that the skills necessary for civic participation are imparted between the eighth and ninth grades. The trial court, by contrast, concluded that productive citizenship "means more than being *qualified* to vote or serve as a juror, but to do so capably and knowledgeably"—to have skills appropriate to the task.
>
> We agree with the trial court that students require more than an eighth-grade education to function productively as citizens, and that the mandate of the Education Article for a sound basic education should not be pegged to the eighth or ninth grade, or indeed to any particular grade level.

CFE, Inc., v. State, 801 N.E.2d 326, 331 (N.Y. 2003) (citations omitted).

54. The state has not fully followed through on these commitments, and a new law suit has been brought by a number of parents, advocacy groups and state wide education organizations that is challenging the state's failure to provide all students in New York City and other parts of the state sufficient funding to support the opportunity for a sound basic education. Aristy-Farer/New Yorkers for Students' Education Rights (NYSER) v. New York, 29 N.Y.3d 501 (N.Y. 2017). The author is cocounsel for NYSER plaintiffs. Litigation papers and current information about the case is available at http://www.nyser.org. A detailed discussion of the remedy issued by the Court in CFE, the history of the state's implementation of the CFE requirements and the reasons why the NYSER case was

filed are set forth in Michael A. Rebell, *Safeguarding the Right to a Sound Basic Education in Times of Fiscal Constraint*, 75 ALB. L. REV. 1855 (2012).

55. In 2012, the legislature did add to a preexisting statute calling for instruction in "civility, citizenship and character education" a sentence stating that such instruction shall include "safe, responsible use of the internet and electronic communications" N.Y. Educ. Law § 801-a, L. 2012 c. 102 § 8, *effective* July 1, 2013, but there has been no serious effort to enforce this requirement.

56. JAMES C. CLINGER ET AL., KENTUCKY GOVERNMENT, POLITICS, AND PUBLIC POLICY 270 (2013). Note also that the curriculum frameworks and teaching guides issued to Kentucky's teachers speak extensively of a concern that "educators and communities must guarantee 21st -century readiness that will prepare learners for college and career success," but contain no references to how teachers can instill in their students the specific knowledge and skills that are needed for effective civic participation. *See* KY. DEP'T OF EDUC., MODEL CURRICULUM FRAMEWORK 2014 4 (2014).

57. Note, however, that in both New York and Kentucky, and in other states where plaintiffs had prevailed in education adequacy cases, the state education departments have adopted the "C3" framework for social studies state standards that incorporates a dynamic approach to civics issues that has been recommended by many of the leading scholars on civic preparation. *See* discussion in chapter 5, at pp. 100–104.

58. CFE v. State, 801 N.E.2d 326, 348 (N.Y. 2003).

59. Montoy v. State, 112 P.3d 923 (Kan. 2005).

60. Lake View Sch. Dist. No. 25 v. Huckabee, 91 S.W.3d 472, 500 (Ark. 2002).

61. The West Virginia Supreme Court explicitly linked the constitutionally-required outcomes for a "thorough and efficient education," with the resources needed to achieve them: "Implicit [in the constitutional requirements] are supportive services: (1) good physical facilities, instructional materials and personnel; (2) careful state and local supervision to prevent waste and to monitor pupil, teacher and administrative competency." Pauley v. Kelly, 255 S.E.2d 859, 877 (W. Va. 1979).

62. *See, e.g.,* William N. Evans, Sheila E. Murray & Robert N. Schwab, *The Impact of Court-Mandated Finance Reform*, *in* EQUITY AND ADEQUACY IN EDUCATION FINANCE: ISSUES AND PERSPECTIVES (Helen F. Ladd et al., eds., 1999) 72 (study of ten thousand school districts from 1972 to 1992 found that court-ordered reform reduced disparities in education funding and increased overall spending on education); R.L. Manwaring & S.M. Sheffrin, *Litigation, School Finance Reform and Aggregate Educational Spending*, 4 INT'L TAX & PUB. FIN. 107 (1995) (noting that litigations increase overall spending on education); C. Kirabo Jackson, Rucker Johnson & Claudia Persico, *The Effects of School Spending on Educational and Economic Outcomes: Evidence from School Finance Reforms*, NBER Working Paper No. 20847 (2015), *available at* http://www.nber.org/

papers/w20847 (study of state supreme court decisions in twenty-eight states between 1971 and 2010 concluded that school finance reforms stemming from court orders have tended both to increase state spending in low-income districts and to decrease expenditure gaps between low- and high-income districts).

63. For example, in a decision issued two decades after the Massachusetts Supreme Judicial Court held the state has a constitutional duty to prepare all of its children "to participate as free citizens of a free State to meet the needs and interests of a republican government," McDuffy v. Sec'y of the Exec. Office of Educ., 615 N.E.2d 516, 548 (Mass. 1993), and one in which it again emphasized that "for its effective functioning, democracy requires an educated citizenry," Hancock v. Comm'r of Educ., 822 N.E.2d 1134, 1137 (Mass. 2005), the court closely examined student progress on achievement test scores, especially in certain high need focus districts, but it did not extend its inquiry into student progress in overcoming the civic engagement gap.

64. The emphasis on academic standards responded to a series of major commission reports in the 1980s that had warned of a "rising tide of mediocrity" in American education—a phenomenon that was said to be undermining the nation's ability to compete in the global economy. NAT'L COMM'N ON EXCELLENCE IN EDUC., A NATION AT RISK: THE IMPERATIVE FOR EDUCATIONAL REFORM 5 (1983). *See also* CARNEGIE FORUM ON EDUCATION & THE ECONOMY, TASK FORCE ON TEACHING AS A PROFESSION, A NATION PREPARED: TEACHERS FOR THE 21ST CENTURY (1986); THEODORE SIZER, HORACE'S COMPROMISE: THE DILEMMA OF THE AMERICAN HIGH SCHOOL (1989). Comparative international assessments had revealed poor performance by American students, especially in science and mathematics. *See* NAT'L ASSESSMENT OF EDUC. PROGRAMS, AMERICA'S CHALLENGE: ACCELERATED ACADEMIC ACHIEVEMENT (1990); *see also* Robert L. Linn & Stephen B. Dunbar, *The Nation's Report Card: Good News and Bad About Trends in Achievement*, 72 PHI DELTA KAPPAN 127, 131 (1990). In response, federal and state policy makers decided that a major effort was needed to develop challenging educational goals and standards that would raise educational expectations and the educational achievement of America's youth, so that the country could again be number one in the intensifying international economic competition.

65. The new state standards aided plaintiffs in the adequacy cases because they provided courts with practical tools for developing judicially manageable approaches for dealing with complex educational issues and for implementing effective remedies. In essence, the states were themselves defining what was an "adequate" education by specifying the academic expectations that all students were supposed to meet. The key question litigants could then pose was whether the state was also providing all students with sufficient resources to allow them a fair opportunity to meet these standards. In most of the cases, the judges decided that the states were not providing such opportunities, and the standards offered the judges workable criteria for crafting practical remedies to imple-

ment their decisions. These issues are discussed in more detail in Rebell, *supra* note 5, ch. 2.

66. Elementary & Secondary Sch. Act of 1965, 20 U.S.C.A. § 6301 (2001).

67. Tina L. Heafner & Paul G. Fitchett, *National Trends in Elementary Instruction: Exploring the Role of Social Studies Curricula*, 103 Soc. Studs. 67 (2012).

68. Seth Schiesel, *Former Justice Promotes Web-Based Civics Lessons*, N.Y. Times, June 9, 2008. O'Connor lamented, "This leaves a huge gap, and we can't forget that the primary purpose of public schools in America has always been to help produce citizens who have the knowledge and the skills and the values to sustain our republic as a nation, our democratic form of government."

69. Ctr. on Educ. Pol'y, Choices, Changes, and Challenges Curriculum and Instruction in the NCLB Era 1, 5 (2007), *available at* http://www.cep-dc.org/McMurrer_FullReport_CurricAndInstruction_072407%20(1).pdf.

70. Richard Rothstein et al., Grading Education 48 (2008). *See also* Campaign for Educ. Equity, Deficient Resources; An Analysis of the Availability of Basic Educational Resources in High Needs Schools in Eight New York State School Districts (2012) (five of thirty-three high-need schools studied were not providing sufficient instructional time or course offerings to meet state requirements in social studies).

71. Elementary & Secondary Sch. Act, 20 U.S.C.A. § 6301 (2015).

72. The new law does, however, permit states to include a measure of school quality or student success such as student engagement, educator engagement, student access to and completion of advanced coursework, postsecondary readiness, school climate, and safety. 20 U.S.C.A. § 6311(c) (4) B (VI).

73. *See, e.g.*, N.Y. State Dep't of Educ., College and Career Readiness Anchor Standards, *available at* http://www.nylearns.org/module/Standards/Tools/Browse?standardId=98862; Ky. Dep't of Educ., Kentucky's College and Career Readiness Anchor Standards, *available at* http://education.ky.gov/curriculum/standards/Documents/Kentucky_Academic_Standards_ELA.pdf.

74. The National Commission on Excellence and Equity in Education recognized this need in its call for new directions for American education:

> To achieve the excellence and equity in education on which our future depends, we need a system of American public education that ensures all students have a real and meaningful opportunity to achieve rigorous college- and career ready standards. . . . But American schools must do more than ensure our future economic prosperity; they must foster the nation's civic culture and sense of common purpose, and create the unified nation that e pluribus unum celebrates. So much depends on fulfilling this

> mission: the shared ideals that enable our governmental system to hold together even in the face of fractious political disagreements; the strength of our diversity; the domestic tranquility that our Constitution promises; and the ability to maintain the influence—as example and power—that America has long projected in the world. We neglect those expectations at our peril.
>
> We cannot have a strong democracy without an informed, engaged citizenry.

U.S. DEP'T OF EDUC., FOR EACH AND EVERY CHILD—A STRATEGY FOR EDUCATION EQUITY AND EXCELLENCE 12 (2013).

75. Anne Mishkind, *Overview: State Definitions of College and Career Readiness* 4 (Am. Inst. for Research 2014), *available at* http://www.ccrscenter.org/sites/default/files/CCRS%20Defintions%20Brief_REV_1.pdf. The New York State Board of Regents also recently announced that its goal is to ensure that each child is prepared for success in "college, career, and citizenship." New York State, Draft Plan to the U. S. Department of Education, The Elementary and Secondary Education Act of 1965, as amended by the Every Student Succeeds Act 6 (July 2017).

76. Bonner *ex rel.* Bonner v. Daniels 885 N.E.2d 673, 691 (Ind. Ct. App. 2008) (quoting statement of delegate Bryant of Warren County, 2 REPORT OF THE DEBATES AND PROCEEDINGS OF THE CONVENTION FOR THE REVISION OF THE CONSTITUTION OF THE STATE OF INDIANA 1850 1890–91).

77. *See, e.g.,* ROGERS M. SMITH, CIVIC IDEALS: CONFLICTING VISIONS OF CITIZENSHIP IN U.S. HISTORY (1997) (discussing systematic exclusion of women, minorities and working class from exercise of the franchise); Thiel v. S. Pac. Cty., 328 U.S. 217, 222 (1946) (discussing systematic exclusion from jury list of those who work for a daily wage); Taylor v. Louisiana, 419 U.S. 522, 538 (1975) (discussing systematic exclusion of women from jury duty).

78. The history of the slow extension of the franchise throughout American history is discussed in detail in ALEXANDER KEYSSAR, THE RIGHT TO VOTE: THE CONTESTED HISTORY OF DEMOCRACY IN THE UNITED STATES (2000).

79. 52 U.S.C.A. § 10101 *et seq.*

80. *See, e.g.,* MOLLY SELVIN & LARRY PICUS, THE DEBATE OVER JURY PERFORMANCE: OBSERVATIONS FROM A RECENT ASBESTOS CASE 45–46 (RAND 1987), *available at* http://www.rand.org/content/dam/rand/pubs/reports/2007/R3479.pdf; ARTHUR D. AUSTIN, COMPLEX LITIGATION CONFRONTS THE JURY SYSTEM: A CASE STUDY (1984); William C. Thompson, *Are Juries Competent to Evaluate Statistical Evidence?* 52 LAW & CONTEMP. PROBS. 9, 24–41 (1989).

81. "If the jury has an Achilles heel, it is the comprehension of legal instructions." Joe S. Cecil et al., *Citizen Comprehension of Difficult Issues: Lessons from Civil Jury Trials*, 40 AM. UNIV. L. REV. 727, 749 (1991). The authors cited an

in-depth examination of jury decision-making in complex cases by the Litigation Section of the American Bar Association, which found that jurors had significant difficulty in understanding and applying judicial instructions and that there was substantial variance in juror comprehension between cases and among jurors. *Id.* at 752–54. *See also* Franklin Strier, *The Educated Jury: A Proposal for Complex Litigation*, 47 DEPAUL L. REV. 49, 53 (1997) (discussing studies indicating that pattern jury instructions are difficult for juries to understand).

82. Warren E. Burger, *The Use of Lay Jurors in Complicated Civil Cases*, Remarks to the Conference of State Chief Justices (3–5) (Aug. 7, 1979) (asserting that technical evidence is too complex for lay juries); *see also* Warren E. Burger, *Agenda for Change*, 54 JUDICATURE 232, 235 (1971) (recommending consideration of use of experts to assist judges in complex cases); Peter Sperlich, *The Case for Preserving Trial by Jury in Complex Civil Litigation*, 65 JUDICATURE 394, 397 (1982) (discussing Chief Justice Burger's concern and its impact).

83. *Burger Suggests Waiving Juries in Complex Civil Trials*, NAT'L L.J., Aug. 13, 1979, at 21.

84. *See, e.g.,* William Luneberg & Mark A. Nordenberg, *Specially Qualified Juries & Expert Nonjury Tribunals: Alternatives for Coping with the Complexities of Modern Civil Litigation*, 67 VA. L. REV. 887, 945–50 (1981); Mark A. Nordenberg & William Luneberg, *Decision-Making in Complex Federal Civil Cases: Two Alternatives to the Traditional Jury*, 65 JUDICATURE 420, 425–27 (1982) (proposing that jurors in complex cases be required to hold a college degree); Strier, *supra* note 81.

85. *See, e.g., In re* Japanese Elec. Prods Antitrust Litig., 631 F.2d 1069, 1084 (3rd Cir. 1980) (denying right to jury in complex litigation); Bernstein v. Universal Pictures, 79 F.R.D. 59 (S.D.N.Y 1978) (same). *But see In re* U.S. Fin. Secs. Litig., 609 F.2d 411 (9th Cir. 1979) (holding that there is no complexity exception to the Seventh Amendment); *see also Ross v. Bernhard*, 396 U.S. 531, 538 n. 10 (noting that in determining whether an issue was of a legal nature and therefore triable by a jury, courts should consider "the practical abilities and limitations of juries"); Note, *The Right to a Jury Trial in Complex Civil Litigation*, 92 HARV. L. REV. 898 (1979).

86. 28 U.S.C. § 1861. The act states that "it is the policy of the United States that all litigants in federal courts entitled to trial by jury shall have the right to grand and petit juries selected at random from a fair cross-section of the community." This right was apparently extended to the states by Taylor v. Louisiana, 419 U.S. 522, 528 (1975), at least in regard to criminal cases. *But see* United States v. Potter, 552 F.2d 901, 905 (9th Cir. 1977) (holding that "the less educated" are not a "cognizable group" entitled to constitutional protections); United States v. Butera, 420 F.2d 564, 571 (1st. Cir 1970) (indicating that the "less educated" are a distinctive group).

87. *See, e.g.,* Batson v. Kentucky, 476 U.S. 79 (1986) (a black defendant may

challenge prosecutors' use of peremptory challenges against racial minorities); Taylor v. Louisiana, 419 U.S. 522 (1975) (banning exclusion of women as a class from jury service).

88. Moore v. New York, 333 U.S. 565, 570 (1948). The New York elite jury panel practice had previously been upheld by the Court in Fay v. New York, 332 U.S. 261 (1946). As late as 1967, 60 percent of federal courts still relied heavily on blue-ribbon juries (results of a 1967 survey of federal courts cited in JEFFREY ABRAMSON, WE, THE JURY: THE JURY SYSTEM AND THE IDEAL OF DEMOCRACY 99 (1994). Juries have historically played a more critical role in America than in other nations, including England. In colonial days, the colonists relied on the jury to restrain governmental excesses, as in the Peter Zenger trial, and juries played an important role in keeping the judicial branch independent. In the nineteenth century, they were an important counter to pro-business judges. For an overview discussion of the historical role of American juries, *see* Stephan Landsman, *The History and Objectives of the Civil Jury System*, *in* VERDICT: ASSESSING THE CIVIL JURY SYSTEM 22 (Robert E. Litan ed., 1993). *See also* LEONARD W. LEVY, THE PALLADIUM OF JUSTICE: ORIGINS OF TRIAL BY JURY (1999).

89. *See, e.g.,* R. Lempert, *Civil Furies and Complex Cases: Taking Stock After 12 Years*, in VERDICT, *supra* note 88; Steven A. Saltzburg, *Improving the Quality of Jury Decision-Making*, *id.* at 341; Barbara Allen Babcock, *Jury Service and Community Representation*, in *id.* at 460. In a 1989 survey, 58 percent of federal judges and 66 percent of state court judges disagreed with the proposition that "in complex civil cases, there should be some minimum level of education or qualifications to avoid jurors who cannot understand the case." Louis Harris & Assocs., Inc., *Judges' Opinions on Procedural Issues: A Survey of State and Federal Trial Judges Who Spend at Least Half Their Time on General Civil Cases*, 69 B.U. L. REV. 731, 747 (1989).

90. *See, e.g.,* Graham C. Lilly, *The Decline of the American Jury*, 72 U. COLO. L. REV. 53 (2001) (long-term trends in the nature of litigation and the selection of juries raise serious questions about the continued viability of the jury system); Beth Z. Shaw, *Judging Juries: Evaluating Renewed Proposals for Specialized Juries from a Public Choice Perspective*, 2006 UCLA J. L. & TECH. 3 (2006) (advocating use of specialized juries in complex cases to increase comprehension and reduce the potential for cascading effects during deliberation); Jennifer F. Miller, *Should Juries Hear Complex Patent Cases?*, 2004 DUKE L. & TECH. REV. 4.

91. HARRY KALVEN, JR., & HANS ZEISEL, THE AMERICAN JURY 149 (2nd ed. 1971). Kalven and Zeisel's study was based on questionnaires of a sample of approximately 3,500 criminal jury trials conducted in the mid-1950s. Among other things, the researchers asked presiding judges how they would have decided cases and found that the actual verdicts reached by the juries corresponded to the judges' views in 78 percent of cases. *Id.* at 63. Judge-jury disagreements tended to be on issues of community values and not on factual issues. *Id.* at 116.

See also John Guinther, The Jury in America 208–09 (1988) (stating that heterogeneous juries recognize and offset each other's biases).

92. Strier, *supra* note 81, at 55.

Chapter Four

1. Only about 2 percent of civil lawsuits filed in the United States go to trial, and the majority of all other cases settle. *See* Marc Galanter & Mia Cahill, *Most Cases Settle: Judicial Promotion and Regulation of Settlements*, 46 Stan. L. Rev. 1301 (1994); John Barkai et al., *A Profile of Settlement*, 42 Court Rev. 35 (2006), *available at* http://aja.ncsc.dni.us/courtrv/cr42-3and4/CR42-3BarkaiKentMartin.pdf.

2. These definitions paraphrase and summarize the concepts in Westheimer & Kahne, *Educating the "Good" Citizen: Political Choices and Pedagogical Goals*, 41 Am. Educ. Res. J. 237 (2004).

3. *See* Character Counts!, at https://charactercounts.org/program-overview/.

4. *See, e.g.,* Mario Carretero, Helen Haste & Angela Bermudez, *Civic Education, in* Handbook of Educational Psychology 295 (2013) (outlining a "new civics" approach that expands the definition of civic participation beyond voting-related behavior and knowledge of political institutions and emphasizes "understanding, skills, agency and motivation through hands-on experiences with civic issues and actions"); Youth & Participatory Pols. Res. Network, *at* http://ypp.dmlcentral.net/pages/about; Helen Haste & Angela Bermudez, *The Power of Story: Historical Narratives and the Construction of Civic Identity, in* International Handbook of Research in Historical Culture and Education (M. Carretero, S. Berger & M. Grever eds., 2015).

5. Westheimer & Kahne, *supra* note 2, at 243–44.

6. *Id.* at 244. *See also* Diana E. Hess, Controversy in the Classroom: The Democratic Power of Discussion 132–35 (2009) (discussing opposing views on how schools should implement flag-salute requirements in the wake of the 9/11 attack).

7. Westheimer & Kahne, *supra* note 2, at 244.

8. Morris Janowitz, The Reconstruction of Patriotism: Education for Civic Consciousness 166 (1983) (quoting Peter Kleinbard, a "keen observer of inner-city educational institutions").

9. Thomas Lickona, Educating for Character: How Our Schools Can Teach Respect and Responsibility 276 (1991).

10. *Id.* at 306.

11. Meira Levinson, No Citizen Left Behind 44 (2012) (adopting the Civic Mission of the Schools definition of citizenship that includes these specific

traits). *See also* JOEL WESTHEIMER, WHAT KIND OF CITIZEN? EDUCATING OUR CHILDREN FOR THE COMMON GOOD 46 (2015) ("Character traits such as honesty, integrity, and responsibility for one's own actions are certainly valuable. . . . But on their own, they are not about democracy").

12. CAMPAIGN FOR THE CIVIC MISSION OF THE SCHOOLS, GUARDIAN OF DEMOCRACY: THE CIVIC MISSION OF THE SCHOOLS (2011), *available at* http://civicmission.s3.amazonaws.com/118/f0/5/171/1/Guardian-of-Democracy-report.pdf. This report was substantially based on the Civic Mission of the Schools report that had been issued in 2003 by the Carnegie Corporation of New York and the Center for Information and Research on Civic Learning and Engagement (CIRCLE).

13. These included the Character Education Partnership, National Conference of State Legislators, the American Enterprise Institute, American Federation of Teachers, and the Coalition for Community Schools. *Id.* at 45.

14. *Id.* at 12.

15. *See, e.g.,* CARNEGIE CORP. & CIRCLE, THE CIVIC MISSION OF THE SCHOOLS 21–28 (2003); CAMPAIGN FOR THE CIVIC MISSION OF THE SCHOOLS ET AL., *supra* note 12, at 16–17; JUDITH TORNEY-PURTA & SUSAN VERMEER LOPEZ, DEVELOPING CITIZENSHIP COMPETENCIES FROM KINDERGARTEN THROUGH GRADE 12: A BACKGROUND PAPER FOR POLICYMAKERS AND EDUCATORS (2006), *available at* http://files.eric.ed.gov/fulltext/ED493710.pdf; DANIELLE ALLEN, EDUCATION AND EQUALITY (2016); Wolfgang Althof & Marvin W. Berkowitz, *Moral Education and Character Education: Their Relationship and Roles in Citizenship Education*, 35 J. MORAL EDUC. 495, 503 (2006).

16. NAT'L COMM'N ON EXCELLENCE IN EDUC., A NATION AT RISK 7 (1983).

17. PETER LEVINE & KEI KAWASHIMA-GINSBERG, CIVIC EDUCATION AND DEEPER LEARNING 1 (2015), *available at* http://www.jff.org/sites/default/files/publications/materials/Civic-Education-and-Deeper-Learning-012815.pdf.

18. *Id.* at 1–2.

19. DANIELLE ALLEN, EDUCATION AND EQUALITY (2016).

20. *Id.* at 10. A recent congressionally requested report by a distinguished panel of the National Academy of Arts and Sciences similarly found that all students need a thorough grounding in the humanities, social sciences, and the natural sciences, to provide "an intellectual framework and context for understanding and thriving in a changing world . . . [and to] learn not only what but how and why." AM. ACAD. OF ARTS AND SCIS., THE HEART OF THE MATTER: THE HUMANITIES AND SOCIAL SCIENCES FOR A VIBRANT, COMPETITIVE, AND SECURE NATION 10 (2013).

21. MARTHA NUSSBAUM, NOT FOR PROFIT: WHY DEMOCRACY NEEDS THE HUMANITIES 2 (2010). *See also* ANNE NEWMAN, REALIZING EDUCATIONAL RIGHTS: ADVANCING SCHOOL REFORM THROUGH COURTS AND COMMUNITIES 37 (2013) ("Of course literacy, numeracy, and a basic understanding of history, economics, science and literature are foundational to understanding political and social is-

sues in an ever-evolving world, and to deliberating there issues with diverse fellow citizens").

22. Ilya Somin asserts that increasing levels of education increase political knowledge only 1.3 to 8 points on a 30-point scale. ILYA SOMIN, DEMOCRACY AND POLITICAL IGNORANCE: WHY SMALLER GOVERNMENT IS SMARTER 98–99 (2016). The large 8-point increase relates to a hypothetical shift from a middle school dropout level of education to a graduate degree; the smaller 1.3-point increase stems from a shift from a high school graduate to a college graduate. The studies he cites examine years of schooling but do not focus on the actual content of the education that students receive in those schools. The greatest increases in political knowledge (11.1 points on a 30-point scale) come from an interest in politics. Somin equates interest in politics with partisanship, but political interest can also be stirred by a broad and deep knowledge base.

23. NUSSBAUM, *supra* note 21, at 81.

24. CLAUS VON ZASTROW WITH HELEN JANC, ACADEMIC ATROPHY: THE CONDITION OF THE LIBERAL ARTS IN AMERICA'S PUBLIC SCHOOLS 9 (Council for Basic Educ. 2004).

25. Nat'l Assessment Governing Bd., *Civics Framework for the National Assessment of Educational Progress* (2014), *available at* https://www.nagb.org/publications/frameworks/civics/2014-civics-framework.html. Over a twenty-year period, NAEP assembled committees of scholars, educators, civic leaders, and interested members of the public and worked with the Center on Civic Education and the American Institutes for Research to identify and refine their concepts of the knowledge, skills, and dispositions that students need to function well as civic participants. Many of the concepts in its framework were taken from the National Standards for Civics and Government, developed by the Center on Civic Education (*available at* http://www.civiced.org/standards). The NAEP framework describes the essential elements of civic education in terms of three interrelated components: intellectual and participatory skills, knowledge, and civic dispositions. *Id.* at 15–31.

26. *Id.* at 16.

27. Elementary & Secondary Sch. Act, 20 U.S.C.A. § 6311(b)(1)(C) (2015). Exit examinations in social studies are required in many states, but these graduation requirements do not drive instructional priorities during the elementary, middle, and early high school years as do the annual federally required achievement tests on which school ratings and individual progress are assessed.

28. *See* discussions in chapter 1, at p. 32, and chapter 3, at pp. 62–63.

29. Rosemary C. Salomone, *The Common School Before and After Brown, Democracy, Equality and the Productivity Agenda*, 120 YALE L.J. 1454, 1486 (2011).

30. NORMAN H. NIE, JANE JUNN & KENNETH STEHLIK-BARRY, EDUCATION AND DEMOCRATIC CITIZENSHIP IN AMERICA 41–42 (1996). *See also* Norman Nie &

D. Sunshine Hillygus, *Education and Democratic Citizenship*, *in* MAKING GOOD CITIZENS: EDUCATION AND CIVIL SOCIETY 30 (Diane Ravitch & Joseph P. Viteritti eds., 2001) (empirical analysis finds that college education, and particularly one grounded in social science curriculum, correlates with higher levels of verbal aptitude; higher levels of political participation, and more civic voluntarism).

31. Nat'l Assessment Governing Bd., *supra* note 25, at 23–26. NAEP also calls for "participatory skills" that include interacting, listening and monitoring, and "influencing" by voting, petitioning, and participating in civic and political activities. *Id.* at 26–29.

32. ALLEN, *supra* note 19, at 40. The kinds of verbal skills that Allen describes are similar to those the courts deemed critical for civic participation in Rose v. Council for Better Educ., 790 S.W.2d 186, 212 (Ky. 1989) ("Sufficient oral and written communication skills to enable students to function in a complex and rapidly changing civilization"), and in CFE v. State, 719 N.Y.S.2d 475, 485 (N.Y. Sup. Ct. 2001) ("An engaged, capable voter needs the intellectual tools to evaluate complex issues, such as campaign finance reform, tax policy, and global warming, to name only a few").

33. Jane Mansbridge et al., *A Systemic Approach to Deliberative Democracy*, *in* DELIBERATIVE SYSTEMS DELIBERATIVE DEMOCRACY AT THE LARGE SCALE 1, 4–5 (John Parkinson & Jane Mansbridge eds., 2012). For other discussions of the theory of deliberative democracy, *see, e.g.*, BENJAMIN BARBER, STRONG DEMOCRACY: PARTICIPATORY DEMOCRACY FOR A NEW AGE (1984); AMY GUTMANN & DENNIS THOMPSON, WHY DELIBERATIVE DEMOCRACY (2004); RONALD DWORKIN, JUSTICE FOR HEDGEHOGS (2011).

34. *See* Joshua Cohen, *Deliberative Democracy and Democratic Legitimacy*, *in* THE GOOD POLITY 21 (A. Hamlin & P. Petit eds., 1989). *See also* Joshua Cohen, *Democracy and Literacy*, *in* DELIBERATIVE DEMOCRACY 193 (Jon Elsner ed., 1998).

35. Civic republicanism began as a movement to emphasize the importance to the drafters of the Constitution of classical republican concepts, such as participatory democracy. *See, e.g.*, GARY WILLS, INVENTING AMERICA: JEFFERSON'S DECLARATION OF INDEPENDENCE (1978); GORDON S. WOOD, THE CREATION OF THE AMERICAN REPUBLIC 1776–1787 (1969), but then developed into a broader political-legal perspective that "embraces an ongoing deliberative process . . . to arrive at the public good." Mark Seidenfeld, *A Civic Republican Justification for the Bureaucratic State*, 105 HARV. L. REV. 1511, 1528 (1992). *See also* Frank I. Michelman, *Law's Republic*, 97 YALE L.J. 1493, 1495 (1988) (advocating republican constitutionalism, which "involves the ongoing revision of the normative histories that make political communities sources of contestable value and self-direction for their members").

36. ANDREW PETERSON, CIVIC REPUBLICANISM AND CIVIC EDUCATION 5 (2011). Peterson also notes that civic republicanism is a renaissance of the idea

that "civic virtue needs to be inculcated within the citizenry." *Id.* at 148. Harvard professor Michael Sandel, a prime proponent of civic republicanism, believes that since the mid-twentieth century, America has come to overemphasize consumerism and a "voluntaristic conception of freedom and the conception of persons as free and independent selves" and has neglected the "republican" tradition of civic involvement that is critical for the functioning of a democratic polity. MICHAEL J. SANDEL, DEMOCRACY'S DISCONTENT: AMERICA IN SEARCH OF A PUBLIC PHILOSOPHY 261 (1996).

37. ROBERT N. BELLAH ET AL., HABITS OF THE HEART 218 (1985).

38. Amy Gutmann & Dennis Thompson, *Moral Conflict and Political Consensus*, 101 ETHICS 64, 86–87 (1990); *see also* Christopher Lasch, *The Communitarian Critique of Liberalism*, in COMMUNITY IN AMERICA: THE CHALLENGE OF HABITS OF THE HEAR 173, 178 (Charles H. Reynolds & Ralph V. Norman eds., 1988) (stating that social solidarity "rests on public conversation").

39. BELLAH ET AL., *supra* note 37, at 135 ("when citizens are engaged in thinking about the whole, they find their conceptions of their interests broadened, and their commitment to search for common good deepens"). *See also* Martha Minow, *Foreword: Justice Endangered*, 101 HARV. L. REV. 10, 72 (1987) (discussing the need to take the perspective of the person you called "different").

40. Seidenfeld, *supra* note 35, at 1539 ("The process of deliberation . . . frequently enables society to come close [to consensus] in the sense of arriving at a set of principles as to which most citizens would agree. Moreover . . . the call for persuasion of others as the goals of the deliberative process is likely to discourage adoption of egregiously coercive principles"). *See also* Terence H. McLaughlin, *Liberalism, Education and the Common School*, 29 J. PHIL. EDUC. 239, 248 (1995) ("Democratic deliberation can often lead to consensus, but even if it does not, it can also result in understanding and acceptance of reasonable differences," and "this enriches respect, and indeed toleration, with principle"); EAMON CALLAN, CREATING CITIZENS: POLITICAL EDUCATION AND LIBERAL DEMOCRACY 176 (1997) (substantive conversations of this kind can "nourish an ever widening web of relations, trust, reciprocal goodwill, and associative loyalty" that are the hallmarks of a positive, engaged community).

41. JOHN RAWLS, POLITICAL LIBERALISM 10 (1992).

42. *Id.* at 9.

43. Rawls uses this approach to develop his well-known theory of justice which asks readers to consider basic questions of justice and fair distribution of wealth and benefits from the perspective of constructing a social contract that assumes that they are operating from behind a "veil of ignorance" about their actual life situation. JOHN RAWLS, A THEORY OF JUSTICE (1971).

44. DIANA C. MUTZ, HEARING THE OTHER SIDE: DELIBERATIVE VERSUS PARTICIPATION DEMOCRACY (2006).

45. *Id.* at 3.

46. *Id.* at 148–50.

47. Jane Mansbridge, *Three Reasons Political Polarization Is Here to Stay*, Wash. Post, Mar. 11, 2016, *available at* https://www.washingtonpost.com/news/in-theory/wp/2016/03/11/three-reasons-political-polarization-is-here-to-stay/.

48. Shanto Iyengar, Gaurav Sood & Yphtach Lelkes, *Affect, Not Ideology: A Social Identity Perspective on Polarization*, 76 Pub. Opin. Q. 405 (2012). On a "thermometer rating" in which feelings of "hot" or "cold" toward members of the opposing party are rated on a scale of 1 to 100, the authors found that in 2008, Democratic and Republican ratings of the opposition party had dropped to just below 32 degrees; in comparison, Protestants gave Catholics a 66 rating, Democrats gave big business a 51 and Republicans rated "people on welfare" at 50. *Id.*

49. Karen Stenner, The Authoritarian Dynamic 134, 196 (2005). The overall theme of Stenner's book is that authoritarianism is not a stable personality trait but a psychological predisposition to become intolerant when the person perceives a certain kind of threat from outsiders who challenge established social norms and the group's shared values. Stenner's thesis may explain why the hyperbolic emphasis on porous borders and Islamic terrorism during the 2016 election campaign provoked increased authoritarian reactions in parts of the population. Stenner warns that "exposure to difference, talking about difference and applauding difference—the hallmarks of liberal democracy—are the surest ways to aggravate those who are innately intolerant." *Id.* at 330. She does note, however, that those prone to authoritarianism—who she estimates represent about 25 percent of the population—are provoked by "apparent variance in beliefs, values and culture . . . [more] than racial and ethnic diversity." *Id.* This would seem to indicate that emphasizing the broad consensus on civic values that exists in our society (see the discussion earlier in this chapter) may have an ameliorative, rather than a provocative, effect on those of an authoritarian bent.

50. Joseph Kahne & Benjamin Bowyer, *Educating for Democracy in a Partisan Age: Confronting the Challenges of Motivated Reasoning and Misinformation*, 54 Am. Educ. Res. J. 6 (2017) (citations omitted). They also note: "Moreover, rather than learning from exposure to new information, individuals who encounter . . . new information that contradicts their prior perspective often become even more favorable to their prior beliefs." *Id.* at 7.

51. *Id.* at 27.

52. Tali Mendelberg, *The Deliberative Citizen: Theory and Evidence*, *in* Political Decision-Making, Deliberation and Participation 151, 180 (Michael X. Delli Carpini, Leonie Huddy & Robert Y. Shapiro eds., 2002).

53. Hochschild and Einstein, after undertaking an extensive analysis of the impact of misinformation on voting patterns and public policy decision making, propose three possible solutions for attaining "Jefferson's ideal" of the active, informed voter: more effectively educating the public on the facts concerning

pending major public policy issues, finding ways to work around, ignore or reject public opinion, and organizing social movements to try to change the terms of the debate. JENNIFER L. HOCHSCHILD & KATHERINE LEVINE EINSTEIN, DO FACTS MATTER? INFORMATION AND MISINFORMATION IN AMERICAN POLITICS (2015). As the authors themselves acknowledge in regard to at least one of these recommendations, however, these approaches are "less a strategy than a hope." *Id.* at 143. Instilling respect for facts in students when they are young and instructing them in the use of critical analytic skills for analyzing policy-related information before their political positions become crystallized would have much greater potential for success in the long run.

54. Quoted in James Youniss, *How to Enrich Civic Education and Sustain Democracy*, *in* MAKING CIVICS COUNT: CITIZENSHIP EDUCATION FOR A NEW GENERATION 116–17 (David E. Campbell, Meira Levinson & Frederick M. Hess eds., 2012).

55. *See* ALLEN, *supra* note 19, at 42–43 ("strategic and tactical understanding of the levers of political change" is an essential aspect of "preparatory readiness" for capable citizenship).

56. JOHN DEWEY, DEMOCRACY AND EDUCATION: AN INTRODUCTION TO THE PHILOSOPHY OF EDUCATION (1963) (1916).

57. Peter Levine, *Education for a Civil Society*, *in* MAKING CIVICS COUNT, *supra* note 54, at 37, 43.

58. Constance Flanagan et al., *School and Community Climates and Civic Commitments: Patterns for Ethnic Minority and Majority Students*, 99 J. EDUC. PSYCH. 421 (2007).

59. ROBERT D. PUTNAM, OUR KIDS: THE AMERICAN DREAM IN CRISIS 174 (2015).

60. Margo Gardner, Jodie Roth & Jeanne Brooks-Gunn, *Adolescents' Participation in Organized Activities and Developmental Success 2 and 8 Years After High School: Do Sponsorship, Duration, and Intensity Matter?*, 44 DEV. PSYCH. 814 (2008). *See also* Jonathan F. Zaff et al., *Implications of Extracurricular Activity Participation During Adolescence on Positive Outcomes* 18 J. ADOLESC. RES. 599 (2003) (adolescents who consistently participated in activities from eighth grade through twelfth grade were more likely to vote, volunteer, or attend college than those who participated only occasionally or those who never participated); SIDNEY VERBA, KAY L. SCHLOZMAN & HARRY E. BRADY, VOICE AND EQUALITY: CIVIC VOLUNTEERISM IN AMERICAN LIFE 424–25 (1995) (study of 2,517 adults concluded that the variable most closely related to current civic participation was high school involvement in student government, clubs, and other activities).

61. Reuben J. Thomas & Daniel A. McFarland, *Joining Young Voting Young: The Effects of Youth Voluntary Associations on Early Adult Voting* (Ctr. for Info. & Research on Civic Learning & Engagement, Working Paper No. 73,

2010), *available at* http://eric.ed.gov/?id=ED512250 (the most robust effects on voting habits resulted from high school involvement in the performing arts).

62. *See, e.g.*, PUTNAM, *supra* note 59, at 174–76, and studies cited therein; Peter Kuhn & Catherine Weinberger, *Leadership Skills and Wages*, 23 J. LABOR. ECON. 395 (2005) (students who were high school team captains or class presidents earned higher incomes ten years later); Robert K. Ream & Russell W. Rumberger, *Student Engagement, Peer Social Capital, and School Dropout Among Mexican American and Non-Latino White Students*, 81 SOC. EDUC. 109 (2008) (participation in extracurricular activities and especially athletics predicts lower dropout rates and higher educational attainment, especially for low-income Latino students); Christy Lleras, *Do Skills and Behaviors in High School Matter? The Contribution of Noncognitive Factors in Explaining Differences in Educational Attainment and Earnings*, 37 SOC. SCI. RES. 888 (2008) (regardless of their educational attainment, students who were perceived by their teachers to relate well with other students, to be less passive during class, and who participated in extracurricular academic and sports activities in high school activities had higher earnings ten years later).

63. Joseph E. Kahne & Susan E. Sporte, *Developing Citizens: The Impact of Civic Learning Opportunities on Students' Commitment to Civic Participation*, 45 AM. EDUC. RES. J. 738, 757 (2008).

64. Daniel Hart, Thomas M. Donnelly, James Youniss & Robert Atkins, *High School Community Service as a Predictor of Adult Voting and Volunteering*, 44 AM. EDUC. RES. J. 197 (2007) (also noting that civic knowledge was related only to greater voting habits but not to other forms of civic participation). *See also* James Youniss, Yang Su & Miranda Yates, *The Role of Community Service in Identity Development: Normative, Unconventional and Deviant Orientations*, 14 J. ADOLESC. RES. 248 (1999) (service experience positively affects development in the areas of political involvement, religion, and substance abuse; students' participation in school government and other types of school activities doubled the likelihood of service).

65. Kahne & Sporte, *supra* note 63. *See also* Shelly Billig, Sue Root & Dan Jesse, *The Impact of Participation in Service Learning on High School Students' Civic Engagement* (Ctr. for Info. & Research on Civic Learning & Engagement, Working Paper No. 33, 2005), *available at* http://www.servicelearningnetwork.org/wp-content/uploads/2014/09/WP33Billig.pdf (finding that service-learning is effective when it is implemented well but no more effective than conventional social studies classes when conditions are not optimal).

66. SUBHI GODSAY ET AL., CENTER FOR INFORMATION AND RESEARCH ON CIVIC LEARNING AND ENGAGEMENT FACT SHEET 9 (Oct. 2012) (data attachment), *available at* http://civicyouth.org/wp-content/uploads/2012/10/State-Civic-Ed-Requirements-Fact-Sheet-2012-Oct-19.pdf.

67. PETER LEVINE, THE FUTURE OF DEMOCRACY: DEVELOPING THE NEXT GEN-

ERATION OF AMERICAN CITIZENS 134 (2007). Levine notes: "In the context of real public schools, however, service-learning often degenerates into cleaning the school playground and then briefly discussing this experience." *Id.*

68. SUSAN M. ANDERSON, SERVICE LEARNING: A NATIONAL STRATEGY FOR YOUTH DEVELOPMENT (1998), *available at* http://www.gwu.edu/~ccps/pop_svc.html.

69. *Id.*

70. *See, e.g.,* MASS. CONST. pt. II, ch. 5, § 2 (referring to "Wisdom and knowledge, as well as virtue, diffused generally among the body of the people, being necessary for the preservation of their rights and liberties"); N.H. CONST. pt. 2, art. 83 (referring to "the principles of humanity and general benevolence, public and private charity, industry and economy, honesty and punctuality, sincerity, sobriety, and all social affections, and generous sentiments, among the people").

71. 1 THE PAPERS OF JAMES MADISON, THE FOUNDERS' CONSTITUTION ch. 12, doc. 36 (William T. Hutchinson et al., eds., 1962–77).

72. *See, e.g.,* N.C. CONST. of 1868 art. 3 ("Religion, morality, and knowledge being necessary to good government and the happiness of mankind, schools, libraries, and the means of education shall forever be encouraged"); MICH. CONST. of 1908 art. XI, § 1; MICH. CONST. of 1963 art. VIII, § 1 (same). *See also* FRED HIRSCH, SOCIAL LIMITS TO GROWTH 147 (1976) ("[Liberalism in the eighteenth and nineteenth centuries] was predicated on an underlying moral, religious base. . . . Men could safely be trusted to pursue their own self-interest without undue harm to the community, not only because of the restrictions imposed by law, but also because they were subject to built-in restraints derived from morals, religions, customs and education").

73. DEWEY, *supra* note 56, at 87.

74. *See, e.g.,* PATHWAYS TO CIVIC CHARACTER: A SHARED VISION FOR AMERICA'S SCHOOLS (signed by, *inter alia*, Assoc. for Supervision & Curriculum, Nat'l Assoc. of Elementary Sch. Principals, Nat'l Assoc. of Secondary Sch. Principals, & Nat'l Sch. Bds. Assoc.), *available at* http://www.utahciviccoalition.org/downloads/Pathways_to_Civic_Character.pdf; CARNEGIE CORP. & CTR. FOR INFO. & RESEARCH ON CIVIC LEARNING & ENGAGEMENT, THE CIVIC MISSION OF SCHOOLS 4 (2003), *available at* http://civicmission.s3.amazonaws.com/118/f7/1/172/2003_Civic_Mission_of_Schools_Report.pdf.

75. *See* discussion in chapter 2, at pp. 34–35.

76. *See, e.g.,* Wolfgang Altof & Marvin W. Berkowitz, *Moral Education and Character Education: Their Relationship and Roles in Citizenship Education*, 35 J. MORAL EDUC. 495, 513 (2006), *available at* https://characterandcitizenship.org/PDF/MoralEducationandCharacterEducationAlthofBerkowitz.pdf (emphasizing "social justice, honesty, personal and social responsibility, equality, etc."); CHARACTER COUNTS!, SIX PILLARS OF CHARACTER (trustworthiness, respect, responsibility, fairness, caring and citizenship), *available at* https://www

.charactercounts.org); R. FREEMAN BUTTS, THE CIVIC MISSION IN EDUCATION REFORM PERSPECTIVES FOR THE PUBLIC AND THE PROFESSION 280 (1989) (proposing twelve categories of civic values including "truth" and "patriotism"); PATHWAYS TO CIVIC CHARACTER, *supra* note 74 (setting forth nine specific qualities, including honesty, personal integrity, caring, social justice, resolving differences in constructive ways); CHARACTER.ORG (caring, honesty, diligence, fairness, fortitude, responsibility, grit, creativity, critical thinking, and respect for self and others), *available at* http://character.org/about/faqs; CONGRESSIONAL MEDAL OF HONOR FOUND., CHARACTER DEVELOPMENT PROGRAM (character values framework emphasizing courage, commitment, sacrifice, patriotism, integrity, and citizenship), *available at* http://www.cmohfoundation.org/#!cdp/c17qn.

77. *See, e.g.*, PATHWAYS TO CIVIC CHARACTER, *supra* note 74 (emphasizing in addition to values of honesty, personal integrity, and respect for others: "Work to counter prejudice and discrimination; [and] think critically and creatively about local issues, state and national affairs, and world events"); FREEMAN BUTTS, *supra* note 76, at 280 (emphasizing in addition to honesty and patriotism, equality, diversity, and due process); COMMUNITARIAN NETWORK, THE ROLE OF CIVIC EDUCATION (1998) (emphasizing, in addition to moral responsibility and self-discipline, respect for the rule of law and willingness to listen, negotiate, and compromise), *available at* http://www.gwu.edu/~ccps/pop_civ.html; Marvin W. Berkowitz, Wolfgang Althof & Scott Jones, *Educating for Civic Character*, *in* THE SAGE HANDBOOK OF EDUCATION FOR CITIZENSHIP AND DEMOCRACY 401–02 (James Arthur, Ian Davies & Carole Hahn eds., 2008) (defining the "civic character" needed to maintain a successful democracy in terms of "the set of dispositions and skills that motivate and enable an individual to effectively and responsibly participate in the public sphere in order to serve the common good").

78. Nat'l Assessment Governing Bd., *supra* note 25, at 30.

79. *Id. See, e.g.*, N.Y. STATE EDUC. DEP'T, PARTICIPATION IN GOVERNMENT, CORE CURRICULUM (2002), *available at* http://www.p12.nysed.gov/ciai/socst/documents/partgov.pdf (defining "civic values" as "those important principles that serve as the foundation for our democratic form of government. These values include justice, honesty, self-discipline, due process, equality, majority rule with respect for minority rights, and respect for self, others, and property").

80. Jennifer Hochschild & Nathan Scovronick, *Democratic Education and the American Dream*, *in* REDISCOVERING THE DEMOCRATIC PURPOSES OF EDUCATION 209, 212 (Lorraine M. McDonnel, P. Michael Timpane & Roger Benjamin eds., 2000).

81. STEPHEN MACEDO, DIVERSITY AND DISTRUST: CIVIC EDUCATION IN A MULTI-CULTURAL DEMOCRACY 234 (2000).

82. *Id.*

83. AMY GUTMANN, DEMOCRATIC EDUCATION 29 (1987).

84. *Id.* at 42.

85. *Id.* at 46.

86. *Id.* at 172.

87. MACEDO, *supra* note 81, at 238. *See also* JOSEPH RAZ, THE MORALITY OF FREEDOM 369–70 (1986) (emphasizing importance of developing in children a sense of autonomy and cognitive skills that will allow people to cope with a constantly changing environment).

88. Terence H. McLaughlin, *Liberalism, Education and the Common School*, 29 J. PHIL. EDUC. 3 239, 248 (1995).

89. MACEDO, *supra* note 81, at 172.

90. WILLIAM GALSTON, LIBERAL PURPOSES: GOODS, VIRTUES, AND DIVERSITY IN THE LIBERAL STATE 253 (1991).

91. Michael McConnell, *Education Disestablishment: Why Democratic Values Are Ill-Served by Democratic Control of Schooling*, *in* MORAL AND POLITICAL EDUCATION 87 (Stephen Macedo & Yael Tamir eds., NOMOS XLIII, 2002).

92. Rob Reich, *How and Why to Support Common Schooling and Educational Choice at the Same Time*, 4 J. PHIL. EDUC. 709, 721 (2007). Terrance McLaughlin notes in this regard that "although the school must make it clear that controversial religious consideration should not have decisive weight in the public domain, the school should not seek to promote a secular view of life as a whole." McLaughlin, *supra* note 88, at 248.

93. *Id.*

94. Harry Brighouse & Adam Swift, *Family Values and School Policy: Shaping Values and Conferring Advantage*, *in* EDUCATION, JUSTICE, AND DEMOCRACY 210 (Danielle Allen & Rob Reich eds., 2013).

95. IAN MACMULLEN, CIVICS BEYOND CRITICS: CHARACTER EDUCATION IN A LIBERAL DEMOCRACY 1 (2015).

96. *Id.* at 20–31. He does not deny that the "orthodox" thinkers do clearly endorse many of the classic civic values like the work ethic, personal and civic responsibility, self-restraint, and self-respect. *See, e.g.,* GALSTON, *supra* note 90 at 223 (quoting with approval a 1987 statement from the American Federation of Teachers); *see also* GUTMANN, *supra* note 83, at 50 (noting that the family plays a large part in developing these values in children, as do "churches and synagogues, civic organizations, friendship circles and work group").

97. MACMULLEN, *supra* note 95, chs. 2–3.

98. *Id.* at chs. 7–8. MacMullen does, however, distinguish the "civic identification" he advocates from "patriotic love," which he associates "with a diminished capacity to think critically about one's polity." He believes that children can be taught to identify with the polity in which they live by learning objectively about its history, including elements of both pride and shame (although he would allow the prideful examples to outweigh the shameful ones). He would eliminate the "use of stirring images, music and rhetoric," which he associates with "patriotic love." *Id.* at 132–39.

99. GALSTON, *supra* note 90, at 221.

100. GUTMANN, *supra* note 83, at 43.

101. MACEDO, *supra* note 81, at 10.

102. CARL F. KAESTLE, PILLARS OF THE REPUBLIC: COMMON SCHOOLS AND AMERICAN SOCIETY, 1780–1860 76 (1983). The thrust of this ideology, though democratic and inclusive in the abstract, was also highly assimilationist in practice: "From their beliefs in Protestantism, republicanism, and capitalism, [the common school founders] justified government intervention at a time of rapid change, to regulate morals, develop institutions, and create a more homogeneous population. . . . Their ideology was part of a culture that was insistently didactic, and it became more assertive as new and threatening groups appeared on the American scene." *Id.* at 77.

103. ELLWOOD P. CUBBERLEY, CHANGING CONCEPTIONS OF EDUCATION 16 (1909).

104. *See, e.g.*, DIANE RAVITCH, THE GREAT SCHOOL WARS: A HISTORY OF THE NEW YORK CITY PUBLIC SCHOOLS chs. 1–7 (1974).

105. NAT'L CTR. FOR EDUC. STATS., RACIAL/ETHNIC ENROLLMENT IN PUBLIC SCHOOLS (2015), *available at* http://nces.ed.gov/programs/coe/indicator_cge.asp.

106. William J. Hussar & Tabitha M. Bailey, *Projections of Education Statistics to 2022*, 41 NAT'L CTR. EDUC. STATS. 33 (2014), *available at* https://nces.ed.gov/pubs2014/2014051.pdf.

107. NAT'L CTR. ON EDUC. STATS., CHILDREN & YOUTH WITH DISABILITIES (2015), *available at* http://nces.ed.gov/programs/coe/indicator_cgg.asp (last updated May 2016).

108. Susan Jones, *Poll: Five Percent of High School Students "Identify as Gay,"* CNS NEWS, July 7, 2008, *available at* http://nces.ed.gov/programs/coe/indicator_cgg.asp. The actual percentage is probably higher, since by the time that they reach college, as many as 12 percent of students self-identify as gay or bisexual. Suzannah Weiss, *About 12 Percent of Students Identify as Gay or Bisexual*, BROWN DAILY HERALD, Nov. 12, 2010, *available at* http://www.browndailyherald.com/2010/11/12/about-12-percent-of-students-identify-as-gay-or-bisexual/.

109. N.Y. CITY DEP'T OF EDUC., OFFICE OF ENGLISH LANGUAGE LEARNERS, 2013 DEMOGRAPHIC REPORT (2013), *available at* http://schools.nyc.gov/NR/rdonlyres/FD5EB945-5C27-44F8-BE4B-E4C65D7176F8/0/2013DemographicReport_june2013_revised.pdf.

110. L.A. UNIFIED SCH. DIST., FINGERTIP FACTS 2015–16 (n.d.), *available at* http://achieve.lausd.net/cms/lib08/CA01000043/Centricity/Domain/32/Fingertip%20Facts15-16_final-updated.pdf.

111. NAT'L CTR. FOR EDUC. STATS., THE STATUS OF RURAL EDUCATION (2013), *available at* https://nces.ed.gov/programs/coe/indicator_tla.asp (last updated May 2013).

112. HOUSING ASSISTANCE COUNCIL, RACE & ETHNICITY IN RURAL AMERICA: RURAL RESEARCH BRIEF (Apr. 2012), *available at* http://www.ruralhome.org/storage/research_notes/rrn-race-and-ethnicity-web.pdf.

113. LINCOLN PUB. SCHS., ENGLISH LANGUAGE LEARNER PROGRAM, *available at* http://home.lps.org/federal/ell-english-language-learner-program (last visited Apr. 18, 2017).

114. MIGRATION POL'Y INST., U.S. IMMIGRATION TRENDS, UNITED STATES IMMIGRANT POPULATION BY COUNTRY OF BIRTH 2000–PRESENT (2013), *available at* http://www.migrationpolicy.org/programs/data-hub/us-immigration-trends#source.

115. *See* J.D. VANCE, HILLBILLY ELEGY: A MEMOIR OF A FAMILY AND CULTURE IN CRISIS (2016).

116. EAMONN CALLAN, CREATING CITIZENS: POLITICAL EDUCATION AND LIBERAL DEMOCRACY 164 (1997).

117. Brown v. Bd. of Educ., 347 U.S. 483 (1954).

118. MARTHA MINOW, IN BROWN'S WAKE: LEGACIES OF AMERICA'S EDUCATIONAL LANDMARK 150 (2010).

119. *See, e.g.,* Green v. Cty. Sch. Bd., 391 U.S. 430, 439 (1968) (invalidating "freedom of choice" desegregation plans and requiring Southern schools to develop and implement "a plan that promises realistically to work and promises realistically to work *now*"); Swann v. Charlotte-Mecklenburg Bd. of Educ., 402 U.S. 1 (1971) (approving busing, numerical goals, and other remedies to promote desegregation).

120. Milliken v. Bradley, 418 U.S. 717 (1974).

121. Bd. of Ed. of Okla. City Pub. Schs. v. Dowell, 498 U.S. 237, 238 (1991).

122. Missouri v. Jenkins, 515 U.S. 70 (1995) (holding that students' academic achievement levels are not "the appropriate test to . . . decid[e] whether a previously segregated district has achieved partially unitary status").

123. Parents Involved in Cmty. Schs. v. Seattle Sch. Dist. No. 1, 551 U.S. 701 (2007). For a detailed overview of the Supreme Court's desegregation decisions, *see* James Ryan, *The Supreme Court and Voluntary Integration*, 121 HARV. L. REV. 131 (2007).

124. Parents Involved, 551 U.S. at 869–71 (Appendix A to opinion of Breyer, J., dissenting). *See also* GARY ORFIELD & CHUNGMEI LEE, WHY SEGREGATION MATTERS: POVERTY AND EDUCATIONAL INEQUALITY 17–18 (HARV. UNIV. CIVIL RIGHTS PROJECT 2005), *available at* https://civilrightsproject.ucla.edu/research/k-12-education/integration-and-diversity/why-segregation-matters-poverty-and-educational-inequality/orfield-why-segregation-matters-2005.pdf (high-poverty schools are defined as schools in which 90 percent to 100 percent of the student population is poor). In recent years, segregation trends seem to have been increasing even more. From school years 2000–01 to 2013–14 the percentage of K–12 public schools that were high poverty (75–100 percent) and comprised mostly black or Hispanic students (75–100 percent) increased steadily from 9 per-

cent in 2000–01 (7,009 schools) to 16 percent in 2013–14 (15,089 schools); the number of students in these schools rose from about 4.1 million to 8.4 million students (or from 10 percent to 17 percent of all K–12 public school students). U.S. GOV'T ACCOUNTABILITY OFFICE, K–12 EDUCATION: BETTER USE OF INFORMATION COULD HELP AGENCIES IDENTIFY DISPARITIES AND ADDRESS RACIAL DISCRIMINATION (Apr. 2016), *available at* http://www.gao.gov/assets/680/676745.pdf.

125. JAMES E. RYAN, FIVE MILES AWAY, A WORLD APART: ONE CITY, TWO SCHOOLS, AND THE STORY OF EDUCATIONAL OPPORTUNITY IN MODERN AMERICA 274–75 (2010). Another significant factor here is that, as Yale law professor Peter Schuck points out, modern America is the first society in history to embrace racial diversity as an affirmative social ideal rather than viewing it as a menace, as most other societies in the world still do. He further notes:

> By almost any definition, assimilation of immigrants to American life is proceeding rapidly, fueled by market incentives, the need and desire to learn English, the allure of sports, and a powerful, mass-media shaped national culture. . . . [T]he rates of intermarriage among different ethnic groups and with whites are both high and increasing, especially for Asians and Hispanics, as is the rate of residential diffusion and integration by these recent immigrant groups. . . . Also facilitating the immigrants' assimilation, perhaps, is the fact that two-thirds of the foreign born population self-identified as white in the 2000 census, compared with only half ten years earlier.

PETER H. SCHUCK, DIVERSITY IN AMERICA: KEEPING GOVERNMENT AT A SAFE DISTANCE 101 (2003). Schuck notes, however, that "immigrant achievers tend to be the ones who assimilate more slowly to American culture, while delinquents tend to abandon their ethnic heritage more quickly." He also thinks that multiculturalism can both promote and impede assimilation, depending on how it is perceived and implemented. *Id.* at 102.

126. JENNIFER HOCHSCHILD, VESLA WEAVER & TRACI BURCH, CREATING A NEW RACIAL ORDER: HOW IMMIGRATION, MULTIRACIALISM, GENOMICS AND THE YOUNG CAN REMAKE RACE IN AMERICA (2012).

127. Hochschild, Weaver, and Burch also note four potential "blockages" or impediments to the new racial order: some people will feel harmed by the new racial order, concentrated poverty, poor education and incarceration may prevent some from benefiting from these changes, wealth disparities, and the potential creation of new pariah groups (*e.g.*, Muslims, unauthorized immigrants). *Id.* at ch. 6.

128. Thomas F. Pettigrew & Linda R. Tropp, *A Meta-Analytic Test of Intergroup Contact Theory*, 90 J. PERSONALITY & SOC. PSYCH. 751 (2006).

129. Michael Kurlaender & John T. Yun, *Measuring School Racial Composi-*

tion and Student Outcomes in a Multiracial Society, 113 AM. J. EDUC. 213 (2007). *See also* AMY STUART WELLS, LAUREN FOX & DIANA CORDOVA-COBO, HOW RACIALLY DIVERSE SCHOOLS AND CLASSROOMS CAN BENEFIT ALL STUDENTS (CENTURY FOUND. 25) (2016), *available at* https://tcf.org/content/report/how-racially-diverse-schools-and-classrooms-can-benefit-all-students/ (summarizing historical and current research on benefits of racial integration in schools).

130. *See, e.g.*, AMY STUART WELLS & ROBERT L. CRAIN, STEPPING OVER THE COLOR LINE: AFRICAN-AMERICAN STUDENTS IN WHITE SUBURBAN SCHOOLS (1997) (study of thirteen thousand black students who transferred to suburban schools graduated at twice the rate of those who remained in St. Louis and were more likely to attend college); Jomills Henry Braddock II & Tamela McNulty Eitle, *The Effects of School Desegregation*, *in* HANDBOOK OF RESEARCH ON MULTICULTURAL EDUCATION (James A. Banks & Cherry A. McGee Banks eds., 2d ed. 2004); Robert L. Crain & Rita El Mahard, *Desegregation and Black Achievement: A Review of the Research School Desegregation: Lessons of the First Twenty-Five Years—Part I: Effects of School Desegregation: A Critical Review of Social Science Research*, 42 LAW & CONTEMP. PROBS. 17 (1978) (meta-analysis indicates that school desegregation does not negatively affect achievement of white students, and in a number of cases also improves their achievement).

131. DANIELLE S. ALLEN, TALKING TO STRANGERS: ANXIETIES OF CITIZENSHIP SINCE *BROWN V. BOARD OF EDUCATION* (2004). "Social trust" in this context simply means "that one is safe . . . that a particular fellow citizen is unlikely to take advantage of one's vulnerability." *Id.* at xiv. *See also* PATRICIA WHITE: CIVIC VIRTUES AND PUBLIC SCHOOLING: EDUCATING CITIZENS FOR A DEMOCRATIC SOCIETY 57 (1996) ("No pluralist democracy could survive simply on the basis of personal trust relationships between individuals, it requires a basis of social trust"). Nancy L. Rosenblum, *Navigating Pluralism: The Democracy of Everyday Life (and Where It Is Learned)*, *in* CITIZEN COMPETENCE AND DEMOCRATIC INSTITUTIONS 67 (Stephen L. Elkin & Karol Edward Soltan eds., 1999) (discussing the importance of treating people identically and with easy spontaneity, and speaking out against ordinary injustice). Robert Putnam has shown how historically a spirit of trust and political and social participation in regional communities in northern Italy resulted in substantial economic and political gains, as compared with regions in southern Italy, where mutual suspicion and lawlessness were regarded as normal. ROBERT D. PUTNAM, MAKING DEMOCRACY WORK: CIVIC TRADITIONS IN MODERN ITALY (1993).

132. Eric M. Uslaner, *Trust and the Economic Crisis of 2008*, 13 CORP. REPUTATION REV. 110, 120 (2010). Uslaner states that the level of trust strongly tracks the level of economic inequality in the United States.

133. PETER LEVINE, THE FUTURE OF DEMOCRACY: DEVELOPING THE NEXT GENERATION OF AMERICAN CITIZENS 88 (2007) (citing evidence that the level of social trust among young people has declined by 50 percent in recent years).

134. LEVINSON, *supra* note 11, at 37.

135. ROBERT D. PUTNAM, OUR KIDS: THE AMERICAN DREAM IN CRISIS 220–21 (2015).

136. ALLEN, *supra* note 19, at 42. Her aim is to integrate diverse individuals and groups into a "wholeness of citizenry: . . . [that] might focus on multilingualism, where citizens all expect to learn each other's languages, rather than on multiculturalism, which seems to set up permanently distinct cultural blocs." ALLEN, *supra* note 131, at 20.

137. ALLEN, *supra* note 131, at 129.

138. The Every Student Succeeds Act (ESSA), 20 U.S.C.A. § 6301. Essentially, this same wording also appeared at the start of the No Child Left Behind Act of 2001 (NCLB), but that statute also contained an unrealistic mandate that 100 percent of American students achieve proficiency in challenging state standards by 2014, an impossible goal and one that clearly was not reached. The 100 percent proficiency requirement has been omitted from the ESSA. For a detailed discussion of the 100 percent proficiency mandate and how it undermined the entire structure of the NCLB, *see* MICHAEL A. REBELL & JESSICA R. WOLFF, MOVING EVERY CHILD AHEAD: FROM NCLB HYPE TO MEANINGFUL EDUCATIONAL OPPORTUNITY (2008).

139. *See, e.g.,* N.Y. BD. OF REGENTS, ALL CHILDREN CAN LEARN: A PLAN FOR REFORM OF STATE AID TO SCHOOLS 1 (1993) ("All children can learn; and we can change our system of public elementary, middle, and secondary education to ensure that all students do learn at world-class levels"); MD. STATE BD. OF ED., MARYLAND STATE PLAN TO ENSURE EQUITABLE ACCESS TO EXCELLENT EDUCATORS (2015), *available at* http://marylandpublicschools.org/MSDE/divisions/leadership/docs/MarylandEquityPlan2015-10-2-15.pdf (referring to Maryland's continuous effort to provide equal educational opportunity to every child, including meaningful opportunities for all students to succeed, regardless of family income or race); N.D. STATE DEP'T OF EDUC., NORTH DAKOTA STATE PLAN TO ENSURE EQUITABLE ACCESS TO EXCELLENT EDUCATORS (2015), *available at* https://www.nd.gov/dpi/uploads/93/NorthDakotaStateEquityPlanApprovedOct2015.pdf ("The State of North Dakota is committed to ensuring every public school student will graduate from high school college or career ready").

140. EQUITY AND EXCELLENCE COMM'N, FOR EACH AND EVERY CHILD: A STRATEGY FOR EDUCATION EQUITY AND EXCELLENCE 12, 14 (2013). The author was a member of the commission.

Chapter Five

1. Jackie Zubrzycki, *Texas Latest State to Consider Requiring High School Civics Test*, EDUC. WK., May 11, 2017, *available at* http://blogs.edweek.org/

edweek/curriculum/2017/05/texas_civics_education.html?cmp=eml-enl-cm-news3.

2. This movement was initiated by the Joe Foss Institute, an organization that sends military veterans into schools to discuss patriotism and American government. Although prospective citizens must answer only six out of ten questions culled from an item bank of one hundred, most of the states adopting the institute's approach are requiring students to answer correctly fifty to seventy questions. These questions include: "What do we call the first ten amendments to the Constitution?" and "Name one war fought by the United States in the 1800s." *See Joe Foss Institute, Civic Education Initiative, available at* http://joefossinstitute.org/civics-education-initiative/; Andrew Ujifusa, *U.S. Citizenship Test Gains Traction as Diploma Criterion*, EDUC. WK., Mar. 25, 2015; Rick Rojas & Motoko Rich, *States Move to Make Citizenship Exams a Classroom Aid*, N.Y. TIMES, Jan. 27, 2015, *available at* http://www.nytimes.com/2015/01/28/us/states-move-to-make-citizenship-exams-a-classroom-aid.html?_r=0; Jackie Zubrzycki, *Eight States Add Citizenship Test as Graduation Requirement*, EDUC. WK., Aug. 18, 2015, *available at* http://blogs.edweek.org/edweek/state_edwatch/2015/08/eight_states_add_citizenship_test_requirement_for_grads.html.

3. MEIRA LEVINSON, NO CITIZEN LEFT BEHIND 277 (2012).

4. *See, e.g.,* CAMPAIGN FOR THE CIVIC MISSION OF THE SCHOOLS ET AL., THE GUARDIAN OF DEMOCRACY: THE CIVIC MISSION OF THE SCHOOLS 6–7 (2011), *available at* http://civicmission.s3.amazonaws.com/118/f0/5/171/1/Guardian-of-Democracy-report.pdf.

5. David E. Campbell, *Civic Education in Traditional, Charter, and Private Schools, in* MAKING CIVIC COUNT: CITIZENSHIP EDUCATION FOR A NEW GENERATION 229, 243 (David E. Campbell, Meira Levinson & Frederick M. Hess eds., 2012). Campbell finds that "adolescents who attended public high schools with a strong civic ethos were more likely to be civically engaged—voting and volunteering—fifteen years after graduating from high school." *See also* DAVID E. CAMPBELL, WHY WE VOTE: HOW SCHOOLS AND COMMUNITIES SHAPE OUR CIVIC LIFE ch. 7 (2010).

6. As Meira Levinson has put it: "Diversity does not magically breed civic virtues. . . . Schools can readily end up exacerbating tensions and prejudices among their diverse members rather than resolving or eliminating the conflicts." Meira Levinson, *Diversity and Civic Education, in* MAKING CIVICS COUNT, *supra* note 5, at 89, 93. The way to build positive outcomes in a diverse setting, according to Walter Parker, an experienced educator and political scientist, is to use the differences among the students as "essential assets" and to increase "the variety and frequency of interaction among students who are different from one another." WALTER C. PARKER, TEACHING DEMOCRACY: UNITY AND DIVERSITY IN PUBLIC LIFE 78 (2003). Methods for creating classroom activities and schoolwide curricular and extracurricular activities that promote positive shared ex-

periences and interactions among students of different backgrounds will be discussed throughout this chapter.

7. *See* discussion in chapter 4, at pp. 76–77. *See also* AM. ACAD. OF ARTS & SCIENCES, COMM'N ON THE HUMANITIES & SOC. SCIENCES, THE HEART OF THE MATTER: THE HUMANITIES AND SOCIAL SCIENCES FOR A VIBRANT, COMPETITIVE, AND SECURE NATION 10 (2013) ("Democratic decision-making is based on a shared knowledge of history, civics, and social studies. A thorough grounding in these subjects allows citizens to participate meaningfully in the democratic process—as voters, informed consumers, and productive workers").

8. CARNEGIE CORP. OF N.Y. & CTR. FOR INFO. & RESEARCH ON CIVIC LEARNING & ENGAGEMENT (CIRCLE), CIVIC MISSION OF THE SCHOOLS 14 (2003). Charles Quigley also points out that the one-semester course in government or civics now is usually taken in twelfth grade and is taken by no more than 85 percent of students: "Unfortunately, this is too little and too late. Add the 15% of students who do not take a civics course, the 15% of the students who do not finish high school and we find that many of the students who arguably need civics the most do not get it at all." CHARLES N. QUIGLEY, THE STATUS OF CIVIC EDUCATION: MAKING THE CASE FOR A NATIONAL MOVEMENT, 4 (Ctr. for Civic Educ. 2004), *available at* http://files.eric.ed.gov/fulltext/ED485827.pdf.

9. SUBHI GODSAY ET AL., CENTER FOR INFORMATION AND RESEARCH ON CIVIC LEARNING AND ENGAGEMENT FACT SHEET 9 (Sept. 2012), *available at* http://files.eric.ed.gov/fulltext/ED536256.pdf; Education Commission of the States reports that "thirty-seven states require students to demonstrate proficiency through assessment in civics or social studies," but its compilation includes items like the very minimal short answer quizzes discussed *supra* note 1. EDUC. COMM'N OF THE STATES, 50-STATE COMPARISON: CIVIC EDUCATION (Dec. 12, 2016), *available at* http://www.ecs.org/citizenship-education-policies/.

10. GODSAY ET AL., *supra* note 9, at 2. *See also* David Berliner, *MCLB (Much Curriculum Left Behind): U.S. Calamity in the Making*, 73 EDUC. FORUM (2009) (arguing that high-stakes testing has dictated an increased emphasis on reading and math, leaving little time for the arts and humanities). ESSA, the successor to NCLB enacted in 2015, continues to require statewide assessments in English language arts, math, and science but not in social studies or civics. Elementary & Secondary Sch. Act 20 U.S.C.A. § 6311(b)(1)(C).

11. POL'Y RES. PROJECT OF CIVIC EDUC. POLY'S & PRACTICES, THE CIVIC EDUCATION OF AMERICAN YOUTH: FROM STATE POLICIES TO SCHOOL DISTRICT PRACTICES (1999).

12. *Id.* at 1. The study also reported that "only one-fourth of the responding teachers reported being extremely familiar with these standards" and that "teachers also are unaware or confused about district and school civic education policies."

13. NAT'L COUNCIL FOR THE SOCIAL STUDIES, THE COLLEGE, CAREER, AND

Civic Life (C3) Framework for Social Studies State Standards: Guidance for Enhancing the Rigor of K–12 Civics, Economics, Geography, and History (2013). In 1994, the Center for Civic Education, with support from the U.S. Department of Education and Pew Charitable Trusts, issued a 179-page set of standards for civics and government that emphasized critical analysis and civic participation, but to a more limited extent than does the C3 Framework. *See* Ctr. for Civic Educ., National Standards for Civics and Government (1994) *available at* http://www.civiced.org/standards?page=912erica#15. The recently developed Common Core standards, adopted in whole or in part by forty-two states and the District of Columbia, cover only mathematics and English language arts, although the latter standards use history and social studies texts as sources for developing skills in nonfiction reading and comprehension. Common Core State Standards Initiative, Standards in Your State (2017), *available at* http://www.corestandards.org/standards-in-your-state/.

14. Nat'l Council for the Social Studies, *supra* note 13, at 32–34. Frederick Hess, the director of education policy studies at the American Enterprise Institute has criticized the C3 standards for overemphasizing critical thinking and neglecting knowledge of basic facts about history and civics. *See* Frederick Hess, *Content-Free Social Studies Standards*, Educ. Wk., Sept. 20, 2013, *available at* http://blogs.edweek.org/edweek/rick_hess_straight_up/2013/09/content-free_social_studies_standards.html. Hess is, of course, correct that a solid grounding in facts is a *sine qua non* for thoughtful knowledge and understanding. A need for deep factual knowledge is implicit in the C3 standards, and it is important that teachers emphasize that reality in their teaching of these analytic skills.

15. Levinson, *supra* note 3, at 53.

16. Ga. Dep't of Educ., Georgia American Government/Civics Social Studies Performance Standards (2012), *available at* https://www.georgiastandards.org/standards/Georgia%20Performance%20Standards/American-Government.pdf.

17. Ky. Dep't of Educ., Academic Standards, High School Social Studies (2015), *available at* http://education.ky.gov/curriculum/standards/kyacadstand/Documents/Kentucky%20Academic%20Standards_Final-9%2011%2015.pdf. Interestingly, the leader of the group that drafted the C3 framework was Kathy Swan from University of Kentucky. The Kentucky Department of Education also specifically features the C3 framework on its website. *See* Ky. Dep't of Educ., Social Studies Curriculum Documents and Resources, *available at* http://education.ky.gov/curriculum/conpro/socstud/Pages/SS-Curriculum-Documents-and-Resources.aspx.

18. Ark. Dep't of Educ., Civics: Social Studies Curriculum Framework (2014), *available at* http://www.arkansased.gov/public/userfiles/Learning_Services/Curriculum%20and%20Instruction/Frameworks/Social_Studies/Civics.pdf (generally emphasizes structures and functions but specifically re-

fers to importance of developing critical analytic skills and includes standards like "construct explanations of the ways citizenship in the United States has changed over time and been affected by public policy, geographic location, state and federal law, and demographics using a variety of sources"). *See also* KAN. DEP'T OF EDUC., KANSAS STANDARDS FOR HISTORY, GOVERNMENT AND SOCIAL STUDIES (2013), *available at* http://www.ksde.org/LinkClick.aspx?fileticket=JDadRGpjfZ0%3d&tabid=472&portalid=0&mid=1585-7 (extensive emphasis on critical analytical skills, such as "Students need to know how concepts of rights have changed over time and how social and governmental institutions have responded to issues of rights and diversity," "Students should know the basic outline of the history of the Civil Rights Movement, the struggle for women's suffrage, and later movements for equality," and "What might justify acts of civil disobedience? Where do your rights end and your neighbor's begin?"). *See also* MD. DEP'T OF EDUC., STATE CURRICULUM, GOVERNMENT: HIGH SCHOOL, STANDARD 1: CIVICS (2016), *available at* http://mdk12.msde.maryland.gov/instruction/hsvsc/government/standard1.html (extensive emphasis on critical analytical skills, like "The student will explain roles and analyze strategies individuals or groups may use to initiate change in governmental policy and institutions"). *See also* N.H. DEP'T OF EDUC., K–12 SOCIAL STUDIES NEW HAMPSHIRE CURRICULUM FRAMEWORK (2006), *available at* https://www.education.nh.gov/instruction/curriculum/social_studies/documents/frameworks.pdf (generally emphasizes structures and functions approach but includes analytic themes, like "Analyze the evolution of the United States Constitution as a living document, *e.g.*, the Bill of Rights or Plessy v. Ferguson"); N.Y. STATE EDUC. DEP'T, NEW YORK LEARNING STANDARDS, CIVICS, CITIZENSHIP AND GOVERNMENT (2002), *available at* http://www.p12.nysed.gov/ciai/socst/documents/sslearn.pdf (emphasizes critical analytic skills: "The study of civics and citizenship requires the ability to probe ideas and assumptions, ask and answer analytical questions, take a skeptical attitude toward questionable arguments, evaluate evidence, formulate rational conclusions, and develop and refine participatory skills"). New York State explicitly implemented the C3 standards in its Civics Learning Standards, Press Release, New York State K–12 Social Studies Toolkit Featured in Special Section of Flagship Social Studies Journal, NYSED, 2015, *available at* http://www.nysed.gov/Press/New-York-State-K-12-Social-Studies-Toolkit-Featured-In-Special-Section-of-Flagship-Social-Studies-Journal. *See also* N.Y. STATE EDUC. DEP'T, PARTICIPATION IN GOVERNMENT, CORE CURRICULUM (2002), *available at* http://www.p12.nysed.gov/ciai/socst/documents/partgov.pdf. *See also* S.C. DEP'T OF EDUC., SOUTH CAROLINA SOCIAL STUDIES ACADEMIC STANDARDS (2011), *available at* http://ed.sc.gov/scdoe/assets/file/agency/ccr/Standards-Learning/documents/FINALAPPROVEDSSStandardsAugust182011.pdf (generally emphasizes structures and functions approach but includes some emphasis on critical analysis, like "Explain how fundamental values, principles, and rights often conflict within the American political system; why these conflicts arise; and how these conflicts are and can be addressed").

19. IND. DEP'T OF EDUC., ACADEMIC STANDARDS, UNITED STATES GOVERNMENT (2014), *available at* http://www.doe.in.gov/standards/social-studies (emphasizes functions and structures of government, *such as* "Discuss the individual's legal obligation to obey the law, serve as a juror, and pay taxes"). *See also* NEB. DEP'T OF EDUC., SOCIAL STUDIES STANDARDS, CIVICS (2012), *available at* https://www.education.ne.gov/AcademicStandards/Documents/NE_Social StudiesStandardsApproved.pdf (emphasizes structures and functions of government, such as: "Analyze the significance and benefits of patriotic symbols, songs, holidays, and activities"). *See also* PA. DEP'T OF EDUC., ACADEMIC STANDARDS FOR GOVERNMENT AND CIVICS (2009), *available at* http://static.pdesas.org/content/documents/Academic_Standards_for_Civics_and_Government_(Secondary).pdf (emphasizes structures and functions of government, but promotes comparative perspectives, *such as*: "Contrast the rights and responsibilities of a citizen in a democracy with a citizen in an authoritarian system"). *See also* IOWA DEP'T OF EDUC., CORE K–12 SOCIAL STUDIES STANDARDS, POLITICAL SCIENCE/CIVIC LITERACY (2008), *available at* https://iowacore.gov/iowa-core/subject/social-studies (emphasizes structures and functions of government, but also includes civic participation and appreciation of diversity, *such as* "understand participation in civic and political life can help citizens attain individual and public goals"). Note that the Iowa Department of Education apparently participated in the development of the C3 standards. *See* IOWA DEP'T OF EDUC., SOCIAL STUDIES UPDATE (Oct. 13, 2013) *available at* https://www.educateiowa.gov/sites/files/ed/documents/October2013SSUpdate.pdf. *See also* UTAH EDUC. NETWORK, CORE STANDARDS, UNITED STATES GOVERNMENT AND CITIZENSHIP (2002), *available at* http://www.uen.org/core/core.do?courseNum=6210 (emphasizes structures and functions of government and responsibilities and obligations, but not rights, of citizens).

20. COLO. DEP'T OF EDUC., COLORADO ACADEMIC STANDARDS, HIGH SCHOOL SOCIAL STUDIES STANDARDS, CIVICS (2009), *available at* https://www.cde.state.co.us/standardsandinstruction/GradeLevelBooks. It should be noted that at the time these standards were adopted, the Colorado Supreme Court had issued a preliminary decision in a major education adequacy case, Lobato v. Colorado, 218 P.3d 358 (Colo. 2009), although in a later ruling on the merits, 304 P.3d 1132 (2013), it ruled for the defendants.

21. LEVINSON, *supra* note 3, at 162 (2012).

22. Consider, for example, the following description of the introductory statement of one of the leading civics textbooks: "The first section of *Civics* explains to students that the purpose of the study of civics is to answer questions like 'What does it mean to be an American? What do we believe about our country and government? How do we know what to expect from our government? How

do we know what is expected of us[?].' . . . Notably absent from this list are questions like 'How do Americans engage as citizens? Why should we civically engage? How can we affect our government functions?'" Anna Rosefsky Saavedra, *Dry to Dynamic Civic Education Curricula*, *in* MAKING CIVICS COUNT, *supra* note 5, at 135, 143.

23. Diana Hess & John Zola, *Professional Development as a Tool for Improving Civic Education*, *in* MAKING CIVICS COUNT, *supra* note 5, at 183, 184; REBECCA BURGESS, CIVIC EDUCATION PROFESSIONAL DEVELOPMENT: THE LAY OF THE LAND (2015), *available at* https://www.aei.org/wp-content/uploads/2015/03/Civics-Education-Professional-Development.pdf.

24. CLAUS VON ZASTROW WITH HELEN JANC, COUNCIL FOR BASIC EDUCATION, ACADEMIC ATROPHY: THE CONDITION OF THE LIBERAL ARTS IN AMERICA'S PUBLIC SCHOOLS 9 (2004).

25. *Id.* at 7.

26. Press Release, U.S. Dep't of Educ., Expansive Survey of America's Public Schools Reveals Troubling Racial Disparities (Mar. 21, 2014) *available at* https://www.ed.gov/news/press-releases/expansive-survey-americas-public-schools-reveals-troubling-racial-disparities.

27. *See* 8 N.Y.C.R.R. § 100.5(a)(3)(iii); 8 N.Y.C.R.R. § 100.2(d)(1)–(2) (Students are also required to complete two units of study in a language other than English by grade 9). Because schools are not required to offer students a choice of world languages, some under-resourced high schools provide no more than the minimum one year of language, and many schools offer only one language, generally Spanish.

28. Angela M. Kelly & Keith Sheppard, *Newton in the Big Apple: Access to High School Physics in New York City*, 46 PHYSICS TCHR. 280 (2008). A more recent study found that forty-six New York City high schools, mainly in low-income and minority areas, offered no courses in Algebra II, chemistry, or physics, and most other schools in the city offered only one or two of these courses. CTR. FOR N.Y. CITY AFFAIRS, NEW SCHOOL, CREATING COLLEGE READY COMMUNITIES: PREPARING NYC'S PRECARIOUS NEW GENERATION OF COLLEGE STUDENTS 19 (2013). *See also* Joseph Kahne & Ellen Middaugh, *Democracy for Some: The Civic Opportunity Gap in High School* (Ctr. for Info. & Research on Civic Learning & Engagement, Working Paper No. 59, 2009) (study of 2,500 California high school students finds that students' race and academic track as well as a school's average socioeconomic status determine the availability civic learning opportunities that promote voting and broader forms of civic engagement).

29. Some small high schools in urban areas or in sparsely populated rural areas that lack the resources to provide a full range of courses on-site should enable students to take such courses at nearby high schools or colleges. Digital courses may also be a reasonable option for these schools, provided that the online courses are based on a "blended learning" approach that combines a digi-

tal distance-learning component with meaningful in-person supervision by certified teachers. *See, e.g.*, 8 N.Y.C.R.R. § 100.5(d)(10)(i)(a) (requiring supervision of online courses by a certified teacher).

30. *See* Eric A. DeGroff, *State Regulation of Non Public Schools: Does the Tie Still Bind?* B.Y.U. Educ. & L.J. 363, 382, 390, 393 (2003) (eighteen states impose no curricular requirements whatsoever on private schools or on schools that have not voluntarily registered); U.S. Dep't of Educ., State Regulation of Private Schools 329 (2009), *available at* http://www2.ed.gov/admins/comm/choice/regprivschl/regprivschl.pdf (based on self-reporting, twenty-three states do not impose curriculum requirements on some or all private schools in the state).

31. As of 2015, nineteen states across the county, nine of which are in the South, had established programs that provide state-funded vouchers and/or state tax credits to support student attendance in private schools. S. Educ. Found., Race & Ethnicity in a New Era of Public Funding of Private Schools: Private School Enrollment in the South and the Nation 2 (2016), *available at* http://www.southerneducation.org/getattachment/be785c57-6ce7-4682-b80d-04d89994a0b6/Race-and-Ethnicity-in-a-New-Era-of-Public-Funding.aspx.

32. Approximately five million students (about 10 percent of all students in the United States) attended private schools in 2011–12; about 80 percent of these students attend religiously oriented schools. *See* Council for Am. Private Educ., Facts and Studies, *available at* http://www.capenet.org/facts.html.

33. CFE v. State of New York, 719 N.Y.S.2d 475, 485 (S. Ct. N.Y. Cty. 2001).

34. Comparative international assessments indicate that on the whole, American students perform poorly in basic intellectual skills; for example, the United States ranked well below the mean score of the sixty-four Organization for Economic Cooperation and Development (OECD) countries that participated in the 2012 test of fifteen-year-olds' skills in mathematics and science. Org. for Econ. Cooperation & Dev., PISA 2012 Results in Focus (2014), *available at* http://www.oecd.org/pisa/keyfindings/pisa-2012-results-overview.pdf. But unpacking the socioeconomic dimensions of these scores reveals that most affluent students in the United States are performing extremely well in the academic subjects, and it is only because of the low level of basic skills of students from low income backgrounds that the United States has a mediocre overall ranking:

> America's youth score remarkably high if they are in schools where less than 10% of the children are eligible for free and reduced lunch. . . . If this group of a few million students were a nation, it would have scored the highest in the world on these tests of mathematics and science. . . .
>
> On the other hand . . . [i]n the schools with the poorest students in America, those where over 75% of the student body is eligible for free and reduced lunch, academic performance is not

> merely low: it is embarrassing. Almost 20% of American children and youth, about 9 million students, attend these schools.

David C. Berliner, *Effects of Inequality and Poverty vs. Teachers and Schooling on America's Youth*, 115 TCHRS. C. REC. 1, 7 (2013) (discussing the 2007 TIMMS test results). *See also* MARTIN CARNOY AND RICHARD ROTHSTEIN, WHAT DO INTERNATIONAL TESTS REALLY SHOW ABOUT U.S. STUDENT PERFORMANCE? (Econ. Pol'y Inst. 2013), *available at* http://www.epi.org/publication/us-student-performance-testing/ (finding that social class inequality is greater in the United States than in any of the countries with which the United States can reasonably be compared, and that the relative performance of American adolescents is better than it appears when countries' average performance is compared).

35. *See also* BENJAMIN R. BARBER, STRONG DEMOCRACY: PARTICIPATORY DEMOCRACY FOR A NEW AGE 178–98 (1984) (discussing the types of verbal empowerment skills that will allow students to engage in authentic democratic deliberation, including the ability to articulate one's interests clearly, to identify the true issues that need to be explored, to be able to attempt to persuade others, and to maintain integrity and autonomy while also being able to discern possible common ground for reasonable compromises); ARTHUR LUPIA & MATHEW D. MCCUBBINS, THE DEMOCRATIC DILEMMA: CAN CITIZENS LEARN WHAT THEY NEED TO KNOW? (discussing the reading of cues from knowledgeable and trustworthy sources and other tools citizens need to know to make reasoned choices).

36. Kei Kawashima-Ginsberg & Peter Levine, *Diversity in Classrooms: The Relationship Between Deliberative and Associative Opportunities in School and Later Electoral Engagement*, 14 ANALYSES OF SOC. ISSUES & PUB. POL'Y 294 (2014); Joseph E. Kahne & Susan E. Sporte, *Developing Citizens: The Impact of Civic Learning Opportunities on Students' Commitment to Civic Participation*, 45 AM. EDUC. RES. J. 738 (2008) (study of four thousand students in fifty-two Chicago high schools finds that classroom practices such as discussing controversial issues and using topics that matter to students, combined with undertaking service learning projects and exposure to civic role models, are highly efficacious means of fostering commitments to civic participation).

37. Kawashima-Ginsberg & Levine, *supra* note 36. The authors also found that opportunities to associate with peers who share common interests through issue-oriented groups and participation in issue-oriented extracurricular and service activities can counter these trends.

38. DIANA E. HESS, CONTROVERSY IN THE CLASSROOM: THE DEMOCRATIC POWER OF DISCUSSION 62 (2009).

39. RONALD DWORKIN, IS DEMOCRACY POSSIBLE HERE: PRINCIPLES FOR A NEW POLITICAL DEBATE 148–49 (2006).

40. JONATHAN ZIMMERMAN & EMILY ROBERTSON, THE CASE FOR CONTENTION: TEACHING CONTROVERSIAL ISSUES IN AMERICAN SCHOOLS 4 (2017).

41. *Id.*

42. HESS, *supra* note 38, at 35.

43. Stephen Arons, *The Myths of Value-Neutral Schooling*, EDUC. WK., Nov. 7, 1984, at 24.

44. HESS, *supra* note 38. *See also* DIANA C. MUTZ, HEARING THE OTHER SIDE: DELIBERATIVE VERSUS PARTICIPATORY DEMOCRACY (2006) (empirical study finds that most people avoid discussing political issues with those holding different opinions).

45. Judith L. Pace, *Supporting Controversial Issues Discussion in the Charged Classroom*, TCHRS. C. REC., July 18, 2016, *available at* http://www.tcrecord.org/Content.asp?ContentID=21471. *See also* Richard Weissbourd, *Teaching Students to Talk Across the Aisle*, EDUC. WK. (May 2, 2017), *available at* http://www.edweek.org/ew/articles/2017/05/02/teaching-students-to-talk-across-the-aisle.html.

46. Pace, *supra* note 45.

47. LEVINSON, *supra* note 3, at 40.

48. *Id.* at 39: "Efficacy is clearly correlated with engagement. The less efficacious one feels, the less likely one is to participate. It is also significantly correlated both with class and with race and ethnicity."

49. SHIRA EVE EPSTEIN, TEACHING CIVIC LITERACY PROJECTS: STUDENT ENGAGEMENT WITH SOCIAL PROBLEMS (2014).

50. *Id.* at 26.

51. *See* DANIELLE ALLEN, EQUALITY AND EDUCATION (2016). *See also* discussion in chapter 4.

52. *See* NICOLE MIRRA, ANTERO GARCIA & ERNEST MORRELL, LANGUAGE, CULTURE, AND TEACHING SERIES: DOING YOUTH PARTICIPATORY ACTION RESEARCH: TRANSFORMING INQUIRY WITH RESEARCHERS, EDUCATORS, AND STUDENTS (2015).

53. DIANA E. HESS & PAULA MCAVOY, THE POLITICAL CLASSROOM: EVIDENCE AND ETHICS IN DEMOCRATIC EDUCATION 124–25 (2015).

54. Hess & Zola, *supra* note 23, at 183, 197.

55. BURGESS, *supra* note 23, at 1.

56. *See* Hess & Zola, *supra* note 23, at 188; CAMPAIGN FOR THE CIVIC MISSION OF THE SCHOOLS ET AL., *supra* note 4, at 38. *See also* Judith Torney-Purta, Wendy Klandl Richardson & Carolyn Henry Barber, *Teachers' Educational Experience and Confidence in Relation to Students' Civic Knowledge Across Countries*, 1 INT'L J. CITIZENSHIP & TCHR. EDUC. 32, 47 (2005) (students score higher on a civics assessment when their teachers have received "in-service professional development in civics"); Dennis J. Barr et al., *A Randomized Controlled Trial of Professional Development for Interdisciplinary Civic Education: Impacts on Humanities Teachers and Their Students*, 117 TCHRS. C. REC. 1 (2015), *available at* http://www.tcrecord.org/library/abstract.asp?contentid=17470 (ran-

domized experiment demonstrated that students of teachers trained to promote "informed civic reflection" in the teaching of history showed stronger skills in analyzing evidence, greater civic efficacy and enhanced tolerance for others with different views).

57. Hess & McAvoy, *supra* note 53, at 209. The need to substantially increase discussion of controversial issues in the classroom also has significant implications regarding teacher academic freedom and teacher tenure.

58. Campaign for the Civic Mission of the Schools et al., *supra* note 4, at 15.

59. Zimmerman & Robertson, *supra* note 40, at 79–82, 88–91.

60. Although the U.S. Supreme Court has not focused specifically on the extent to which schoolteachers have a right under the First Amendment to express opinions or shape discussion on controversial issues in the classroom, school boards clearly do possess substantial authority to direct curriculum policy. In Garcetti v. Cebellos, 547 U.S. 410 (2006), the Supreme Court held that speech of a government employee (in this case an assistant district attorney) acting in his or her official capacity does not have First Amendment protection from employer discipline, but the Court also specifically stated: "We need not, and for that reason do not, decide whether the analysis we conduct today would apply in the same manner to a case involving speech related to scholarship or teaching." *Id.* at 425. *See also* Mayer v. Monroe Cty. Cmty. Sch. Corp., 474 F.3d 477 (7th Cir. 2007) (First Amendment did not entitle public elementary school teacher to advocate her viewpoint on an antiwar demonstration during a classroom session on current events, in contravention of school board policy to keep her opinions to herself).

61. Pew Research Center, Teens, Social Media & Technology Overview 2015 (April 9, 2015), *available at* http://www.pewinternet.org/2015/04/09/teens-social-media-technology-2015/.

62. Joseph Kahne & Ellen Middaugh, *Digital Media Shapes Youth Participation in Politics*, Phi Delta Kappan 52 (Nov. 2012), *available at* http://ypp.dmlcentral.net/sites/default/files/publications/Digital_Media_Shapes_Participation.pdf; Joseph Kahne, Erica Hodgin & Elyse Eidman-Aadahl, *Redesigning Civic Education for the Digital Age: Participatory Politics and the Pursuit of Democratic Engagement*, 55 Theory & Res. in Soc. Educ. 1 (2016), *available at* http://www.tandfonline.com/doi/full/10.1080/00933104.2015.1132646. For an extensive discussion of how to use the Internet and social media to build a participatory culture among youth, *see* Henry Jenkins et al., Confronting the Challenges of Participatory Culture: Media Education for the 21st Century 10 (2006), *available at* https://www.macfound.org/media/article_pdfs/JENKINS_WHITE_PAPER.PDF.

63. Malcolm Gladwell, *Small Change: Why the Revolution Will Not Be Tweeted*, New Yorker (Oct. 4, 2010). *See also* Cass Sunstein, #Republic:

Divided Democracy in the Age of Social Media (2017) (social media impede deliberation).

64. W. Lance Bennett, Chris Wells & Deen Freelon, *Communicating Civic Engagement: Contrasting Models of Citizenship in the Youth Web Sphere*, 61 J. Comm. 1 (2011), *available at* http://onlinelibrary.wiley.com/doi/10.1111/j.1460-2466.2011.01588.x/abstract. *See also* W. Lance Bennett & Chris Wells, *Civic Engagement: Bridging Differences to Build a Field of Civic Learning*, 1 Int'l J. Learning & Media 6 (2009).

65. Robert B. Putnam, Bowling Alone: The Collapse and Revival of American Community (2000).

66. Chris Wells, *Two Eras of Civic Information and the Evolving Relationship Between Civil Society and Young Citizens*, 16 New Media & Soc'y 615, 621 (2014), *available at* http://nms.sagepub.com/content/16/4/615.abstract.

67. Archon Fung & Jennifer Shkabatur, *Viral Engagement: Fast, Cheap and Broad: But Good for Democracy?*, *in* From Voice to Influence: Understanding Citizenship in a Digital Age 155, (Danielle Allen & Jennifer S. Light eds., 2015). The authors also point out that as this "persuasion industry develops," large money interests may come to dominate the making of "asks" that go viral on digital social networks. *Id.* at 170. They also point out, however, that "viral engagements can contribute to the quality of public deliberation by articulating a counter point to the prevailing currents of discussion and action," and "The perspectives and interpretations of a viral campaign are never the last or only word, and seldom are they the most powerful voice." *Id.* at 172.

68. Kahne & Middaugh, *supra* note 62, at 55. *See also* discussion of media use in Stanford History Educ. Grp., *Evaluating Information: The Cornerstone of Civic Online Reasoning* (2016).

69. Howard Gardner, *Reclaiming Disinterestedness for the Digital Age*, *in* From Voice to Influence, *supra* note 67, at 232, 243.

70. Robert Putnam, Our Kids: The American Dream in Crisis 212 (2015).

71. *See, e.g.*, Am. Assoc. of College and Research Libraries, Framework for Information Literacy for Higher Educ., (2016) *available at* http://www.ala.org/acrl/sites/ala.org.acrl/files/content/issues/infolit/Framework_ILHE.pdf.

72. Schools with fewer than seven hundred students must have at least a part-time certified school librarian. Schools with 700–1,999 students must have at least one full-time librarian, 2,000–2,999 students require two full-time librarians, 3,000–3,999 need three, and so on, adding another librarian for every 1,000 students. 8 N.Y.C.R.R. § 91.2.

73. Michael A. Rebell, Jessica R. Wolff & Joseph R. Rogers, Jr., Campaign for Educ. Equity, Deficient resources: An Analysis of the Availability of Basic Educational Resources in High Needs Schools in Eight New York State School Districts, 32–33, 50 (2012), *available at* http://www.equitycampaign.org/i/a/document/25804_DeficientResources2-21-13.pdf.

74. Howard Rheingold, *Using Participatory Media and Public Voice to Encourage Civic Engagement*, *in* CIVIC LIFE ONLINE: LEARNING HOW DIGITAL MEDIA CAN ENGAGE YOUTH 97, 104 (W. Lance Bennett ed., 2008).

75. *See* Joseph Kahne & Benjamin Bowyer, *Educating for Democracy in a Partisan Age: Confronting the Challenges of Motivated Reasoning and Misinformation*, 54 AM. EDUC. RES. J. 3 (2017). *See also* discussion in chapter 4.

76. Lauren Feldman et al., *Identifying Best Practices in Civic Education: Lessons from the Student Voices Program*, 114 AM. J. EDUC. 75, 79 (2007), *available at* http://repository.upenn.edu/cgi/viewcontent.cgi?article=1370&context=asc_papers. Joseph Kahne, Jacqueline Ullman, and Ellen Middaugh describe a similar program, Civic Action Project, in which "Students identify a problem, a policy, or an issue and design an action project with a tangible civic goal. Engagement with digital media is woven into this curriculum. Students create project blogs, learn how to use multimedia sources to persuade and inform others, and gain the necessary skills to navigate online sources of information about their chosen topic." Joseph Kahne, Jacqueline Ullman & Ellen Middaugh, *Digital Opportunities for Civic Education*, *in* MAKING CIVIC COUNT: CITIZENSHIP EDUCATION FOR A NEW GENERATION 207, 221 (David E. Campbell, Meira Levinson & Fredrick M. Hess eds., 2012).

77. Feldman, *supra* note 76, at 93. Another interesting finding of this study was that the Student Voices program had "equal impact across ethnic and racial groups." *Id.* at 94. Lance Bennett has also studied the Student Voices program. He found that the program worked effectively in some well-resourced schools, even with at-risk students who had the strongest antipathy to government and politics, but the program withered in other schools due to lack of time, technology resources, and other support. W. Lance Bennett, *Changing Citizenship in the Digital Age*, *in* CIVIC LIFE ONLINE: LEARNING HOW DIGITAL MEDIA CAN ENGAGE YOUTH 1, 17 (W. Lance Bennett ed., 2008).

78. Rheingold, *supra* note 74, at 97.

79. Kahne, Hodgin & Eidman-Aadahl, *supra* note 62, at 10–12.

80. Deanna Kuhn, Laura Hemberger & Valerie Khait, *Dialogic Argumentation as a Bridge to Argumentative Thinking and Writing*, 39 J. STUDY EDUC. & DEV. 25 (2016), *available at* http://www.tandfonline.com/doi/full/10.1080/02103702.2015.1111608?src=recsys.

81. Kahne, Ullman & Middaugh, *supra* note 73, at 227. The portfolios could be placed within a network so that teachers and students could see and comment on one another's work.

82. *Id.* "One could imagine earning badges for engaging in a service activity, for sharing an informed perspective on a societal issue with a large audience, or for seeking out diverse perspectives on a controversial issue." *Id.* For a more detailed discussion of the potential of digital badges to motivate positive digital activities and broaden assessment possibilities, *see* Felicia M. Sullivan, *New and*

Alternative Assessment: Digital Badges and Civics: An Overview of Emerging Themes and Promising Directions (Ctr. for Info. & Research on Civic Learning & Engagement, Working Paper No. 77, 2013), *available at* http://www.civicyouth.org/wp-content/uploads/2013/03/WP_77_Sullivan_Final.pdf.

83. *See* Youth & Participatory Politics Research Network, *available at* http://ypp.dmlcentral.net.

84. Ernest Morrell et al., Critical Media Pedagogy: Teaching for Achievement in City Schools 4 (2013).

85. The challenges for teachers in promoting media literacy were well illustrated for me by the experiences of a New York City social studies teacher who recounted that after he had brought home to his students the importance of questioning the values and ideological perspectives behind all sources of information (including, for example, the *New York Times*), some of the students decided that no information could be considered objective and that, therefore, they should just go with their own ideological preferences.

86. Elizabeth Stearns & Elizabeth J. Glennie, *Opportunities to Participate: Extracurricular Activities' Distribution Across and Academic Correlates in High Schools*, 39 Soc. Sci. Res. 296 (2010), *available at* https://www.researchgate.net/publication/248571987_Opportunities_to_participate_Extracurricular_activities'_distribution_across_and_academic_correlates_in_high_schools.

87. Associated Press, *Field Trips Becoming History at Some Ohio Schools*, Cincinnati Enquirer, Oct. 8, 2012, *available at* http://www.northjersey.com/news/education/field-trips-becoming-history-at-some-ohio-schools-1.383829. *See also* Daniela Altimari, *Field Trips Fading Fast in an Age of Testing*, Hartford Courant, Dec. 9, 2007, *available at* http://www.hartfordinfo.org/issues/documents/education/htfd_courant_120907.asp (field trips cut back due to budget cuts and perceived need to use more time to boost scores on standardized tests).

88. June Kronholz, *Academic Value of Non-Academics: The Case for Keeping Extracurriculars*, 12 Educ. Next (2012), *available at* http://educationnext.org/academic-value-of-non-academics/.

89. Rebell, Wolff & Rogers, *supra* note 73, at 11.

90. *See* Stephanie Simon, *Public Schools Charge Kids for Basics, Frills*, Wall St. J., May 25, 2011, *available at* http://www.wsj.com/articles/SB10001424052748703864204576313572363698678. *See generally* Note, *Pay-to-Play: A Risky and Largely Unregulated Solution to Save High School Athletic Programs From Elimination*, 39 Suffolk L. Rev. 583 (2005–06).

91. Hartzell v. Connell, 679 P.2d 35, 43 (Cal. 1984).

92. Gannon v. State, 2017 WL 8335 (Kan. 2017).

93. Moran v. Sch. Dist. No. 7, 350 F. Supp. 1180 (D. Mont. 1972).

94. *See, e.g.*, Paulson v. Minidoka Cty. Sch. Dist. No. 331, 463 P.2d 935, 938 (Idaho 1970) (noting that there is no constitutional prohibition of fees for extra-

curricular activities); Kelley v. E. Jackson Pub. Schs., 372 N.W.2d 638, 640 (Mich. App. Ct. 1985) (holding that fees for interscholastic sports are constitutional *because* they are extracurricular in nature).

95. PUTNAM, *supra* note 70, at 176–77. The "scissors gap" statistics refer to both school-based and community-based extracurricular activities. The participation gap in school-based extracurricular activities rose from about 10 percent in 1972 to about 21 percent in 2002. *Id.* at 177.

96. Ralph McNeal, *High School Extracurricular Activities: Closed Structures and Stratifying Patterns of Participation*, 91. J. EDUC. RES. 183 (1998). McNeal also reports the following participation patterns: "Another notable ethnic effect is that Asian American students have higher participation rates for academic activities, newspaper/yearbook participation, and student service/government organizations. . . . Girls have substantially lower rates of participation in the high-status athletic activities (although higher participation rates in cheerleading). However, girls have greater participation rates than boys do in fine arts (34% vs. 21%), academic organizations (41% vs. 31%), newspaper/yearbook (13% vs. 8%), and student service/government (25% vs. 14%)." *Id.* at 186.

97. Doninger v. Niehoff, 514 F. Supp. 2d 199 (D. Conn. 2007).

98. Bd. of Educ. of Indep. Sch. Dist. No. 92 of Pottawatomie Cty. v. Earls, 536 U.S. 822 (2002). *See also* Veronica Sch. Dist. 47J v. Acton 515 U.S. 646 (1995) (student barred from playing football for failure to submit to mandatory urinalysis drug test).

99. D.N. *ex rel.* Huff v. Penn Harris Madison Sch. Corp., 2006 WL 2710596 (N.D. Ind. 2006). A poignant example of how some schools inappropriately use the denial of opportunities for social interactions as a disciplinary device in regard to a student with disabilities was recounted by. Michael Gregory, a clinical associate professor at Harvard Law School:

> The archetype case that we teach in our special education clinic—based on a case we actually did in the early days of the clinic—involves a student being placed on the "behavior list" in 5th grade, which prohibited him from engaging in Field Day activities and the school pizza party. He had to eat his lunch every day in the principal's office rather than in the cafeteria with the other children. The irony is that children who lack social skills and self-regulation abilities –the cornerstones of effective social participation and civic engagement—are the very children most likely to be denied access to the parts of the school day that are designed to foster these competencies.

Personal e-mail communication to the author from Prof. Michael Gregory, Jan. 18, 2016.

100. MASS. CODE REGS. 603, § 53.11 (2016).

101. U.S. DEP'T OF EDUC., CIVIL RIGHTS DATA COLLECTION, DATA SNAPSHOT: DISCIPLINE (2014), *available at* http://www2.ed.gov/about/offices/list/ocr/docs/crdc-discipline-snapshot.pdf. A recent analysis of the OCR data that focused on Southern states found that although blacks constitute 24 percent of students in those areas, they accounted for 50 percent of suspensions and expulsions. EDWARD J. SMITH & SHAUN R. HARPER, CTR. FOR THE STUDY OF RACE AND EQUITY, DISPROPORTIONATE IMPACT OF K–12 SCHOOL SUSPENSIONS AND EXPULSION ON BLACK STUDENTS IN SOUTHERN STATES (2015), *available at* http://www.gse.upenn.edu/equity/SouthernStates.

102. These policies originally required schools to expel students suspected of involvement with on-campus drug use (or possession), violence, or gang-related activity. Over the years, the policies have been applied to a broader range of behavioral problems, such as cigarette smoking and other forms of school misconduct (e.g., cheating, swearing, disrupting class). K.C. Monahan, S. VanDerhei, J. Bechtold & E. Cauffman, *From the School Yard to the Squad Car: School Discipline, Truancy, and Arrest*, *43* J. YOUTH & ADOLESCENCE 1110–11 (2014).

103. Russell J. Skiba et al., *The Color of Discipline: Sources of Racial and Gender Disproportionality in School Punishment*, 34 URBAN REV. 317, 319 (2002), *available at* http://indiana.edu/~equity/docs/ColorofDiscipline2002.pdf. These researchers also noted: "There also appeared to be differences in the type of punishment meted out to students of different social classes. While high-income students more often reported receiving mild and moderate consequences (e.g., teacher reprimand, seat reassignment), low-income students reported receiving more severe consequences, sometimes delivered in a less-than-professional manner (e.g., yelled at in front of class, made to stand in hall all day, search of personal belongings)." *Id.*

104. *See* Belinda Hopkin, *Restorative Justice in the Schools*, 17 SUPPORT FOR LEARNING 144 (2002), *available at* http://www.transformingconflict.org/system/files/libraryfiles/Doc%205%20-%20Restorative%20Justice%20in%20Schools%202002%20-%20Support%20for%20Learning%2017.3.pdf; Brenda Morrison, *Restorative Justice in Schools*, *in* NEW DIRECTIONS IN RESTORATIVE JUSTICE: ISSUES, PRACTICE, EVALUATION (Elizabeth Elliot & Robert M. Gordon eds., 2011); N.Y. STATE PERMANENT JUDICIAL COMM'N ON JUSTICE FOR CHILDREN ET AL., RESTORATIVE PRACTICES IN ACTION JOURNAL: FOR SCHOOL AND JUSTICE PRACTITIONERS (2015), *available at* https://www.nycourts.gov/ip/justiceforchildren/PDF/RestorativePracticeConf/RP_Journal.pdf.

105. A school that creates the kind of inclusive climate that is supportive of students from all backgrounds—which is also the type of positive climate that is most conducive for civic preparation—tends to have fewer discipline issues because students perceive the rules to be fair and clear and believe that they have the ability to shape school policies, and there is a system of shared values and

a pattern of caring relationships among students and staff. AARON KUPCHIK, HOMEROOM SECURITY: SCHOOL DISCIPLINE IN AN AGE OF FEAR 16 (2010). *See also* Kei Kawashima-Ginsburg & Peter Levine, *Policy Effects on Informed Political Engagement*, 58 AM. BEHAV. SCI. 655 (2014) (research finds that "students who attend schools with positive school climate can develop a positive sense of belonging, connection to peers, and trust in institutions and eventually in the broader society and its democratic system"); Campbell, *supra* note 5, at 243 ("adolescents who attended public high schools with a strong civic ethos were more likely to be civically engaged"); ANTHONY BRYK, VALERIE LEE & PETER HOLLAND, CATHOLIC SCHOOLS AND THE COMMON GOOD (1993) (Catholic schools are successful because they promote a strong sense of community, centered on trust).

106. JOEL WESTHEIMER, WHAT KIND OF CITIZEN? EDUCATING OUR CHILDREN FOR THE COMMON GOOD 52 (2015).

107. *Id.* at 63.

108. Hugh McIntosh, Sheldon Berman & James Youniss, *A Five Year Evaluation of a Comprehensive High School Civic Engagement Initiative* (Ctr. for Info. & Res. on Civic Learning and Engagement, Working Paper No. 70, 2010), *available at* http://eric.ed.gov/?id=ED509713.

109. PETER LEVINE, WE ARE THE ONES WE HAVE BEEN WAITING FOR: THE PROMISE OF CIVIC RENEWAL IN AMERICA 122 (2013). Levine also correlates this extensive youth political involvement with the fact that almost 80 percent of Hampton's young residents voted in the 2004 election, compared to 43 percent in Virginia as a whole. *Id.*

110. *See* DANIEL LAUTZENHEISER & ANDREW P. KELLY, CHARTER SCHOOLS AS NATION BUILDERS DEMOCRACY PREP AND CIVIC EDUCATION 6 (Am. Enter. Inst. 2013).

111. Kahne, Hodgin & Eidman-Aadahl, *supra* note 62, at 21.

112. *Id.* at 21–22.

113. The iCivics initiative is *available at* the website https://www.icivics.org/games. *See also* "Zora," a virtual city built and operated by eleven- to fifteen-year-olds described in Marina Umaschi Bers, *Civic Identities, Online Technologies: From Designing Civics Curriculum to Supporting Civic Experiences*, *in* CIVIC LIFE ONLINE, *supra* note 74, at 139. A survey of video games played by 1,100 teenagers found that 43 percent of teens played games such as Quest Atlantis and Civilization, in which they help make decisions about the operations of a community, city, or nation, and 52 percent reported playing games in which they think about moral and civic issues. The study also found that teens had the same civic gaming experiences, regardless of family income race and ethnicity. *See* JOSEPH KAHNE, ELLEN MIDDAUGH & CHRIS EVANS, MACARTHUR FOUND., THE CIVIC POTENTIAL OF VIDEO GAMES (2009), *available at* http://www.civicsurvey.org/sites/default/files/publications/Civic_Pot_Video_Games.pdf.

114. Richard Weissbourd, The Parents We Mean to Be: How Well Intentioned Adults Undermine Children's Moral and Emotional Development 116 (2009).

115. Quoted in Paul Tough, How Children Succeed: Grit, Curiosity and the Hidden Power of Character 59 (2013).

116. *See, e.g.,* Alfie Kohn, *How Not to Teach Values: A Critical Look at Character Education, in* Character and Moral Education: A Reader, 130, 134 (Joseph De Vitis and Tianlong Yu eds., 2011) (criticizing selective listing of only traditional values and presenting them in a way that uses them as "euphemisms for uncritical deference to authority"); Michael Davis, *What's Wrong with Character Education?*, 110 Am J. Educ. 32 (2003), *available at* http://www.journals.uchicago.edu/doi/pdfplus/10.1086/377672 (criticizing "simple" character education).

117. Tough, *supra* note 115, at 60. *See also* Russell J. Sojourner, The Rebirth and Retooling of Character Education in America 9 (2012), *available at* https://www.character.org/wp-content/uploads/Character-Education.pdf. Character education actually predated President Clinton's State of the Union declaration. It emerged in reaction to the values clarification movement, popular in many areas in the 1970s and 1980s. Values clarification considered the inculcation of any set of values to be objectionable, given the diversity of political, religious, and moral beliefs among contemporary students. Proponents of this approach sought to help students analyze, understand, and choose those values that ware most appropriate for their own lives. *See, e.g.,* S. Simon, L. Howe & H. Kirschenbaum, Values Clarification: A Handbook of Practical Strategies (1972); B. Chazen, Contemporary Approaches to Moral Education (1985). Critics claimed that values clarification offered merely manipulation of "desires and self-gratification" and "an endless succession of conflicts and dilemmas." William J. Bennett & Edwin J. Delattre, *Moral Education in the Schools*, 50 Pub. Int. 81, 86, 98 (1978).

118. Sojourner, *supra* note 117, at 12.

119. Wolfgang Althof and Marvin W. Berkowitz, leaders of the contemporary character education movement, write that it is "now a consensual idea that a competent, engaged and effective citizenship—necessary for full political, economic, social and cultural participation"—requires civic and political knowledge, intellectual skills, social and participatory skills, and certain values, attitudes, and "dispositions" with a motivational power. Wolfgang Altof & Marvin W. Berkowitz, *Moral Education and Character Education: Their Relationship and Roles in Citizenship Education*, 35 J. Moral Educ. 495, 503 (2006), *available at* https://characterandcitizenship.org/PDF/MoralEducationandCharacterEducationAlthofBerkowitz.pdf.

120. N.C. Gen. Stat. § 115C-81 (h). The statute defines each of these traits in some detail.

121. Aaron Cooley, *Legislating Character: Moral Education in North Carolina's Public Schools*, *in* CHARACTER AND MORAL EDUCATION, *supra* note 116, at 69.

122. Michael H. Romanowski, *Through the Eyes of Students: High School Students' Perspectives on Character Education*, *in* CHARACTER AND MORAL EDUCATION, *supra* note 116, at 123–24.

123. Paul Tough presents a striking example of how values of respect, self-control and hard work were taught realistically and successfully to street-smart students through the KIPP Academy's behavior modification program. KIPP combined the motivational aspects of academic success and college admission with an acceptance of "code switching," techniques that advised the students to use these behavior patterns in the school environment, but not necessarily when they were operating in their street cultures. TOUGH, *supra* note 115, at 89.

124. SCOTT SEIDER, CHARACTER COMPASS: HOW POWERFUL SCHOOL CULTURE CAN POINT STUDENTS TOWARD SUCCESS 126–27 (2012).

125. *Id.* at 128–29.

126. *Id.* at 180–81.

127. Diane Ravitch, *Celebrating America*, *in* PLEDGING ALLEGIANCE: THE POLITICS OF PATRIOTISM IN AMERICA'S SCHOOLS 92 (Joel Westheimer ed., 2007). Ravitch adds: "The public school is itself an expression of the nation's democratic ideology, a vehicle created to realize the nation's belief in individualism, self-improvement and progress. It was in the public schools that students not only would learn what it meant to be an American but would gain the education necessary to make their way in an open society, one in which rank and privilege were less important than talent and merit." *Id.* at 92–93.

128. MORRIS JANOWITZ, THE RECONSTRUCTION OF PATRIOTISM: EDUCATION FOR CIVIC CONSCIOUSNESS 84 (1983).

129. *Id.* at 94.

130. *Id.* at 111.

131. Sigal Ben-Porath, *Education for Shared Fate Citizenship*, *in* EDUCATION, JUSTICE & DEMOCRACY 80 (Danielle Allen & Rob Reich eds., 2013).

132. Joel Westheimer, *Introduction* in PLEDGING ALLEGIANCE, *supra* note 127, at 4.

133. STANFORD CTR. ON ADOLESCENCE, YOUTH CIVIC DEVELOPMENT & EDUCATION: A CONFERENCE REPORT 19 (2014). *See also* CTR. FOR CIVIC EDUC., NATIONAL STANDARDS FOR CIVICS AND GOVERNMENT, STANDARD IV. D. 3 (1994), *available at* http://www.civiced.org/standards?page=912erica#15 (patriotism means "loyalty to the values and principles underlying American constitutional democracy as distinguished from jingoism and chauvinism"); Joseph Kahne and Ellen Middaugh similarly espouse a patriotism that

> applaud[s] some actions by the state and criticize[s] others in an effort to promote positive change and consistency with the

> nation's ideals. For example, imperialistic actions, though often advantageous to the imperialist nation's citizens, should be rejected as inconsistent with democratic values. Rather than view critique or debate as unpatriotic . . . constructive patriots consider a wide range of perspectives and enact what Ervin Straub calls "critical loyalty." . . . The point is not to downplay . . . the promise of America's democratic commitments to equality and justice. Rather, it is to help students use their love of country as a motivation to critically assess what is needed to make it better.

Joseph Kahne & Ellen Middaugh, *Is Patriotism Good for Democracy*, *in* PLEDGING ALLEGIANCE 115, *supra* note 127, at 119.

134. Ben-Porath, *supra* note 131, at 90.

135. *Id.*

136. NAT'L CTR. FOR EDUC. STATS., BULLYING AT SCHOOL AND CYBER-BULLING ANYWHERE (2015), *available at* http://nces.ed.gov/pubs2015/2015056.pdf.

137. *See Policies and Laws*, STOPBULLYING.GOV, *available at* http://www.stopbullying.gov/laws/index.html (summarizing laws and policies regarding anti-bullying laws in the fifty states).

138. N.J. Stat. Ann. 18A: 37-13-18A:37-31.

Chapter Six

1. *See* discussion in chapter 3, at pp. 61–64.

2. See chapter 3 for a discussion of the various phrases used in the different state constitutions to describe the minimal level of education to which all students are entitled.

3. *See* MICHAEL A. REBELL, COURTS AND KIDS: PURSUING EDUCATIONAL EQUITY THROUGH THE STATE COURTS, 22–29 (2009).

4. McDaniel v. Thomas, 285 S.E.2d 156, 165 (Ga. 1981).

5. Rose v. Council for Better Educ., 790 S.W.2d 186, 212 (Ky. 1989). The other three capacities cited by the Court that did not relate specifically to civic preparation were "sufficient self-knowledge and knowledge of his or her mental and physical wellness," "sufficient training or preparation for advanced training in either academic or vocational fields so as to enable each child to choose and pursue life work intelligently," and "sufficient levels of academic or vocational skills to enable public school students to compete favorably with their counterparts in surrounding states, in academics or in the job market."

6. *See* discussion and citations in chapter 3 at note 37.

7. *See* Pauley v. Kelly, 255 S.E.2d 859, 877 (W.Va. 1979) (defining a "thorough and efficient education" among other things, as including "knowledge of government to the extent that the child will be equipped as a citizen to make informed

choices among persons and issues that affect his own governance" and "social ethics, both behavioral and abstract, to facilitate compatibility with others in this society").

8. The motivation for the trial judge to undertake this extensive process to define constitutional standards, and the Supreme Court's acceptance of them, may have been influenced by the especially low levels of civic participation that commentators had noted in Kentucky at the time. *See* PENNY M. MILLER, KENTUCKY POLITICS AND GOVERNMENT 3 (1994) (finding that Kentucky's political culture has been characterized by low levels of political participation and general deference to a small set of politically active elites).

9. The select committee actually recommended the four capacities that centered exclusively on civic participation concepts together with knowledge to attend to their own wellness. The two additional capacities relating to vocational skills were added by the Court. Kern Alexander et al., *Constitutional Intent: "System," "Common," and "Efficient" as Terms of Art*, 15 J. of EDUC. FIN. 142, 154 (1989).

10. Molly A. Hunter, *All Eyes Forward: Public Engagement and Educational Reform in Kentucky*, 28 J. L. & EDUC. 485, 495 (1999). For additional discussion of the extensive public engagement process led by the Prichard Committee that both preceded and followed the court decisions, *see* MICHAEL PARIS, FRAMING EQUAL OPPORTUNITY: LAW AND THE POLITICS OF SCHOOL FINANCE REFORM pt. 3 (2010).

11. Campaign for Fiscal Equity (CFE), Inc. v. State, 801 N.E.2d, 326, 332 (NY 2003). This definition was also substantially adopted by the Connecticut Supreme Court in Conn. Coal. for Justice in Educ. Funding v. Rell, 990 A.2d 206 (Conn. 2010).

12. CFE v. State, 719 N.Y.S.2d 475, 485 (N.Y. Sup. Ct. 2001). Justice DeGrasse apparently meant that a capable voter or juror needs sufficient skills to follow arguments made by experts on complex subjects, not that voters and jurors necessarily need to master the intricacies of campaign finance reform or DNA themselves. In essence, these standards are, in contemporary terms, equivalent to the "Jefferson ideal" of the kinds of knowledge and skills that an active informed citizen should possess. *See* JENNIFER L. HOCHSCHILD & KATHERINE LEVINE EINSTEIN, DO FACTS MATTER/INFORMATION AND MISINFORMATION IN AMERICAN POLITICS 4–6 (2015).

13. CFE v. State, 655 N.E.2d 66, 666–67 (N.Y. 1995).

14. *See* Michael A. Rebell, *Adequacy Litigations: A New Path to Equity?, in* BRINGING EQUITY BACK: RESEARCH FOR A NEW ERA IN AMERICAN EDUCATIONAL POLICY 291, 307–15 (Janice Petrovich & Amy Stuart Wells eds., 2005).

15. McCleary v. State, 269 P.3d 227, 246–47 (Wash. 2012).

16. McCleary v. State, 2010 WL 9073395 (Wash. Super. 2010), *aff'd* 269 P.3d 227, 229 (Wash. 2012).

17. McCleary v. State, 269 P.3d at 231–46.

18. Deborah Meier, Response to Danielle Allen, *New Democracy Forum*, BOSTON REV., 8, 14 May–June, 2016, *available at* https://bostonreview.net/forum/what-education/deborah-meier-deborah-meier-responds-danielle-allen.

19. Specifically, the Center for Information and Research on Civic Learning and Engagement (CIRCLE) analyzed the correlation between the twenty-two states in which plaintiffs had prevailed in education adequacy cases as of June 2016, as listed at the Schoolfunding website (http://www.schoolfunding.info), and the seven indicators listed previously. It found the following correlations: state-required civics course, 0.03; civics test, 0.00; state social studies assessment, 0.00; test plus course required, 0.014; social studies standards, 0.11; number of years of required social studies, –0.14; and service learning 0.06. Personal correspondence from Peter Levine, the Tufts associate dean responsible for CIRCLE, to Michael A. Rebell, July 1, 2016. Note, however, that there appears to have been a pattern of greater acceptance of rigorous social studies standards related to civic education in states in which there had been a successful adequacy litigation. *See* discussion in chapter 5, at pp. 102–3.

20. The expectation would be that "while the judiciary has the duty to construe and interpret the word 'education' by providing broad constitutional guidelines, the Legislature is obligated to give specific substantive content to the word and to the program it deems necessary to provide that 'education' within the broad guidelines." McCleary v. State, 269 P.3d at 247.

21. GERALD N. ROSENBERG, THE HOLLOW HOPE: CAN COURTS BRING ABOUT SOCIAL CHANGE 32 (1991).

22. The mere filing of school-funding-adequacy litigation have tended to move fiscal equity issues to the top of the political agenda, whether or not the plaintiffs actually prevail in a particular litigation. *See* G. Alan Hickrod et al., *The Effect of Constitutional Litigation on Education Finance: A Preliminary Analysis*, 18 J. EDUC. FIN. 180 (1992).

23. *See, e.g.,* judicial order requiring annual reporting by the legislature in McCleary v. State, Sup. Ct. Order No. 84362-7 (Wash. 2012), *available at* http://www.courts.wa.gov/content/publicUpload/News/McCleary%20v.%20State%20order%207.18.12.pdf. Among other things that order specified: "The court's review will focus on whether the actions taken by the legislature show real and measurable progress toward achieving full compliance with Article IX, section 1 by 2018 . . . the State must demonstrate steady progress according to the schedule anticipated by the enactment of the program reforms in [the relevant legislation]."

24. *Cf.* Claremont Sch. Dist. v. Governor, 794 A.2d 744, 751 (N.H. 2002): "Accountability means that the State must provide a definition of a constitutionally adequate education, the definition must have standards, and the standards must be subject to meaningful application so that it is possible to determine whether,

in delegating its obligation to provide a constitutionally adequate education, the State has fulfilled its duty."

25. *Cf., e.g.*, Castaneda v. Pickard, 648 F.2d 989, 1010 (5th Cir. 1982): ("The court's second inquiry would be whether the programs and practices actually used by a school system are reasonably calculated to implement effectively the educational theory adopted by the school").

26. *Cf., e.g.*, Conn. Coal. for Justice in Educ. Funding, Inc. v. Rell, 990 A.2d 206, 254 (Conn. 2010), quoting Pauley v. Kelly, 255 S.E.2d 859 (W. Va. 1979): (constitutionally adequate system requires "careful state and local supervision to prevent waste and to monitor pupil, teacher and administrative competency").

27. *See* discussion in chapter 4, at pp. 74–75.

28. Cal. Task Force On K–12 Civic Learning, Revitalizing K–12 Civic Learning in California (2014), *available at* http://www.cde.ca.gov/eo/in/documents/cltffinalreport.pdf.

29. *See* Robert R. McCormick Found., Illinois Civic Blueprint (2d ed., 2013), *available at* http://documents.mccormickfoundation.org/pdf/Civic-Blueprint-2013.pdf.

30. Educ. Comm'n of the States, National Center for Learning and Civic Engagement, State Civic Education Policy Framework (2014), *available at* http://www.ecs.org/clearinghouse/01/16/12/11612.pdf.

31. *See* Frances L. Kidwell, The Relationship Between Civic Education and State Policy: An Evaluative Study (May 2005) (unpublished Ph.D. dissertation, Univ. S. Cal.), *available at* http://cms-ca.org/Kidwell_Civic%20Education%20and%20State%20Policy.pdf (dissertation analyzing practices in all fifty states finds that although civic education curriculum standards exist in most states, they play a far less significant role in assessments, classroom instruction and curriculum development).

32. For this reason, litigators in state which have already-articulated judicial standards might seek a remedial order that incorporates those standards but supplements them with proposals for additional judicial standards or with a request that the state be required to develop and implement additional standards in areas not covered by existing judicial standards.

33. Abbott v. Burke, 710 A.2d 450 (N.J. 1998).

34. Subhi Godsay et al., Fact Sheet 9 (Ctr. for Info. & Res. on Civic Learning and Engagement, Oct. 2012), *available at* http://files.eric.ed.gov/fulltext/ED536256.pdf.

35. The College, Career, and Civic Life (C3) Framework for Social Studies State Standards: Guidance for Enhancing the Rigor of K–12 Civics, Economics, Geography, and History (2013). The fact that these standards were developed by the American Bar Association together with a number of major civic education and educational organizations would add to their credibility for many judges. *See* discussion in chapter 5, at pp. 100–101.

36. *Id.* at 32–34.

37. Paulson v. Minidoka Co. Sch. Dist. 463 P.2d 935, 938 (Idaho 1970). The U.S. Court of Appeals for the Sixth Circuit has held that under the Individuals with Disabilities Education Act (IDEA), school districts are not obligated to provide extracurricular activities to students with disabilities. Rettig v. Kent City Sch. Dist., 788 F.2d 328 (N.D. Ohio 1986).

38. The California Supreme Court, one of the few state courts that have upheld the importance of extracurricular activities, did note when it declared fees for extracurricular activities to be unconstitutional in Hartzell v. Connell 679 P.2d 35,43 (Cal. 1984) that "in addition to the particular skills taught, group activities encourage active participation in community affairs, promote the development of leadership qualities, and instill a spirit of collective endeavor. These results are directly linked to the constitutional role of education in preserving democracy, as set forth in article IX, section 1, and elaborated in Serrano [v. Priest,] 487 P.2d 1241."

39. Ctr. for Info. & Research on Civic Learning and Engagement, *State Civic Ed Policies Update* (as of Jan. 13, 2014), annexed to correspondence dated July 1, 2016, from Peter Levine to Michael A. Rebell.

40. MD. REGS. CODE tit. 13A § 03.02.06.

41. *See* discussion in chapter 5, at pp. 120–23.

42. Quoted in MAGGIE CLARK, GOVERNING ST. AND LOCAL GOV'T, 49 STATES NOW HAVE ANTI-BULLYING LAWS. HOW'S THAT WORKING OUT? (Nov. 2013), *available at* http://www.governing.com/news/headlines/49-States-Now-Have-Anti-Bullying-Laws-Hows-that-Working-Out.html. *See also* Deborah Temkin, *All 50 States Now Have a Bullying Law. Now What?* HUFFINGTON POST, Apr. 27, 2015, *available at* http://www.huffingtonpost.com/deborah-temkin/all-50-states-now-have-a_b_7153114.html ("Without any mechanism to ensure that schools and districts actually follow through with their obligations, these anti-bullying laws do essentially nothing to help prevent bullying"). Eleven states identify a source of funding to assist school districts in satisfying the various mandates imposed by state bullying laws; six of those states provide for appropriations, and five rely on private donations. Programs in some other states are funded through competitive grant programs. *See* DENA T. SACCO ET AL., AN OVERVIEW OF STATE ANTI-BULLYING LEGISLATION AND OTHER RELATED LAWS 12 (Feb. 2012), *available at* http://www.meganmeierfoundation.org/cmss_files/attachmentlibrary/State-Anti-Bullying-Legislation-Overview.pdf.

43. After nine students and former students of the Anoka-Hennepin School District in Minnesota had committed suicide over a two-year period, five students filed a civil rights suit against the district for inaction against antigay bullying. The U.S. Department of Justice and the Office for Civil Rights of the U.S. Department of Education joined as intervenors in the case. The district subsequently entered into a consent decree that included a comprehensive plan to

counter and prevent future harassment in district education programs and activities. Key features of the plan included a thorough evaluation of the district's anti-harassment policies and procedures, tailored actions to improve the school climate and enhance the training of staff and students and monitoring by the U.S. Department of Education. *See* Doe v. Anoka-Hennepin Sch. Dist., No. 11-CV-01999-JNE-SER (2012), *available at* https://www.justice.gov/sites/default/files/usao-mn/legacy/2012/03/06/Anoka-Hennepin%20FINAL%20Consent%20Decree.pdf.

44. The federal courts have understood the importance of schools taking effective stances against bullying in upholding school policies enforcing anti-cyberbullying activities. *See, e.g.,* Kowalski v. Berkeley Cty. Schs., 652 F.3d 565 (4th Cir. 2014) (student suspended for creating and posting to a webpage on a home computer that ridiculed a fellow student), S.J.W. v. Lee's Summit R-7 Sch. Dist., 696 F.3d 771 (8th Cir. 2015) (students suspended for creating website with blog containing variety of offensive, racist, and sexist comments about school and classmates). *See also* Erwin Chemerinsky, *Can the First Amendment Survive the Internet?*, CHRON. HIGHER EDUC., Jan. 9, 2015.

45. David E. Campbell, *Civic Education in Traditional, Charter, and Private Schools Moving From Comparison to Explanation*, *in* MAKING CIVICS EDUCATION COUNT: CITIZENSHIP EDUCATION FOR A NEW GENERATION 229, 230–31 (David E. Campbell, Meira Levinson & Frederick M. Hess eds., 2012).

46. GODSAY ET AL., *supra* notc 34.

47. Elementary & Secondary Sch. Act, 20 U.S.C.A. § 6311(c) (4) B (VI) (2015).

48. *See* WASH. OFFICE OF SUPERINTENDENT OF PUB. INSTRUCTION, CIVICS ASSESSMENT FOR HIGH SCHOOLS, *available at* http://www.k12.wa.us/socialStudies/Assessments/HighSchool/HSCivics-ChecksandBalances-CBA.pdf.

49. *See* LINDA DARLING-HAMMOND ET AL., LEARNING POLICY INST., PATHWAYS TO NEW ACCOUNTABILITY THROUGH EVERY STUDENT SUCCEEDS ACT, 14–15 (2016).

50. *See* Diane Ravitch, *A New Paradigm for Accountability: The Joy of Learning*, HUFFINGTON POST, Jan. 12, 2015, *available at* http://www.huffingtonpost.com/diane-ravitch/a-new-paradigm-for-accoun_b_6145446.htm.

51. MEIRA LEVINSON, NO CITIZEN LEFT BEHIND (2012).

52. RICHARD DAGGER, CIVIC VIRTUES: RIGHTS, CITIZENSHIP, AND REPUBLICAN LIBERALISM 31, 34 (1997).

53. DIANA E. HESS, CONTROVERSY IN THE CLASSROOM: THE DEMOCRATIC POWER OF DISCUSSION 171 (2009). Note also that the higher drop-out rates associated with under-funded schools in and of themselves appear to have a detrimental impact on civic participation: "An additional year of [secondary] schooling increases voter participation by 3.8 percent, an increase of approximately 5 percent. These results also imply that another year of schooling significantly increases the index of newspaper readership (by 0.104, an increase of 3 percent)

and the number of group memberships (by .222, an increase of 12 percent). Another year of schooling also appears to increase support for free speech by a statistically significant 2.2 to 3.6 percentage points, depending on who is doing the speaking." Thomas S. Dee, *Are There Civic Returns to Education?*, 88 J. PUB. ECON. 1697, 1713 (2004).

54. Letter from Catherine E. Lhamon, Assistant Secretary for Civil Rights, to colleagues (Oct. 1, 2014), *available at* http://www2.ed.gov/about/offices/list/ocr/letters/colleague-resourcecomp-201410.pdf.

55. NAT'L CTR. FOR EDUC. STATS., SCHOOL DISTRICT EXPENDITURES PER PUPIL 2011–2012, *available at* http://nces.ed.gov/edfin/Fy11_12_tables.asp. A recent analysis by the Education Trust took into account not only the differences in the number of dollars allocated by state and local sources to poor and affluent districts but also the additional resources needed to provide comprehensive supplemental services to students from disadvantaged background. NATASHA USHOMIRSKY & DAVID WILLIAMS, FUNDING GAPS 2015: TOO MANY STATES STILL SPEND LESS ON EDUCATING STUDENTS WHO NEED THE MOST 5 (Educ. Trust 2015), *available at* http://edtrust.org/wp-content/uploads/2014/09/FundingGaps2015_TheEducationTrust1.pdf. Using what they considered a conservative estimate that a 40 percent increase in *per capita* funding was needed to provide meaningful educational opportunities to students of poverty, they found that on average nationally the highest poverty districts receive about $2,200, or 18 percent, less per student than low-poverty districts. By their calculations before accounting for the additional needs of low-income students, seventeen states provide substantially more funding (at least 5 percent) to the highest-poverty districts, but after the adjustment for necessary supplemental services, only four still do. *See also* BRUCE BAKER, DANIELLE FARRIE, THERESA LUHM & DAVID G. SCIARRA, IS FUNDING FAIR? A NATIONAL REPORT CARD (2016), *available at* http://www.schoolfundingfairness.org/National_Report_Card_2016.pdf (finding that fourteen "regressive" states provide less funding to school districts with higher concentrations of low-income students); BRUCE D. BAKER & SEAN P. CORCORAN, CTR. FOR AM. PROGRESS, THE STEALTH INEQUITIES OF SCHOOL FUNDING HOW STATE AND LOCAL SCHOOL FINANCE SYSTEMS PERPETUATE INEQUITABLE STUDENT SPENDING (2014), *available at* https://cdn.americanprogress.org/wp-content/uploads/2012/09/StealthInequities.pdf (discussing how often-overlooked features of school funding systems tend to exacerbate inequities in per-pupil spending).

56. A recent study of state supreme court decisions in twenty-eight states between 1971 and 2010 concluded that school finance reforms stemming from court orders have increased state spending in lower-income districts, decreased expenditure gaps between low- and high-income districts, improved graduation rates, and resulted in higher earnings for graduates. C. Kirabo Jackson, Rucker Johnson & Claudia Persico, *The Effects of School Spending on Educational and*

Economic Outcomes: Evidence from School Finance Reforms (Nat'l Bureau of Econ. Research, Working Paper No. 20847, 2015), *available at* http://www.nber.org/papers/w20847.

57. See *Summary of School Funding Court Cases* (1973–2017), *available at* www.schoolfunding.info. Since 1989, when most funding cases have been based on "adequacy" rather than "equity" claims, plaintiffs have been a bit more successful, winning about 60 percent of these decisions. *Id.*

58. UNICEF, Innocenti Report Card No. 13, 10 (2016), *available at* https://www.unicef-irc.org/publications/pdf/RC13_eng.pdf.

59. *Id.*

60. *See, e.g.*, Robert Lenzer, *The Wealthiest 20% Own 72%; The Poorest 20% Only 3%*, Forbes (2013), *available at* http://www.forbes.com/sites/robertlenzner/2013/04/19/the-growing-disparity-in-wealth-made-the-great-recession-worse-and-the-recovery-weaker-than-ever-before/#52d43e0a69c4 (top 20 percent of the population own 72 percent of the nation's wealth; the poorest 20 percent of the U.S. population own only 3 percent of the wealth); Alyssa Davis & Lawrence Mishel, *CEO Pay Continues to Rise as Typical Workers Are Paid Less*, Econ. Pol'y Inst. (2014), *available at* http://www.epi.org/publication/ceo-pay-continues-to-rise/ (the ratio of CEO compensation to average worker pay in 2013 was 296 to 1, compared to a ratio of 22 to 1 in 1973).

61. Richard Rothstein, Class and Schools: Using Social, Economic and Educational Reform to Close the Black-White Achievement Gap 11(2004). *See also* David C. Berliner, *Our Impoverished View of Educational Research*, 6 Tchrs. C. Rec. 949, 956–61 (2006) (discussing the impact of poverty on efforts for school reform); Jeanne Brooks-Gunn & Greg J. Duncan, "The Effects of Poverty on Children," 7 Future of Children 55 (1997) (summarizing studies of the effects of long-term poverty on children's welfare and cognitive abilities); Whitney C. Allgood, *The Need for Adequate Resources for At-Risk Children* (Econ. Pol'y Inst., Working Paper No. 277, 2006) (comprehensively reviewing studies and literature on impact of poverty on children's readiness to learn and setting forth a model for determining the components and costs of an adequate education for at-risk children.); James E. Ryan, *Schools, Race and Money*, 109 Yale L.J. 249, 284–96 (1999) (providing overview of research on impact of concentrated poverty school performance); Russell W. Rumberger, *Parsing the Data on Student Achievement in High Poverty Schools*, 85 N.C. L. Rev. 1293, 1310–11 (2007) (discussing national longitudinal study of ten thousand students that indicates that attending a high poverty school has a significant negative effect on achievement of students from poverty backgrounds).

62. I discuss these issues in detail in Michael A. Rebell, *The Right to Comprehensive Educational Opportunity*, 47 Harv. Civ. Rts.–Civ. Liberties L. Rev. 47 (2012).

63. *See* Michael A. Rebell, *Safeguarding the Right to a Sound Basic Educa-*

tion in Times of Fiscal Constraint, 75 ALB. L. REV. 1855, 1921–26 (2012) (discussing how billions of dollars can be saved, without compromising services to students, by such steps as cutting back unnecessary state mandates, reforming special education, promoting school district consolidation, improving teacher retention rates, and eliminating abuses in teacher pension programs). Educational funding analyses and expenditures should also be subject to on-going cost-effective analyses. *See* Michael A. Rebell, Henry M. Levin, Robert Shand & Jessica R. Wolff, *A New Constitutional Cost Methodology for Determining the Actual Cost of a Sound Basic Education* (paper presented at the 41st annual conference of the Assoc. for Educ. Fin. & Pol'y, 2016), *available at* http://www.equitycampaign.org. It has also been demonstrated that investments in education are returned to society many times over in terms of increased work productivity, higher taxes paid, and lower expenditures on prisons, welfare, health, and other costs. *See, e.g.*, THE PRICE WE PAY: THE ECONOMIC AND SOCIAL CONSEQUENCES OF INADEQUATE EDUCATION (Clive M. Belfield & Henry M. Levin eds., 2007).

64. William S. Koski & Rob Reich, *When "Adequate" Isn't: The Retreat from Equity in Educational Law and Policy and Why It Matters*, 56 EMORY L.J. 545, 611 (2006). *See also* Isabel V. Sawhill & Daniel P. McMurrer, *American Dreams and Discontent: Beyond the Level Playing Field*, USIA, U.S. SOC. & VALUES (Jan. 1997) ("With the closing of the frontier around the turn of the [twentieth] century, Americans increasingly looked to education as the primary source of opportunity").

65. "Once the government provides this framework, individuals are on their own, according to the ideology. . . . Put more positively, it is up to individuals to go as far and as fast they can in whatever direction they choose." JENNIFER L. HOCHSCHILD & NATHAN SCOVRONICK, THE AMERICAN DREAM AND THE PUBLIC SCHOOLS 10 (2003).

66. One observer summarized current attitudes as follows: "Surveys continue to show that Americans, in large numbers, still believe in many of the tenets of the American dream. For example, majorities of Americans believe that hard work will lead to success. But, their belief in the American dream is wavering. Between 1986 and 2011, around 50 percent of those polled by Pew consistently said they felt that the American dream was 'somewhat alive.' However, over that same time period, the share who said it was 'very alive' decreased by about half, and the share that felt it was 'not really alive' more than doubled." Marianne Cooper, *The Downsizing of the American Dream*, ATLANTIC, Oct. 2, 2015, *available at* http://www.theatlantic.com/business/archive/2015/10/american-dreams/408535/.

67. *See, e.g.*, Elise Gould, *U.S. Lags Behind Peer Countries in Mobility: Economic Snapshot*, ECON. POL'Y INST. (2012), *available at* http://www.epi.org/publication/usa-lags-peer-countries-mobility/ (finding that the intergenerational

correlation between the earnings of fathers and sons among OECD countries was stronger—meaning less mobility—for the United States than for a number of other countries, including Denmark, Norway, Finland, Canada, Australia, Sweden, New Zealand, Germany, Japan, Spain, France, and Switzerland).

68. *See* JENNIFER HOCHSCHILD, FACING UP TO THE AMERICAN DREAM: RACE, CLASS AND THE SOUL OF THE NATION (1995). An in-depth survey of Americans' attitudes toward the American dream found that a broad range of families believed in the tenets of the dream, even while acknowledging that different schools provide vastly different opportunities for children: "The more privileged parents interviewed acknowledge the advantages they have received through family wealth, and acknowledge advantageous educational opportunities they are now able to pass along to their children. What is really intriguing, however, is that at the same time, these same families hold close to their hearts the idea that they have earned and deserved what they have, and they argue vehemently that their privileged positions have resulted from their individual hard work, efforts and achievements." HEATHER BETH JOHNSON, THE AMERICAN DREAM AND THE POWER OF WEALTH CHOOSING SCHOOLS AND INHERITING INEQUALITY IN THE LAND OF OPPORTUNITY 21 (2015).

69. Jeremy Reynolds & He Xian, *Perceptions of Meritocracy in the Land of Opportunity*, 36 RES. SOC. STRATIFICATION & MOBILITY 121, § 7.1 (2014), *available at* http://www.sciencedirect.com/science/article/pii/S0276562414000122. *See also* KARLYN BOWMAN ET AL., IS THE AMERICAN DREAM ALIVE? EXAMINING AMERICANS' ATTITUDES 11–12 (Am. Enterprise Inst. 2014) (about 70 percent of Americans still believe in the American dream), *available at* https://www.aei.org/wp-content/uploads/2014/12/Is-the-American-Dream-Alive_Dec2014.pdf; Andrew Kohut & Michael Dimock, *Resilient American Values: Optimism in an Era of Growing Inequality and Economic Difficulty* 5–6 (Council on Foreign Relations, Working Paper, 2013) ("while the public rates its current financial situation as low as it has at any point over the past twenty-five years, it remains bullish about the ability of the American people to overcome challenges").

70. JUSTIN GEST, THE NEW MINORITY: WHITE WORKING CLASS POLITICS IN AN AGE OF IMMIGRATION AND INEQUALITY 155 (2016).

71. As the evidence concerning the correlation between pre-kindergarten education and school readiness has grown in recent years, the public has increasingly been willing to pay for expanded public prekindergarten programs. Between the 2001–02 and 2014–15 school years, despite the impact of the Great Recession in 2008, total state pre-K spending has increased from about $2.4 billion to about $6.2 billion. NAT'L INST. FOR EARLY EDUC. RES. (NIEER) YEARBOOKS, 2002 and 2015, *available at* http://nieer.org/research/state-preschool-2015.

72. For example, the 2014 Phi Delta Kappan and Gallup polls of a representative national sample of one thousand adults found that the public believes that the biggest problem facing the public schools is "a lack of financial support."

Democrats, Republicans, and Independents all listed this as the biggest problem. William J. Bushaw & Valerie J. Calderon, *The 46th Annual PDK/Gallup Poll of the Public's Attitudes Toward the Public Schools; Part I* (Phi Delta Kappan & Gallup 2014), *available at* http://www.pdkintl.org/noindex/PDK_Poll46_2014.pdf. In 2016, voters in California adopted by a margin of two to one a ballot initiative that would raise personal income taxes for twelve years to provide increased funding for education. *See* Ballotopedia, *California Proposition 55: Extension of the Proposition 30 Income Tax Increase (2016), available at* https://ballotpedia.org/California_Proposition_55,_Extension_of_the_Proposition_30_Income_Tax_Increase_(2016). Voters in Minneapolis approved a property tax increase by a 71 percent to 29 percent margin. *See* Emily Lowthar, *Strong Schools Strong City Referendum Passes in Minneapolis*, HMONG TIMES ONLINE, Nov. 18, 2008, *available at* http://www.hmongtimes.com/main.asp?SectionID=37&SubSectionID=183&ArticleID=1486&TM=6672.087. Voters in Maine narrowly approved a statewide income tax increase education. Ballotopedia, *Maine Tax on Incomes Exceeding $200,000 for Public Education, Question 2 (2016), available at* https://ballotpedia.org/Maine_Tax_on_Incomes_Exceeding_$200,000_for_Public_Education,_Question_2_(2016).

73. *See* discussion in chapter 4, at pp. 93–94.

74. Keyes v. Sch. Dist. No. 1, Denver, 413 U.S. 189 (1973).

75. Sheff v. O' Neill, 678 A.2d 1267 (Conn. 1998). Court orders and consent decrees in this case have resulted in a number of open choice programs that allow students to transfer to suburban or urban districts, interdistrict magnet and "Lighthouse" schools intended to draw students to residentially segregated districts, as well as interdistrict exchange programs. These efforts have led to more than 1,600 Hartford students taking part in open choice, and over 5,400 Hartford students and over 8,000 suburban students attending thirty-seven regional magnet schools; overall, 42 percent of Hartford schoolchildren now attend integrated schools. *See* AM. CIVIL LIBERTIES UNION, SHEFF V. O'NEILL, A GROUNDBREAKING SCHOOL DESEGREGATION CASE IN HARTFORD, CONNECTICUT (Mar. 11, 2014), *available at* https://www.aclu.org/cases/sheff-v-oneill. The ACLU and other plaintiffs entered into a new consent agreement with the state in 2015 in an attempt to provide integrated schooling opportunities for rest of Hartford's students. Sheff v. O'Neill, Stipulation and Order (Feb. 23, 2015), *available at* https://www.aclu.org/legal-document/sheff-v-oneill-stipulation-and-order?redirect=racial-justice/sheff-v-oneill-stipulation-and-order.

76. Art. I, § 8, of the Connecticut Constitution provides that "no person shall be denied the equal protection of the law *nor be subjected to segregation* or discrimination in the exercise or enjoyment of his or her civil or political rights because of religion, race, color, ancestry, national origin, sex or physical or mental disability" (emphasis added). Art. I, § 9 of the Hawaii Constitution states: "No

citizen shall be denied enlistment in any military organization of this State nor be segregated therein because of race, religious principles or ancestry."

77. Parents Involved in Cmty. Schs. v. Seattle Sch. Dist. No. 1, 72 P.3d 151, 162–63 (Wash. 2003). *See also* Booker v. City of Plainfield, 212 A.2d 1 (1965) (holding that *de facto* segregation violates the "thorough and efficient" education clause of the state constitution). In Paynter v. State, 797 N.E.2d 1225 (N.Y. 2003), a group of African American students attending schools in the Rochester City School District claimed that the extreme racial isolation in their schools, whose students were 90 percent low income and 80 percent students of color, was denying them the opportunity for a sound basic education guaranteed by Art. I § 11 of the state constitution. The Court of Appeals rejected their claim. It held that 'if the State truly puts adequate resources into the classroom,' it has satisfied its obligation under the Education Article." *Id.* at 1229. To interpret the constitutional obligation to provide all students the opportunity for a sound basic education any more broadly, it reasoned, "would be to subvert the important role of local control and participation in education.'" *Id.* Judge Smith issued a strong dissent, saying: "There is no merit to the argument that allowing plaintiffs' suit to go forward is inconsistent with local control of education. First of all, as it stands now, the State's control over *its* public schools through laws and regulations is pervasive. Second, plaintiffs are not arguing for the elimination of local school boards. They argue that the State should not draw district lines in a manner that encircles poor and minority students, and sets them up for failure. There is nothing sacrosanct about district lines. . . . Moreover, local control has always taken a backseat to larger state interests. . . . Here, the larger interest is the need to insure that plaintiffs have access to a sound education." *Id.* at 1249 (Smith, J., dissenting.) The *Paynter* plaintiffs supported their arguments for interpreting the constitutional right to the opportunity for a sound basic education to encompass desegregation by proffering evidence showing a correlation between concentrated poverty and racial isolation on the one hand and poor educational performance on the other. They did not, however, emphasize the link between concentrated poverty, racial isolation, and a civic empowerment gap that substantially undermines the goal of preparing all students to function productively as civic participants that this same court had declared in *CFE* to be the purpose of the state's public school system.

78. Parents Involved in Cmty. Schs. v. Seattle Sch. Dist. No. 1, 551 U.S. 701 (2007).

79. Justice Kennedy's decisive concurring opinion specifically held that school authorities "are free to devise race-conscious measures to address the problem in a general way and without treating each student in different fashion solely on the basis of a systematic, individual typing by race. School boards may pursue the goal of bringing together students of diverse backgrounds and races

through other means, including strategic site selection of new schools; drawing attendance zones with general recognition of the demographics of neighborhoods; allocating resources for special programs; recruiting students and faculty in a targeted fashion; and tracking enrollments, performance, and other statistics by race." *Id.* at 788–89. Justice Kennedy also stated that "individual racial classifications . . . may be considered legitimate . . . if they are a last resort to achieve a compelling interest." *Id.* at 790.

80. Consolidation plans that combine a large city and its neighboring suburbs into one single countywide school district have historically led to the emergence of stable, integrated school systems in North Carolina and many other locales. *See, e.g.,* Swann v. Charlotte-Mecklenburg Bd. of Educ., 402 U.S. 1, 6 (1971) (describing sprawling school district that "encompasses the city of Charlotte and surrounding Mecklenburg County, North Carolina. The area is large—550 square miles—spanning roughly 22 miles east-west and 36 miles north-south"). *See also* ANSLEY ERIKSON, MAKING THE UNEQUAL METROPOLIS: SCHOOL DESEGREGATION AND ITS LIMITS (2016) (substantial racial integration achieved in county school system encompassing Nashville, Tennessee).

81. *See* Kara S. Finnegan & Jennifer Jellison Holme, *Learning from Interdistrict School Integration Program*, 24 POVERTY & RACE 13 (2015) (describing eight successful interdistrict programs and reasons they have succeeded).

82. Erica Frankenberg & Elizabeth Debray, *Federal Legislation to Promote Metropolitan Approaches to Educational and Housing Opportunity*, *in* INTEGRATING SCHOOLS IN A CHANGING SOCIETY: NEW POLICIES AND LEGAL OPTIONS FOR A MULTIRACIAL GENERATION 281 (Erica Frankenberg & Elizabeth Debray eds., 2011). The authors specifically propose a federal housing for integration initiative but a similar program could be initiated by state legislatures—or by state courts. *See, e.g.,* S. Burlington Twp. NAACP v. Mt. Laurel, 336 A.2d 713 (N.J. 1975).

83. U.S. DEP'T OF JUSTICE, CIVIL RIGHTS DIVISION & U.S. DEP'T OF EDUC., GUIDANCE ON THE VOLUNTARY USE OF RACE TO ACHIEVE DIVERSITY AND AVOID RACIAL ISOLATION IN ELEMENTARY AND SECONDARY SCHOOLS (2008), *available at* http://www2.ed.gov/about/offices/list/ocr/docs/guidance-ese-201111.pdf. *See also* Frankenberg & Debray, *supra* note 82 (more than two dozen authors set forth detailed proposals for promoting school integration consistent with current federal law).

84. *See* Richard D. Kahlenberg, *Socioeconomic School Integration: Preliminary Lessons from More than 80 Districts*, *in* INTEGRATING SCHOOLS IN A CHANGING SOCIETY, *supra* note 82.

85. In 2012–13, 45 percent of the students in high poverty schools were black, 45 percent were Hispanic, and only 8 percent were white. Nat'l Ctr. for Educ. Stats., *Condition of Education 2016*, *available at* https://nces.ed.gov/programs/coe/pdf/coe_clb.pdf.

86. For a detailed discussion of these efforts, *see* Kathryn A. McDermott, Erica Frankenberg & Sarah Diem, *The "Post-Racial" Politics of Race: Changing Student Assignment Policy in Three School Districts*, 29 EDUC. POL'Y 504, 531–39 (2015).

87. *See, e.g.*, Jennifer B. Ayscue et al., *School Segregation and Resegregation in Charlotte and Raleigh, 1989–2010*, EDUC. POL'Y 1 (2016), *available at* http://journals.sagepub.com/doi/abs/10.1177/0895904815625287. Note that in late 2016, the Charlotte-Mecklenburg school board adopted a new diversity-driven magnet lottery plan that seeks to maximize integration based on students' socioeconomic status. *See* Ann DossHelms, *Choice, Diversity and Schools: How the New CMS Magnet Lottery Will Work*, CHARLOTTE OBSERVER, Nov. 3, 2016, *available at* http://www.charlotteobserver.com/news/local/education/article112262392.html.

88. *See* discussion in chapter 4, at pp. 94–95.

89. THE RESEGREGATION OF SUBURBAN SCHOOLS: A HIDDEN CRISIS IN AMERICAN EDUCATION 2 (Erica Frankenberg & Gary Orfield eds., 2012).

90. *Id.* at 234.

91. *Id.* at 234. Residents in some communities appear to agree and are taking active steps to promote diverse schools. *See* Rachel M. Cohen, *Can Charlotte-Mecklenburg Desegregate Its Schools . . . Again?* AM. PROSPECT, Mar. 18, 2016, *available at* http://prospect.org/article/battle-royal-over-segregation-queen-city-0 (grassroots coalition of residents organizing to making Charlotte-Mecklenburg a place where diverse individuals live, work, and attend school together). Note also studies that indicate that whites, blacks, and Latinos all state a preference for living in racially diverse neighborhoods, although interestingly the neighborhoods in which they search for houses and in which they eventually live do not fully correspond to these stated desires. *See* Esther Havekes, Michael Bader & Maria Krysan, *Realizing Racial and Ethnic Neighborhood Preferences? Exploring the Mismatches Between What People Want, Where They Search, and Where They Live*, 35 POP. RES. POL'Y REV. 101 (2016).

92. AMY STUART WELLS, LAUREN FOX & DIANA CORDOVA-COBO, CENTURY FOUND., HOW RACIALLY DIVERSE SCHOOLS AND CLASSROOMS CAN BENEFIT ALL STUDENTS 25 (2016), *available at* https://tcf.org/content/report/how-racially-diverse-schools-and-classrooms-can-benefit-all-students/. The authors argue that policy makers have emphasized the benefits of diversity in higher education but have neglected the increasing evidence that diversity in K–12 education has important educational and social advantages for all students.

93. *See* JUSTIN GEST, THE NEW MINORITY: WHITE WORKING CLASS POLITICS IN AN AGE OF IMMIGRATION AND INEQUALITY (2016).

94. *Id.* at 145.

95. *Id.*

96. STUART WELLS, FOX, & CORDOVA-COBO, *supra* note 92, at 15.

97. *Id.* at 25. *See also* AMY STUART WELLS, NAT'L EDUC. POL'Y CTR., DIVERSE HOUSING, DIVERSE SCHOOLING: HOW POLICY CAN STABILIZE RACIAL DEMOGRAPHIC CHANGE IN CITIES AND SUBURBS, 3 (2015), *available at* http://nepc.colorado.edu/files/pb-wells_housing_nexus.pdf.

98. ANSLEY T. ERICKSON, MAKING THE UNEQUAL METROPOLIS: SCHOOL DESEGREGATION AND ITS LIMITS (2016).

99. *Id.* at 305.

100. *Id.* at 315.

101. Erickson notes, for example, that in Tennessee white elites undermined the bussing plan by refusing to purchase enough school busses to make the plan work effectively and as a result "to transport students without sufficient buses, [the school district] staggered school start times from as early as 7:00 a.m. to as late as 10:00:am, with the school day ending at a variety of points from 12:30 to 4:30. This schedule, which ill-matched many parents' work schedules, left children home in the morning unsupervised or had them walking home from the bus stop after day (in the winter)." *Id.* at 194. *See also* Alison Morantz, *Desegregation at Risk: Threat and Reaffirmation in Charlotte*, *in* DISMANTLING DESEGREGATION: THE QUIET REVERSAL OF BROWN v. BOARD OF EDUCATION 179, 182–83 (Gary Orfield & Susan Eaton eds., 1996) (busing plans needed to rely on constant adjustments to remain viable, and frequent school reassignments became a source of community discord); J. HARVIE WILKINSON III, FROM BROWN TO BAKKE: THE SUPREME COURT AND SCHOOL INTEGRATION 1954–1978, chs. 8–9 (describing the history and results of busing to promote school desegregation); MICHAEL J. KLARMAN, FROM JIM CROW TO CIVIL RIGHTS: THE SUPREME COURT AND THE STRUGGLE FOR RACIAL EQUALITY (2004) (describing the depth of resistance of Southern whites and how judicial indecision in implementing Brown's requirements contributed to that resistance).

102. Individuals With Disabilities Education Act, 20 U.S.C.A. § 1401 et seq. The rapidity and measure of support with which this law was enacted is also striking. In the early 1970s, two lower federal court decisions, both of which were quickly settled and never reached the U.S. Supreme Court, determined that students with disabilities had a right to attend an appropriate public education. Mills v. Bd. of Educ., 348 F. Supp. 866 (D.D.C. 1972), and Pa. Ass'n for Retarded Children (PARC) v. Pennsylvania, 334 F. Supp. 1257 (E.D. Pa. 1971), *modified* 343 F. Supp. 279 (E.D. Pa. 1972). Congress then responded quickly to the concerns of advocates for the disabled and recognized the rights of students with disabilities to appropriate educational services by enacting the predecessor to the IDEA, the Education of all Handicapped Children's Act, Pub. L. No. 94-142, even though no court had ordered them to do so, and the Supreme Court had never—and still has not—held that there is a constitutional right in this area. The law now provides extensive procedural and substantive rights to almost six million students, constituting almost 13 percent of all six- through twenty-one-

year-olds in the United States. Nat'l Ctr. for Educ. Stats., *Digest of Statistics for School Year 2011–2012*, Table 204.70, *available at* https://nces.ed.gov/programs/digest/d13/tables/dt13_204.70.asp.

103. Specifically, states must ensure that "to the maximum extent appropriate, children with disabilities, including children in public or private institutions or other care facilities, are educated with children who are not disabled, and special classes, separate schooling, or other removal of children with disabilities from the regular educational environment occurs only when the nature or severity of the disability of a child is such that education in regular classes with the use of supplementary aids and services cannot be achieved satisfactorily." IDEA, 20 U.S.C. § 1412 (a)(5)(A).

104. Bd. of Educ., Sacramento Unified Sch. Dist. v. Holland, 786 F. Supp. 874 (E.D. CA, 1992), *aff'd* 14 F.3d 1398 (9th Cir., 1993). "Further, in considering the relative educational benefits available in integrated and non-integrated settings, the school district must demonstrate that it has considered whether supplemental aids and services would permit satisfactory education in the regular classroom." *Id.*

105. Sixty-one percent of all students with disabilities were educated in regular classes in 2011, and an additional 20 percent were educated in regular classes 40–79 percent of the time. U.S. DEP'T OF EDUC., DIGEST OF EDUCATION STATISTICS, 2013 ch. 2 (Nat'l Ctr. for Educ. Stats. 2015), *available at* https://nces.ed.gov/fastfacts/display.asp?id=59.

106. Nat'l Ctr. for Educ. Stats., *Fast Facts: Charter Schools* (2016), *available at* https://nces.ed.gov/fastfacts/display.asp?id=30.

107. Erica Frankenberg, Genevieve Siegel-Hawley & Jia Wang, *Choice without Equity: Charter School Segregation*, 1 EDUC. POL'Y ANALYSIS ARCHIVES (2011), *available at* http://epaa.asu.edu/ojs/article/view/779. For example, one study cited in this article found that 70 percent of black charter school students in the country attended hyper-segregated minority schools that had a 90–100 percent minority composition. *Id.* at 6–7. *See also* Iris C. Rotberg, *Charter Schools and the Increased Risk of Segregation*, EDUC. WK., Mar. 27, 2014 (summarizing findings of many studies that document trends of segregation), *available at* http://www.edweek.org/ew/articles/2014/02/01/kappan_rotberg.html. A recent study of charter school enrollments in North Carolina found that they were either overwhelmingly black or overwhelmingly white—in contrast to traditional public schools, which are more evenly mixed. Helen F. Ladd, Charles T. Clotfelter & John B. Holbein, *The Growing Segmentation of the Charter School Sector in North Carolina* (Nat'l Bureau of Econ. Research, Working Paper No. 21078, 2015).

108. U.S. GOV'T ACCOUNTABILITY OFFICE, CHARTER SCHOOLS: ADDITIONAL FEDERAL ATTENTION NEEDED TO HELP PROTECT ACCESS FOR STUDENTS WITH DISABILITIES (2012), *available at* http://www.gao.gov/products/GAO-12-543

(during the 2009–10 school year, the percentage of students with disabilities at charter schools across the country was 8.2 percent, compared with 11.2 percent at traditional schools).

109. Frederick Hess, *Our Achievement Gap Mania*, NAT'L AFFAIRS, 127–28 (Fall 2011), *available at* http://www.nationalaffairs.com/publications/detail/our-achievement-gap-mania.

110. Ctr. for Research on Educ. Outcomes at Stanford Univ. (CREDO), *How Charter Schools Affect Student Outcomes* (2009) (longitudinal study of charter school outcomes in five cities and three states finds that across locations, there is little evidence that charter schools are producing, on average, achievement impacts that differ substantially from those of traditional public schools), *available at* http://www.rand.org/pubs/monographs/MG869.html; CREDO, *National Charter School Study* (2013) (comprehensive study of charter schools in twenty-seven states finds that African American and Hispanic students from poverty backgrounds perform better than traditional public schools, but other groups do not, and charter school quality is uneven from state to state and school to school), *available at* http://credo.stanford.edu/documents/NCSS%202013%20Final%20Draft.pdf; Will Dobbie and Roland G. Fryer, *Charter Schools and Labor Market Outcomes* (Nat'l Bureau of Econ. Research, Working Paper No. 22502, Aug. 2016), *available at* http://www.nber.org/papers/w22502 (finding that charter schools in Texas, on average, had no impact on test performance and a negative influence on income).

111. *See, e.g.,* AARON KUPCHIK & THOMAS J. CATLAW, DISCIPLINE AND PARTICIPATION: THE LONG-TERM EFFECTS OF SUSPENSION AND SCHOOL SECURITY ON THE POLITICAL AND CIVIC ENGAGEMENT OF YOUTH (2013), *available at* https://civilrightsproject.ucla.edu/resources/projects/center-for-civil-rights-remedies/school-to-prison-folder/state-reports/discipline-and-participation-the-long-term-effects-of-suspension-and-school-security-on-the-political-and-civic-engagement-of-youth/kupchik-discipline-engagement-ccrr-conf-2013.pdf.

Chapter Seven

1. In 2014, per-pupil spending was $10,352 in Philadelphia, $10,851 in Los Angeles, and $21,154 in New York City. Educ. Fin. Branch, U.S. Census Bureau, *Public Education Finances 2014* tbl. 18 (2016), *available at* https://www2.census.gov/govs/school/14f33pub.pdf.

2. URBAN INST., MAKING THE GRADE IN AMERICA'S CITIES ASSESSING STUDENT ACHIEVEMENT IN URBAN DISTRICTS 4, *available at* http://www.urban.org/sites/default/files/alfresco/publication-pdfs/2000821-Making-the-Grade-in-America's-Cities-Assessing-Student-Achievement-in-Urban-Districts.pdf.

3. JONATHAN KOZOL, THE SHAME OF THE NATION: THE RESTORATION OF APARTHEID SCHOOLING IN AMERICA 249 (2006).

4. Carl F. Kaestle, *Equal Educational Opportunity, the Federal Government, and the United States Constitution: An Interpretive Synthesis* 38 (S. Educ. Found. Study Grp., Working Paper, 2006) (on file with author). *See also* ANNE NEWMAN, REALIZING EDUCATIONAL RIGHTS: ADVANCING SCHOOL REFORM THROUGH COURTS AND COMMUNITIES 43 (2013) ("The importance that Americans ascribe to public education, some argue, makes it a de facto national right"); CASS R. SUNSTEIN, THE SECOND BILL OF RIGHTS: FDR'S UNFINISHED REVOLUTION AND WHY WE NEED IT MORE THAN EVER 185 (2004) (right to education is indispensable for citizenship).

5. Statement of Ted Shaw, former executive director, NAACP Legal Defense Fund, quoted in KOZOL, *supra* note 3, at 254. Reflecting this perspective, African American leaders like Jesse Jackson and Robert Moses have called for a constitutional amendment that would ensure that "all persons shall enjoy the right to a public education of equal high quality." *See* QUALITY EDUCATION AS A CONSTITUTIONAL RIGHT (Theresa Perry et al. eds., 2010).

6. Elementary & Secondary Sch. Act of 1965, 20 U.S.C.A. § 6301 (2002).

7. 147 CONG. REC. 26,593 (2001) (statement of Sen. Russ Feingold).

8. *Id.* at 26,601 (statement of Sen. Blanche Lincoln).

9. *Id.* at 26,588 (statement of Sen. John Edwards).

10. Elementary & Secondary Sch. Act of 1965, 20 U.S.C.A. § 6301 (2002). This provision has been slightly revised in ESSA to read that "the purpose of this subchapter is to provide all children significant opportunity to receive a fair, equitable, and high-quality education." 20 U.S.C.A. § 6301 (2015).

11. *See* MICHAEL A. REBELL & JESSICA R. WOLFF, MOVING EVERY CHILD AHEAD: FROM NCLB HYPE TO MEANINGFUL EDUCATIONAL OPPORTUNITY 99 (2007).

12. S. EDUC. FOUND., NO TIME TO LOSE: WHY AMERICA NEEDS AN EDUCATION AMENDMENT TO THE US CONSTITUTION TO IMPROVE PUBLIC EDUCATION 5 (2009). *See also* Stephen Laurie, *Why Doesn't the Constitution Guarantee the Right to Education?*, ATLANTIC, Oct. 16, 2013, *available at* http://www.theatlantic.com/education/archive/2013/10/why-doesnt-the-constitution-guarantee-the-right-to-education/280583/. Susan Bitensky, a professor at Michigan State University, College of Law, has explained what the impact of a federal right to education would be: "Were education to be recognized as an affirmative right under the Constitution . . . [it would make] the federal government the ultimate guarantor of education for school-age children. . . . Reform efforts could be freed from the hobbling strictures of state and local governments' piecemeal and often resource poor responses, as the federal government would bring its uniquely national perspective, powers, and resources to bear upon what has become, in scope and consequence, a truly national problem." Susan H. Bitensky, *Theoretical Foundations for a Right to Education Under the U.S. Constitution: A Beginning to the End of the National Education Crisis*, 86 NW. L. REV. 552–53 (1992).

13. *See* EDWARD S. CORWIN, THE HIGHER LAW BACKGROUND OF AMERICAN CONSTITUTIONAL LAW (1928).

14. ALEXANDER MEIKLEJOHN, FREE SPEECH AND ITS RELATION TO SELF-GOVERNMENT 32 (1948) ("the court holds a unique place in the cultivating of our national intelligence"); Eugene V. Rostow, *The Democratic Character of Judicial Review*, 66 HARV. L. REV. 193, 208 (1952) (the "Supreme Court is, among other things, an educational body, and the Justices are inevitably teachers in a vital national seminar"); Christopher L. Eisgruber, *Is the Supreme Court an Educative Institution?*, 67 N.Y.U. L. REV. 961 (1992) (arguing that the Supreme Court cannot be fully understood except as an institution with educative responsibilities); JOHN RAWLS, POLITICAL LIBERALISM 252–53 (1993) (the Supreme Court's approach to judicial review provides an educative model of the kind of public reasoning and deliberation that all citizens should pursue).

15. ROBERT G. MCCLOSKEY, THE AMERICAN SUPREME COURT 16 (1960). *See also* Owen Fiss, *The Forms of Justice*, 93 HARV. L. REV. 1, 12 (1979) (judges have a special role in upholding the "public values" of the constitution).

16. SANFORD LEVINSON, CONSTITUTIONAL FAITH 73 (1988). *See also* MICHAEL J. PERRY, THE CONSTITUTION, THE COURTS AND HUMAN RIGHTS 100–01 (1982) (discussing the courts' role in promoting the "moral evolution of the polity"); Archibald Cox, *The Supreme Court and the Federal System*, 50 CAL. L. REV. 800 (1962) ("Certainly no other people has gone so far in committing fundamental and divisive issues, whether social, economic, governmental, or even philosophical, to a court for decision according to law").

17. Brown v. Bd. of Educ., 347 U.S. 483 (1954).

18. Baker v. Carr, 369 U.S. 186 (1962); Reynolds v. Sims, 377 U.S. 533 (1964).

19. Roe v. Wade, 410 U.S. 113 (1973).

20. District of Columbia v. Heller, 554 U.S. 570 (2006).

21. Citizens United v. FEC, 558 U.S. 310 (2010).

22. United States v. Virginia, 518 U.S. 515 (1996).

23. Lawrence v. Texas, 539 U.S. 558 (2003); Obergefell v. Hodges, 135 S. Ct. 2584 (2015).

24. Fiss, *supra* note 15, at 12. *See also* RONALD DWORKIN, TAKING RIGHTS SERIOUSLY (1977) (discussing the courts' "principled" decision-making mode). From a comparative institutional perspective, courts do, in fact, act in a more principled manner than do legislative and executive bodies. *See* MICHAEL A. REBELL & ARTHUR R. BLOCK, EDUCATIONAL POLICY MAKING AND THE COURTS: AN EMPIRICAL STUDY OF JUDICIAL ACTIVISM (1982) (empirical analysis of sixty-five education cases concludes that judges decide cases largely on principled bases); MICHAEL A. REBELL & ARTHUR R. BLOCK, EQUALITY AND EDUCATION: FEDERAL CIVIL RIGHTS ENFORCEMENT IN THE NEW YORK CITY SCHOOL SYSTEM (1985) (finding that courts tend to decide affirmative action issues from a prin-

cipled rational-analytic perspective, legislatures through a mutual adjustment decision making mode and a federal regulatory agency through a pragmatic-analytic mode).

25. For discussions of the range of factors that affect reactions to court decisions, *see, e.g.*, WILLIAM K. MUIR, JR., LAW AND ATTITUDE CHANGE (1967) (school prayers); James W. Soutenborough, Donald P. Haider-Market & Mahalley D. Allen, *Reassessing the Impact of Supreme Court Decisions on Public Opinion: Gay Civil Rights Cases*, 59 POL. RES. Q. 419 (2006).

26. Paul B. Sheatsley, *White Attitudes Toward the Negro*, AM. ACAD. ARTS & SCI., 219 (1966), *available at* http://files.eric.ed.gov/fulltext/ED013274.pdf. These are national figures. Looking solely at white Southerners, positive attitudes toward racial integration rose from 2 percent before the issuance of the *Brown* decision to 14 percent in 1956 and 34 percent in 1963. *Id. See also* MILDRED A. SCHWARTZ, TRENDS IN WHITE ATTITUDES TOWARD NEGROS, NATIONAL OPINION RESEARCH CENTER (Univ. of Chicago 1967), *available at* http://www.norc.org/PDFs/publications/NORCRpt_119.pdf.

27. PEW RESEARCH CTR., CHANGING ATTITUDES ON GAY MARRIAGE (2016), *available at* http://www.pewforum.org/2016/05/12/changing-attitudes-on-gay-marriage/.

28. Tinker v. Des Moines Indep. Sch. Dist., 393 U.S. 503, 507 (1969).

29. Plyler v. Doe, 457 U.S. 202, 221 (1982).

30. San Antonio Indep. Sch. Dist. v. Rodriguez, 411 U.S. 1, 36–37 (1973). *See also* Papasan v. Allain, 478 U.S. 265, 284 (1986) (stating that the Court still has not definitively settled the question whether a minimally adequate education is a fundamental interest). *See also* discussion in chapter 2.

31. Rodriguez, 411 U.S. at 37. Note also that in another context, the Supreme Court also emphasized the importance of jury service to a vibrant democracy: "Indeed, with the exception of voting, for most citizens the honor and privilege of jury duty is their most significant opportunity to participate in the democratic process." Powers v. Ohio, 499 U.S. 400, 407 (1991).

32. *Id.* at 36: "Even if it were conceded that some identifiable quantum of education is a constitutionally protected prerequisite to the meaningful exercise of either right, we have no indication that the present levels of educational expenditures in Texas provide an education that falls short." *Id.* at 24: "The State repeatedly asserted in its briefs . . . that it now assures 'every child in every school district an adequate education.' No proof was offered at trial persuasively discrediting or refuting the State's assertion."

33. DANIELLE ALLEN, EDUCATION AND EQUALITY 40–41 (2016).

34. MEICKLEJOHN, *supra* note 14, at 103. *See also* NEWMAN, *supra* note 4, at 36: "The ability to evaluate others' claims carefully is foundational to substantive political agency, understood as the capacity to exercise one's political liber-

ties in a meaningful, not merely procedural, way. Cognitive autonomy enables individuals to carry out these evaluations—to develop a view of what course public policies should take, and to assess proposed options accordingly."

35. Samuel L. Popkin & Michael A. Dimock, *Political Knowledge and Citizen Competence*, *in* CITIZEN COMPETENCE AND DEMOCRATIC INSTITUTIONS 122 (Stephen L. Elkin & Karol Edward Soltan eds., 1999). *See also* Serrano v. Priest, 5 Cal.3d 584, 608 (Cal. 1971 *en banc*) ("At a minimum, education makes more meaningful the casting of a ballot. More significantly, it is likely to provide the understanding of, and the interest in, public issues which are the spur to involvement in other civic and political activities").

36. Bd. of Educ., Island Trees Union Free Sch. Dist. No. 26 v. Pico, 457 U.S. 853, 876 (1982) (Blackmun, J., concurring) ("the Constitution presupposes the existence of an informed citizenry prepared to participate in governmental affairs"). *See also* W. Va. Bd. of Educ. v. Barnette, 319 U.S. 624, 631 (1943) ("The State may require teaching by instruction and study of all in our history and in the structure and organization of our government, including the guarantees of civil liberty, which tend to inspire patriotism and love of country") (citation omitted).

37. Tinker, 393 U.S. at 512 (the "Nation's future depends upon leaders trained through wide exposure to that robust exchange of ideas which discovers truth 'out of a multitude of tongues, [rather] than through any kind of authoritative selection"). *See also* Island Trees, 457 U.S. at 869 ("just as access to ideas makes it possible for citizens generally to exercise their rights of free speech and press in a meaningful manner, such access prepares students for active and effective participation in the pluralistic, often contentious society in which they will soon be adult members"); Barnette, 319 U.S. at 644 (1943) (Black, J., & Douglas, J., concurring) ("These laws must, to be consistent with the First Amendment, permit the widest toleration of conflicting viewpoints consistent with a society of free men"); Weiman v. Updegraff, 344 U.S.186, 196 (1952) (Frankfurter, J., & Douglas, J, concurring) ("Public opinion is the ultimate reliance of our society only if it be disciplined and responsible. It can be disciplined and responsible only if habits of open-mindedness and of critical inquiry are acquired in the formative years of our citizens"); Schuette v. Coal. to Defend Affirmative Action, 134 S. Ct. 1623, 1626 (2014) ("This Nation's constitutional system also embraces the right of citizens to speak and debate and learn and then, as a matter of political will, to act through a lawful electoral process").

38. Goss v. Lopez, 419 U.S. 565 (1975) (schools must provide students fundamental due process rights in school suspension situations).

39. Ambach v. Norwick, 441 U.S. 689, 676 (1979) ("The importance of public schools . . . in the preservation of the values on which our society rests, long has been recognized by our decisions").

40. Bethel Sch. Dist. No. 403 v. Fraser, 478 U.S. 675, 681 (1986) (schools must

inculcate the "fundamental values necessary to the maintenance of a democratic political system . . . [which] must, of course, include tolerance of divergent political and religious views").

41. The concept of the federal system allowing a "laboratory" of the states originated with Justice Louis Brandeis, who stated, "It is one of the happy incidents of the federal system that a single courageous state may, if its citizens choose, serve as a laboratory; and try novel social and economic experiments without risk to the rest of the country." New State Ice Co. v. Liebmann, 285 U.S. 262, 311 (1932), (Brandeis, J., dissenting).

42. JACK M. BALKIN, LIVING ORIGINALISM 210 (2011).

43. Bowers v. Hardwick, 478 U.S. 186 (1986).

44. Lawrence v. Texas, 539 U.S. 558 (2003).

45. BALKIN, *supra* note 42, at 212–13. Balkin also discussed the impact of changes in public attitudes and state laws on major U.S. Supreme Court decisions regarding the legality of the use of contraceptives in the 1960s. *Id.* at 212.

46. Obergefell v. Hodges, 135 S. Ct. 2584 (2015).

47. *Id.* at 2605.

48. Rodriguez, 411 U.S. at 42 (notes omitted).

49. *Id.* The correlation between expenditures and educational quality would, in any case, be less directly relevant to a claim based on preparation for civic participation than to the fiscal equity issues that were before the Supreme Court in *Rodriguez* because funding *per se* would not be the central focus, although ultimately such a case might result in increased expenditures.

50. For a discussion of the state court's extensive treatment of this subject, *see* Michael A. Rebell, *The Courts' Consensus, Money Does Matter for Educational Opportunity*, 674 ANNALS AM. ACAD. POL. & SOC. SCI. 184 (2017).

51. Eric Hanushek, who has been the primary witness for the defendants on this issue in most of these cases, specifically acknowledged that "money spent wisely, logically, and with accountability would be very useful indeed." Montoy v. State, No. 99-C-1738, 2003WL 22902963 49 (Kan. Dist. Ct., Shawnee Cty., Dec. 2, 2003), *aff'd* 112 P.3d 923 (Kan. 2005).

52. Clive R. Belfield & Henry M. Levin, *The Economics of Education on Judgment Day*, 28 J. EDUC. FIN. 182, 205 (2002).

53. Plyler v. Doe, 457 U.S. 202 (1982).

54. *Id.* at 223–24.

55. *Id.* at 224.

56. *Id.* at 230.

57. *Id.*

58. *See* discussion in chapter 5, at pp. 104–5, 114–15.

59. *See* discussions in chapter 1, at pp. 21–23.

60. In some cases, the Supreme Court has applied rational relationship with "bite," a concept that arguably should also apply in this situation *See, e.g.*, Zobel

v. Williams, 457 U.S. 55 (1982) (invalidating Alaska's policy of providing a monetary "dividend," stemming from windfall oil revenues to its residents in accordance with the number of years that each individual had lived in the state); Att'y Gen. of N.Y. v. Soto-Lopez, 476 U.S. 898 (1986) (denial of civil service benefits to veterans who were not state residents at the time they entered the armed services was a violation of constitutional right to travel).

61. Parents of students in Detroit have filed a complaint alleging that the state of Michigan has disinvested in education in Detroit to such an extent that children lack fundamental access to literacy. Gary B. v. Snyder, No. 16-CV-13292 (E.D. Mich. 2016), *available at* http://www.publiccounsel.org/tools/assets/files/0812.pdf. The plaintiffs claim: "Achievement data reveal that in Plaintiffs' schools, illiteracy is the norm. The proficiency rates in Plaintiffs' schools hover near zero in nearly all subject areas." The plaintiffs' legal theory in this case is based on the proposition that there is a constitutional right to literacy under the Fourteenth Amendment to the United States Constitution, citing both *Rodriguez* and *Plyler.*

62. The full text of the first section of the Fourteenth Amendment reads: "All persons born or naturalized in the United States, and subject to the jurisdiction thereof, are citizens of the United States and of the State wherein they reside. No State shall make or enforce any law which shall abridge the privileges or immunities of citizens of the United States; nor shall any State deprive any person of life, liberty, or property, without due process of law; nor deny to any person within its jurisdiction the equal protection of the laws."

63. Slaughter-House Cases, 83 U.S. 36, 72 (1873).

64. BALKIN, *supra* note 42, at 192.

65. Slaughter-House Cases, *supra* note 63.

66. *Id.* at 79.

67. *Id.* at 97 (Field, J., dissenting). Justice Field stated that if the Congress that had adopted the Fourteenth Amendment intended that "privileges and immunities" be read so narrowly, then "it was a vain and idle enactment, which accomplished nothing, and most unnecessarily excited Congress and the people on its passage. With privileges and immunities thus designated or implied no State could ever have interfered by its laws, and no new constitutional provision was required to inhibit such interference. The supremacy of the Constitution and the laws of the United States always controlled any State legislation of that character. But if the amendment refers to the natural and inalienable rights which belong to all citizens, the inhibition has a profound significance and consequence." *Id.* at 96.

68. Goodwin Liu, *Education, Equality and National Citizenship*, 116 YALE L.J. 330, 349 (2006).

69. Stephen G. Calabresi & Sarah E. Agudo, *Individual Rights Under State Constitutions When the Fourteenth Amendment Was Ratified in 1868: What Rights Are Deeply Rooted in American History and Tradition?*, 87 TEX. L. REV. 7, 108 (2008).

70. *Id. See also* Derek Black, *The Constitutional Compromise to Guarantee Education*, 70 STAN. L. REV. (forthcoming, 2018) (arguing that the original intent of the Fourteenth Amendment was to guarantee education as a right of state citizenship).

71. Saenz v. Roe, 526 U.S. 489, 524 (1999) (Thomas, J., dissenting). *Saenz* was only the second Supreme Court decision to invoke the privileges and immunities clause since the *Slaughter-House Cases* (the other case that had invoked the clause had been overruled five years earlier). *Id.* at 510. In *Saenz*, the Supreme Court held that a newly arrived citizen claiming welfare benefits is entitled to the same privileges and immunities enjoyed by other citizens of the state and not only by the new arrival's status as a state citizen but also by her status as a citizen of the United States. The majority's opinion stated that the right to travel was one of the specific rights included in the narrow definition of "privileges and immunities" articulated by the majority opinion in the *Slaughter-House Cases. Id.* at 503. Therefore, the majority of the justices in *Saenz* indicated that they were not disputing or expanding the definition of privileges and immunities in that decision. A decade later, in upholding the applicability of the Second Amendment's right to bear arms to the states, the Court again held that it saw no need to reconsider the *Slaughter-House* holding: "For many decades, the question of the rights protected by the Fourteenth Amendment against state infringement has been analyzed under the Due Process Clause of that Amendment and not under the Privileges or Immunities Clause." McDonald v. Chicago, 561 U.S. 742, 758 (2010). Justice Thomas filed a separate opinion, agreeing with the Court's judgment, but arguing at great length that the decision should have been based on the privileges and immunities clause rather than the due process clause. Justice Stevens, in his dissenting opinion in *McDonald*, took issue with Justice Thomas's view: "For the very reason that it has so long remained a clean slate, a revitalized Privileges or Immunities Clause holds special hazards for judges who are mindful that their proper task is not to write their personal views of appropriate public policy into the Constitution." *Id.* at 860.

72. Saenz, 526 U.S. at 528. *See also* Clarence Thomas, *The Higher Law Background of the Privileges or Immunities Clause of the Fourteenth Amendment*, 12 HARV. J. L. & PUB. POL'Y 63 (1989). Justice Thomas has tied his efforts to bolster the status of the privileges and immunities clause to a belief that doing so might lessen the Court's reliance on the equal protection and due process clauses: "We should also consider whether the Clause should displace, rather than augment, portions of our equal protection and substantive due process jurisprudence. The majority's failure to consider these important questions raises the specter that the Privileges or Immunities Clause will become yet another convenient tool for inventing new rights, limited solely by the predilections of those who happen at the time to be Members of this Court." *Saenz*, 526 U.S. at 526 (citation omitted).

73. *See Rodriguez*, 411 U.S. at 33–35 (discussing potential precedential significance of an equal protection ruling in *Rodriguez* on housing and welfare cases).

74. Brown v. Bd. of Educ., 347 U.S. 483, 493 (1954).

75. Liu, *supra* note 68, at 369. *See also* JOHN HART ELY, DEMOCRACY AND DISTRUST: A THEORY OF JUDICIAL REVIEW 28 (1980): "The most plausible interpretations of the Privileges or Immunities Clause is, as it must be, the one suggested by its language—that it was a delegation to future constitutional decision-makers to protect certain rights that the document neither lists, at least not exhaustively, nor even in any specific ways gives directions for finding."

76. *Id.* at 115.

77. BALKIN, *supra* note 42, at 209. *See also* Philip B. Kurland, *The Privileges or Immunities Clause: Its Hour Come Round at Last?* WASH. UNIV. L.Q. 405, 406 (1972) ("only the privileges or immunities clause speaks to matters of substance; certainly the language of due process and equal protection does not"). Yale law professor Akhil Reed Amar also argues that the privileges and immunities clause, together with the retention of the rights "by the people" in the Ninth Amendment, opened the door for the assertion of new constitutional rights that reflect important components of national citizenship. AKHIL REED AMAR, AMERICA'S UNWRITTEN CONSTITUTION: THE PRECEDENTS AND PRINCIPLES WE LIVE BY (2012). According to Amar, although responsibility for education was not vested in the federal government in the original text of the constitution, the adoption of the Thirteenth, Fourteenth, and Fifteenth Amendments after the Civil War substantially transformed the scope of the Constitution and the manner in which many of its original provisions must now be read. *Id.* at 408. The establishment of national citizenship, and its privileges and immunities, has also infused the Ninth Amendment's reservation of the rights of the people, with substantive new meanings: "One of the core unenumerated rights of the people under the Ninth Amendment is the people's right to discover and embrace new rights and to have these new rights respected by government, so long as the people themselves do indeed claim and celebrate these rights in their words and/or actions." *Id.* at 108.

78. Akhil Reed Amar, *The Central Meaning of Republican Government: Popular Sovereignty, Majority Rule and the Denominator Problem*, 65 U. COLO. L. REV. 749 (1994).

79. *See* Thomas C. Berg, *The Guarantee of Republican Government: Proposals for Judicial Review*, 54 UNIV. CHI. L. REV. 208, 231 (1987): "The guarantee of republican government thus embodies two values. The first, accountability of government decision makers to the people, is evident in the framers' clear intent that the clause would prohibit monarchy or aristocracy in any state. The second value is that government decisions be made deliberatively and by reference to a public value, rather than by simply deferring to the interests of powerful private groups. This value is evident in the framers' particular concern with control of

governmental processes by self-interested factions—a concern that specifically led to adoption of the guarantee clause—and in the Madisonian device of representation as a tool for increasing deliberation in government."

80. Quoted in R. FREEMAN BUTTS, THE CIVIC MISSION IN EDUCATION REFORM 104–05 (1989). *See also* Black, *supra* note 70, at 5 (education inherent to republican government).

81. Wisconsin v. Yoder, 406 U.S. 205, 221 (1972).

82. MINN. CONST. art. VIII, § 1 (emphasis added). *See also, e.g.,* S. DAK. CONST. art VIII, § 1 ("The stability of a republican form of government depending on the morality and intelligence of the people, it shall be the duty of the Legislature to establish and maintain a general and uniform system of public schools"); CALIF. CONST. art. IX, § 1 ([a] "general diffusion of knowledge and intelligence [is] essential to the preservation of the rights and liberties of the people"); ARK. CONST. art. XIV, § 1 (1874) ("Intelligence and virtue being the safeguards of liberty and the bulwark of a free and good government, the State shall ever maintain a general, suitable and efficient system of free public schools").

83. Luther v. Borden, 48 U.S. 1 (1849).

84. "Under this article of the Constitution it rests with Congress to decide what government is the established one in a State. For as the United States guarantee to each State a republican government, Congress must necessarily decide what government is established in the State before it can determine whether it is republican or not. And when the senators and representatives of a State are admitted into the councils of the Union, the authority of the government under which they are appointed, as well as its republican character, is recognized by the proper constitutional authority. And its decision is binding on every other department of the government, and could not be questioned in a judicial tribunal." *Id.* at 35.

85. BALKIN, *supra* note 42, at 241.

86. *See* Baker v. Carr, 369 U.S. 186, 223–26 (1962), and cases cited therein. In *Baker*, the Court delineated the standards for determining whether or not a claim constituted a political question for purposes of the equal protection clause, but not for purposes of the republican guarantee clause.

87. New York v. United States, 505 U.S. 144, 185 (1992). The Court in that case also cited a number of books and articles that advocated invoking the clause in various situations. *Id. See also* Plessy v. Ferguson, 163 U.S. 537, 563–64 (1896) (Harlan, J., dissenting) (racial segregation is "inconsistent with the guarantee given by the Constitution to each State of a republican form of government").

88. *See* Erwin Chemerinsky, *Cases Under the Guarantee Clause Should Be Justiciable*, 65 U. COLO. L. REV. 849 (1994) (arguing that individual claims under the republican guarantee clause should be deemed justiciable).

89. *See* Arthur E. Bonfield, *The Guarantee Clause of Article IV, Section 4: A Study in Constitutional Desuetude*, 46 MINN. L. REV. 513, 559–60 (1962) (arguing that the republican guarantee clause should be interpreted in light of the con-

temporary views of natural justice and opining that under that standard "universal free public education, not a requisite to such government 150 years ago, must unavoidably be deemed so today").

90. Some scholars have also argued that federal constitutional provisions other than equal protection, privileges and immunities, and the republican guarantee should be interpreted to provide a national right to education. *See, e.g.,* Julius Chambers, *Adequate Education for All: A Right, an Achievable Goal*, 22 HARV. CIV. RTS.–CIV. LIBERTIES L. REV 69 (1987) (setting forth a number of constitutional and international law bases for recognizing a federal right to education); Note, *A Right to Learn? Improving Educational Outcomes Through Substantive Due Process*, 120 HARV. L. REV. 1341–44 (2007) (arguing that the compulsory nature of public education provides a substantive due process right to education based on the precedent of Youngberg v. Romeo, 457 U.S. 307 (1982); Susan H. Bitensky, *Theoretical Foundations for a Right to Education Under the U.S. Constitution: A Beginning to the End of the National Education Crisis*, 86 NW. L. REV. 550 (1992) (finding a variety of constitutional anchors for a right to education in the Fourteenth Amendment's due process clause, the privileges or immunities clause, the First Amendment's free speech clause, the right to vote, and other implied constitutional rights); Nicholas A. Palumbo, Note, *Protecting Access to Extracurricular Activities: The Need to Recognize a Fundamental Right to a Minimally Adequate Education*, BYU EDUC. & L.J. 393 (2004) (arguing that the decision in Lawrence v. Texas, 539 U.S. 558 (2003) provides relevant precedent for the existence of fundamental interests that are not explicitly mentioned in the constitution); Kimberly Jenkins Robinson, *The Case for a Collaborative Enforcement Model for a Federal Right to Education*, 40 U.C. DAVIS L. REV. 1712–16 (2007) (proposing that Congress recognize a more than minimal right to education based on the International Covenant on Economic, Social and Cultural Rights and the Convention on the Rights of the Child); Barry Friedman & Sara Solow, *The Federal Right to an Adequate Education*, 81 GEO. WASH. L. REV. 92 (2013) (arguing that there is a federal right to education under the due process case precedent).

91. Pierce v. Soc'y of Sisters, 268 U.S. 510 (1925). *See* discussion in chapter 2, at pp. 37–39.

92. Tinker, 393 U.S. at 503.

93. Island Trees, 457 U.S. at 853.

94. Jackson v. City of Joliet, 715 F.2d 1200, 1203 (7th Cir. 1093).

95. Laurence H. Tribe, *The Abortion Funding Conundrum: Inalienable Rights, Affirmative Duties, and the Dilemma of Dependence*, 99 HARV. L. REV. 330, 332 (1985).

96. Cass R. Sunstein, *Lochner's Legacy*, 87 COLO. L. REV. 873, 889 (1987). *See also* David P. Currie, *Positive and Negative Constitutional Rights*, 53 CHI. L. REV. 864, 887 (1986) ("From the beginning there have been cases in which the Supreme Court, sometimes very persuasively, has found in negatively phrased

provisions constitutional duties that can in some sense be described as positive"); Susan Bandes, *The Negative Constitution: A Critique*, 88 MICH. L. REV. 2271, 2279 (1990) ("The definitional difficulties in distinguishing action from inaction are manifold").

97. Liu, *supra* note 68, at 337.

98. Tribe, *supra* note 95, at 334.

99. *Id.* Note also that to implement the Supreme Court's school desegregation ruling during the civil rights era of the 1960s and 1970s, numerous federal courts utilized "structural reform injunctions." *See* OWEN M. FISS, THE CIVIL RIGHTS INJUNCTION (1978), which ordered affirmative steps that often revamped entire school systems to ensure continuing compliance. Through the structural injunction, courts were "cast in an affirmative, political—activist, if you must—role." Abram Chayes, *The Supreme Court, 1981 Term, Foreword: Public Law Litigation and the Burger Court*, 96 HARV. L. REV. 4 (1982). Federal courts continue to issue such affirmative remedial injunctions today in areas like prison reform. *See* Brown v. Plata 563 U.S. 493 (2011) (serious overcrowding of prisons justifies order capping prison population), and ensuring adequate care for the developmentally disabled (Youngberg v. Romeo, 457 U.S. 307 (1982)). *See also* Myriam Gilles, *An Autopsy of the Structural Reform Injunction: Oops . . . It's Still Moving!*, 58 U. MIAMI L. REV. 143 (2003).

100. Many of the state courts have issued declaratory judgments as the sole remedy in their equity and adequacy decision. For example, in Brigham v. State, 692 A.2d 384 (Vt. 1997), the Vermont Supreme Court ruled that the state's educational finance system was violating the state constitution's requirement that all students receive an equal educational opportunity. It did not purport to tell the legislature how to fix this major constitutional violation. Instead, it said, "although the Legislature should act under the Vermont Constitution to make educational opportunity available on substantially equal terms, the specific means of discharging this broadly defined duty is properly left to its discretion." *Id.* at 269.The legislature promptly enacted a thoroughgoing reform bill. The bill did create substantial controversy, which led to further legislative deliberations and statutory modifications. *See* Michael A. Rebell & Jeffrey Metzler, *Rapid Response, Radical Reform: The Story of School Finance Litigation in Vermont*, 31 J. L. & EDUC. 167 (2002). Since the *Brigham* decision in 1997, the issue has never returned to the state supreme court.

101. Lau v. Nichols, 414 U.S. 563 (1974). The Court held that the district was violating regulations issued under Title VI of the 1964 Civil Rights Act and that, therefore, it did not need to reach the constitutional issue of whether the district's policies violated the equal protection clause.

102. *Id.* at 564–65.

103. Rachel Moran, *The Story of Lau*, *in* EDUCATION LAW STORIES (Michael A. Loivas & Ronna G. Schneider eds., 2008).

104. TASK FORCE FINDINGS SPECIFYING REMEDIES AVAILABLE FOR ELIMINATING PAST EDUCATIONAL PRACTICES RULED UNLAWFUL UNDER LAU V. NICHOLS (1975). *See* Lau Index maintained by Prof. Kenji Hakuta, *available at* http://web.stanford.edu/~hakuta/www/LAU/IAPolicy/IA3ExecLauRemedies.htm.

105. Equal Educ. Opportunities Act of 1974, 20 U.S.C. § 1703(f).

106. Pub. L. No. 93–380, § (a)(4)(A). The Bilingual Education Act had mainly been a research statute with little funding; after Lau, it became largely a civil rights act and its funding was increased tenfold. The act has gone through many modifications over the years and is now incorporated in the Every Student Succeeds Act, 20 U.S.C.A. §§ 6811–8621 (2015).

107. *See, e.g.,* Serna v. Portales Municipal Schs., 499 F.2d 1147 (10th Cir. 1974) (court approves a bilingual-bicultural program to assure that Spanish surnamed children receive meaningful education); Castaneda v. Pickard, 648 F.2d 989 (5th Cir. 1981) (establishing judicial standards for assessing whether state programs for English-language learners comply with federal laws and regulations); Horne v. Flores, 557 U.S. 433 (2009) (reciting long history of judicial supervision of implementation of ELL programs in Arizona and remanding the case for further factual findings).

108. U.S. CONST. Amend XIV, § 5: "The Congress shall have power to enforce, by appropriate legislation, the provisions of this article."

109. Elementary & Secondary Educ. Act, 20 U.S.C. § 6311(b)(1)(A) ("Each State, in the plan it files under subsection (a), shall provide an assurance that the State has adopted challenging academic content standards and aligned academic achievement standards"). For a discussion of the Clinton administration's unsuccessful attempt to impose national opportunity to learn standards in its Goals 2000 legislation in 1994, *see* PATRICK J. MCGUINN, NO CHILD LEFT BEHIND AND THE TRANSFORMATION OF FEDERAL EDUCATION POLICY, 1965–2005 (2006).

110. Chris Cantrill, *U.S. Government Spending*, *available at* http://www.usgovernmentspending.com/year_spending_2011USbn_17bs2n_20#usgs302.

111. Educ. Fin. Branch, U.S. Census Bureau, *Public Education Finances: 2013* tbl. 8 (2015), *available at* http://www2.census.gov/govs/school/13f33pub.pdf.

112. BRUCE BAKER, DAVID SCIARRA & DANIELLE FARRIE, SCHOOL FUNDING: A NATIONAL REPORT CARD (4th ed. 2015).

113. U.S. Census Bureau, 2015 *supra* note 111, at tbl. 12.

114. BAKER, SCIARRA & FARRIE, *supra* note 112, at 18.

115. *See, e.g.,* MCGUINN, *supra* note 109, at 30 (initial enactment of Title I funding for disadvantaged students required "spreading money around to a majority of congressional districts"); JACK JENNINGS, PRESIDENTS, CONGRESS AND THE PUBLIC SCHOOLS: THE POLITICS OF EDUCATION REFORM 38–39 (2015) (discussing how members of Congress "voted [their] district").

116. Brown v. Bd. of Educ., 349 U.S. 294 (1955).

117. *Id.* at 300–01.

118. The argument in the text presumes that the Court would emphasize the importance of ensuring *access* to such programs for all students, and that such judicial emphasis would in and of itself encourage many more students to enroll in such programs. Some have proposed that all young people be *required* to participate in a national service program, either in the military, AmeriCorps, a revived Civilian Conservation Corps or some other form of civilian service. *See, e.g.*, Morris Janowitz, The Reconstruction of Patriotism: Education for Civic Consciousness 194 (1983) ("there can be no reconstruction of patriotism without a system of national service"); Benjamin Barber, Strong Democracy: Participatory Politics for a New Age 300 (1984) (proposing that every American citizen—male and female alike—be required to enlist either in the military or an Urban Projects Corps, a Rural Projects Corps, an International (Peace) Corps or a Special Services Corps); William Galston, *Compulsory National Service Would Strengthen American Citizenship*, U.S. News & World Rep., Oct. 19, 2010, *available at* https://www.usnews.com/opinion/articles/2010/10/19/compulsory-national-service-would-strengthen-american-citizenship. Such a mandate would be unwise, however, since it would likely raise fierce political resistance and encounter substantial practical implementation difficulties. *See* Melissa Bass, The Politics and Civics of National Service: Lessons from the Civilian Conservation Corps, VISTA, and AmeriCorps (2013) (describing the history of civilian national service programs and the problems their implementation and expansion have encountered). However, strongly encouraging young citizens to engage in a year or two of voluntary national service could bolster civic preparation and long-term commitments to civic participation. For recent calls for such efforts, *see* Stanley McCrystal, *Lincoln's Call to Service—and Ours*, Wall St. J., May 29, 2013, *available at* https://www.wsj.com/articles/SB10001424127887324809804578511220613299186, and the Aspen Institute's Franklin project, *available at* https://www.aspeninstitute.org/programs/service-year-alliance/.

119. Pierce, 268 U.S. at 510.

120. *Id.* at 534.

121. *See* discussion in chapter 2, at pp. 39–43.

122. *See* Anthony S. Bryk, Valerie E. Lee & Peter B. Holland, Catholic Schools and the Common Good (1992) (arguing that Catholic schools today are informed by a vision, similar to that of John Dewey, of the school as a community committed to democratic education and the common good of all students); Michael McConnell, *Education Disestablishment: Why Democratic Values Are Ill-Served by Democratic Control of Schooling*, *in* Moral and Political Education 87, 126 (Stephen Macedo & Yael Tamir eds., NOMOS XLIII, 2002) ("Religious schools seem to be more successful than public schools in inculcating habits of democratic participation"); James S. Coleman, *Changes in the Family and Implications for the Common School*, 1991 U. Chi. Legal Forum

153 (Catholic schools have access to more social capital to develop positive values in students), *available at* http://chicagounbound.uchicago.edu/uclf/vol1991/iss1/8. A recent random national survey of high school social studies teachers in public and private schools found that 43 percent of private school teachers were "very confident" that their students had learned "to be tolerant of people and groups who are different from themselves," compared with 19 percent among public school teachers. In addition, the survey found that private school teachers reported an overall more positive school atmosphere for conveying the importance of citizenship, that their high school has a community service requirement for graduation (82 percent versus 37 percent), and that their high school encourages involvement in student government and other issues-oriented clubs (91 percent versus 73 percent). Steve Farkas & Ann M. Duffett, Am. Enterprise Inst., High Schools, Civics and Citizenship: What Social Studies Teachers Think and Do 7 (2011), *available at* https://www.aei.org/wp-content/uploads/2014/09/High-Schools-Civics-Citizenship-Full-Report.pdf.

123. *See* Cheryl Mills & Robin Lake, Am. Enterprise Inst., Strengthening the Civic Mission of Charter Schools (2012), *available at* https://www.aei.org/wp-content/uploads/2012/01/-strengthening-the-civic-mission-of-charter-schools_171609180133.pdf. Mills and Lake refer to exemplary programs at Democracy Prep Public Schools, the United Neighborhood Organization (UNO) Charter School Network, the KIPP schools and the César Chávez Public Charter Schools for Public Policy, and they note that charter schools have great potential for promoting civic participation: "As public schools of choice, charter schools are freed from many rules and regulations that can inhibit innovation and improvement. They can readily adopt best practices in civic education and encourage (or even mandate) extracurricular activities to enhance civic learning." Because many other charter schools have not taken advantage of this potential, the bulk of their reports recommend specific actions to promote civic preparation that all charters should take.

124. John E. Chubb and Terry M. Moe, after analyzing an extensive data base of information about sixty thousand students in public and private schools concluded: "In terms of general goals, public schools place significantly greater emphasis on basic literacy, citizenship, good work habits, and specific occupational skills, while private schools regardless of type-are more oriented by academic excellence, and personal growth." John E. Chubb & Terry M. Moe, *Politics, Markets and the Organization of Schools*, 82 Am. Pol. Sci. Rev. 1065, 1080 (1988).

125. *See* discussion of ultra-Orthodox Jewish schools that do not teach civics, social studies, or other secular subjects in chapter 2, at pp. 42–43.

126. *See, e.g.*, Jonathan Merritt, *Segregation Is Still Alive at These Christian Schools*, Daily Beast, Sept. 18, 2016, *available at* http://www.thedailybeast.com/articles/2016/09/18/segregation-is-still-alive-at-these-christian-schools.html.

127. This is the legal requirement that is already on the books in a number of

states, but often is not consistently enforced. *See, e.g.*, N.Y. EDUC. LAW § 3204.2 (instruction provided to a minor in a private school shall be "shall be at least substantially equivalent to the instruction given to minors of like age and attainments at the public schools of the city or district where the minor resides"); ALASKA STAT. § 14.30.010(b)(1) (the academic education in private schools must be "comparable to that offered by the public schools in the area"); Ill. 105 ILCS 5/26-1 (children in private schools must be "taught the branches of education taught to children of corresponding age and grade in the public schools").

128. Keyes v. Sch. Dist. No. 1, 413 U.S. 189 (1973).

129. Milliken v. Bradley, 418 U. S. 717 (1974).

130. Parents Involved in Cmty. Schools v. Seattle Sch. Dist. No. 1, 551 U.S. 701 (2007).

131. Mike Rose, *The Language of Schooling: Recapturing the Purposes of Education*, *in* LEARNING FROM THE FEDERAL MARKET-BASED REFORMS 3, 4 (William Mathis & Tina Trujillo eds., 2016) ("think of how rarely we hear of commitment to public education as the center of a free society").

Chapter Eight

1. Brown v. Bd. of Educ., 347 U.S. 483 (1954).

2. Brown v. Bd. of Educ., 349 U.S. 294 (1955).

3. J. HARVIE WILKINSON III, FROM BROWN TO BAKKE: THE SUPREME COURT AND SCHOOL INTEGRATION 1954–1978 6 (1979) ("the Court sired the movement"). *See also* RICHARD KLUGER, SIMPLE JUSTICE 749–52 (1977) (discussing the "mass movement" triggered by *Brown*); Kevin J. MacMahon & Michael Paris, *The Politics of Rights Revisited*, *in* LEVERAGING THE LAW: USING THE COURTS TO ACHIEVE SOCIAL CHANGE (David A. Schultz ed., 1998) (discussing the influence of *Brown* in inspiring the Montgomery, Alabama, bus boycott). *Cf.* MICHAEL J. KLARMAN, FROM JIM CROW TO CIVIL RIGHT: THE SUPREME COURT AND THE STRUGGLE FOR RACIAL EQUALITY (2004) (arguing that *Brown* reflected the broader social and political context of the times).

4. Abram Chayes, *The Role of the Judge in Public Law Litigation*, 89 HARV. L. REV. 1281 (1976). For a detailed discussion of how the federal courts have carried out this role, *see* MICHAEL A. REBELL & ARTHUR R. BLOCK, EDUCATIONAL POLICY MAKING AND THE COURTS: AN EMPIRICAL STUDY OF JUDICIAL ACTIVISM (1982); MICHAEL A. REBELL & ARTHUR R. BLOCK, EQUALITY AND EDUCATION: FEDERAL CIVIL RIGHTS ENFORCEMENT IN THE NEW YORK CITY SCHOOL SYSTEM (1985). For a detailed discussion of the role of the state courts in education and adequacy litigations, *see* MICHAEL A. REBELL, COURTS AND KIDS: PURSUING EDUCATIONAL EQUITY THROUGH THE STATE COURTS (2009); MICHAEL A. REBELL, COURTS AND KIDS: PURSUING EDUCATIONAL EQUITY THROUGH THE

STATE COURTS (Supp. 2017), *available at* http://press.uchicago.edu/ucp/books/book/chicago/C/bo8212990.html.

5. Lau v. Nichols, 414 U.S. 563 (1974); Castaneda v. Pickard, 648 F.2d 989 (5th Cir. 1981).

6. United States v. Virginia, 518 U.S. 515 (1996).

7. Goss v. Lopez, 419 U.S. 565 (1975).

8. Endrew F. v. Douglas Cty. Sch. Dist., 137 S. Ct. 988 (2017); Bd. of Educ. v. Rowley, 458 U.S. 176 (1982); Pa. Assoc. for Retarded Children (PARC) v. Commonwealth, 334 F. Supp. 1257 (E.D. Pa. 1971), 343 F. Supp. 279 (E.D. Pa. 1972); Mills v. Bd. of Educ., 348 F. Supp. 866 (D.D.C. 1972).

9. Plyler v. Doe, 457 U.S. 202 (1982).

10. Wyatt v. Stickney, 344 F. Supp. 373 (M.D. Ala. 1972), *aff'd in part sub nom*, Wyatt v. Aderholt, 503 F.2d 1305 (5th Cir. 1974). N.Y. State Assoc. of Retarded Children v. Rockefeller, 357 F. Supp. 752 (E.D.N.Y.1973).

11. Griggs v. Duke Power Co., 401 U.S. 424 (1971).

12. *See, e.g.*, Gautreaux v. Chi. Hous. Auth., 304 F. Supp. 736, 737–39 (N.D. Ill. 1969); Gautreaux v. Landrieu, 498 F. Supp. 1072, 1073 (N.D. Ill. 1980); Gautreaux v. Chi. Hous. Auth., 4 F. Supp. 2d 757, 758 (N.D. Ill. 1998).

13. Hutto v. Finney, 437 U.S. 678 (1978); Brown v. Plata, 131 S. Ct. 1919 (2011).

14. *See* OWEN FISS, THE STRUCTURAL INJUNCTION (1978).

15. *See, e.g.*, Wayne D. Brazil, *Special Masters in Complex Cases: Extending the Judiciary or Reshaping Adjudication?* 53 U. CHI. L. REV. 394 (1986); James S. DeGraw, *Rule 53, Inherent Powers, and Institutional Reform: The Lack of Limits on Special Masters*, 66 N.Y.U. L. REV. 800 (1991).

16. Jed S. Rakoff, *The Cure for Corporate Wrongdoing: Class Actions vs. Individual Prosecutions*, 62 N.Y. REV. BOOKS 38 (2015).

17. MALCOLM M. FEELEY & EDWARD L. RUBIN, JUDICIAL POLICY MAKING AND THE MODERN STATE: HOW THE COURTS REFORMED AMERICA'S PRISONS 344 (1998). Many judges agree with this perspective. For example, Richard Posner, a veteran judge on the U. S. Court of Appeals for the Seventh Circuit, recently wrote:

> Judges tend not to be candid about how they decide cases. They like to say they just apply the law—given to them, not created by them—to the facts. They say this to deflect criticism and hostility on the part of the losing parties . . . and to reassure the other branches of government . . . that they are not legislating . . . or usurping executive-branch powers. . . .
>
> [F]ederal court of appeals judges most of the time do decide appeals formalistically. But it is not always possible. The reasons include the absence of disciplined legislative processes in the American governmental system, as a result of which legisla-

> tion is often insolubly ambiguous, the difficulty of amending the Constitution and resulting pressure on federal courts to engage in loose interpretation of it (which, realistically, means making constitutional law); and the breadth of explicitly judge-made law (common law—both state common law. . . . And federal common law, which federal judges make up). Other reasons the judges can't just be law appliers [include]. . . . limitations of human foresight and language.

RICHARD A. POSNER, REFLECTIONS ON JUDGING 106–08 (2013). *See also* Frank M. Johnson, Jr., *The Role of the Federal Courts in Institutional litigation*, 32 ALA. L. REV. 271 (1981) ("The new form of judicial activism is attributable to . . . the increasingly prominent role government has come to play in our society").

18. Paul Gewirtz & Chad Goldner, Op-ed, *So Who Are the Activists?*, N.Y. TIMES, July 6, 2005, at A19. Gewirtz and Goldner also point out that the Court's most conservative members tended to be the most "activist": Justice Thomas voted to strike down 65.63 percent of these congressional provisions, and Justice Scalia 56.25 percent, in contrast to only 39.06 percent for Justice Ginsberg and 28.13 percent for Justice Breyer. *Id. See also* Barry Friedman, *The Importance of Being Positive: The Nature and Function of Judicial Review*, 72 U. CINN. L. REV. 1257, 1261–63 (2004) (arguing that the Rehnquist Court is one of the "most activist in history").

19. Parents Involved in Cmty. Schs. v. Seattle Sch. Dist. No. 1, 361 U.S. 701 (2007).

20. Citizens United v. FEC, 558 U.S. 310 (2010).

21. Nat'l Fed. of Indep. Bus. v. Sebelius, 132 S. Ct. 2566 (2010).

22. Obergefell v. Hodges, 135 S. Ct. 2584 (2015).

23. Brown, 349 U.S. at 300–01.

24. *See* discussion in chapter 4, at pp. 93–94. *See also, e.g.,* Jenkins v. Missouri, 515 U.S. 701 (1995) (reversing injunctive decree promoting "desegrative attractiveness" of urban magnet schools and requiring maintenance of quality education programs until achievement scores of minority students substantially improve); MARTHA MINOW, IN BROWN'S WAKE: LEGACIES OF AMERICA'S EDUCATIONAL LANDMARK ch. 1 (2010); James Ryan, *The Supreme Court and Voluntary Integration*, 121 HARV. L. REV. 131, 139–42 (2006); ERICA FRANKENBERG, CHUNGMEI LEE & GARY ORFIELD, THE CIVIL RIGHTS PROJECT, A MULTIRACIAL SOCIETY WITH SEGREGATED SCHOOLS: ARE WE LOSING THE DREAM? 17–20 (2003), *available at* https://www.civilrightsproject.ucla.edu/research/k-12-education/integration-and-diversity/a-multiracial-society-with-segregated-schools-are-we-losing-the-dream/frankenberg-multiracial-society-losing-the-dream.pdf.

25. *See, e.g.,* Horne v. Flores, 557 U.S. 433, 450–52 (2009) (reversing and remanding district court order requiring State of Arizona to take appropri-

ate action to overcome language barriers for non-English speaking students in state's public schools).

26. Charles F. Sabel & William H. Simon, *Destabilization Rights: How Public Law Litigation Succeeds*, 117 HARV. L. REV.1015, 1018–19 (2004). Sabel and Simon also noted:

> The particular forms of this activity, however, have evolved. . . . The evolution of structural remedies in recent decades can be usefully stylized as a shift away from command-and-control injunctive regulation toward experimentalist intervention. Command-and-control regulation is the stereotypical activity of bureaucracies. It takes the form of comprehensive regimes of fixed and specific rules set by a central authority. These rules prescribe the inputs and operating procedures of the institutions they regulate.
>
> By contrast, experimentalist regulation combines more flexible and provisional norms with procedures for ongoing stakeholder participation and measured accountability. In the most distinctive cases, the governing norms are general standards that express the goals the parties are expected to achieve—that is, outputs rather than inputs. Typically, the regime leaves the parties with a substantial range of discretion as to how to achieve these goals. At the same time, it specifies both standards and procedures for the measurement of the institution's performance. Performance is measured both in relation to parties' initial commitments and in relation to the performance of comparable institutions.

Id. at 1019. *See also* John C. Jeffries, Jr., & George A. Rutherglen, *Structural Reform Revisited*, 95 CAL. L. REV. 1387 (2007) (reviewing history of structural reform litigations and their current status); David Zaring, *National Rulemaking Through Trial Courts: The Big Case and Institutional Reform*, 51 UCLA L. REV. 1015 (2004) (arguing that the law in structural reform cases is spreading horizontally from trial court to trial court, building into a network of national standards for the administration of state and local institutions).

27. Brown v. Plata, 563 U.S. 493, 511 (2011). *See also* Frew *ex rel.* Frew v. Hawkins, 540 U.S. 431 (2004) (reinstating court enforcement of consent decree overseeing implementation of state Medicaid program).

28. Goodridge v. Dep't of Pub. Health, 798 N.E.2d 941 (Mass. 2003); *In re* Marriage Cases, 183 P.3d 384 (Cal. 2008).

29. S. Burlington Cty. NAACP v. Twp. of Mount Laurel, 336 A.2d 713 (N.J. 1975); S. Burlington Cty. NAACP v. Twp. of Mount Laurel, 456 A.2d 390 (N.J. 1983).

30. *See, e.g.,* Lascari v. Bd. of Educ. of Ramapo Indian Hills Regional High Sch. Dist., 560 A.2d 1180 A-50 (N.J. 1989); L.A. Unified Sch. Dist. v. Garcia, 314 P.3d 767 (2013); *Allen v. McDonough* (Mass. Sup. Ct., 1974), discussed in Michael A. Rebell, *Allen v. McDonough: Special Education Reform in Boston, in* BARBARA FLICKER, JUSTICE AND SCHOOL SYSTEMS: THE ROLE OF THE COURTS IN EDUCATION LITIGATION 70 (1990); Office of the General Counsel, Boston Pub. Schs., Allen v. McDonough Working Files, 1974–1998, *available at* http://www.cityofboston.gov/Images_Documents/Guide%20to%20the%20Allen%20Case%20Working%20files_tcm3-23344.PDF.

31. League of Women Voters of Wash. v. Washington, 355 P.3d 1131 (Wash. 2015); Craven v. Huppenthal, 338 P.3d 324 (Ariz. Ct. App. 2014).

32. Up-to-date information regarding the history and current status of these cases can be found at the Schoolfunding.info website maintained by the Center for Educational Equity at Teachers College, Columbia University, at http://www.schoolfunding.info.

33. Burt Neuborne, *Toward Procedural Parity in Constitutional Litigation*, 22 WM. & MARY L. REV. 725, 732 (1981).

34. MATTHEW H. BOSWORTH, COURTS AS CATALYSTS: STATE SUPREME COURTS AND PUBLIC SCHOOL FINANCE EQUITY 99 (2001).

35. Judith S. Kaye, *Contributions of State Constitutional Law to the Third Century of American Federalism*, 13 VT. L. REV. 49, 56 (1988).

36. Adam Liptak, *Rendering Justice, with One Eye on Re-Election*, N.Y. TIMES, May 25, 2008 at A1.

37. Burt Neuborne, *Forward: State Constitutions and the Evolution of Positive Rights*, 20 RUTGERS L.J. 881, 900 (1989). *See also* Douglas S. Reed, *Popular Constitutionalism: Toward a Theory of State Constitutional Meanings*, 30 RUTGERS L. REV. 871 (1999) (arguing that the meaning of state constitutions is generated through an exchange between popular mobilization and judicial interpretation, especially in states where the initiative mechanism exists).

38. Helen Hershkoff, *Positive Rights and State Constitutions: The Limits of Federal Rationality Review*, 112 HARV. L. REV. 1131, 1137 (1999). *See also* Helen Hershkoff & Stephen Loffredo, *State Courts and Constitutional Socio-Economic Rights: Exploring the Underutilization Thesis*, 115 PENN ST. L. REV. 923 (2011) (discussing the underutilized potential of state courts to enforce socioeconomic rights); Robert F. Williams, *The Brennan Lecture: Interpreting State Constitutions as Unique Legal Documents*, 27 OKLA. L. REV. 189, 192 (2002) ("State constitutions often contain positive or affirmative rights, while federal constitutional rights are primarily negative in nature"); Robert A. Schapiro, *Judicial Deference and Interpretive Coordinacy in State and Federal Constitutional Law*, 85 CORNELL L. REV. 656 (2000) (noting that state constitutions often establish affirmative obligations that the government must discharge); Jonathan Feldman, *Separation of Power and Judicial Review of Positive Rights*

Claims: The Role of State Courts in an Era of Positive Government, 24 RUTGERS L. REV. 1057 (1993) (distinguishing "positive" separation of powers from "negative" separations of powers); Robert F. Williams, *Equality Guarantees in State Constitutions*, 63 TEX. L. REV. 1195 (1985) (describing how concepts of equality in state constitutions differ from federal equal protection concepts). *Cf.* Frank B. Cross, *The Error of Positive Rights*, 48 UCLA L. REV. 857 (2001) (discussing the difficulties for courts in enforcing positive rights).

39. McCleary v. Washington, 269 P.3d 227, 248 (Wash. 2012). *See also* REBELL, *supra* note 4 at 47 (quoting statement of Albert Rosenblatt, former judge of the New York Court of Appeals: "The state constitutions are different [from the federal constitution] . . . the state constitutions are the sources of expanded educational opportunities").

40. Quoted in REBELL, *supra* note 4, at 114–15.

41. Vergara v. State, 209 Cal. Rpt. 3d 558 (Cal. Ct. App. 2016), *review denied* Cal. Aug. 22, 2016. Note, however, that a New York trial court has denied a motion to dismiss claims that teacher tenure and seniority layoff statutes are denying students the opportunity for a sound basic education. Davids v. State, No. 101105/14, Decision & Order (N.Y. Sup. Ct., Mar. 20, 2015, & N.Y. Sup. Ct. Oct. 22, 2015), appeal pending; and a trial court in Connecticut has struck down as unconstitutional the state's standards for high school graduation, elementary school promotion, teacher evaluation, and special education identification, intervention and funding. Conn. Coal. for Justice in Educ. Funding, Inc. v. Rell, 2016 WL 4922730 (Conn. Sup. Ct. 2016), appeal pending. *See also* Note, *The Misguided Appeal of a Minimally Adequate Education*, 130 HARV. L. REV. 1458 (2017).

42. Cruz-Guzman v. State of Minnesota, 892 N.W.2d 533 (Minn. Ct. App., 2017); Paynter v. State, 797 N.E.2d 1225 (N.Y. 2003).

43. Brown v. State, 39 N.Y.S.3d 327 (N.Y. App. Div., 4th Dep't, 2016); J.D. ex rel. Scipio-Derrick v. Davy, 2 A.3d 387, 397 (N.J. App. Div. 2010).

44. REBELL & BLOCK, *supra* note 4. A comparative analysis of the fact-finding capabilities of Congress and the courts reached similar conclusions, *see* Neal Devins, *Congressional Factfinding and the Scope of Judicial Review: A Preliminary Analysis*, 50 DUKE LAW JOURNAL 1169 (2001).

45. REBELL & BLOCK, *supra* note 4.

46. This is not to say, of course, that the executive and legislative branches do not have significant strengths in regard to policy making that the courts lack. Our studies found, for example, that the legislatures' mutual adjustment decision-making processes more effectively fostered political compromises and that the administrative pragmatic-analytic decision making approach was most effective for grassroots implementation.

47. DONALD L. HOROWITZ, THE COURTS AND SOCIAL POLICY (1977). *See also* GERALD N. ROSENBERG, THE HOLLOW HOPE: CAN COURTS BRING ABOUT SO-

CIAL CHANGE? 16 (1991) ("courts lack . . . any degree of specialization . . . expertise and planning, often crucial in issues involving significant social reform are seldom present"); JEREMY RABKIN, JUDICIAL COMPULSIONS: HOW PUBLIC LAW DISTORTS PUBLIC POLICY 113 (1989) (asserting that judges are "amateur policy makers"); ERIC A. HANUSHEK & ALFRED A. LINDSETH, SCHOOLHOUSES, COURTHOUSES AND STATEHOUSES: SOLVING THE FUNDING-ACHIEVEMENT PUZZLE IN AMERICA'S PUBLIC SCHOOLS 282 n. 66 (2009) (citing Horowitz and discussing the "institutional difficulties" of courts to "bring about social change").

48. Neil K. Komesar, *A Job for the Judges: The Judiciary and the Constitution in a Massive and Complex Society*, 86 MICH. L. REV. 657 (1988).

49. Alfred A. Lindseth, *The Legal Backdrop to Adequacy*, *in* COURTING FAILURE: HOW SCHOOL FINANCE LAWSUITS EXPLOIT JUDGES' GOOD INTENTIONS AND HARM OUR CHILDREN 33 (Eric A. Hanushek ed., 2006).

50. This history is discussed in more detail in REBELL, *supra* note 4, at 51–52.

51. Mills v. Bd. of Educ., 348 F. Supp. 866 (D.D.C., 1972); Pa. Assoc. for Retarded Children, 334 F. Supp. at 1257. *See* H.R. Rep No. 332, 94th Cong., 1st Sess., 3–4 (1975).

52. ALEXANDER M. BICKEL, THE LEAST DANGEROUS BRANCH: THE SUPREME COURT AT THE BAR OF POLITICS 962 (1986).

53. Campaign for Fiscal Equity (CFE) v. State, 655 N.E.2d 661, 666 (N.Y. 1995).

54. *See* Colleen McMahon & David L. Kornblau, *Chief Judge Judith S. Kaye's Program of Jury Selection Reform in New York* 10 J. CIV. RIGHTS & ECO. DEV. 263 (1995), *available at* http://scholarship.law.stjohns.edu/cgi/viewcontent.cgi?article=1411&context=jcred.

55. N.Y. JUDICIARY LAW art. 16, as amended by L. 1995, c. 86, § 1.

56. Author's interview with Chief Judge Judith Kaye, New York Court of Appeals (Ret.), Nov. 6, 2015. Judge Kaye also expressed surprise when I told her that the New York Court of Appeals had, in fact, been the first court in the country to include jury service specifically in their definition of civic participation. Judge Kaye's perspective is consistent with evidence that service on a jury (which about one-third of American citizens will experience at some point in their lifetimes) is correlated with increased voting and greater civic engagement in community affairs and deliberative discussion. *See* JOHN GASTIL ET AL., THE JURY AND DEMOCRACY: HOW JURY DELIBERATION PROMOTES CIVIC ENGAGEMENT AND POLITICAL PARTICIPATION (2010).

57. *See* CALIFORNIA COURTS, *available at* http://www.courts.ca.gov/20902.htm.

58. *See* CAL. TASK FORCE ON K–12 CIVIC LEARNING, REVITALIZING K–12 CIVIC LEARNING IN CALIFORNIA: A BLUEPRINT FOR ACTION (2014), *available at* http://www.cde.ca.gov/eo/in/documents/cltffinalreport.pdf.

59. *Id.*

60. *Id.*

61. These examples are taken from NAT'L CTR. FOR STATE COURTS, CIVICS RESOURCE GUIDE, *available at* http://www.ncsc.org/Education-and-Careers/Civics-Education/Resource-Guide.aspx. The guide lists similar civics outreach activities of courts and bar association in numerous other states.

62. *See* DISCOVERING JUSTICE: THE JAMES D. ST. CLAIR COURT EDUCATION PROJECT, *available at* http://discoveringjustice.org/our-programs/suyr/.

63. The program included the following:

> (i) Extending the circuit's "Inns of Court program" to "our younger society," including junior high school students, high school students and college students;
>
> (ii) Hosting evenings at the Courthouse to enable lawyers and non-lawyers to explore the historic Courthouse, visit courtrooms and participate in educational programs;
>
> (iii) Sponsoring more organized programs enabling school classes to visit the Courthouse; and
>
> (iv) Hosting civic teachers and making use of already existing materials to develop modules about the courts which could be part of school curricula.

Robert Katzmann, *State of the Circuit Report* (2014), *available at* http://www.ca2.uscourts.gov/docs/jc_reports/2014/1_State_of_the_Circuit.pdf. Two years later, Judge Katzmann reported that this program had been substantially implemented. Robert A. Katzmann, *State of the Circuit Report* (2016), *available at* http://www.ca2.uscourts.gov/Docs/2016%20State%20of%20the%20Circuit.pdf.

64. Sandra Day O'Connor, former U.S. Supreme Court justice, keynote speech at the Civic Learning California Summit (Feb. 28, 2016), *excerpts available at* http://www.courts.ca.gov/17158.htm.

65. SANDRA DAY O'CONNOR INST., *available at* http://oconnorinstitute.org.

66. *See* ICIVICS, *available at* https://quest.icivics.org/our-story.

67. *See* Mark Walsh, *High Court Justice Spotlights Civics Education at 9th Circuit Conference*, EDUC. WK., July 18, 2017, *available at* http://blogs.edweek.org/edweek/school_law/2017/07/high_court_justice_spotlights_.html.

68. HOROWITZ, *supra* note 47, at 25 (1977) ("The generalist character of judges . . . unfits them for processing specialized information.") Note, however, that in formulating remedial decrees, judges actually tend to either rely on negotiations among the parties and their policy experts, REBELL & BLOCK, *supra* note 4, at 210–11, or allow state defendants a wide range of policy discretion in complying with judicial orders. REBELL, *supra* note 4, at 70–71.

69. For detailed discussions of this resistance in the South, *see* MICHAEL J. KLARMAN, FROM JIM CROW TO CIVIL RIGHTS: THE SUPREME COURT AND THE STRUGGLE FOR RACIAL EQUALITY (2004); ANSLEY ERIKSON, MAKING THE UNEQUAL METROPOLIS: SCHOOL DESEGREGATION AND ITS LIMITS (2016). For a dis-

cussion of resistance to a desegregation decree in the North, *see* J. ANTHONY LUKAS, COMMON GROUND: A TURBULENT DECADE IN THE LIVES OF THREE AMERICAN FAMILIES (1985).

70. Examples of initial resistance to court decrees in education adequacy cases are described in REBELL, *supra* note 4, at 31.

71. CAMPAIGN FOR THE CIVIC MISSION OF SCHS. ET AL., GUARDIAN OF DEMOCRACY: THE CIVIC MISSION OF THE SCHOOLS 28 (2011), *available at* http://www.civicmissionofschools.org/the-campaign/guardian-of-democracy-report.

72. For example, in a 2004 poll, 71 percent of adults said that it was important to "prepare students to be competent and responsible citizens who participate in our democratic society." PETER LEVINE, THE FUTURE OF DEMOCRACY: DEVELOPING THE NEXT GENERATION OF AMERICAN CITIZENS 100 (2007).

73. McCollum v. Bd. of Educ., 333 U.S. 203, 216 (1948) (Frankfurter, J., concurring).

74. Lorraine M. McDonnell & M. Stephen Weatherford, *Seeking a New Politics of Education*, *in* REDISCOVERING THE DEMOCRATIC PURPOSES OF EDUCATION 174, 192 (Lorraine M. McDonnel, P. Michael Timpane & Roger Benjamin eds., 2000).

75. As Robert Putnam has noted, "In virtually all societies 'have-nots' are less trusting than 'haves,' probably because haves are treated by others with more honesty and respect. In America blacks express less social trust than whites, the financially distressed less than the financially comfortable." ROBERT PUTNAM, BOWLING ALONE: THE COLLAPSE AND REVIVAL OF AMERICAN COMMUNITY (2000).

Index